# INSIGHT GUIDE

# Kenya

APA PUBLICATIONS

Part of the Langenscheidt Publishing Group

2

# ABOUT THIS BOOK

2

*Editorial*

*Project Editor*
**Jeffery Pike**
*Managing Editor*
**Emily Hatchwell**
*Editorial Director*
**Brian Bell**

*Distribution*

*UK & Ireland*
**GeoCenter International Ltd**
The Viables Centre
Harrow Way
Basingstoke
Hants RG22 4BJ
Fax: (44) 1256-817988

*United States*
**Langenscheidt Publishers, Inc.**
46–35 54th Road
Maspeth, NY 11378
Fax: (718) 784-0640

*Worldwide*
**APA Publications GmbH & Co.**
**Verlag KG (Singapore branch)**
38 Joo Koon Road
Singapore 628990
Tel: (65) 865-1600
Fax: (65) 861-6438

*Printing*

**Insight Print Services (Pte) Ltd**
38 Joo Koon Road
Singapore 628990
Tel: (65) 865-1600
Fax: (65) 861-6438

©1999 APA Publications GmbH & Co.
Verlag KG (Singapore branch)
*All Rights Reserved*
*First Edition 1985*
*Fourth Edition 1999*

**CONTACTING THE EDITORS**
Although every effort is made to
provide accurate information in
this publication, we live in a
fast-changing world and would
appreciate it if readers would
call our attention to any errors or
outdated information that may
occur by writing to us at:
**Insight Guides, P.O. Box 7910,
London SE1 8ZB, England.
Fax: (44 171) 620 1074.
e-mail:
insight@apaguide.demon.co.uk**

This guidebook combines the interests and enthusiasms of two of the world's best known information providers: Insight Guides, whose titles have set the standard for visual travel guides since 1970, and Discovery Channel, the world's premier source of nonfiction television programming.

The editorial team at Insight Guides provide both practical advice and general understanding about a destination's history, culture, institutions and people. Discovery Channel and its Web site, www. discovery.com, help millions of viewers to explore their world from the comfort of their own home and also encourage them to explore it firsthand.

### How to use the book

To understand Kenya today, you need to know something of its ancient past. The **Features** section, with a yellow colour bar, covers the history of the area from prehistoric times through to the struggle for independence and the formation of the modern state. The cultural scene and everyday life in Kenya today are explored in lively essays by experts, and for this edition

EXPLORE YOUR WORLD
**Discovery**
CHANNEL

several new chapters have been added to describe the country's fascinating flora and fauna.

The **Places** section, with a blue bar, gives a full and detailed run-down of the major sights, including Kenya's numerous National Parks and Reserves, its many mountains, lakes and wilderness areas, and, last but not least, the spectacular coast with its beautiful beaches and ancient towns. The main places of interest are coordinated by number with full-colour maps.

The **Travel Tips** listings section, with an orange bar, provides all the addresses and telephone numbers you'll need. You can locate infor-mation quickly by referring to the index on the back cover flap, which also serves as a handy bookmark.

### The contributors

The new edition was edited by **Jeffery Pike**, a London-based jour-nalist and photographer who has travelled extensively in Africa since 1984. He has also introduced sev-eral new chapters on wildlife, plants and active pursuits for the visitor.

Jeffery Pike drew on the last edition of *Insight Guide: Kenya*, which was originally put together by the late **Mohamed Amin**, a native of Kenya who died tragically in an air-craft hijacking in 1996, **John Eames**, an award-winning cameraman, and **Ian Parker**. The writing that they did not do themselves, was contributed by a team of other writers.

**Edward Rodwell**, **Chege Mbitiru**, **Dr Daniel Stiles**, **Alastair Matheson** and **David Round-Turner** were each responsible for different chapters in the history section, while other contributions were made by **Peter Usher**, **Jean Hartley**, **Kathy Eldon** and **Mary Anne Fitzgerald**.

All the material from previous editions of the guide has been thoroughly checked and updated by Kenyan **Suzie Sardelli**, who now lives in Nairobi but was born on a farm in Naro Moru; she really got to know the country well when she worked surveying the route for the famous Safari Rally. Suzie has also enlarged and updated the Travel Tips section, which was originally put together by **Joan Egan**. She introduced much more information on places to stay and eat in Kenya.

The book was proofread by **Barbara Balletto** and indexed by **Isobel McLean**.

## Map Legend

| | |
|---|---|
| — ·· — | International Boundary |
| — — — — | Province Boundary |
| — ·— ·— | National Park/Reserve |
| — — — — | Ferry Route |
| ✈ ✈ | Airport: International/ Regional |
| 🚌 | Bus Station |
| P | Parking |
| ❶ | Tourist Information |
| ✉ | Post Office |
| ✝ ✝ | Church/Ruins |
| † | Monastery |
| ☾ | Mosque |
| ✡ | Synagogue |
| 🏰 | Castle/Ruins |
| ∴ | Archaeological Site |
| ∩ | Cave |
| 👤 | Statue/Monument |
| ★ | Place of Interest |
| ■ | Safari Lodge |
| △ | Tented Camp |

The main places of interest in the Places section are coordinated by number with a full-colour map (e.g. ❶), and a symbol at the top of every right-hand page tells you where to find the map.

# CONTENTS

## Maps

**Inside front cover:** Kenya

**Inside back cover:** Kenya
Parks & Reserves

## Introduction

## History

## Features

## Wildlife

**Beautiful Diani Beach, south of Mombasa**

## Insight on ...

## Information panels

## Travel Tips

## Places

# THE ESSENCE OF AFRICA

*From snow-capped peaks to white-sand beaches, via forests and open plains,*
*the Kenyan landscape encapsulates the entire African continent*

Kenya is a country of dramatic extremes and classic contrasts. Desert and alpine snows; forests, both lowland and montane; acacia woodlands and open plains; vast freshwater lakes and the superb coastline pounded by the Indian Ocean. Overall, it can be seen as almost the entire African continent in microcosm.

In terms of geography, Kenya is bounded to the north by Ethiopia whose highland bastions are the site of an ancient civilisation, partly Christian. To the northeast is Somalia, a hot, arid lowland of semi-desert. The nomads and camels spill over into modern Kenya, and the fall of the dictator Siad Barre in 1991 brought a flood of refugees into the country.

Most of the Kenya's eastern border – 480 km (300 miles) of it – is warm, unruffled and translucent ocean. Along the parallel strip of beach and tropical hinterland, the environment has all the attributes – and more – of a South Seas island.

To the south is Tanzania, the border a division between political and economic ideologies, and also between people of the same tribal origins – the Digo on the coast, and the Maasai and the Kuria in the west, where the frontier ends at the inland sea of Lake Victoria. On the western flank is Uganda, scene of terrible civil war in 1994, which shocked the world for its ferocity, but now peaceful and stable.

Geophysically, Kenya divides into a number of distinct zones, by far the largest of which is the low-lying arid land in the north and northeast. This comprises about two-thirds of the country, most of it at an altitude of up to 900 metres (3,000 ft). It is hot and dry, with sparse groundwater and it is populated almost entirely by nomad pastoralists who are forever chasing

the odd shower of rain and the short-lived green flush that follows it. Although this is the largest sector of the country, it inevitably supports few people, and they subsist almost exclusively on their stock of cattle, camels, sheep and goats.

Kenya's coastal plain is well-watered in two monsoon seasons off the Indian Ocean, and the land is lush, but cultivated only in patches with coconut groves, sugar and other crops. The gentle warm climate induces a pervasive attitude of "mañana" – *kesho* in Swahili – which encourages a far more relaxed pace of life than found elsewhere in the country.

The third and by far the most productive sector of Kenya is the high tableland in the southwest, much of it above 1,500 metres (5,000 ft). This raised, volcanic block is split from north to south by the Great Rift Valley, leaving one-third of the land area in the east, two-thirds in the west. Of the two parts, the east is the more dramatic since it is dominated by the mass of Mount Kenya, a giant extinct volcano

**PRECEDING PAGES:** Mount Kenya's twin peaks, Batian and Nelion; a Maasai warrior gazes over the Maasai Mara; greater flamingos ignore the rain in one of the Rift Valley lakes; local life on an Indian Ocean beach. **LEFT:** African legends narrated through wood-carving. **RIGHT:** a dugout canoe off the coast at Mombasa.

once higher than Everest. Its rim has long since fallen away, leaving the eroded plugs as twin snow-covered peaks that reach a height of around 5,200 metres (17,000 ft).

Close by, in a north-south traverse of this eastern Rift area, is the Aberdares or Nyandarua range. The mountains do not match the grandeur of Mount Kenya, but are nonetheless impressive, with the blunted peaks of Satima and Kinangop at well over 3,600 metres (12,000 ft).

The whole mass confronts the easterly winds

## AN INLAND SEA

Kenya's fertile western highlands are watered by rainfall not from the Indian Ocean but from Lake Victoria, which is so vast that it creates its own weather systems.

in on itself along the line of the crack. The wall of the range rises above 3,000 metres (10,000 ft) into an "Afro-Alpine" zone, with the land falling away gently all the way to Lake Victoria. The highest point west of the Rift is another isolated and extinct volcano, Mount Elgon, whose western flank is bisected by the Kenya-Uganda border. At above 4,200 metres (14,000 ft), Elgon's peak is not high enough for a permanent white cap although there is brief snow cover from time to time.

of the Indian Ocean and drains them of the moisture they have carried – fairly meanly – across the dry lands separating the highlands from the coast. This rainfall, landing on fertile volcanic soil, has been mulched over the centuries by cycles of dense forest, making the eastern highlands among the world's richest agricultural lands. Nairobi, Kenya's capital, stands at the southern approaches to the Aberdare range.

On the other flank of the Rift in the west, the ridges and peaks of the Mau Range are generally highest along the wall of the valley itself. It is almost as though they were scuffed upwards when the earth's crust faulted and fell

## Immigrants and inhabitants

The earliest inhabitants of east Africa were probably hunter-gatherers. Linguistically, they are related to the Khoisan hunters of southern Africa. Roughly 2,000 years ago, a wave of migrants from what is now Ethiopia settled in the region. These south Cushitic herders brought with them not only their own cattle but also skills in cereal growing. Some two thousand years later, Bantus, mainly from southern Zaire, settled in east Africa. Waves of Nilotic pasturalists also headed southeast from the Nile, in what is now Sudan. More recent immigrants include the Oromo-speaking tribes from the north of the African continent, who arrived in the 16th century, and east Cushitic Somalis in the 19th century.

Today, the different origins of Kenya's people are still apparent in a variety of languages, dress, customs and physical features. There are distinctive tribes that may appear to be Cushitic or Bantu, for example, but intermarriage between the tribes and Christian and Muslim missionaries have blurred the cultural boundaries.

While the people of inland Kenya evolved in their various ways, the coast was settled by mariners and colonists from other continents. After the rise of Islam, Arabs and Persians sailed into the embryo ports of what was then demand for ivory which had resulted from the West's industrial revolution, that the coast men turned their attention to the "dark interior".

## Forays into the hinterland

The first caravans organised by coastal traders – Arabic and Swahili – did not reach the highlands of what is now Kenya until around the 1840s. Soon after, though, they fought, bartered and cajoled their way into the country as far west as Lake Victoria. Their methods and manners did not make them popular with the indigenous tribes, which became increasingly hostile over the next four or five decades.

called the "Land of Zinj (black)" and some of them stayed. They intermarried with the locals, and the Arab and African mix gave rise to the Swahili people, who retained a predominantly Islamic culture. Eventually, a chain of city-states formed along the coast – from north to south: Lamu, Mambrui, Malindi, Takaungu, Mtwapa, Mombasa and Vanga. The Swahili people lived – some of them thrived – on exports gleaned from the hinterland, such as ivory, rhino horn and gum arabic. But it was not until the 19th century, with the rocketing

**LEFT:** cheetahs in Nairobi National Park.
**ABOVE:** on the train to Mombasa.

By then, Europe's eyes were on Africa, and in the mid-1880s the continent was divided into European "spheres of interest". Kenya went to Britain, which initially gave authority and right of exploitation in the area to a private company, the Imperial British East Africa Company (IBEAC). From 1887, the company men began moving inland along the coastal caravan routes, and they were received no less hospitably than were the Swahilis and Arabs.

They found the interior a feuding, warring Balkans of tribal territories, but dominated by the wide-ranging armies of the Maasai. Everyone, including the caravan traders, paid "tribute" for permission to cross Maasailand. The IBEAC did some exploring, but found nowhere near sufficient resources to rule and develop the country. So, in 1895, the British Government took over responsibilities for the territories that were to become Kenya and Uganda.

Believing that rapid communications were the key to efficient administration and economic development, the British decided to build a railway from Mombasa on the coast to Lake Victoria. It was started in 1896 and completed five years later, at a cost of over £5 million – an

between Europeans and Africans, which erupted in the Mau Mau rebellion in the 1950s.

Even so, from then until 1963, when Britain relinquished control, the presence of a large white community in Kenya led to a more diverse and competitive economy than in most other African countries under colonial rule. Its positive aspects included giving the African people greater exposure to modern agricultural methods, to which they were quick to adapt, joining the national cash economy in the process.

The country's remarkable economic growth was also attributable, in part, to a large community of traders and professional people from India and Pakistan. The skills, industry and capital investments of this Asian community contributed much to Kenya's prosperity, and still do.

Agriculture remains the base of the national economy, but tourism ranks as Kenya's largest foreign exchange earner, thanks to a vast rise from 10,000 visitors in 1963 to 800,000 today. In recent years, the traditional wildlife-based aspects of Kenyan tourism have been exceeded by the attraction for sun-starved Europeans of the uncrowded white-sand beaches.

To some extent, all this makes up for the fact that the country has no oil – as yet – nor any substantial mineral resources. A brief gold rush occurred in western Kenya in the 1930s, but deposits were soon mined out. The only other minerals with any economic potential are fluorspar, soda and gemstones.

Constitutionally, Kenya has been a republic since 1964, governed by two long-serving presidents. The first, Jomo Kenyatta, will probably be rated by history as among the most outstanding politicians of the 20th century. Tough and shrewd, he remained in office until he died in 1978, having led Kenya well along the road to a liberal, capitalist system.

This has not been substantially changed by his successor, the present incumbent, Daniel Toroitich arap Moi. Kenya has remained relatively stable, in sharp contrast to many other African countries, which have been on the point of political and economic collapse. ❑

extraordinarily expensive undertaking for that time. To recoup the capital, the railway needed to carry freight. Since the tribes of inland Kenya were not involved in cash economies or crops during this period, the decision was taken to bring in white settlers to farm or ranch the land along the route of the rail track.

## Sequestration and alienation

A steady influx of Europeans – principally Britons – began to settle, and eventually they built up a modern agricultural economy in the Kenyan highlands that was without peer in the tropics. But this sequestration of mainly Kikuyu land led to alienation and bitter feelings

**LEFT:** a memorial to the first president, Jomo Kenyatta, in Nairobi.
**RIGHT:** a young Maasai woman.

# Decisive Dates

**2.4 million BC** A hominid (man-like ape) known as *Australopithecus africanus* lives in East Africa.
**2 million BC** Evidence of *Homo habilis* ("Handy Man"), the first tool-maker, from Lake Turkana.
**1.6 million BC** *Homo erectus* makes hand-axes and cleavers; spreads throughout East Africa.
**300,000 BC** *Homo sapiens* active near Lake Baringo.
**5,000 BC** Kenya is inhabited by hunter-gatherers.
**c2,000 BC** Cushitic nomads arrive from Ethiopia.
**c1,000 BC** The Yaaku, a tribe of Eastern Cushites, arrive in central Kenya.

**c600 BC** Egyptian pharaoh Nacho sends an expedition to the East African coast.
**500 BC–AD 500** Bantu migrants arrive in Kenya, bringing metalworking skills. Kenya enters the Iron Age.
**AD 130** The geographer Ptolemy (Claudius Ptolemaeus) produces a map showing the source of the Nile and the whole of the Kenyan coast. (Mombasa is called "Tonika", Malindi "Essina" and Lamu "Serapion".)
**c900** Islamic Arabs occupy Mombasa and other seaports. The beginning of the coast's golden age.
**1300s** Swahili community emerges. Arab and Persian settlers develop coastal trade and caravan routes to the interior.
**1498** Vasco da Gama arrives in Malindi, signalling the start of Portuguese influence.

**1500** Portuguese admiral Cabral sacks Mombasa.
**1593** Portuguese begin construction of Fort Jesus overlooking Mombasa harbour.
**1600s** Portugal imposes strong and sometimes harsh regime all along the coast.
**1696** Arabs and allies begin siege of Fort Jesus.
**1699** After 33 months, Arabs take Fort Jesus and kill the surviving Portuguese defenders.
**1720** Portugal withdraws from Kenya for good. For 100 years the coast is ruled by the Imam of Oman, with the Mazrui family as governors of Mombasa.
**1822** Mazrui chief Suleiman bin Ali requests British help against Seyyid Said of Oman.
**1824** British ship HMS *Leven* arrives in Mombasa. Captain Owen declares the town a British protectorate.
**1827** British Government repudiates Owen's action, protectorate of Mombasa is removed.
**1832** Seyyid Said transfers his court from Mombasa to Zanzibar.
**1830–1880** Slave trade flourishes under Seyyid Said and his successors.

## THE AGE OF EXPLORATION

**1846** Missionaries Johannes Krapf and Johannes Rebmann make evangelical journeys into the interior.
**1848** Rebmann is the first European to see Mount Kilimanjaro. His reports of permanent snow on the summit are disbelieved in London.
**1849** Krapf is the first European to see Mount Kenya.
**1854** Krapf produces a rough map of the interior, showing a large inland "sea", possibly Lake Victoria.
**1856** Richard Burton and John Hanning Speke set out to find if this "sea" is the source of the Nile.
**1862** Ahmed Fumoluti al-Nabahani declares himself Sultan of Witu, which becomes briefly an independent state, "Swahililand".
**1883** Explorer Joseph Thomson travels from Mombasa to Lake Victoria, makes first contact with the Maasai, redraws the map of East Africa.
**1887** Austrian Count Samuel Teleki von Szek leads an expedition via Mount Kenya to Lake Turkana.
**1888** British East Africa Company builds headquarters in Mombasa; mints money, prints stamps.
**1890** The Treaty of Berlin brings all Kenya and Uganda under British jurisdiction.
**1892** Johnstone Kamau, later known as Jomo Kenyatta, is born in the Highlands north of Nairobi.
**1895** The British Government acquires the assets of the British East Africa Company and takes over what is now Kenya and Uganda as "British East Africa".
**1896** Construction of the railway from Mombasa to Uganda begins. It takes six years to complete.
**1899** Railway headquarters established at Nairobi,

soon followed by commercial enterprises and finally the government centre.

**1901** The railway reaches Port Florence (now Kisumu) on Lake Victoria.

**1902** First daily newspaper founded in Mombasa.

**1918** After World War I, the British Government offers war veterans land in the Kenyan Highlands.

## THE NATIONALIST MOVEMENT

**1922** Harry Thuku, leader of the first Kenyan nationalist organisation, is arrested. Kenyans protesting outside Nairobi's police station are massacred.

**1924** The Kikuyu Central Association (KCA) is formed with Jomo Kenyatta as its secretary.

**1929** Kenyatta goes to England to plead the cause of Kenyan liberation.

**1939–45** In World War II, Britain uses Kenya as a base for operations in Ethiopia (then Abyssinia). Many Kenyan Africans fight in the British army.

**1940** The KCA and other African organisations are outlawed and their leaders detained under new "defence regulations".

**1944** Start of Mau Mau, an underground independence movement with an oath of allegiance against the British.

**1946** Jomo Kenyatta becomes chairman of the newly-formed Kenya African Union (KAU).

**1952** State of emergency declared following attacks on white settlers. Kenyatta and 82 other nationalists are arrested and imprisoned. War declared on Mau Mau.

## INDEPENDENCE ACHIEVED

**1955** Africans allowed to form political parties.

**1956** First elected African representatives in the Legislative Council include Daniel arap Moi. Mau Mau rebellion ends: 13,500 have been killed.

**1959** Kenyatta released from prison but immediately put under house arrest.

**1960** State of emergency ends. Lancaster House Conference endorses the principle of majority rule.

**1961** Kenyatta released, becomes president of Kenya African National Union (KANU).

**1963** Kenya becomes independent with Jomo Kenyatta as Prime Minister.

**1964** Kenya becomes a republic with Kenyatta as the first President, Oginga Odinga as Vice-President.

**1968** Thousands of Kenyan Asians emigrate in the

---

**PRECEDING PAGES:** volcanic hills near Lake Turkana.
**LEFT:** petrified wood in Sibiloi National Park dates back over 20 million years.
**RIGHT:** Ahmed Fumoluti al-Nabahani, briefly the Sultan of "Swahililand".

face of government "Africanisation" policies. Many hurry to Britain to beat tightening of immigration laws.

**1977** The hunting of wild animals is outlawed.

**1978** Kenyatta dies, is succeeded as President by Daniel arap Moi.

**1982** Attempted coup d'état by the Kenyan Air Force is put down.

**1989** Richard Leakey is appointed head of the Kenya Wildlife Service (KWS) with broad powers. Institutes a strong policy against ivory poachers.

**1990** World Bank and major donors suspend aid, demanding social and economic reforms in Kenya.

**1992** First multi-party elections for 25 years. Three parties oppose KANU, but Daniel arap Moi is returned as

President, amid accusations of electoral irregularities.

**1993** Economic crisis: Kenyan shilling devalued by 25 percent, inflation soars to 50 percent. World Bank withholds aid until Moi agrees to economic reforms.

**1995** Tribal clashes after 2,000 Kikuyu farmers are forcibly relocated from Rift Valley. Moi rebukes Richard Leakey for trying to set up a new opposition party.

**1997** Amid continuing accusations of corruption in government, police clash with protesters demanding constitutional reform. With the opposition split along tribal lines, Moi and KANU are re-elected.

**1998** Heavy rains caused by El Niño cause devastation in large areas of Kenya. Islamic terrorists plant a car bomb near the US Embassy in Nairobi: more than 200 killed, thousands injured, mostly Kenyans. ❑

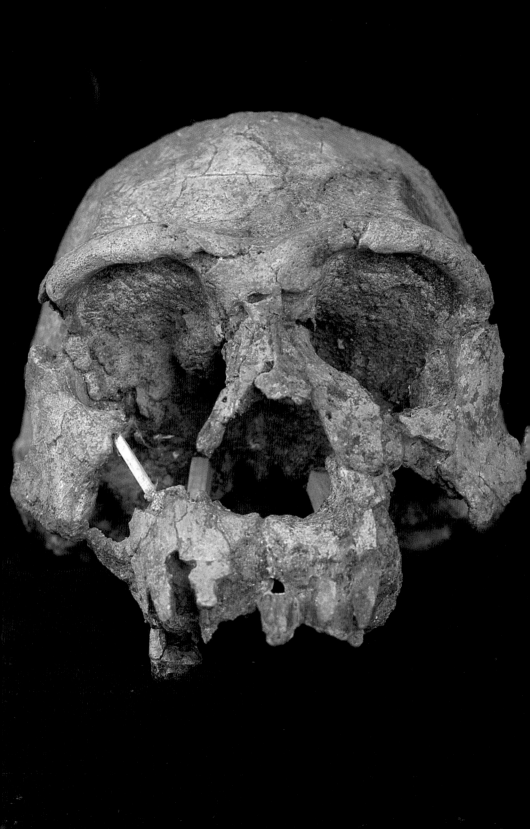

# THE CRADLE OF MANKIND

*Kenya's Rift Valley has yielded spectacular archaeological finds which suggest that this was the first home of human beings*

Some 25 million years ago, Kenya was an extensive plateau gently sloping towards the Indian Ocean in the east. A vast forest covered most of the land, in which lived various species of apes called *dryopithecine*. One of them was the ancestor of humankind.

This primordial world was shattered when molten rock from deep below broke through the crust of the plateau to form huge volcanoes, since worn down to the present stumps of Mounts Kilimanjaro, Kenya and Elgon. The crust cracked from north to south. In the west, the land sagged into a great depression, creating the inland sea of Lake Victoria.

Violent earthquakes over millions of years widened the crack, which joined with other fissures to form the immense Rift Valley, running from Jordan to Mozambique. In Kenya, streams flowed from the high ground on both sides into its rugged trough, laying down a series of lakes.

The formation of giant volcanic mountains and the Rift had a profound effect on the vegetation and wildlife in prehistoric Kenya. The highlands created rain shadows on their leeward sides, and the forests died out in the lower and hotter sections of the valley floor. The new ecological zone was savannah.

## Evolution of the ape man

One of the ape species on the fringe of the forest later moved into the open grassland, adapting and learning to exploit the area's resources. They lived on the shores of the lakes and by the streams which fed them. Ancient campsites, together with remains of animal meals and stone tools, were covered and preserved by silts or sands from the rising lake water or by ash from erupting volcanoes. The Rift Valley and its environs amount to a repository of the history of human evolution over 8 million years.

Little was known of this until an energetic, forceful and perhaps eccentric Kenyan called

**LEFT:** skull ER 3733, found beside Lake Turkana and later identified as *Homo erectus*.
**RIGHT:** Richard Leakey made some of the major finds.

Louis Leakey first dug out the Rift's treasure trove of fossils in 1926. As a student and later a researcher for Cambridge University, he led several archaeological expeditions in Kenya and from these amassed tons of stone artifacts and numerous hominid (human) and ape fossils ranging over 25 million years. In 1935

Leakey and his wife Mary embarked on a joint career that was to shape much of our understanding of human evolution. Their most important finds were at Olduvai Gorge in Tanzania, confirming the theory that two different forms of man lived side by side during the early Pleistocene era. One was small and tagged gracile (or "thin"), known today as *Australopithecus africanus*, while the other was larger and heavier, called *Australopithecus robustus*.

## The first tool-maker

But Louis Leakey was convinced that they had found a third hominid type, more closely related to the *Homo* genus. They pieced him together from bits of fossils and called him *Homo habilis* ("handy man") because they believed he made the crude stone tools found in the lower deposits of the gorge. The Leakeys thought it was "handy man" who had survived, whereas the *Australopithecus* had died out, leaving no descendants.

Throughout the 1960s and 1970s, scientists all over the world debated their interpretation. Some insisted there was only one species of early man, and that the *robust* and *gracile* forms were simply the male and female of the

**HOMO ANONYMUS**

The important skull found in 1972 was never named, but is known to posterity simply by its catalogue number – KNM-LR 1470 (Kenya National Museum-Lake Rudolph).

tified as part of a hominid's skull. When reconstructed, the fragments revealed a skull that stunned the academic world.

Its high forehead and relatively large cranial capacity put it squarely within the *Homo* genus, although the upper jaw is curiously primitive. Most significant, however, was that it had been found in deposits thought to date back 2.9 million years. The Leakeys were elated: this single skull seemed to prove that humanity descended not from the little *Australopithecus* ape-man,

same species. Others agreed on two hominid types or supported the Leakey count of three.

Then the Leakeys' second son, Richard, got into the argument. In 1968, he established a camp on a sandy pit on the eastern shore of Lake Rudolph (now Turkana) at a place called Koobi Fora. For the next 15 years, this arid, wind-blasted land would yield the most impressive collection of Plio-Pleistocene hominid and animal fossils the world has ever seen.

In 1972 Bernard Ng'eneo, a member of Richard Leakey's team, made one of the most dazzling fossil finds of the century. In sandy deposits in the side of a steep gully, he came across some scraps of bone, which were iden-

but from the contemporary third species Louis Leakey had proposed. He died that year, content that he had been right.

## The Homo jigsaw

For a while, the Leakey theory was accepted reluctantly by most former doubters. But after a series of tests, it was finally agreed that the skull was closer to 2.2 million years old. So it was suggested that he could have been an early split from *Australopithecus*: the argument is still open. In 1976, another skull was unearthed.

**ABOVE:** Louis and Mary Leakey inspect a dig.
**RIGHT:** a prehistoric turtle unearthed at Koobi Fora.

It belonged to *Homo erectus*, a descendant of "handy man" and an undisputed ancestor of *Homo sapiens*, modern man. This was dated to 1.6 million years, when *A. robustus* was still alive and well – and *H. erectus* was clearly not a female of the species.

Current theories for the complex evolution of man can be summarised as follows:

Between 2.2 million and 1.8 million years ago, *Australopithecus africanus* split into two branch lines, *A. robustus* and *Homo habilis*, which developed separately by adapting to different foods and lifestyles. *A. robustus* concentrated on plant foods, developing huge rear teeth to crush and grind fibrous matter. *Homo habilis* became a meat-eater, scavenging for kills and practising opportunistic hunting. He also used tools to help him hunt, hence developing the creature's capacity to think.

Around 1.6 million years ago, *H. habilis* evolved into *Homo erectus,* a creature which in most respects resembled modern man. In 1984, Richard Leakey discovered the almost complete skeleton of a 12-year-old *Homo erectus* boy on the west side of Lake Turkana. Apart from his head, with its jutting brow ridges, low forehead and protruding jaw, he probably looked very similar to a young human of today.

## A MILLION YEARS OF STONE TOOLS

*Homo habilis'* first tools were pieces of stone crudely chipped into shape, a class of tool-making known by archaeologists as *Oldowan*, after the Olduvai Gorge. The evolution of *Homo erectus* brought a more skilled style, known as *Acheulian* (after St Acheuls in France, where typical artifacts were first found). Hand axes, cleavers and other tools were now honed on both sides to produce a sharper blade. The basic designs remained unchanged for over 1 million years. The crude hand axe made from a piece of lava 1½ million years ago at Koobi Fora has the same design as the slim, fine-honed stone axe made 200,000 years ago at Kariandusi.

By 300,000 years ago, the first *Homo sapiens* were beginning to evolve from *H. erectus*, but there is such variation in the fossil record and uncertainty about dating that no clear picture yet exists. By now, man was a proficient hunter of antelope and other wildlife of the savannahs.

Fully modern man, in the anatomical sense, emerged only around 40,000 years ago during the Middle Stone Age period. By 20,000 years ago, he was learning to use stone tools, often with a handle of wood or bone, to make instruments used in daily life. The Stone Age technology continued until the arrival of Bantu farmers from the Congo Basin, who brought metalworking skills. ❏

# THE COAST SINCE ADAM

*Long before Western Europeans set foot on Africa's east coast,*
*Mombasa and its neighbours were centres of trade and culture*

The Indian Ocean, tumbling over the reefs and shores of Kenya, is awash with history. At the centre of this coast, the industrial port of Mombasa is a museum of memories which date from the earliest days of marine navigation.

According to the 17th-century poet John Milton in *Paradise Lost*, the seaports of Mombasa and Malindi were there soon after the Creation around 4026 BC. This was when the angel Michael was apparently providing a vision of the world to Adam:

*Nor could his eyes not ken*
*The empire of Negus to the utmost port.*
*Ercooco and the less Maritime Kings;*
***Mombasa** and Quiloa and **Melind**;*
*And Sofala, thought Ophir to the realm*
*Of Congo and Angola, further south.*

## Old Testament connection

Noah, the owner of a vineyard and a notable imbiber of the wine, is Kenya's other Old Testament connection. It seems that the old man, "in his cups" one day, exposed himself to his family and started a row involving his son Ham and his grandson Canaan. Noah ended up cursing this filial branch of the Hamites and Canaanites, for which reason they were beaten in battle by Joshua and had to leave Palestine for the barren wastes of North Africa. Later, they were joined by the related tribes of Shem and started a long migration south and east through the Horn to the coastal hinterland of Kenya.

Solomon and Sheba were later active in the area, with the queen's domain extending from the Red Sea down to Mozambique, according to the Ethiopian *Book of the Glory of Kings*. Solomon's navy was bringing up gold from the port-city of Ophir, mentioned by Milton, but now as mysteriously lost as Atlantis. (According to recent research, it may have been well

---

**LEFT:** a deserted beach on Kenya's north coast.
**RIGHT:** the ruins of Gede, a great Islamic city in the 14th century, mysteriously abandoned in the 17th.

south in the area of Mozambique.) The king's fleets were also collecting ivory, apes and peacocks from ports on the way back, which presumably included Mombasa.

Then the Egyptians took their turn at exploring the coastal strip. A record of an expedition is depicted in the temple of Deir el Bahri at Thebes

on the Nile, with one tablet showing a scene remarkably like that of Old Mombasa harbour. Ships are shown loading frankincense and myrrh, and there are orange trees in tubs and monkeys playing in the rigging.

Another expedition was dispatched in 600 BC by Nacho, the last of the pharaohs. They explored harbours in the "Land of *Punt*" which, according to Egyptologist Professor Petrie, is pronounced "Pwane", the name still applied to the Kenya coast by Arab navigators.

So it would appear that even before Christ, coastal towns, particularly Mombasa and Malindi, were thriving centres of trade. It was then, we can assume, that the Swahili language was established as a hybrid of Arabic and the local vernacular. Arabic script was also adopted.

In Egypt, the Greek traders prospered under the settled rule of the Roman Empire. Among them was one Diogenes, who landed at Rhaptum (Pangani) and claimed to have travelled inland to the vicinity of "two great lakes and the snowy range of mountains from which the Nile draws its two sources". He said it took him 25 days – which would have been an amazingly swift safari.

In any event, it was to Claudius Ptolemaeus (Ptolemy) that credit should go for noting the true source of the Nile, which was not officially "discovered" for another 17 centuries. Ptolemy remained the authority on the geography of Africa until the Middle Ages. He termed this coast *Parvum Litus*; Lamu he called *Serapion*, Malindi *Essina* and Mombasa *Tonika*. The earliest version of Ptolemy's map is dated AD 130.

## Trade and prosperity

Arab Christians continued to settle and trade in and around places like Mombasa and Malindi. But it wasn't until the emergence of Prophet Mohamed that the trickle turned into a flood of immigrants fleeing southwards from Islamic political and religious dissension of the time.

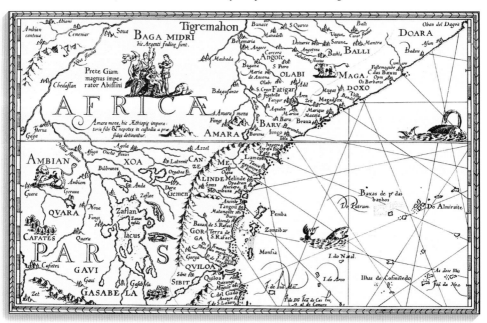

It was also then that the east coast cities began their Golden Age. The Arabs occupied Mogadishu, Mombasa, Malindi, Lamu and seaports farther south. In the process, mud and coral houses and stores made way for buildings of architectural merit; agriculture flourished and the people were well-dressed. The Arab historian Mahsaudi, who visited the east coast in the 9th century, recorded in his *Meadows of Gold and Mines of Precious Stones* that Mombasa and Malindi were rich in gold and ivory.

After that, the Hegira Arabs began to trade with an empire which, in the 8th and 9th centuries, spread from the south of France through the Mediterranean, the Red Sea and beyond to the borders of China and India. Trade with the Arab Empire brought substantial benefits to east Africa. Technology, new goods, concepts and business practices brought the coastal towns in line with the cultures the trade connection had to offer.

As it happened, the east coast of Africa was never part of the Arab Empire proper. But substantial benefits occurred from the regular trade with the Arab world. Technology, new goods, concepts and business practices brought the African coastal

> ### TRIANGLE TECHNOLOGY
>
> Arab nautical trade was built on the invention of the triangular lateen sail – something of a revolution in the history of the sea since it meant vessels could sail into and across the wind.

## The arrival of the Portuguese

Towards the end of the 15th century, the ordered East was assailed by Western explorers. King John of Portugal and his son, Prince "Henry the Navigator" inspired the extraordinary record of exploration and conquest manifested by Portugal up to 1700 or so. For the Kenyan coast, the year of the Portuguese was 1498. This was after Vasco da Gama had received orders from Prince Henry to round the Cape and find the sea route to India.

towns in line with the cultures the trade connection had to offer.

These were moderately peaceful days, and remained so for five or six centuries, until the arrival of the Portuguese. Towns were thriving; the business of the ports brought stability and much contentment. Narrow streets were crowded with slaves bearing parcels of freight to chanting oarsmen who ferried commodities to and from the vessels riding in the harbours.

**LEFT:** a 16th-century map of the coast shows "Mombaza", "Melinde" and "Lamo".
**ABOVE:** the triangular sail – Arabia's bequest to East Africa.

His small fleet reached Mozambique, where it found the principal inhabitants to be Arabs. According to the record, "a few merchant dhows lay in the harbour, laden with rings and a quantity of pearls, jewels and rubies". The Arabs, possessive of their position in the area, were not pleased to see the Europeans. Dissension broke out and the Portuguese left in a hurry, vowing to return and teach the Arabs a lesson.

As they sailed, a small dhow set off to warn fellow Arabs farther north of what might be in store for them. Thus, when the Portuguese fleet arrived at Mombasa, a seaborne guerrilla attack was launched to cut the anchor ropes. To avoid a confrontation, da Gama retreated to Malindi where, finally, he found a friendly Sultan who entertained da Gama and his crew royally.

It was altogether a pleasant visit, according to da Gama's record: "Malindi houses are lofty and whitewashed and have many windows. On the land side are palm groves and all around it, maize and vegetables are being cultivated. For nine days we had fetes, sham fights and musical performances." At the end of it, the Portuguese ships were loaded with fruit, vegetables

### LOW CONVERSION RATE

The Portuguese brought Christian missionaries with them – but they had little success in converting either the Muslim Arabs or the "pagan" Africans.

and meat; the Sultan produced a pilot who knew the route to "Calicut" (Calcutta), and the voyage to India was accomplished.

The friendly association of the Portuguese and Malindi lasted for almost 200 years, but other ports on the coastline suffered reprisals for the impolite way they had received the first Europeans. Mombasa was sacked in 1500 by Cabral, in 1505 by Almeida and in 1528 by Nuña da Cunha.

In their chronicles, the Portuguese wrote a description of the port: "Mombasa is a very fair place with lofty stone and mortar houses well aligned in streets; the wood is well-fitted with excellent joinery work. The men and women

go very bravely attired with many fine garments of silk and gold in abundance. This is a place of great traffic and has a good harbour in which are moored crafts of many kinds."

In 1593, the Portuguese started to build a fortification overlooking Mombasa harbour, which was to become Fort Jesus. At first it was little more than a walled compound, but soon developed into the huge fortress that can be seen today. With this massive stronghold, they felt safe. Victualled, gunned and shotted, and defended with regular soldiers, they thought they would have a solid edge on the belligerent Arabs and local tribes. And for a while they were right.

The Arabs fought desperately on land and by sea to regain control, but were unsuccessful even with the support of Ali Bey, a Turk. They also had unlikely allies in the *Wa-Simba*, a warlike tribe which had suffered at the hands of the Portuguese in Mozambique. These *Wa-Simba* ("lions" in Swahili) trekked northwards to Mombasa, destroying everything in sight. Unfortunately they made no impression on the garrison at Mombasa, and so carried on to Malindi where they suffered a second defeat. They then withdrew and were not heard of again.

The Portuguese gradually spread along the coastline, demanding the payment of levies. Every part of the coast suffered under the harsh regime and there was severe retribution for the slightest offence.

### A losing battle

The Portuguese were in fact in a losing situation. All their supplies to Mombasa, except food, had to be imported from Goa in India. When their soldiers sickened and died from malaria and other scourges, the ships bringing relief and reinforcements had to fight their way into the port. Finally, in 1696, the Arabs and their allies began a siege of Fort Jesus that was to break Portuguese dominance forever.

It started on 15 March, when an Arab fleet began to bombard Mombasa. Some 50 Portuguese, together with 2,500 local people, took to the fort and stayed there for nine months, living on short rations that were smuggled in at night. Their spirits rose when, on Christmas Day, four Portuguese warships sailed into harbour. But the elation was short-lived: the Arab guns were turned on the incoming ships, which pulled out and sailed away.

A month later bubonic plague broke out in the fort, and only a few stuck it out – the commandant, two children, a few local men and 50 women. A month later the commandant died.

In September 1697, the fort was re-manned with 150 Portuguese and 300 Indian troops, from Mozambique, but the siege continued for another 15 months until, with the help of a passing Welsh captain and crew, the Arabs were finally able to scale the fortress walls.

Only 11 men and two women remained alive; all of them were immediately run through with swords. The siege of Fort Jesus was over after 33 months.

In 1720, the Portuguese – bloody and bowed – left the Kenya coast for good. From Pate to Vanga, the Arabs would again be masters until the coming of the British and Germans towards the end of the 19th century.

Although the Imam of Oman was then ruler of the coast, he was ineffectual. He appointed governors from the Nahaban family in Pate, the Mazruis in Mombasa and the El-Hathis in Zanzibar. The governors quarrelled among themselves and the people of the coast suffered. Trade dwindled; the wealth of the coast disappeared. It was not until the early 19th century when a new ruler in Oman came to East Africa that the coast recovered, politically and economically.

This was Seyyid Said who, in 1822, sent an army to quell Pate, Pemba and Mombasa, then occupied by the Mazruis. With this began the story of British intervention in the area since the Mazrui chief, Suleiman bin Ali, invoked the protection of England.

The following year, two British survey ships, HMS *Leven* and HMS *Barracouta*, were on a mission to survey the east coast of Africa. When the *Leven* arrived at Mombasa, Captain Owen was begged by the local Mazrui Arabs to raise the Union Jack over the fort and place the island and its surrounding territory in the hands of His Britannic Majesty. Owen agreed to establish a "Protectorate".

Thus, on 7 February 1824, the British flag was hoisted over the fort. In return, the Mazruis promised to abolish the slave trade. A lieutenant of the *Leven* was appointed Commandant and Captain Owen's decision to assume authority was transmitted to London to await ratification.

After three years, London's response was received. Captain Owen's action was repudiated and the British Protectorate over Mombasa was removed. This opened the way for Seyyid Said of Oman to restore his sovereignty, which he did in 1828. He brought in a fleet, placed a Baluchi garrison in the Fort and, in Zanzibar, began to lay out the clove plantations which have since brought considerable wealth

to the island. In 1832, Seyyid transferred his court from Oman to Zanzibar and a period of prosperity followed. Within a few years the east African coast, from Cape Guardafui to Cape Delgado, was an acknowledged dominion of the Sultan, and his dreams of an African empire began to materialise.

## Slave trails open

From this time, the coast was opened up for trade. German, British and American merchants established themselves and slave trails were run up through the hinterland to the great lake.

There was little thought of partition on the mainland during Seyyid's lifetime, but when

---

**LEFT:** a yoked slave en route to the coast.
**RIGHT:** Sir William Mackinnon, who brought the first scheduled steamship to Mombasa.

he died in 1856, France, Italy and Germany began to show interest in East African colonisation. King Leopold of the Belgians had an eye on Malindi as the potential starting point of a railway to the Congo, and three Egyptian warships sailed down to the coast under McKillop Pasha in the hope of securing a foothold at Mombasa, Malindi or Lamu. The warships were replenished by Seyyid Majid, the new Sultan of Zanzibar, on the condition that the fleet returned to Egypt.

When Majid died in 1870, his brother Seyyid Bharghash took over, and it was during his reign that the partition of East Africa took

place. It began with the arrival of European explorers and missionaries, followed soon after by the vanguard officers of imperial interests.

In 1886, Britain and Germany agreed to the extent of the Zanzibar dominion. Tanganyika (now Tanzania) became a German colony, and Kenya and Uganda were assigned to Britain. The Sultan of Zanzibar would retain the coastline to a depth of 10 miles (16km), but as a British Protectorate. It was to stay this way right up to the Independence of Kenya in 1963, when Sultan Seyyid Khalifa ceded the territory to the new Kenyan Government.

In 1887, an administrative and trading concession was granted to a "British East Africa Association", which covered all coast from Vanga to Kipini. A year later, the company was incorporated under a Royal Charter, but by July 1895 was virtually bankrupt. So for £200,000, the British Government acquired the company's assets and took over what is now the territory of Kenya as "British East Africa". The Sultan in Zanzibar was paid an "honorarium" of £17,000 a year for British protection of his 10-mile strip of coastline.

A Scotsman, Sir William Mackinnon, the former chairman of the company, brought the first scheduled steamship line to the East African ports and built a road from Mombasa upcountry to Kibwezi. Trade from the coast to the hinterland was then started up and brought about the building of the Uganda Railway and the end of the slave trade.

Construction of the railway out of Mombasa began in 1896 and reached Nairobi three years later, in May 1899. On 2 December 1901, an engine finally steamed into Port Florence (now Kisumu) on Lake Victoria. Commerce quickly moved from Zanzibar to Mombasa with its railway terminus and ports. Steamships had replaced sailing vessels from Europe, although dhows remained in use for the Arabian and Indian trade.

Malindi, which had lost all of its former glory, became a centre of plantation activity which sadly died in the early stages when the bottom fell out of the copra (dried coconut kernels) and rubber markets. European and Asian companies set up agencies in Lamu. Although the railway had brought prosperity to Mombasa, the resident companies soon acknowledged that their future lay in Nairobi. As they moved up the line, so did the planters' associa-

## THE LION OF WITU'S BRIEF REIGN

In the 1860s, the sleepy village of Witu became the seat of a sultanate and the capital of the short-lived state of "Swahililand". The "Sultan of Witu", in fact, came from Pate in 1862 to escape the powerful Sultan of Zanzibar, with whom he had unwisely quarrelled. Calling himself Simba ("Lion"), the sultan minted his own currency and issued Swahililand stamps.

His sultanate came to an end in 1888, when he signed an alliance pact with the Dendhart brothers from Germany, in effect making Witu a German Protectorate. Two years later the Treaty of Berlin brought the whole of Kenya under British jurisdiction.

tion, the commercial associations and, finally, the Government. Old Mombasa harbour was left to the sailing vessels and plans were made to build deep water berths at Kilindini harbour.

By 1902 there was a daily newspaper at Mombasa and a steam laundry. Electricity came in 1908; a motorcar appeared and a Mr Jeevanjee imported a motor launch. Barclays Bank stood in Treasury Square, soon to be joined by the Standard Bank. Shipping lines employed local agencies and importing agencies began to handle almost

### Money Talks

As if to emphasise the trading links with Asia, at the turn of the century the official currency in Mombasa was the Indian rupee.

There was little trade. Coffee prices slumped. Wages were negligible, but those companies that were able to keep going began to pick up substantially in the 1930s, with World War II in the offing. From 1937, Kenya's economy improved and then boomed, so much so that the past 60 years have seen more vigorous growth than ever.

## Modern Mombasa and Malindi

Those who knew the country in the 1930s would find themselves in another world if they

the entire Uganda trade. Produce had begun to flow outwards and the railway was being used more and more for freight and passengers.

### The world wars and their effects

World War I boosted Mombasa's economy, with troops and goods from overseas moving through the port. A new ferry was established from the island to Likoni on the south coast. After the war, the impetus lasted for a few years, but then the world slump hit Kenya.

**LEFT:** the coast in the 19th century…
**ABOVE:** and today – Bamburi Beach Hotel, north of Mobasa.

returned to the coast today. Mombasa and Malindi have expanded beyond imagination, with the seaport of Mombasa now the largest on the northeast coast of the continent. Light and heavy industry is abundant. The old Wilson Airways runway at Bamburi has given way to a vast Moi International Airport at Changamwe.

Tourist amenities have developed from a group of palm frond huts at Bamburi to the ribbon development of hotels all along the coast, which cater for hundreds of thousands of tourists from all over the world. Mombasa and the other coastal centres have learned to be hospitable to visitors – after all, they have had several millennia of experience. ❑

# EXPLORING THE INTERIOR

*A combination of Christian missionary zeal, imperial ambition and a
simple desire to explore sent Europeans deep into the "Dark Continent"*

While Britain and Germany were still seeking to impose their influence on the East African coast, explorations inland had already revealed some of its secrets to Europeans. Among the first white explorers were two German missionaries, Johannes Krapf and Johannes Rebmann, whose evangelical journeys into the interior from 1846 took them to within sight of Mount Kilimanjaro and Mount Kenya. Their reports of snow at the equator were at first disbelieved in Europe.

In 1854 Krapf produced a rough map of the interior, showing both mountains and a huge inland "sea". Four years later the Englishman John Hanning Speke reached the lake, named it after Queen Victoria and concluded (correctly) that it was the source of the Nile.

So far, it had been exploration for exploration's sake, but it was not long before the European powers started to show a more colonial interest in the territory. The Germans led the way in 1882, when Dr Gustav Fischer led a well-armed expeditionary force as far as Lake Naivasha at the territorial border of the Il-Purrko division of the Maasai. The tribe ambushed his army in a gorge now called "Hell's Gate" and Fischer lost the fight around a tall obelisk of basalt rock which still carries his name: Fischer's Tower.

## Thomson's tattered army

The way was open for a young British nature student to take on the Maasai with a quarter of the German strength and fire-power, and fulfil the prophecy of Batian, the Maasai's greatest medicine man. The old man had foreseen the imminent arrival of three plagues from the north which, by 1890, would virtually annihilate his people and leave the survivors to witness Kenya's great leap forward into the era of European civilisation. The horsemen of the Maasai Apocalypse were smallpox, rinderpest and the

white man, beginning with the Scottish-born Joseph Thomson, then aged 29.

Thomson rode in on a donkey at the head of a tattered enterprise by the Royal Geographical Society in March 1883. Born the working-class son of a stonemason in Dumfriesshire, Scotland, he talked his way into a job as second

assistant field naturalist on an expedition to the Central African lakes in 1875. Five years later, he was the only experienced Africa hand willing to approach the Maasai with anything short of an artillery regiment.

He eventually took 143 men, only a dozen of whom could fire a rifle. His second-in-command was an illiterate Maltese sailor named James Martin; the rest he described as "the very off-scourings of the Zanzibar waterfront". Inevitably, they mutinied a few miles out of Mombasa, but Thomson tried his Scottish brogue and the men responded, not to what he was saying – they understood not a word of it – but to the warm inflections in his voice. The

---

**LEFT:** Joseph Thomson at the start of his 1883 trek.
**RIGHT:** a confrontation between 19th-century colonials from the coast and local tribesmen.

fine-tuned African antenna had picked up the fact that the young man, the *kijana*, might be a lunatic in the head but was "good in the heart".

They were persuaded to go on, but only as far as Kibonoto, north of Kilimanjaro, where they caught sight of an advance guard of the Maasai *moran* (warriors) who had routed the Fischer expedition. It made no difference what Thomson said; they prepared to take off at dawn for Mombasa and beyond. But the young Scot was fascinated. His reaction to the sight of "the savages so long the subject of my waking dreams" was: "Oh what splendid fellows!" He then led a peace party of the *moran* war-

riors into the camp, where they delivered "a mostly friendly and encouraging greeting, and with great cheerfulness, relieved us of the care of nearly 10 loads of goods".

But the cheerfulness was short-lived. "The warriors grew boisterous and rude. One of them tried to stab me because I pushed him away, and we had to remain under arms from morn till night. On the morning of the third day, our worst fears were realised. We had been deluded and entrapped and we knew they were about to take their revenge on our small party for their failure to annihilate Fischer."

So, "with bitter disappointment, much chagrin, and the gravest doubts about the manifest cowards" of his crew, Thomson decided to return to the coast. They jogged all the way back to Mombasa, covering the 390 km (240 miles) in six days. Undeterred, Thomson refitted at the port, engaged a few more men and set off on his second foray into Maasailand.

## Encounter with the Maasai

He was heading north from Kilimanjaro, on a direct bearing to Lake Victoria towards Amboseli, when his "miseries started in earnest" in an encounter with the Matapato division of the Maasai. Thomson and his men were compelled to live wretchedly among the "most unscrupulous and arrogant savages in Africa". In spite of full defensive precautions, including surrounding himself with two thick thorn fences, Thomson was harassed daily by the *moran,* who merely strolled past the armed guards and walked into camp. "They would frequently push me aside and swagger into the tent, bestowing their odiferous, greasy, clay-clad persons on my bed or wherever it suited their ideas of comfort. I would have to say how delighted I was to see them and give them string after string of beads in the hope of hastening their departure."

He was not seriously threatened until he deviated out of the Rift Valley towards *Ol-Doinyo Keri*, "the striped mountain", which was what the Maasai called Mount Kenya. The atmosphere there so reminded Thomson of home that he renamed the *Satima* range the "Aberdares". But nostalgia soon vanished with the arrival of a battalion of *moran* to subject him to the most severe and sustained provocation he had yet endured. He kept moving, but took a month on the journey which should have taken 10 days. Thomson reached Lake Victoria in December 1883, and redrew the map of eastern Africa, putting in more water surfaces than were known previously. He toured Mount Elgon in the northwest and found the great caves in the mountain which Sir Rider Haggard would later use as a main set in his novel *She*.

### WHITE MAGIC

Thomson gained a reputation among the Maasai as a great *laibon* or "wizard". Tricks that got him out of trouble included frothing at the mouth with the help of Eno Fruit Salts and the removal of two false teeth.

Thomson completed his survey and was ready to start back to the coast on New Year's Eve 1883, but decided he would first treat himself to a traditional Scottish Hogmanay. In the absence of grouse on the Elgon moors, he opted for a buffalo steak and duly shot a large bull – then discovered why hunters were later to rate the buffalo the most dangerous sport in the bush.

The "dead" animal got up, drove a horn into his thigh and tossed him several feet in the air. He landed on his head and laid there in a state of stunned euphoria, calmly waiting to be "pounded to jelly". Someone fired a shot as the bull advanced. Thomson opened his eyes and "with glad surprise, I found the beast's tail presented to my delighted contemplation." The buffalo was then dispatched with a fusillade from the bearers.

The explorer was borne away down through the Rift Valley to Naivasha. He convalesced at the lakeside for a while and recovered enough to go off on a side trip to map the country north of Lake Baringo. But he then went down with a near-fatal attack of dysentery and was again put on a litter and carried the rest of the way to Mombasa, arriving in May 1884.

## The first African safaris

Thomson, a genuinely modest man, was a hero back in Britain. His adventure in the wilds of Africa fired the Victorian imagination and started the safari business. From then on, there were almost back-to-back tours to Kenya for gentlemen and politicians who were to carve East Africa into British and German spheres of influence. But prior to that, there were two other major path-finding missions into un-

charted areas to the east of Thomson's route. An Anglican bishop, James Hannington, set off in 1885 to start a diocese in Uganda. On the way he found a lake Thomson had missed just below Baringo, later named after Hannington and today called Bogoria. He then went on as far as the Nile, where he was killed, thus putting the bishop's mission to an end before it had even started.

The following year, preparations were made for an ambitious safari through the Kikuyu

heartland in central Kenya and on to Lake Turkana, which at that time was still called *Embasso Narok*, the "black lake" of the Maasai. The leader of this 700-strong expedition was a rich Austro-Hungarian count named Samuel Teleki von Szek. He took a diligent biographer with him, Lt. Ludwig von Höhnel, so that every step of the epic journey would be recorded for posterity.

Von Höhnel was also quartermaster for the trip and his inventory list was a volume in itself. It included 24,000 metres of *amerikani* calico; 115 loads of iron, copper and brass wire; and a ton of fashionable glass beads from Paris and the House of Filonardi in Italy. Teleki's

**LEFT:** Count Samuel Teleki von Szek, the first European to see Lake Turkana, in 1887.
**RIGHT:** Ernest Gedge climbed Mount Elgon in 1890.

"natives", mainly the Kikuyu as it turned out, were never so elegant.

The aristocratic count led his caravan of tinkers up from the coast in January 1887. They went across the dry Taru Desert to Kilimanjaro. By April, they were camped on the Ngong Hills in the Kikuyu region, within range of the Kikuyu's poisoned arrows. Nothing happened until Teleki moved up to the forest edge, fired a couple of shots to attract attention and thereafter received a few tattered Ndorobo hunters sent out as trade consuls.

### ROYAL LAKE

Count Teleki named Lake Turkana "Rudolf", after Austria's crown prince, who later shot himself and his mistress at Mayerling.

### Honorary chief

They were returned alive with samples of the count's haberdashery, after which hordes of the tribal women appeared with goats, chickens and a vast array of crops. Finally, the men arrived in full battle-dress, looking much like the Maasai – robed, red-painted and their hair in long ringlets set solid in mud and animal fat. In the trade-off, the Kikuyu received mirrors, cowries and cavalry swords, while Teleki received a cape of colobus monkey skins as the mark of an honorary chief.

His position was only slightly inferior to the chief of what was probably the Waiyaki clan, which still command great respect in Kenya.

The Waiyaki chief then protected Teleki's march up and down the ridges of Kikuyuland, harassed only occasionally by archers on the hills. They were deterred by a demonstration of the return firepower of the white man's "spears", which could puncture a buffalo hide shield at 100 metres. Once out of Waiyaki's protection, they had several scraps with more aggressive Kikuyu.

As for the country, up from the Ngong Hills through the Aberdares to Mount Kenya, the Austrian count found it green and pleasant. It was observed to "grow nearly all the cereals and crops native to East Africa and it is, in fact, the granary of a very extended district". Listed among the main produce were millet, maize, potatoes, beans, yams, sugar cane and bananas.

Once out of the area, the caravan split for a while. Von Höhnel went to trade ivory and map the northern Laikipia shoulder of Mount Kenya and followed the Ewaso Ngiro, the "brown river", north into Samburu country. Teleki climbed the mountain, taking his "perishing barefoot companions" up to 4,100 metres (13,600 ft) and then going on alone up to the jagged peaks of the mountain.

From there on, the safari continued to a spur of the Marmanet range, and on to Lake Turkana, where the landscape today is unchanged from the volcanic wasteland von Höhnel saw as "recently flung from some monstrous forge". Teleki's men made their way across a vast field of sharp-pleated lava and leapt into the clear water, which turned out to be full of soda and drinkable only in a fizz of tartaric acid.

Three years later two Britons, Ernest Gedge and Frederick Jackson, climbed Mount Elgon and traversed its huge crater from north to south. Next, a couple of Americans, Donaldson Smith and William Chandler, surveyed the Tana River and the featureless *Commiphora* bush of the northeast. After that, the main structures of the land and people of Kenya were known to the outside world. It remained for the British to plough, build and reorganise in the colonial process they started in 1888. ❏

**LEFT:** the Maasai *laibon* Lenana with Sir Arthur Hardinge in 1898.
**RIGHT:** John Hanning Speke, who found the source of the Nile at Lake Victoria.

# THE RED BARON AND THE WHITE SETTLERS

*Britain's growing control over Kenya involved bloody battles with*
*tribesmen, eccentric agricultural schemes and a "lunatic" railway*

The natives were restless in 1895 when the British Crown took over from the British East Africa Company. Detachments of the British Army were brought over from India to deal initially with the Mazrui family, which had organised attacks on Mombasa and Malindi in a unilateral declaration of independence for the coastal strip.

It then took four expeditions against sections of the Kamba tribe to persuade them to accept the British administration. Further up-country, more troops were garrisoned at Fort Smith to control an opportunist territorial expansion of the Kikuyu out of the highland forests. Around Lake Victoria, the Nandi and other tribes started a guerrilla resistance in 1895 which was to last more than 10 years until the Nandi *laibon* and chief strategist was shot dead at peace talks.

## The warlike Maasai

Only the Maasai came into the Protectorate of their own accord. At that time they were having difficulty dealing with predatory raids of the Kikuyu and Kamba since the prophesied plagues of rinderpest and smallpox had seriously weakened them. In the north, a revival was started with food-aid cattle from the Protectorate and a couple of seasons of good rain. The Maasai *moran* picked themselves up and replenished the tribe with cattle and women collected in reprisal raids against the Kikuyu, and the Meru and Embu on the eastern shoulder of Mount Kenya.

By the end of 1895, the British rated the Maasai "a menace and a force to be reckoned with" after they massacred half a caravan of 1,100 men in the Kedong section of the Rift Valley above Nairobi. A passing trader, Andrew Dick, decided to exact retribution on behalf of

the Crown. He attacked the Maasai sentries guarding the cattle, made off with a large herd, and was halfway up the eastern escarpment before the main body of the *moran* caught up with him. Trader Dick was thus added to the casualty list, which also included 452 Kikuyu and 98 Swahili. At the official Court of Inquiry, the Maasai were found to have been unreasonably provoked but were charged compensation for the massacre in the amount of the cattle taken by the deceased Mr Dick.

## The "line to nowhere"

The following year, the British started to build the Uganda Railway from Mombasa to Lake Victoria. The original purpose of the line was strategic, to get a permanent line of communication into Uganda ahead of the Germans coming up from the south. A vocal opposition group in the British Parliament called it a monumen-

---

**LEFT:** the 1913 Provincial Commissioner's office in Nairobi, overshadowed by its 1983 successor.
**RIGHT:** a funicular was built to help the Uganda Railway down the steep wall of the Rift Valley.

tal waste of time and money, "a lunatic line to nowhere". But the scheme went ahead in 1896, with the import of 32,000 Indian labourers from Gujarat and the Punjab.

The railway was driven along the divide between Maasai and hostile Kamba territory until a temporary halt was called at mile peg 327, on the banks of the Nyrobi River. The ground was higher and healthier a few miles further on, but not so flat. Thus, the town of Nairobi was founded as a tented depot on a dank, evil-smelling swamp, infested with frogs

and larger wildlife wandering in from the Athi Plains.

The Maasai stayed aloof from it all, but the Kikuyu came in to market their crops and livestock. The first coffee was planted by Catholic fathers at St Austin's mission on the outskirts of the township, and tea was started on the wooded uplands of Limuru close to the 600-metre (2,000-ft) precipitous drop into the Rift Valley. This, the worst of the natural obstacles in the way of the line, was negotiated first by a funicular system of cables and winches. Later a zigzag slant was cut out on the face of the scarp.

From there on it was fairly easy going across the Rift floor, up the gentler wall of the Mau Range to an English country landscape around Njoro, and on down to the shores of Lake Victoria. The last spike was driven in at Port Florence (later Kisumu) on 19 December 1901, just over five years after construction started.

## Rail returns

Commissioner Sir Charles Eliot decided that the huge cost of the railway should be recouped through European settlement along the line, wherever the land could be farmed or ranched. Thomson's Scottish-looking Aberdares, with their cool climate and fertile valleys, offered the best prospect for arable development. Several of the first farmer-settlers were the rootless younger sons of the minor British aristocracy. In a sense, these "White Highlands" became the officers' mess of colonial Africa, with the Asians barred from owning land in the area and the Kikuyu either retained as labour or asked to remove themselves to a patchwork reserve on the range's lower eastern slopes.

The Rift Valley itself and the western highlands of the Mau were occupied off and on by the Maasai, whom Eliot both admired and disdained. He liked their manly appearance, but, because of their top dressing of red ochre and rancid animal fat, preferred "to interview them out of doors and at a distance".

In a dispatch to London he rated the Maasai

**LEFT:** the grave in Nairobi of British officer Lt. Alfred Harrison, killed by a Tsavo lion in 1898.
**RIGHT:** the "Red Baron", Lord Delamere (*centre*), with leaders of the Colonists' Association in 1908.

the most advanced and worthwhile of the local natives. He recommended that the *moran* armies be broken up and the tribe dispersed into the highlands as farm labour and perhaps later as tenant farmers of the new landed gentry. But he was overruled by a British Parliament, which had acquired a liberal "Native Affairs" lobby. The tribe would stay intact and merely move out of the way of the white settlement.

A few stayed in the Rift on a 40,000-hectare (100,000-acre) ranch one extraordinary settler had acquired between Nakuru and Njoro. Lord Delamere, from stately Vale Royal in Cheshire, had a touch of what was to become a common rash of European admiration for the tribe – called "Maasaiitis". At first the *moran* did nothing but look on sardonically as the cranky, red-haired gnome of a man lost a fortune trying to farm sheep in the Rift (see panel below).

After failing with sheep, the "Red Baron" tried cattle, mixing good beef stock looted from the Vale Royal estate with the hump-backed, long-horned Boran cattle of the northern tribes. The progeny were resistant to most of the local viruses, but not to a new East Coast fever from German East Africa, which wiped out the Delamere herd. After that, the "mad" Englishman was a soul-mate of the Maasai.

## Maasai managers

They took over Delamere's stock management and, aided by imported veterinary science, built up the cattle on sections of the ranch they knew could support the herds. Delamere was greatly obliged and from then on supported the Maasai in land battles with the British administration led by their own advocate, *Ole Legalishu.*

With ranching back on track, the baron took on more rich and benign-looking acres of the Rift Valley and all the violent African blights and pest infestations they produced. In an expensive process of trial and error he demonstrated how his fellow settlers might ruin themselves over a range of agricultural enterprise, including coffee, flax, and sisal for hemp ropes.

His next venture was wheat, ploughed over a vast acreage by oxen brought up from South Africa. The wheat grew thick on Delamere's rolling downs, and became a favoured breakfast cereal for every wild plains animal in the Rift Valley. What the game left was destroyed by several species of wheat rust. Delamere defeated the disease with a full-scale research laboratory which eventually produced the national rust-resistant strain. He defeated the game by shooting everything in sight.

But Delamere was serious and effective in leading the settlers' political opposition against government policy, which tended towards support for the rights of the dispossessed Africans. As minister at the Colonial Office, Winston Churchill supported the policy of the Protectorate Government. On a visit to Kenya, he made plain his opinion of the 4 million Africans who then inhabited the Protectorate: "Just and honourable discipline, careful education, sym-

### THE SHEEP'S TALE

The first flock of high-grade Australian sheep that Lord Delamere introduced could not survive on the mineral-deficient vegetation, and died. He then ploughed in English clover, brought in new sheep and watched the clover fail – the local African bees were unable to pollinate it. The Red Baron's solution was to import European bees from England, and it worked. However, with no winter to keep the crop down in a dormant period, and no frost to kill off the pests, the clover grew into a giant green jungle and the sheep died of foot rot.

Further up the valley, in Molo District, flocks of hybrid local and imported stock did well, and still do.

pathetic comprehension are all that are needed to bring a very large proportion of the tribes of East Africa to a far higher social level than that at which they now stand. *And it is, after all, their Africa.*"

Delamere met Churchill on this visit and, while doubtless arguing the cause of the white settlers, also laid on entertainment in the form of a pig-sticking party at Elmenteita. Once they had seen Churchill off on the train to Uganda, Delamere and his disciples set about consolidating the White Highlands. By 1912 they had the Protectorate paying its way on the basis of a mixed agricultural economy.

### War in Africa

The 1914–18 war in Europe did not leave East Africa untouched. At first the African campaign was a series of minor but highly cinematic episodes. The German commander in Africa, Paul von Lettow-Vorbeck, first defeated the British embarrassingly at Tanga and then led a hit-and-run campaign against the railway supply line from behind the Taita Hills.

Two-thirds of some 3,000 British settlers left their wives to manage the farms while they rode after Germans in irregular cavalry units. Delamere himself took off into the Maasai reserve with a party of *moran* scouts, but they soon became bored and returned to the ranch. There-

after the Maasai resisted strenuous attempts to conscript them into the regular army.

But the British successfully attacked at Lake Victoria, where the galloping settler brigades captured the German post at Bukoba. Finally, Jan Smuts from South Africa drove Vorbeck into a fighting retreat around Central Africa – which achieved the German general's objective of occupying a large force of the British Army for the duration of the war. He was leading 155 Germans and 3,000 Africans into Portuguese Angola in November 1918, when he received news of the armistice.

### The outcome of the war

Vorbeck was thus undefeated, but his country lost Tanganyika in the Treaty of Versailles in 1919. Britain was assigned to govern the larger part of it under a League of Nations mandate and began thinking of an economic federation of the three East African territories.

Another significant consequence of the war was the British Government's decision to offer estates in the highlands to veterans of the European campaign in what was called the "Soldier Settlement Scheme". By 1920, when the country was designated the "Colony of Kenya", the white population was around 9,000. The coastal strip remained detached for a few years on a courtesy lease from the Sultan of Zanzibar.

For Delamere settlers, all this advanced their objective of a permanent white man's Kenya – but they were soon disillusioned. A government White Paper in 1923 revived and reinforced the policy of Africa for the Africans. In what was seen as a Bill of Rights for the black Kenyans, the key paragraph stated that "Primarily, Kenya is an African country. H.M. Government think it necessary to record their considered opinion that the interests of the African native must be paramount, and that if and when those interests and the interests of the immigrant races should conflict, then the former should prevail."

From then on a succession of colonial governors were obliged to apply the paper policy, with or without personal conviction, against the cantankerous and abusive opposition of Delamere and his "Kenya Cowboys" on a

**LEFT:** the white settlers tried to domesticate some of the local wildlife.
**RIGHT:** air travel from Britain to Kenya was pioneered by Imperial Airways.

national Legislative Council. A takeover attempt by the settlers was always a possibility, but there were never enough of them for any open rebellion or for the political fight, which was probably lost when the administration's power base at Nairobi began a rapid expansion from the mid-1920s.

The Africans streamed in to enlarge the one-street frontier town with sprawling settlements along the Nyrobi River and around the railroad. It was a major social revolution of mostly the adaptable Kikuyu – the great leap from the African bush to the European town with its complex lifestyle and cash economy.

A few young Kikuyu formed community groups as channels for government protection of their tribal interests. But the fundamental issue was land, and the early associations of the Kikuyu in Nairobi were revivalist meetings for the return of the "alienated" highlands.

About this time, a remarkable former herd-boy called Johnstone Kamau took a job reading water meters for the Municipal Council. He later changed his name to Jomo Kenyatta as he increased his involvement in the political organisation of the Kikuyu in what was to become a long and eventually traumatic struggle with the settlers. ❑

## HIGH LIFE IN THE HIGHLANDS

The Muthaiga Country Club was the settlers' political headquarters in Nairobi, and also the venue for the hunt balls, the occasional elegantly wild party and other revels said to include half-clandestine wife-swapping in an extension of what was also said to be the permissive scene up-country in the *Wanjohi* or "Happy Valley" of the highlands. One moment of serious drama in all this was the unsolved shooting of the noted ladies' man, Lord "Joss" Erroll, a close friend of the lady who was to become the wife of Lord Delamere's son and heir.

Another casualty of the period was the first Baroness (Karen) Blixen, whose hunter husband, Bror, went off with another woman and left her to go bankrupt on a suburban Nairobi coffee farm under the Ngong Hills. Her memoir, *Out of Africa* – remarkable for its stylish insight on the country and people – was also eloquent on the since exaggerated and romanticised high life of Kenya in the 1920s and 1930s. She entertained Edward, Prince of Wales, and she had her own romantic interlude with a raffish member of the club, the Hon. Denys Finch-Hatton.

But the overall impression was that of a slightly desperate gaiety, rather like that of pre-Revolutionary Russia in *The Cherry Orchard*. The peasant revolution, in the form of the Kikuyu independence movement, was close at hand.

# THE STRUGGLE FOR INDEPENDENCE

*Kenya's transition from British colony to independent state involved four decades of fervent political debate and, at times, bloody armed conflict*

One day in early March 1922, a crowd of Africans gathered outside the Central Police Station where the main campus of the University of Nairobi stands today. A few settlers stood watching outside the nearby Norfolk Hotel. It was generally calm, as one European noted, except for the squalling of Nairobi's prostitutes. Inside the police station, under arrest, was Harry Thuku, leader of the "Young Kikuyu Association".

There are conflicting reports about what happened. One was that a woman lifted her skirt and derisively told the men to give the women their trousers. "Our leader is there", she cried, "Why don't you go and get him?" It was then that shots rang out from the police station and, according to some reports, from the direction of the Norfolk Hotel. Officially, 21 people died, but the Africans claimed over 100 were killed.

The episode marked the beginning of a sustained fight for political, economic and social rights for Kenya's Africans. Even at that early date, many were determined to take over from the British and run the country themselves. Their objective was *Uhuru* – Swahili for "freedom" – and it was to be a long struggle before they achieved it.

## Land grievances

Since the 1902 Land Acquisition Order in Council, white settlers had acquired the most fertile land in Kenya. They had also become politically dominant in a Legislative Council in Nairobi, which allocated more and more land to Europeans and passed laws that forced Africans to seek employment from settlers. These laws were ruthlessly enforced through an elaborate system of chiefs and headmen established in the early 1900s.

A local newspaper reported in 1922: "Out at Pangani village [close to Nairobi], the Natives

are very busy these days holding meetings of the mass kind. Every Sunday, thousands of *Njoroges* and *Kamaus* may be seen listening raptly to others of their kind holding forth on presumably the question of the hour… And it is fairly apparent that these meetings have a savour of politics about them and that the

Natives are discussing matters connected with registration, taxation and so on."

These meetings were attended by up to 5,000 people and were multi-tribal in character. The main complaints were over the forced labour practices and the imposition of a "hut tax", which most people couldn't afford. Among the many Africans who attended these rallies of discontent was the young Kikuyu Johnstone Kamau. Born before the British settlement, he grew up as an orphan and was educated by missionaries. As Jomo Kenyatta, his name would leave an indelible mark on Kenya.

Initially, the Colonial Government was not fully aware of the extent to which the Africans

**LEFT:** the late Chief Njiri displaying his loyalty to the Crown in the 1950s.
**RIGHT:** Jomo Kenyatta celebrates his release from house arrest in 1961.

were prepared to fight. The first sign of organised resistance came in 1924 when the Kikuyu Central Association (KCA) was formed with Kenyatta as its secretary. The KCA complained against the government's policy of dividing the tribes and asked for the establishment of a Central Native Council. Instead, they were fobbed off with Local Native Councils made up of chiefs and appointed members and charged with giving "the younger and more educated Natives a definite avenue along which to develop".

> **LAND GRABBING**
>
> By 1928 about 26,400 sq. km (10,200 sq. miles) of Kenya's best arable land had been allocated to European settlers.

him somewhat as a "stooge". Many of his supporters joined the KCA. Meanwhile, Kenyatta had gone to London to present the Africans' case. He reported back, but then went off again in 1931 for what would be a 15-year odyssey in the Western world, including some time in Stalin's Soviet Union.

Three years later, a commission inquiring into the disposition of land in Kenya heard views presented forcefully and articulately by the Africans, but nevertheless disallowed all African claims to the "White High-

## Social conflicts

In 1929, there was another complicated social controversy over female circumcision. The church expelled anyone who supported the practice, and many Kikuyu regarded this as another interference with tribal tradition. The affair led to the formation of independent schools and church movements, and these splinter developments were to become useful to Kenyatta and the KCA, as it was in the independent schools that the Kikuyu sense of identity and African nationalism were inculcated.

Harry Thuku was released from jail in 1930 on the condition that he would cooperate with the government. When he agreed, it isolated

lands". As a result, the "social" organisations proliferated. In addition to the Kikuyu KCA, the Luo around Lake Victoria formed the North Kavirondo Central Association; the Taita Hills Association represented the Taita people west of Mombasa; and the numerous Kamba tribe southeast of Nairobi founded the Ukamba Members Association.

In May 1940, 23 leaders of these associations were detained under newly promulgated "defence regulations". They were held on suspicion of consulting with the Italian Consulate in Nairobi, a potential enemy of the king. A copy of Adolf Hitler's *Mein Kampf* found at the KCA headquarters compounded the felony.

## The Kenya African Union

Although the KCA and other associations were banned in 1940, a more potent political organisation came into being following the appointment of Eliud Mathu – a graduate of Balliol College, Oxford – as the first African member of the Legislative Council. Recognising the need to have a base, in 1944 Mathu formed the Kenya African Study Union, with its constitution written by Indian lawyers.

**REBELS UNITED**

The Kikuyu-dominated Mau Mau began in 1948 as a loose but vigorous association of secret societies. The origin of the name Mau Mau is obscure.

In 1946 the organisation changed its name to the Kenya African Union (KAU). Although it had an inter-tribal outlook, its leadership was dominated by former KCA Kikuyu members. So it was not surprising that when Jomo Kenyatta returned the same year, after 16 years abroad, he was elected president of KAU. He was the only man who had a chance of uniting the Africa challenge to the colonialists.

With Kenyatta at the helm and using the Kikuyu independent schools and churches machinery, KAU grew in strength in Nairobi, Central Province and among Africans working in the "White Highlands". It also stepped up confrontation with the government. There was a KAU-supported strike at Mombasa docks, which was ruthlessly suppressed. At Uplands, a few miles north of Nairobi, police shot several strikers at a bacon factory. In the same year, 1947, police fired at Africans demonstrating against the intimidation of a Kikuyu chief.

## Oaths of allegiance

As a reaction to the strict enforcement of regulations against Africans squatting in the highlands, Kikuyus started forming secret societies. New members were sworn in at "oathing" ceremonies, at which oaths of loyalty to political objectives were often accompanied by vows to kill Europeans and their collaborators.

The authorities, including African chiefs, viewed the oathing as a threat to law and order, and the missionaries and their Christian African followers saw the ceremonies as anti-Christian. This caused a deep social rift, so that when the

**LEFT:** Jomo Kenyatta pleads his cause in Trafalgar Square, London, in 1938.
**ABOVE:** a mural depicting Kenyatta's midnight arrest in October 1952.

Mau Mau war started, the Christian Kikuyu were prime targets. Many of them were killed.

As political fervour increased, oathing spread among other tribes – the Maasai, the Luo, the Luhya and, to some extent, the Kamba and the Kipsigis. There was a wave of destruction of settlers' property, as well as murders of chiefs and other Africans loyal to the government. The "Mau Mau Rebellion" had begun.

On 21 October 1952, Governor Sir Evelyn Baring declared a "state of emergency". Keny-

atta and 82 other nationalists were arrested and detained. Military reinforcements were flown into Kenya and war was declared on the Mau Mau. Before the month was over, Kenyatta and five of his colleagues were charged with managing this "unlawful organisation". And, despite a spirited defence by a team of international lawyers, Kenyatta was convicted and sentenced to serve seven years in jail.

Walter Odede, a Luo, took over leadership of KAU, but the party was banned soon afterwards and the new leaders detained. By then, accordingly to the colonial government, at least 59 leading Africans had been murdered. The reprisal – the arrest of the KAU leaders – only made the matters worse. It was followed by an outpouring of Kikuyu from the "White Highlands" and many urban areas into the forest enclaves of the Mau Mau around the Aberdares and Mount Kenya.

The government used drastic measures to deal with the rebellion. They herded rural communities together, cramming people into "protected villages" surrounded with barbed wire. Anyone found outside during a strict night curfew was shot. To augment the police and the army, 20,000

**DEATH TOLL**

Between 1952 and 1960, the casualty count of the Mau Mau rebellion was 13,577 killed and 3,959 wounded. Of the dead, only about 100 were Europeans.

Central Province – "to encourage a simple and orderly development of African political life".

A majority of the settlers were far from accepting Africans as partners in the government, while a majority of Africans no longer cared what the Europeans thought. The following year saw yet another Constitution which gave the Africans eight seats in the Legislative Council – this time elected by all constituents in the country's eight provinces.

These first full representatives of the Kenyan

Kikuyu "Home Guards" were recruited, a move that, along with Christian opposition to the Mau Mau, expanded the rebellion to civil war.

During 1953 and 1954, a number of pitched battles took place between Mau Mau fighters and government troops. After these, the rebels were more or less on the run. The Colonial Secretary, Oliver Lyttelton, turned up in Kenya, and subsequently produced a document known as the "Lyttelton Constitution". This created a multi-racial Council of Ministers, which infuriated the settlers.

In June 1955, the government announced that Africans could form political parties at district levels – except in the Mau Mau heartland of

majority included Daniel Toroitich arap Moi, later President; Tom Mboya, assassinated after independence; Ronald Ngala, who died in a road accident; and Oginga Odinga, an important political figure.

Six months before Kenyatta's jail term ended, the Africans on the Legislative Council started a clamour for his release. The government gave way to agitation and lifted the "state of emergency" in 1960, not without resistance at first. But it was clear that a settler-dominated government could no longer be sure of maintaining law and order in Kenya. This, together with the continued agitation of the African elected members, led the British Government to convene the 1960 "Lancaster House Conference" on the future of the colony.

Advising the Africans was a future US Supreme Court Justice, Thurgood Marshall, but as usual, they failed to get what they wanted. Even so, the principle of majority rule and ultimate independence for Kenya as an African – not a white man's – country was endorsed.

At its first meeting as a legal political party, KAU changed its name for no apparent reason to the Kenya African National Union (KANU). But there was almost instant division. The coast's man, Ronald Ngala, with other leaders from the Luhya, the Kalenjin and the Maasai, formed

safeguard the rights of the minorities; it also had support from a considerable number of the settlers. For a while Kenyatta toyed with the idea of forming his own political party. But, because of his long association with the people and ideas that dominated KANU, he eventually agreed to take over as president of the party.

## Uhuru at last

Kenyatta led KANU's delegation to another round of talks at Lancaster House in London in November. Haggling, threats and compromise went on for two years until the Colonial Office finally got KADU and KANU to agree on

the Kenya African Democratic Union (KADU), with Ngala as president.

Finally, Kenyatta was released in August 1961, and returned to Nairobi to find two hostile groups of African nationalists in the Legislative Council. Apart from their mutual insistence on *Uhuru,* the two parties had nothing in common. KANU wanted a unitary form of government with firm control from Nairobi. KADU wanted a federal type of government to

**LEFT:** British soldiers guard Mau Mau rebels after mass arrests in Nairobi.

**ABOVE:** Prime Minister Kenyatta welcomes returning freedom fighters to Independence celebrations in 1963.

a date for the end of colonial rule – 12 December 1963.

It rained the night before, but the crowds were impervious to it as they gathered in their thousands towards midnight at a makeshift "Independence Square". This was barely 5 km (3 miles) from the site of the 1922 shooting. Men and women all over the country had their ears tuned to their radio sets. Then it happened: midnight and "freedom" – the embattled, long-delayed *Uhuru.* The lights at the square were dimmed. When they were turned on again, the Union Jack was nowhere to be seen. From the flagstaff flew the black, red and green ensign of the new independent Kenya. ❑

# THE MODERN REPUBLIC

*The years since 1963 have not been easy for any African state, but Kenya*
*has coped better than most with natural disasters and political unrest*

As the flag of independent Kenya was being raised for the first time on 12 December 1963, there was a momentary hitch as the rope snagged. The visiting Duke of Edinburgh, never at a loss for a quip, asked Jomo Kenyatta: "Do you want to change your mind? There's still time!"

The story may be apocryphal, but it matches the spirit of joviality with which Kenya entered its new era as a free nation, after a bitter and bloody struggle during which relations with the colonial power had been strained to the limit. In the years since that historic moment, Kenya has fared better than most of the 50 or so independent African nations on a continent plagued by climatic hardships and natural disasters, as well as by civil strife and numerous military coups and insurrections.

Hardly had Independence been granted when all of East Africa was set aflame by revolutions and coups, and rumours of Communist subversion were rife. Jomo Kenyatta and the ruling party, the Kenya African National Union (KANU), were committed to a policy of strict non-alignment, and hoped to exist with both Capitalism and Communism.

Within a month of Kenya becoming a self-governing state within the Commonwealth, a bloody revolution not only ousted the Sultan of Zanzibar but also led to a pogrom of Arabs by the non-Arab (mostly African) majority. The dust had hardly settled when the army mutinied in neighbouring Tanzania. President Julius Nyerere was forced into hiding and had to call in British troops to overpower the mutineers.

Mutinies also broke out in Uganda, and then in Kenya. About 5,000 British troops were stationed in East Africa and some were deployed to quell all three mutinies. While Communists may have been involved on Zanzibar, the mainland troubles showed no such external influ-

ences; trade unions were seen as the main instigators. Nevertheless several leaders in Kenya became jittery about the "Red menace", especially at the time when the Chinese and Soviets were trying to expand their influence in Africa. Luo leader Oginga Odinga, the first Vice-President of the new republic, was seen as a sym-

pathiser with China and the Eastern Bloc countries, while Tom Mboya, the Minister for Economic Affairs, was accused of being a tool of the imperialists.

Meanwhile Kenya had become a *de facto* one-party state, with the voluntary dissolution of the opposition KADU (Kenya African Democratic Union) in November 1964. It seemed tribal rivalries had been put aside in favour of a "coalition" type government.

Amid allegations that Odinga was plotting to overthrow the government, he was eased out of the top KANU hierarchy by 1966. Infuriated, he resigned as Vice-President of Kenya and later formed his own rival party with many of

---

**PRECEDING PAGES:** Prime Minister Kenyatta is sworn in as President in 1964.
**LEFT:** the Uhuru (Freedom) Monument, Nairobi.
**RIGHT:** President Daniel arap Moi.

his supporters. He named it the Kenya People's Union (KPU), and once more the country had an opposition party. Odinga was replaced as Vice-President by Joseph Murumbi. A so-called "little general election" was called the following year to test the newly-formed KPU at the polls. It won only nine seats

But by this time others were sniping at the up-and-coming Mboya, including some influential Kikuyu, who feared that the young and ambitious Luo confidante of Kenyatta might have ideas about

---

**ANIMAL FARM**

In the 1966 election KANU's voting symbol was a cockerel (*jogoo*) and the KPU's a bull (*dume*). Accordingly this was labelled the "cock and bull election".

---

reaching hospital. A young Kikuyu of the KANU party was duly charged and convicted of the killing. The murder of one of Africa's most promising young statesmen soon aroused tribal tension and violence spilled out in the capital, with a near-riot during the memorial service. The body had to be moved to a distant grave on Rusinga Island in Lake Victoria to avoid any problems with over-emotional mourners.

There was renewed violence, this time in Kisumu – in the Luo heartland and base of

succeeding the President. It was not long before an amendment was made to the Constitution raising the age limit for a President from 35 to 40, which effectively ruled out young Mboya from the presidential stakes.

Within months of Daniel arap Moi's appointment as Vice-President in 1967 (after Murumbi resigned through ill health), several other important constitutional changes were made, including a provision to enable a Vice-President to succeed automatically – but for 90 days only – on the death of a President.

After a relatively peaceful interval, tragedy again struck Kenya in July 1969 with the gunning down of Tom Mboya, who died before

Oginga Odinga – when President Kenyatta paid the town a visit some months later. Eleven bystanders in a crowd were killed when his bodyguards opened fire on what they regarded as a hostile demonstration. Odinga was promptly blamed for the trouble and was immediately detained, along with most of his leading supporters. The KPU party was banned.

In 1973, Kenya celebrated its 10th year of Independence and a decade of Jomo Kenyatta's rule. Achievements noted were a doubling of the country's national income, free education up to the first four grades, school attendance up by 150 percent, a tripling of tea production and a 50 percent rise in coffee production. In the 1974 elections, however, more than half the sitting members, including four ministers, lost their seats.

By 1977, the subject of who would succeed Jomo Kenyatta had ceased to be academic in view of the President's rapidly failing health. His deteriorating condition caused the cancellation of the KANU party elections – in spite of the fact that none had been held for 11 years. Kenyatta finally died in Mombasa on 22 August 1978, while on a "working holiday" at the coast.

### MOI AS "MR AFRICA"

In 1981, President Moi was elected Chairman of the Organisation of African Unity (OAU) at its Nairobi summit, an office he held for an unprecedented two years.

No significant changes were made in the Cabinet, but there was a major shake-up in the security services and Immigration Department. The new President announced a stern crackdown on corruption, smuggling and nepotism, but promised that political detention would be only "a last resort". The new Moi era was known as *Nyayo* ("footsteps") – the implication being that Moi was following closely Kenyatta's policies.

The President made it known in the middle of 1980 that all tribal societies would be dis-

banded immediately. The Kikuyu society's chairman, Njenga Karume, tried to prevaricate, saying it would destroy the tribe's cultural heritage. But the ban was enforced in order "to stamp out the negative aspects of tribalism", even to the extent of changing household names such as Luo Union and the Luo tribe's soccer team, Gor Mahia.

After what the government saw as a dangerous Leftist tendency developing at the University of Nairobi and other higher education institutions, it clamped down on demonstrations and closed the university several times. The mounting tension between the government and the university continued into 1982 and was

## A new president

Vice-President Moi temporarily took over the running of the country, while making arrangements for the obligatory presidential elections within 90 days. The election became a formality when a groundswell of public support for Moi was clearly apparent. There was no opposition despite rumours of a prominent Kikuyu contesting the post. Mwai Kibaki, the Minister for Finance and Planning, became Vice-President.

**LEFT:** three presidents – Jomo Kenyatta, Julius Nyerere of Tanzania and Kenneth Kaunda of Zambia. **ABOVE:** the State Opening of Parliament in Nairobi.

heightened when doctors went on strike. Unrest then developed among Kenya's many teachers.

## Coups and corruption

In August 1982, it was announced on the official Voice of Kenya radio that the armed forces had deposed Moi's government and a People's Redemption Council had been set up. In fact, it was an attempted coup by junior personnel of the Kenya Air Force.

It was swiftly crushed, two self-confessed ringleaders and 10 other airmen were sentenced to death for treason, and the entire Kenya Air Force was replaced by a new unit called the

"82 Air Force". Civilians suspected of being involved in the abortive coup were thrown into detention, including former MP George Anyona (earlier accused of planning to form an opposition political party with Oginga Odinga) and a prominent Nairobi human rights lawyer, Dr John Khaminwa.

They were detained without trial in June 1982 before Parliament passed a constitutional amendment which made Kenya a one-party state and prohibited the formation of other political parties in the future. Odinga and Anyona were expelled from KANU in the same year following a crackdown on "dissidents".

Less than a year later, President Moi startled the citizens with his announcement that a "traitor" within his government was being secretly groomed by unnamed foreign powers to take over the Presidency. The Minister for Constitutional Affairs, Charles Njonjo, was suspended from the Cabinet, and voluntarily resigned his seat in Parliament only hours before being expelled from KANU.

A year ahead of schedule, general elections were held in September 1983 by President Moi, "to give the country time to clean up its house". A judicial commission was later set up to inquire into allegations against Njonjo, and in 1984 found him guilty of corruption, involvement in the illegal import of firearms, and an attempt to topple the government of the Seychelles. He was given a presidential pardon, but the 64-year-old former minister could not rejoin KANU and his career in government was over.

The Njonjo enquiry was one of the most sensational disclosures of disturbing events which plagued this period of Kenya's history. In 1985 party elections from grass-roots to national levels were held in order to rid the party and the government of "disloyal" and "anti-*Nyayo*" elements. President Moi then embarked on a wide-ranging re-organisation of the party, turning it into his own power base.

The growing dissatisfaction with the financial and political mismanagement of the country, under a party that did not allow any political opposition, came to a head in 1990. The unexplained murder in February of the Minister for Foreign Affairs, Dr Robert Ouko, was followed a few months later by the death of an outspoken government critic, the Rev Alexander Muge, in a road accident. There were strong rumours

### SENSITIVE TO ATTACK

After 1985, KANU became increasingly intolerant of criticism from any quarter. Within the party, it reverted to a system of warnings and vilification. Some 45 members were expelled from the party for dissent, many others suspended for varying periods – and membership of KANU was a requirement for anybody seeking election or appointment to public office. Outside the party, critical lawyers, clergymen and others were branded as "tribalists", "unpatriotic" and "in the pay of foreign masters". A number of prominent non-party citizens were picked up by police for questioning. Some were released, others detained.

of government involvement in both deaths.

Meanwhile, following the political turmoil in the Soviet Union and Eastern Europe, Kenya was pressured by Western aid donor countries to set up multi-party elections. Pro-democracy demonstrations in July and subsequent government crackdowns by its paramilitary security forces resulted in 20 deaths and led to the detentions without trial of Raila Odinga (son of Oginga Odinga) and two former cabinet ministers, Kenneth Matiba and Charles Rubia.

### VOTE-RIGGING CLAIMS

Observers monitoring the 1992 election reported that there were electoral irregularities favouring KANU, but nothing that would have affected the overall result.

## A multi-party state again

Yielding to external and internal pressure, President Moi released the detainees and rescinded the constitutional one-party status: a handful of new political parties were registered to contest the 1992 election. The principal opposition to KANU came from two branches of the Forum for the Restoration of Democracy (FORD). Using several blatant tactics to ensure success, KANU and Moi were re-elected, with FORD-Asili's Kenneth Matiba as Vice-President. Oginga Odinga, who was the candidate for FORD-Kenya, had played his last political role. He died in 1994 at the age of 82.

In 1995, Raila Odinga succeeded his father as leader of FORD-Kenya, while Richard Leakey entered Kenyan politics for the first time, launching his Safina party. But Moi's acceptance of a multi-party Kenya was thrown into question when Leakey's application to register his party was initially rejected. Amid demands for changes in the Constitution to bring harmony to Kenya's new political system, a Constitutional Review Commission was set up. Towards the end of the year, the main opposition parties formed an alliance against KANU, but this disintegrated early in 1996. Within months one of those parties, FORD-Kenya, itself split into two, with Raila Odinga moving to the National Democratic Party of Kenya.

When Moi opened the final session of the 7th Parliament in March 1997, after five years of a multi-party state, nothing significant had changed. Just before Madaraka Day (1 June)

an unlicensed opposition rally in Nairobi was dispersed by riot police and the main opposition leaders were placed under house arrest. Discussion was held to replace the Public Order Act – probably the most unpopular law in Kenya – with a Peaceful Assemblies Bill. In June the opposition attempted to disrupt the budget reading, chanting "No Reforms, No budget".

Before the 1997 election, all Kenyan citizens had to apply for new identity cards, under threat of fines. Complaints were made about that the

lack of organisation and registration centres hampered the exercise. The election eventually took place in a fairly orderly manner on 30 December. KANU won again, primarily because the opposition parties remained split along tribal lines.

At the start of the new Parliament in 1998, the President made promises to eradicate poverty and corruption, and to stimulate the economy. At the time of going to press, the post of Vice-President was still vacant, and there was no clue as to who will succeed Moi at the end of his fifth (and constitutionally last) term. The Review Commission on constitutional reform was still sitting. ❑

LEFT: Kenya's youth applaud 28 years of independence.
RIGHT: Parliament Building, Nairobi.

# A MODEL FOR AFRICA

*Kenya has made great economic and social advances since*

*Independence, despite its enormous population growth*

The liberal social and economic policies introduced by Jomo Kenyatta and pursued by his successor, Daniel arap Moi, have encouraged a steady expansion of Kenya's economy while also satisfying many of the more urgent political problems which faced the newly independent state. There have been fewer setbacks than might have been expected, though in recent years accusations of government corruption and economic mismanagement have raised fears among foreign states, who have traditionally given financial support.

The end of the Cold War has had some far-reaching consequences for developing countries; for one thing, they can no longer play off one superpower against the other for economic gain. The World Bank and the International Monetary Fund (IMF) argue that corruption and mismanagement are the main obstacles to increasing economic prosperity, and in this regard, Kenya's economy has not been given a clean bill of health. By the mid-1990s inflation was running at over 50 percent and Moi's government was coming under increasing attack.

But the social and economic achievements of independent Kenya's first 30 years set a foundation which could – if current problems are speedily resolved – ensure a prosperous and stable future for the republic.

## Sharing out the land

In the years following Independence, the new government ushered in a period of sustained stability which, although far from trouble-free, brought far-reaching changes in Kenya's major industries and economic structure.

Changes were implemented most rapidly in agriculture. Before 1963, the large-scale farms in the "White Highlands" – which produced most of the grains, meat and dairy products that fed a steadily increasing population – were in

**PRECEDING PAGES:** Jomo Kenyatta International Airport, Nairobi.
**LEFT:** Kenyatta International Conference Centre.
**RIGHT:** an enterprising street trader in Mombasa.

the hands of some 4,000 settler farmers. They viewed the advance to Independence with alarm and dismay. Handing over their hard-won land to appease political and social demands of an independent government was unthinkable. There was talk of a "scorched earth" policy, of abandonment. Production slumped.

But Jomo Kenyatta put many fears to rest, announcing his commitment to an orderly and fair redistribution and transfer of land. "Willing buyer, willing seller" was to be the criterion. This statement of the new government's respect for the sanctity of title restored confidence and a mammoth programme of land purchase started, funded largely by Britain.

Thousands of hectares were involved in a new agricultural revolution. First to be bought out were the mixed farms (that is, those producing both crops and livestock), which were split into smallholdings for the purpose of settling African families. Within five years of Independence, more than 45,000 families had been settled and more than 800,000 hectares (2 million acres) were transferred to Africans, mainly in cooperative societies formed for that specific purpose.

The success produced more funds to extend the scheme to the larger farms. While many were acquired for settlement, others were bought as units and left intact. The buyers were sometimes local companies, but usually individual Africans. However, the enormous cattle ranches in the arid northern area of the country were little sought after. The exten-

**GOING TO POT**

Coffee is Kenya's single most valuable cash crop – closely followed by tea. Kenya is the world's third largest tea producer, after India and Sri Lanka.

Coffee and tea had long been vital export commodities and the new government encouraged development. Programmes to stimulate smallholder growing were introduced, and soon a substantial proportion of the total production came from cooperatives, producing high-quality tea and coffee crops.

The favourable and diverse climate has allowed the horticultural industry to produce a wide variety of high-quality crops such as French beans, tomatoes, grapes, mangoes, bananas, pineapples,

sive style of livestock ranching held little attraction for new farmers in the early years. Many ranches still remain under their long-standing settler ownership, while a few have been bought by ultra-rich Continental Europeans and Middle East oil barons. Cattle and sheep production, despite vulnerability to drought, has risen, and a significant livestock surplus is exported to new markets in the Middle East and within Africa.

The big coffee and tea plantations remained intact, as shareholdings were often held overseas. But shares gradually passed into local hands and few of the large plantations today are owned entirely by outside interests.

avocados, oranges and flowers. The horticultural sector earns about 18 percent of Kenya's total agricultural income, exporting to expanding markets in Europe, North America, the Middle East, Japan and the former Soviet Union.

## Coffee boom and bust

In the mid-1970s an unprecedented high price for coffee brought a boom in a steady but unspectacular property market, and commercial constructions increased, as did sales and transfers. Many borrowers were also able to pay off loans and to dispense with the professional management demanded by the lenders. But, as coffee prices subsided to more realistic levels, the property market declined and then stagnated, and many borrowers found that their revenue expectations had been too optimistic. Subsequent business failures sparked a new boom for accountancy firms specialising in receivership.

This period coincided with the world recession and for Kenya a severe foreign exchange fall-back. Effective, though unpopular, measures were taken to stem the flow of imports generated by the coffee boom. Interest rates rose and curbs were imposed on spending. Aid donors rescheduled debt repayments. As a result, foreign reserves, which had fallen to a near-crisis

dividends was allayed by the "Certificate of Approved Enterprise". This guaranteed foreign industrialists that, under the approval system, repatriation of capital and royalties was assured. Factories burgeoned and industrial areas expanded as a result.

Kenya launched a major export drive by relaxing import tariffs and duties; simplifying investment regulations; promoting manufacturing under bond; strengthening investment and export promotion bodies; and establishing export promotion zones – all designed to make Kenya a producer and exporter of processed goods rather than of primary products.

level, rose again. As the recession was worldwide, tourism earnings dropped sharply and underlined an over-reliance on agricultural exports and fluctuations in world prices.

The uncertainty in agriculture was shared by the urban industrial community. Currency controls were introduced early, made necessary by the flight of capital immediately before and after Independence. But Kenyatta's liberal policies slowly restored business confidence, and investment from abroad gathered momentum. Concern over the repatriation of capital and

**RIGHT:** the soil is rich in the verdant highlands.
**ABOVE:** graduation day at Nairobi University.

## AUTOMOBILES AND THE "WA-BENZI"

Restrictions on the import of cars have boosted Kenya's motor manufacturing industry. Associated Vehicle Assemblers in Mombasa build pick-ups, saloon cars, trucks and vans, while their rivals Kenya Vehicle Manufacturers turn out Land-Rovers and other vehicles in Thika. In addition, the US giant General Motors has been assembling in Nairobi for over 20 years.

Despite the restrictions on imports, there has been no apparent reduction in the demand for sleek Mercedes Benz saloons, long the accepted symbol of position in Kenyan society, where the monied elite are known as the Wa-benzi ("Benz people").

## Border wars

In the years immediately following Independence, economic growth was slowed by a border dispute with neighbouring Somalia, which led to a war against the Somali *shifta* rebels. (The Kenya-Somalia border cuts across an area inhabited by people of Somali origin, and claims by Somalia to the area had lain dormant during the colonial era.) Kenyan armed forces were deployed for many months in the arid Northeastern Province. The cost was one which Kenya could ill afford.

The guerrilla fighting dragged on and loss of life seemed interminable. Eventually the dispute was resolved at a meeting in Tanzania, through the diplomacy and negotiation of Kenyatta himself. The possibility of oil lying beneath the vast desert wastes may have added impetus to the Somali claims for an otherwise empty and problematic area. But although large reserves have apparently been discovered in Sudan, the quantities are not exploitable.

## The *harambee* principle

The *harambee* ("all pull together") system may not be unique to Kenya, but it was endorsed by Jomo Kenyatta and has been very successful in providing a source of capital and revenue for rural projects starved of funds.

The principle involves the public collection of funds from within the community, including urban-based relatives, at meetings presided over by a prominent personality. Since Kenyatta's days, the system has been extended to raise funds to build dams and provide water supplies, to create higher education establishments and other amenities such as cattle dips. However, following growing abuses of the system, a 1990 report by the then Vice-President, Professor George Saitoti, concluded that, although the *harambee* movement had played a pivotal role in Kenya's development, its function as a strategy for future development needed to be critically and urgently re-examined.

The argument was that *harambee* undermines the importance of the function of planning, assessment and budgeting, and places undue pressure on political leaders, encouraging corruption because civil servants have to raise the Harambee money to meet their bosses' targets. Stricter auditing was to be instituted at all levels. Following the report, the President banned civil servants from presiding at *harambee* meetings, then suspended the *harambee* meetings completely. However, the *harambee* principle has since been reinstated and is functioning strongly.

## Modern-day tourism

For most of the 20th century, East Africa was a tourist destination only for the wealthy. But the introduction of package tours has transformed the industry, which is now a major earner of foreign exchange. Few people foresaw the explosion in tourist development that occurred after around 1969. In that year, 275,000 visitors came to Kenya and tourist revenue was

### THE UN IN NAIROBI

In the early 1970s, Nairobi was chosen as the home for a new United Nations Environment Programme (UNEP). It was a momentous decision in that, at the time, Geneva and Vienna were the only cities outside New York in which UN headquarters were located.

UNEP was first housed in the new Kenyatta Conference Centre, but later transferred to a specially designed $30 million complex at Gigiri, 16 km (10 miles) north of the city centre, which now also houses the United Nations Centre for Human Settlements (Habitat), as well as a number of other UN agencies and programmes employing 3,000 people.

US$2 million. By 1984, nearly 400,000 visitors were recorded, with receipts at around $15 million. By the late 1990s, with long-haul tour operators bringing in wide-bodied aircraft, the annual visitor count is nearer 800,000.

The introduction of luxury cruise ships to tourist destinations on the East African coast and the Indian Ocean islands greatly increased Kenya's share of the world tourist trade, and by the 1990s some 14 luxury cruise ships a year were docking at Mombasa.

The stable environment, the profusion of wildlife and a friendly population all made Kenya an attractive destination, but the flow of tourists has faltered significantly seven times since Independence – first, after the worldwide fuel crises of 1973; second, following the attempted coup d'état in August 1982 by the Kenyan Air Force; third, after the murder of a British tourist, Julie Ward, in the Maasai Mara Game Reserve in 1989; fourth, because of the possibility of instability due to the elections in 1992 and the currency crisis; fifth, by reports that Somali refugees had been moving south; sixth, before and after the 1997 elections, following tribal clashes, bad weather and general social unrest; and seventh, after the 1998 bomb that caused such destruction and loss of life at the US Embassy in Nairobi. Despite all this, tourism continues to be a lucrative industry.

## The Asian tradition

The record of achievements in post-Independence Kenya would be incomplete without recognition of the role of the Asian population. The word "population" is used rather than "community", since it comprises a spectrum of religions, cultures and castes found elsewhere only on the continent of Asia.

They have invested heavily in industry, transport and in financial services; they fill many vital roles in the economy and their contribution to industry and commerce is immense. Through their involvement in the welfare sector, Asians are also a mainstay of many charity institutions and programmes. Kenya's culture and economy are all the richer for the Asian presence, and there are many vital areas where Asian capital, expertise and hard work make an immeasurable contribution.

**LEFT:** Kenya Airways, the national carrier.
**RIGHT:** harvesting tea in the highlands near Kericho.

## Aid in the balance

Through the 1990s, changes in the world political climate and the end of the Cold War brought Kenya under increasing pressure from foreign aid donors, who first threatened to withhold funds unless the country held multi-party elections. To comply, President Moi staged the elections in 1992, won – and then threw the IMF out of Kenya in 1993.

He later reversed this bold expulsion, and donors released US$40 million. But the years that followed have seen uneasy relations between Moi's government and international aid donors, who have frequently expressed dis-

satisfaction with his social and economic programmes, and more than once withheld aid completely.

In 1994 the German government cut its funding of Kenya's development programme from Kshs 4.5 billion to Kshs 1.5 billion, as a statement of dissatisfaction with the government's approach to political reform. In particular, Germany cited government officials' harassment of opposition politicians; renewed pressure on the critical press, both local and international; the hampering of the activities of NGOs (non-governmental organisations); and the government's apparent dwindling concern for constitutional reform.

The following year, dismayed by what they saw as a resurgence of corruption and a reluctance on Moi's part to implement promised economic reforms, donor countries again threatened to withhold aid. The government promptly announced measures to relax import controls, to encourage foreign investment, and to privatise Kenya Airways and other state-owned concerns.

The donor countries were appeased by this effort to stabilise the economy, and in 1996, the World Bank approved a

**CLASS CONSCIOUSNESS**

There is no shortage of qualified schoolteachers in Kenya, thanks to a large education programme funded by Britain and to teacher-training colleges paid for by Sweden and Canada.

the tottering economy was devastated by bad weather. Heavy rains, caused in part by El Niño, destroyed crops, livestock, roads and communications. Crops rotted or were washed away; the main artery highway between Mombasa and Nairobi was closed for over a month after a bridge collapsed and the ill-maintained road literally fell to pieces; there were major traffic jams and delays in Nairobi and at the port of Mombasa. The net result was another rise in the prices of basic foodstuffs, coupled with a further devaluation of the shilling and a rise in domestic interest rates from 18 to 26 percent.

$115 million loan to help rehabilitate Kenya's roads. The British government pledged to release £5 million in aid, and later in the year the IMF agreed to release a loan of $216 million that had been blocked since 1994.

But Kenya's economy was slowing down. Growth dropped to 4.6 percent in 1996 – attributed to low rainfall, the high cost of domestic credit and power rationing. Meanwhile, inflation rose to 9 percent – basically due to the upward price adjustments of petroleum products, the reduced availability of basic food items and the gradual extension of VAT on consumer goods and services.

At the end of 1997 and the beginning of 1998

## A growing population

The economy stands vulnerable to one major threat which lurks in the background, but one which is in the forefront of the minds of economic planners – that of a rapidly increasing population that has doubled since Independence and still grows at around 4 percent annually. A growing population may mean a growing labour pool, but it also means that the provision of goods and services must rise faster than the birthrate.

Infant mortality is declining and life expectancy has increased from 35 years in 1948 to the current 56 years. The great majority of the population is under 20 years old. Kenya has not escaped urban drift and consequent overemployment in unskilled sectors. On the other hand, there is underemployment in the rural areas and, if Kenya is to remain self-sufficient in food, a reliable as well as an adequate workforce is essential to maintain the massive contribution which agriculture makes to the country's economy.

With a population of 28.6 million and with one of the world's highest population growth rates, the Kenyan government, through the National Council for Population and Development and with the help of voluntary organisations, is trying to educate its people on the need for family planning. The objective is to reduce the population growth rate to the desired level of around 3 percent by the next century. But it is a race against time. ❏

**LEFT:** a day at the Ngong Race Track, Nairobi.
**RIGHT:** farm produce on sale at a local market.

# THE ANCESTRAL PEOPLE

*For centuries tribes have migrated into this fertile region from throughout Africa, and today Kenya's population contains at least 30 different ethnic groups*

Culturally and linguistically, Kenya is one of the most diverse countries in Africa. You can walk down Nairobi's main street and in 10 minutes you will pass people representing almost every major language stock in Africa and every other continent in the world – and they could all be Kenyan citizens.

To reconstruct the history of its various people is not easy, but the research of many scholars in the fields of archaeology, historical linguistics, oral traditions, Arabic and colonial records has resulted at least in a general idea of how the people arrived in Kenya.

Language is the most common factor in classifying different groups of people, partly because of the close correlation between language and culture, and also because a language can be described accurately and compared with others. This comparison has become a useful tool in reconstructing the history of non-literate peoples and is based on the principle that the more similar two languages are, the more closely the people are related historically.

Linguists have attempted to estimate the dates of language divergence, which usually occur at times of geographical separation. Migration patterns have been reconstructed and word borrowings from other languages have been used as evidence of contact between groups. Archaeology and oral tradition have also both helped in unravelling the intricate weave of Kenya's history.

There are no written sources in East Africa and so the work of linguists and archaeologists has a special importance. In the 1960s linguists devised a method of measuring not just the extent of the relationship between languages, but also the intervals between any changes in the language. Using their findings, the dates of

PRECEDING PAGES: Maasai warriors wearing ostrich-plume and lion's-mane headdresses; a Luo warrior with hippo-teeth horns and cowrie-shell necklace.
LEFT: a Giriama flute player.
RIGHT: Islamic women in Lamu with their all-concealing cloaks.

population movements from north and south can be established, as well as the routes that were taken and the contacts that were made between the tribal groups. About 30 different African tribes now live in Kenya, each with their own language.

The American linguist J. Greenberg has

found four language groups in Africa, and three of them are to be found in Kenya. Bantu, which belongs to the Niger-Congo language group, is spoken by 65 percent of Kenyans, while Nilotic – a member of the Nilo-Saharan group of languages – is spoken by about 30 percent of the population. Cushitic, the only Afro-Asiatic language, is spoken by only 3 percent of Kenyans. Khoisan is the fourth language group but it is no longer spoken in Kenya.

## The first immigrants

There has been a long series of migrations, which lasted until the 19th century. This was the ancestral influx of ethnic groups found in

Kenya today. The first immigrant wave was tall, lean nomadic peoples speaking Cushitic languages from Ethiopia. They moved south from Lake Turkana, beginning sometime around 2000 BC. In addition to living off livestock, they possibly cultivated sorghum and made stone tools and vessels including bowls from lava and pumice.

Later, when rainfall began to decrease and the lake levels fell, these Southern Cushites restarted their migration in search of better grazing. They encountered little resis-

the continent. A tide of Cushitic, Nilotic and Bantu groups arrived as inquisitive tourists and then chose to stay on, attracted by good farming and grazing land, and the abundant water flowing from the forest-clad highlands around Mount Kenya.

## The Kalenjin group

The ancestors of the present Kalenjin group, for instance, arrived from the area of the Nile Valley between 2,000 to 2,500 years ago. They began pushing the Southern Cushites and Yaaku out of their

tance from the indigenous people, whoever they were, and moved leisurely southwards all the way into central Tanzania.

Another group of pastoralists followed the trail of the Southern Cushites approximately 3,000 years ago. These were a group called the Yaaku, a tribe of Eastern Cushites, who occupied a large part of central Kenya for several centuries. Today they are represented by a small and little-known group called the Mukogodo, who live near the forest of Mukogodo, northwest of Mount Kenya.

Over the next millennium, between 500 BC and AD 500, the roots of almost all of present-day Kenyans spread in from every section of

territories and eventually occupied much of the rich highland area in western Kenya. Later this Kalenjin group, who took up the practice of male and female circumcision from the Southern Cushites, developed into the present Kipsigis, Nandi, Marakwet, Tugen and other tribes. They were originally pastoralists, but also cultivated sorghum and finger millet.

The Kalenjin still live today mainly in the western highlands around Kitale, Kericho, Eldoret, the Uasin Gishu plateau and the Cherangani Hills. (Kenya's President, Daniel arap Moi, is a member of the Kalenjin.) A related tribal group, the pastoral Pokot, occupy the drier lowlands north of Lake Baringo.

One other splinter group of Kalenjin-speaking people are the Okiek, who until very recently were scattered in the mountain forest of central and western Kenya. These people, who are called the Dorobo by the Maasai, live by hunting and pot-making, and the gathering of wild plant foods and honey.

Their origins are not known but, most likely, the Okiek are the product of interbreeding between the first Kalenjin immigrants and the ancient hunters.

**PRODUCTIVE FARMERS**

Kenya's Bantu people live mainly on the rich farmland around Mount Kenya, with the Kamba to the southeast. Together they produce most of Kenya's food and export cash crops.

southeastern Nigeria, was explosive. Today, Bantu-speakers occupy a great deal of central, southern and eastern Africa.

In Kenya, the Bantus were influenced by the Southern Cushites and Southern Nilotes who, in turn, were influenced by the Bantus. After many complicated migrations, mixings and splittings, the Bantus ended up at their present locations as late as the 19th century – and movements into new lands are still going on. Today, the main cluster of Bantus is in central

Farming has largely replaced pastoralism as the mainstay of the Kalenjin economy, and they produce much of Kenya's tea.

## The Bantu

At about the same time as these Southern Nilotes were entering Kenya from the north-west, different groups of Bantu peoples were streaming in from the west and south. The movements of these iron-making farmers are still not known with any certainty, but their expansion, which began 2,000 years ago in

Kenya, and comprises the Kikuyu (about 4½ million); the Kamba (about 2.2 million); the Meru (about 1.1 million); and many other related sub-groups.

Another group of "lacustrine" Bantu lives, as the name implies, near a lake – in this case, Lake Victoria. These tribes, such as the numerous Luyha (about 3.1 million), the Gusii (about 1.3 million) and the Kuria (110,000), have been influenced greatly by the Kalenjin and other Nilotic people from a long history of close – but not always friendly – interaction. They live to the east of the lake around the towns of Kisii, Bungoma and Kakamega and are famous, or rather notorious, for their high birth rate.

**LEFT:** tribal traditions are incorporated into school life.
**ABOVE:** schoolchildren perform on Independence Day.

## People of the coast

There is no doubt that some Bantu groups had reached the coast when early Arab traders arrived in the 8th century. These Arabs, together with Persian traders, came in dhows in search of ivory, slaves and skins ,and some settled in African villages close to the beach. They built in stone, using coral and lime, and introduced Islamic architecture and culture, eventually developing sizeable townships such as Shanga, Gedi and Takwa.

### COMMON TONGUE

The Swahili language, which is essentially Bantu, with an infusion of Arabic, Asian and European words, has become the *lingua franca* for about 60 million people in eastern Africa.

By the 14th century, a new civilisation and language called Swahili were fully developed. (Some think the name Swahili, comes from the Arabic word *sahel* meaning "coast".) Swahili culture has in effect turned away from the African hinterland towards the sea and the countries of the East, which gave the people their sense of identity, their religion and their markets. Until Kenya's independence in 1963, the coastal strip was nominally under the authority of the Sultan of Zanzibar.

Another set of coastal Bantu, distinct from the Swahili mix, are the Mijikenda, made up of nine related tribes (Giriama, Kauma, Chonyi, Jibana, Kambe, Ribe, Rabai, Duruma and Digo). They claim they originated from Shungwaya, which is thought to have been in southern Somalia on or near the coast. It was said to have been a kingdom, with a capital city of stone buildings, where people lived peacefully until the coming of the Galla marauders from the north.

These Oromo-speaking tribesmen had originally moved into southern Somalia in the 16th century, driving the previous occupants before them. They then continued as far south as the hinterland of Mombasa and are today they are known as the Orma people.

The Mijikenda were casualties of this Boran-Galla drive south, but they held out; their descendants still occupy a long swath of land inland from the coast from the Tana River well down into Tanzania. No one knows for sure whether Shungwaya really existed, but it is mentioned frequently in the local oral traditions, in particular those of the Bajun sub-group of the Swahili.

Back in the dry north of Kenya, an Eastern Cushitic language group had developed from the original immigration into the area 2,000 years before. These were the Sam people, the name for some reason derived from their word for "nose". They were pastoralists and ranged out to occupy most of Kenya east of Lake Turkana, reaching to the Lamu hinterland and then north into Somalia.

Over time, these Sam have diversified into numerous sub-groups, such as the Rendille nomads and the Aweer or Boni hunter-gatherers of Lamu District. About 500,000 of their kin, the Somali, occupy most of northeastern Kenya, with another 4 million living in the neighbouring Republic of Somalia.

## The myth of the Hamites

To outsiders, perhaps the best known of the peoples of East Africa are the Maasai. Like the Kalenjin, the ancestors of these proud cattle people came in from the Nile Valley. On arrival in the Lake Turkana region, they interacted with Eastern Cushites, and it may have been from them that the Maasai acquired many of their cultural and social traditions, including possibly the class system as well as injunctions against eating most wild game, fowl and fish.

Although there is little Eastern Cushitic

influence on the Maasai or Maa language, the tendency among writers is to refer to both the Maasai and the "off-shoot" Samburu as "Nilo-Hamites", reflecting a recognition of Cushitic influence on them. An emerging recognition of Cushitic imprint on the peoples of Kenya, however, is somewhat embarrassing to African historians who have spent much time and effort trying to dispose of the "Hamitic myth".

This dates from the early part of this century, most explicitly propounded by C.G. Seligman, who wrote: "The incoming Hamites were pastoral Caucasians, arriving wave after wave, better armed as well as quicker-witted than the dark agricultural Negroes."

The implication was that the "superior" Hamites introduced just about everything of value into Africa, bestowing the Caucasian civilisation on the backward locals.

With its racist connotations, the "Hamitic" tag is therefore usually replaced by the term "Cushitic". The Cushites did not, in fact, come from Caucasia as has always been asserted, but from the Ethiopian uplands, from where many East Africans originated. According to the most recent classification, they are not strictly "Nilo-Hamites" but South Nilotic (for example the Kalenjin) or East Nilotic (the Maasai and Turkana). The "pure" Nilotic tribes, like the Luo, are now called West Nilotic.

On pages 202–3 there is a full discussion of the Maasai, and their unique combination of warlike and pastoral traits. Their cousins, the Samburu (105,000), live in the desert north and a third Maa-speaking group, in a small sub-tribe called the Ilchamus or Njemps, lives on the southern shore of Lake Baringo.

## Group affinity

There is clearly some affinity between the Maasai groups and the peoples previously referred to as "Hamites" – the Oromo. Of these, there are about 36,000 Gabbra, a tribe of hardy camel nomads who roam the arid northern lands around the Chalbi Desert (over an area the size of Switzerland). About 80,000 of their cousins, the Boran, live to their east, reaching with their livestock well north into their original Ethiopian homeland and also south as far as Isiolo.

The Oromo-speaking tribes, numbering about the same as the Gabbra, live along the Tana River in arid bush country and can often be seen driving herds close to the coast either to market or in search of pasture. The Sakuye are a small group of mainly camel-herding people who live to the east of Mount Marsabit. Some say that their name derives from the mountain, which in Oromo is called Saku.

All these people have complicated age-set systems which strictly control their social and economic life, although to some extent these are now breaking down with the intrusions of modern life.

**LEFT:** a Bok woman with a water pitcher in the Mount Elgon area.
**RIGHT:** a Nubian elder in Nairobi.

Finally, the remaining major tribal group in Kenya is the Nilotic Luo, numbering about 2.7 million and forming the third largest group after the Kikuyu and Luhya. Originally from the Bahr-al-Ghazal region of southern Sudan, now occupied by the related Dinka and Nuer, the Luo began to move into western Kenya through Uganda in the early 16th century. Small groups pushed into western Kenya between 1520 and 1750, displacing or absorbing the resident Bantu speakers. They then spread south around Lake Victoria to occupy and proliferate in their present Nyanza homelands.

At first they were nomadic herdsmen, but as their population increased they settled as farmers and fishermen (they are particularly noted as skilled fishermen with both hooks and floating nets). But the Luo are still itinerant people – they compare themselves to water which flows until it finds its own level – and they have spread across the country in their tens of thousands, into major cities including Nairobi and Mombasa, and north to the shores of Lake Turkana and south to Lake Jipe.

## Later immigrants

In addition to this complex, indigenous African element make-up of Kenya, there are a number of immigrant communities. Some 40,000 Kenyans claim to be Arab, most of them descendants of the early coastal traders but infused with African culture over generations. Many families still maintain contacts with Oman, the Yemen and Saudi Arabia.

Not so well-known or documented are the early arrival and settlement of the coast by people from India and Pakistan. Immigrants from Gujarat and Kutch in southwest India probably began settling in the coastal Afro-Arab trading towns as early as the 10th–12th centuries, although there is no evidence that they mixed with the local population as the Arabs did. The Indian influence on Swahili culture is most evident in the architecture and artifacts.

Most of Kenya's present-day Asian community arrived in the late 1800s as workmen on the British railway or as small-scale businessmen. They number about 80,000 today and are mostly settled in the larger towns and cities which bear the exotic stamp of their culture in mosques, temples, bazaars and suburbs of squat, pastel-coloured villas. The Asians have also prospered in all sectors of the economy.

There are also some 40,000 inhabitants of European descent, most of whom arrived in the late 19th or early 20th century from Britain, South Africa, Italy, Greece and elsewhere to establish farms in the rich highland areas. An additional community of about 40,000 European and American expatriates now live in Kenya, many of them employed on short-term contracts in commerce, the diplomatic corps, the United Nations and many other institutions. ❑

### DESERT DWELLERS

In the harsh semi-desert and scrub southeast of Lake Turkana live the Rendille, a tribe related to the Somalis. According to their legend, nine Somali warriors once lost their way and wandered for days with their camels until they reached the Samburu region. Before the Samburu elders allowed them to marry women from their tribe, they had to renounce Islam and give up their traditions. They agreed and, as a result of this union, the Rendille tribe was born. They now live in semi-permanent settlements but spend much of their time herding their camels across the Kaisut Desert, Kenya's most inhospitable terrain.

**LEFT:** an Okiek woman in bridal headdress.
**RIGHT:** a Samburu warrior, wearing traditional ivory earplugs.

# AFRICA'S BIG FIVE

*These are the animals that every old-time hunter wanted to bag – and*

*the dramatic quintet that every safari visitor wants to see*

The idea of a "Big Five" dates from the days when White Hunters led safaris whose principal objective was to shoot wild beasts for trophies. Inevitably, some creatures were regarded as more desirable targets than others, reflecting the skill it took to track them, the risk involved in confronting them, and the quality of the trophy retrieved from a successful kill.

In time, five mammals which qualified on all counts were recognised as the ultimate objectives of a hunting safari: the elephant, rhino, lion, leopard and buffalo – the Big Five. Today, hunting is outlawed in Kenya (and strictly controlled elsewhere in Africa) but the Big Five still have their cachet. They're still dangerous beasts, or can be, and first-class photographs or video footage of any one of them make worthwhile trophies.

## Gentle giants

The African elephant (*Loxodonta africana* or *tembo* in Swahili) is the largest living land animal, growing to over 3 metres (10 feet) at the shoulder and up to five tonnes in weight. It is remarkable in other respects, too, with its disproportionately large head; toenails instead of hooves; two breasts between the forelegs; tusks nearly worth their weight in gold; a unique trunk; enormous ears and a 60-year life span.

Elephants once roamed throughout Africa. Now they occupy only one-fifth of the continent. Although they still number between 700,000 and one million, their range and numbers are dwindling rapidly. Poaching for ivory over the past 30 years has reduced most East African populations by 90 percent and, despite international concern for their threatened status, their future in the wild is still precarious at best.

They are found in all African habitats from near desert to closed canopy forest. They are very mobile animals, which means they can select foods from a variety of habitats over a home range which may cover thousands of square kilometres. The availability of grass for a good part of the year is important; the presence of perennial water is essential. Elephants move daily and seasonally between different

### THE CALL OF THE WILD

Recent research has shown that elephants are highly vocal animals. Low-frequency sound, well below or at the very edge of human perception, is a very efficient means of communicating over great distances – even amid thick vegetation. It enables elephants to maintain contact for up to 10 km (6 miles).

The deep rumble we hear from time to time is a contact vocalisation ("Here I am – where are you?") which just enters the range of human hearing. Elephants also roar and scream audibly through the trunk to produce the classic trumpeting, either in anger or exultation, depending on the situation.

**PRECEDING PAGES:** a herd of wildebeest head off on their great migration; a pool of wallowing hippos.
**LEFT:** a magnificent female leopard.
**RIGHT:** elephants play-fighting by Ewaso Ngiro River.

parts of the habitat: from woodland to grassland, from bushland to swamp, and back again. They spend up to 16 hours a day feeding.

The basic social group is the family unit, comprising several related adult females and their immature offspring. The family is led by the eldest cow, the matriarch. There is no such creature as a herd bull. Adult males who tag along with a family group for a while, in the hope of mating with females, have no leadership role in the group, although they will assist in defence.

Bulls drift from family unit to family unit, and from time to time into loosely-knit bull groups of two to 20 males.

A family unit of 15 is large. Beyond that size the group is likely to split into two, each new group going its own way, one led by the old matriarch, the other by one of her sisters or cousins. But with the rains and abundant grass growth, families may join together in larger herds which, in places like Tsavo, have numbered more than 1,000.

The only serious threat to an adult elephant is humankind. Elephants do, rarely, get their own back. An unarmed human has little chance at close range against an angry elephant. The frequently observed head shake, often accompanied with an audible ear snap, is a warning to keep away. In a serious charge the elephant runs at 35 km/h (22 mph), ears out, head lowered, trunk curled under, and making suprisingly little sound.

### HEALTHY APPETITES

An adult elephant eats 70–90 kg (150–200 lb) of vegetation a day. Water is essential for cooling and for helping digestion: they drink up to 200 litres (50 gallons) daily.

## Horns of a dilemma

The sad truth is that, in our lifetimes, the black and white rhinoceros (*Diceros bicornis* and *Ceratotherium simum*) are doomed in the wild, outside small protected areas. Rhinos' horns are leading the beast to the brink of extinction, for the unabated and apparently uncontrollable problem of poaching is more than the rhino's naturally very low population density and slow reproductive rate can support.

African rhinos have two long horns, one set behind the other (unlike their cousin, the Indian rhino, which has just one). Horns are not bone, but tightly packed bundles of hair-like structures, similar to hooves and toenails, mounted on roughened areas of the skull. Apart from this, rhinos are virtually hairless.

The alleged qualities of rhino horn as a nerve tonic and general restorative (rather then the oft-mentioned aphrodisiac) have long supported relatively modest markets in the Far East. But most of the recent poaching in East Africa has been to fulfill the demand for dagger handles, a male status symbol in the Yemen, where a well-wrought *jambia* made from one full-grown horn can fetch up to US$15,000.

Rhinos are odd-toed ungulates, like horses. Their footprints, with three large toes, are unmistakable. The two distinct African species, "black" and "white" rhinos, are in fact both grey. "White" is a corruption of the Afrikaans word for "wide", referring to its mouth. (Zoologists now prefer the terms "narrow-lipped" and "wide-lipped".) The white rhino's broad upper lip is designed for grazing. Black rhinos have longer, nearly prehensile upper lips, and longer necks, which allow them to browse small twigs, leaves, fruit and vines.

Both species have lost the front biting teeth altogether and rely on their lips to gather vegetation. The habitat of black rhinos ranges from moist, montane forest to semi-arid bushland. The white rhino prefers the drier habitat of open or wooded grassland.

The rhinos' keen senses of smell and hearing compensate for their weak eyesight. They can turn their ears to locate the source of any disturbance. Man is the rhino's main predator, although lions and hyenas may try to attack very young calves. Rhinos are able to rout or dispatch most intruders after a short 50 kph (30 mph) charge. Disturbed rhinos are prone to attack – often before they have properly located the source of disturbance, so the charge may not be directly towards the intended target. Other charges may stop short, as though the real purpose is to get close enough to identify and intimidate the disturbance.

## The king of beasts

The lion (*Panthera leo,* or *simba* in Swahili) is the largest of the big cats, twice the weight of its cousin, the leopard. Lions are far more social than other cats, and also show greater differences between the sexes. Males have manes that are fully developed after four years, and they are up to 50 percent heavier than females. Young lions have a spotted coat which, over the first two years, becomes a nearly uniform tawny.

Lions are widespread in wooded and bushed habitats. Although they are often seen in completely open grasslands, they prefer areas which have cover for hunting and hiding young. They maintain healthy populations in most of Kenya's national parks and reserves.

They are predominantly active in the evening, early morning, and intermittently through the night. They tend to spend nearly all daylight hours resting or asleep in the shade.

Lions are the only really social cats. Prides are built around up to 15 related lionesses and their dependent offspring, accompanied by a coalition of males, many of whom are probably brothers unrelated to the females. When young females mature they join their mothers and aunts as breeding pride members, but young males leave and seek unrelated prides to attempt to take over.

Lion prides are ever changing: males hold sway over a group of females for an average of only 18 months, before they are ousted, sometimes even killed, by stronger or more numerous newcomers.

Nomadic male lions regularly kill the cubs of others – presumably to eliminate from the population the genetic material of rivals. Young cubs are also at risk from other predators such as hyenas and leopards. Lionesses try to keep their brood well hidden and move the hiding places if disturbed.

Most of the lion's prey are medium to large ungulates, such as wildebeest and zebra, but they will also take smaller creatures such as warthogs and gazelles, and even rodents, fledgling birds or ostrich eggs. Males need to eat approximately 7 kg (20 lb) of meat a day; females 5 kg (11 lb).

### HUNTING PARTIES

Lions routinely tackle prey, such as buffalos, that are beyond the ability of other predators. They stalk and ambush their prey but, unlike cheetahs and leopards, lionesses hunt as a group (with the males tagging behind). Although they can reach 60 kph (35 mph), most of their prey can sprint faster, so lions must get within 30 metres (100 ft) before charging, slapping down and grabbing the victim, which is then suffocated with a quick neck bite or a sustained bite over the muzzle. Larger prey may be overcome by several lions together and other members of the pride may begin to tear open the victim while one lion is still suffocating it.

**LEFT:** a black rhino grazes under a giant euphorbia.
**RIGHT:** the intense gaze of an alert lioness.

## The solitary hunter

The leopard (*Panthera pardus,* or *chui* in Swahili) is the largest spotted cat, distinguished from the more slender cheetah by its heavy build, pug-mark spots and thick, white-tipped tail. It is also the most elusive of the large cats, mainly due to its nocturnal and secretive habits. Leopards have been little studied, so not much is known about their behaviour in the wild. They are active day and night, but veer towards nocturnalism, to avoid harassment.

> **BRANCHING OUT**
>
> Of all the African cats, the leopard is the most adept at climbing trees, which assures it protection from lions, concealment for ambush and a safe place to store its kill for later consumption.

availability of food. Males and females defend their own, often overlapping, territories from members of their own sex. Males mark trees and logs throughout their area by clawing bark and spraying urine. Female territories tend to be smaller and several may be encompassed within one male territory.

Leopards, like all other cats except lions, are solitary breeders. Males court, consort and mate, but there the honeymoon ends: they leave and take no part in cub rearing. The only long-

The leopard is found in all except the driest African habitats – namely, woodland, bushland, wooded grassland and forest. It is the most widespread member of the cat family, even commonly occurring in suburban areas. *Kopjes* (rocky outcrops) and large trees along rivers are favourite resting sites. As long as there is an adequate food supply and a minimum of persecution, the leopard is at home. However, despite its adaptability, persecution by those involved in the fur trade and competition with man for living space have reduced leopard numbers drastically.

Leopards are solitary animals. They occupy and defend home ranges which can extend up to 30 sq. km (12 sq. miles) depending on the

term social bond is between a leopardess and her cubs, which are weaned after three months and become independent after two years.

The leopard's diet includes most small to medium herbivores (impala are a favourite), large birds, rodents and primates, as well as smaller carnivores, such as servals and jackals.

Leopards mainly use stealth and surprise to capture their prey. Like cheetahs and lions, they are stalkers, but their tree-climbing habit adds a third dimension to their hunts: it is a common tactic to leap out of trees onto prey and seize it by the throat. But the leopard is not keen on long chases. If the prey is not secured after a rush of a few metres, it invariably gets away.

## A dangerous bovine

The African buffalo (*Syncerus caffer*, or *nyati* in Swahili) is traditionally known as the meanest beast in the bush, prone to launch a charge at the drop of a hat – and many an old-time hunter was maimed by this giant herbivore. It is an understandable reaction if one is being shot at, and solitary males hate being disturbed. But the majority of buffalos in cow-calf herds are nearly as docile as cattle.

As grazers, buffalos are generally found in grassland, where they do most of their feeding and moving around at evening, night and early morning. They spend the rest of their time lying

prides of lions. It is not uncommon, though, for lions to be fatally injured during a prolonged battle with a wounded buffalo.

Buffalos live in herds of relatively stable size. They may number up to 2,000, but large herds tend to fragment during the dry season and regroup in the wet. This spreads the grazing load when grass is in short supply.

Bachelor groups of 10 to 15 are common, and consist either of old, retired bulls who no longer bother to keep competing for females, or younger bulls nearing their prime. Solitary old males or small bull groups are the animals most likely to charge intruders. ❏

down and ruminating, in shade if available, rather like cows in a field. Buffalos, which weigh up to 800 kg (1,750 lb), must drink daily, so are never found more than 15 km (9 miles) from water. Like domestic cattle, they probably sleep for no more than an hour a day.

The massive, bossed horns and exceptional size of the animal afford considerable protection. This has allowed blind, lame, even three-legged individuals to survive longer than could have been expected. Solitary bulls, without the protection of numbers, commonly fall prey to

### GRASS-ROOTS DEMOCRACY

A group of buffalo cows and their calves does not appear to have an obvious leader. Decisions about which way a resting group should move next seem to be taken by a form of popular vote.

When the herd are resting and ruminating, individual females occasionally stand up, face a particular direction for a few moments, then lie down again to continue chewing the cud. After a couple of hours, the whole herd moves off in the direction most buffalos faced when standing. "Voting" appears to pay off, since it usually seems to take the herd in the direction of the greatest amount of grass in the neighbourhood.

**LEFT:** a male lion feasts on a zebra kill.
**ABOVE:** a buffalo cow, with a red-billed oxpecker.

# THE PREDATORS

*There are cats, there are dogs, there are relatives of the weasel – and plenty*
*of other creatures besides – all living by hunting and killing*

The cheetah (*Acinonyx jubatus*) is a lean and muscular cat, standing taller than a leopard but weighing only about half as much (40–60 kg/90–130 lb). Its rounded spots are dotted all over its body, not grouped in rosettes like a leopard's, and it has a distinctive a "tear stripe" running from eye to jaw. Its silhouette is long and lanky. Unlike the rest of the cat family, the cheetah does not have retractable claws.

You have a reasonable chance of observing cheetahs in Nairobi and Amboseli national parks, or in the Maasai Mara National Reserve. They are gazelle-hunting specialists, so their distribution roughly corresponds to the open dry range of the antelopes. They are the most endangered of the three large cats perhaps because, unlike leopards, they are unable to adapt easily to the changes wrought to their habitat by humans, who are gradually forcing them into marginal areas.

Cheetahs are diurnal animals which prefer to hunt at dawn. But in game parks where they are hassled by tourist vehicles, they have taken to hunting during the heat of the day, when tourists return to the lodges for lunch.

Cheetahs are generally silent, solitary animals except for consorting pairs and females with dependent offspring. Young animals which have just left their mother tend to stay together for a time and males sometimes band together temporarily to defend a territory.

Males and females socialise only whilst the female is on heat. They select breeding areas that have a reasonable number of gazelles, with good hiding places for cubs, perennial water and relatively low densities of possible cub predators. Males congregate in these areas which allows them to mate with local females.

After a gestation period of three months, cheetah cubs are born blind, naked and helpless. Litter size varies from one to eight (usually three) cubs. Females hide them away for two to three weeks in dens, often in dense vegetation

or among rocks. Mothers hunt for food, leaving the cubs in hiding, and periodically returning to suckle them. Every few days she moves her litter between dens. Although adults are not very vulnerable to predators, cheetah cubs are preyed on by hyenas, lions and leopards.

Cubs may be born at any time of year, but

### EDUCATION IN SURVIVAL

At five to six weeks cheetah cubs venture out after their mother to join her at kills. This is an important period for the cubs since, unlike other young cats, they do not know instinctively how to stalk, chase, catch and kill their prey.

A cheetah cub, when presented with a mouse for the first time, will stare stupidly at it, or perhaps even run away. In contrast, other young cats, such as a young leopard or a young serval, will pounce on the mouse without hesitation. Therefore, cheetah mothers must bring dazed or half-dead young gazelles or hares to their offspring and patiently instruct them in the process of being a hunter.

**LEFT:** a cheetah and her cubs on the Mara plains.
**RIGHT:** one of the smaller cats – the elusive serval.

there is a peak which coincides with the appearance of gazelle fawns, which are easy prey for females.

Cheetahs prey on relatively small animals such as Thomson's gazelles, relying on sight to locate, stalk and initiate pursuits. They select the least vigilant animal on the edge of the group as victim. Although cheetahs are the world's fastest land mammal, they cannot maintain their top speed of 95 kph (56 mph) for more than about 300 metres (330 yards), so unless they can get close

### JUST LIKE TIDDLES

All the smaller cats make typical feline sounds, communicating by variations on the "miaow" theme, snarling and spitting as a warning, and purring when content.

a thick-set domestic tabby cat. It's a solitary hunter and prowls mostly at night. It is found in a variety of habitats, from wooded areas to semi-arid bush, but is not common. Near human settlements it often interbreeds with the domestic cat.

Slightly larger, and much rarer, is the golden cat (*Felis aurata*), a reddish-brown feline that is almost entirely nocturnal. It's a forest-dweller and the only recorded sightings in Kenya have been in the Mau Forest and around Mount Elgon.

to their prey undetected before starting their chase, they are rarely successful.

In a typical kill, cheetahs use their forefeet to knock the running animal off balance, then clamp tightly on to its neck to strangle it. The dead prey is invariably dragged into cover, where the cheetahs will feed. Females will call their cubs to the kill with a soft, bird-like chirrup. Adults will not hunt again until about four days after a successful kill.

### Smaller cats

There are several other cats living in Kenya, but you will be lucky to see any of them. The African wild cat *(Felis lybica)* looks rather like

The serval (*Felis serval*) is more widespread but still elusive. It's a large tawny-yellow spotted cat, around 50 cm (20 ins) tall at the shoulder, with long legs and large oval ears. It favours areas of scattered bush, tall grass, or dry reedbeds near streams.

Last of the smaller cats is the caracal (*Felis caracal*), slightly smaller than the serval, sleek and reddish-brown with tufted ears. It favours open woodlands and semi-arid bush country, but is not common anywhere in Kenya. Like all its cousins, it is rarely seen in daytime.

All these small cats have several features in common. They do not have a very good sense of smell, but on the other hand their hearing is excellent and keenly directional; also, their eye-sight is acute in dim light.

The small cats' main enemies are big raptors and other large predators. Their basic defence is alertness and the avoidance of open areas monitored by birds of prey. They are entirely carnivorous. Small living prey is stalked, pounced upon, hooked with extended claws, and then killed.

Killing techniques depend on the size of the prey: very small animals – insects, lizards, mice – are simply bitten to

### MIGHTY BITE

The hyena, with the strongest jaws of any mammal, can eat large bones – a source of nutritious marrow. Hyena droppings are often white because of all the calcium they contain.

## Hyenas

The spotted hyena (*Crocuta crocuta*) has powerful forelegs and shoulders, a long neck and a heavily-built skull with formidable teeth. Ears are round and the coat is spotted. They are found in dry acacia bushland, open plains and rocky country where there is abundant wildlife. They are not common in heavily wooded country or in forests, but can live at high altitudes, up to 4,000 metres (13,000 ft).

The striped hyena (*Hyaena hyaena*), its far

death or squeezed in the jaws until suffocated. Larger animals – rats, hyraxes, large birds – are characteristically killed with a prolonged bite to the nape of the neck, which effectively breaks it. Caracal and serval are able to bring down large birds, such as bustards, and the kids of gazelles and other small antelopes.

In some cases wild cats take domestic stock. But it rarely becomes a habit, and such small depredations are more than offset by their importance in controlling rodent pests.

---

**LEFT:** the fearsome jaws of the spotted hyena.
**ABOVE:** one hyena family feeds while another waits impatiently its turn.

less common cousin, shares the powerfully-built shoulders and head, but has longer legs and forefeet much larger than the hindfeet. It has a light-coloured body, with a crest of hair running down the back to a very bushy tail, and bold stripes on the outer sides of the legs. Striped hyenas inhabit the drier regions, and have been found in desert areas where water is not available for many kilometres.

Both species are very vocal. The characteristic "whoop whoop" howl can be heard throughout the African night. When fighting, they issue a hoarse "ahh ahh" sound. When excited, the hyenas' uneven-pitched howl is eerily reminiscent of the laughter of a demented soul.

Man and lions are the hyenas' prime enemies.

Spotted hyenas are usually seen alone or in pairs, but where there is plenty of available prey they may form temporary or even permanent groups which share, patrol and defend a hunting territory against other clans. They are not individually territorial, but once a group has been formed they defend their territory fiercely.

Both species are opportunistic hunters and scavengers, taking advantage of wastes left by other animals or man. Hyenas in general will take weaker or sick animals in preference to healthy ones. Spotted hyenas show a primitive form of cooperative hunting which is generally

more successful and is better able to resist the consequences of a counter-attack by another wildebeest, for example. Both species will eat the dead of almost any mammal, bird, reptile or fish, irrespective of size or species. Striped hyenas are more omnivorous than spotted hyenas. Insects, birds, reptiles and fruit seem to be their main diet.

## Jackals and foxes

Three species of jackal are found in Kenya, but two are extremely rare. You are most likely to see the black-backed (or silver-backed) jackal (*Canis mesomelas*), a versatile hunter that is found in open plains, bush coun-

try and light woodlands. They hunt alone, in pairs or in family parties. Much less common are the side-striped (*Canis adustus*) and the golden (*C. aureus*) jackals.

All of them have a striking similarity with domestic dogs in the way they move, lift their legs, raise their hackles, scratch, bury food and roll in something rotten. Their senses of sight, hearing and smell are all very well developed. They are all active 24 hours a day; their tendency to be active at night is reinforced by human persecution.

Jackals are very sociable animals. The basic social unit is a pair – either permanent or for a few seasons. Several adults form more or less permanent social groups within a home range, but essentially a pair marks and defends a small territory which includes one or more subterranean dens. Pairs tend to stay together beyond one season – at least six years in the black-backed jackal, and probably longer.

The young are born helpless, just like dog puppies, and will stay in the safety of the burrow, suckled by mother. When they emerge from the den, they are fed on regurgitated food by adults – and not just their own parents. Black-backed jackals, and probably the other species, have non-breeding "helpers", usually the young of previous seasons, which assist in care of the current young. This ensures a higher rate of survival of the pups.

Jackals are opportunistic carnivores who will feed on almost anything they can catch or unearth – small vertebrates, invertebrates of any size, young animals, eggs, carrion, even some fruits. They also scavenge for food killed by others. As many as 30 jackals can be seen, often

---

### A DISAPPEARING DOG

The African wild dog (*Lycaon pictus*) is about the size of a labrador, but slimmer and long-legged, with a coat of brown, black, yellow and white. They are efficient pack hunters, which enables them to take prey as large as a wildebeest, though their usual diet consists of small antelopes such as impala and Thomson's gazelle.

Wild dogs were once found in savannah grassland all across Kenya. But in recent years they have fallen prey to diseases carried by domestic dogs, notably distemper and rabies. The two packs that roamed the Maasai Mara have not been seen for several years. They may have been the last survivors in Kenya.

along with vultures, at the fringes of a lion or hyena kill, waiting for a chance to dash in and grab a piece of meat from the carcass.

The bat-eared fox (*Otocyon megalotis*) looks like a small, greyish jackal with a black face and legs and a black-tipped bushy tail. But the unmistakeable feature which gives it its name is a pair of enormous ears.

This fox is found all over Kenya, but not in great numbers, and since it is mainly active at night it is not commonly seen. It feeds on a variety of small creatures, but 80 percent of its diet is insects, mainly *Hodotermes* termites. Bat-eared foxes pair for life.

### EXCEPTIONAL EARS

The bat-eared fox has very acute, directional hearing. It can pinpoint termites moving underground and digs furiously to unearth them before they can burrow away.

large grey mongoose, which also frequents the edges of lakes and swamps but is also found in woodland and thick bush; the slender or black-tipped mongoose, found in a variety of habitats from woodlands to neglected cultivated ground; and the white-tailed mongoose, a common species in wooded areas and bush.

Both of the social species, the dwarf mongoose and the banded mongoose, frequent wooded and bushed grassland; the latter prefer a somewhat more open habitat. They occur in packs averag-

## Mongooses

There are a least six species of mongoose in Kenya. These are small, lively mammals which move with weasel-like gait, pausing from time to time to stand upright and look around. Some are solitary creatures, others live in fairly large social groups. In the former category are the marsh mongoose, a nocturnal creature living mainly beside swamps, lakes and rivers; the

**LEFT:** grooming time for two black-backed jackals.
**ABOVE:** an inquisitive pair of dwarf mongooses.

ing around a dozen animals, but up to 30 in the case of the dwarf mongoose. The pack's home range includes a number of burrow sites, such as termite mounds or loosely aggregated rock piles, which are used for night-time dens, as breeding sites and as lookouts.

Social mongooses are very vocal, and have a large vocabulary of squeaks and twitters. Their main enemies are larger carnivores and birds of prey. Alertness, speed and a readiness to dive into nearby holes are their main defences.

Mongoose packs tend to change dens every few days, which ensures that a particular predator cannot focus its attention on one area, and also allows the neighbourhood food supply to recover from the depredations of the ravenous hoard. They eat virtually any small terrestrial living creature, both vertebrate and invertebrate, as well as birds' and reptiles' eggs and occasionally fruits. Poisonous snakes are frequently killed by the pack.

## Genets and civets

These relatives of the mongooses are low-slung, long-tailed, largely nocturnal carnivores, with a variety of striking spottings, stripings or conspicuous tails. All members of the group have large eyes, facing front, and outstanding night vision.

Their habitat stretches from forest edge to semi-desert. The large-spotted and small-spotted genets and the African palm civet are semi-arboreal – they spend much of their life in trees. The African civet, the largest of the family, is more likely to seek refuge in crevasses, holes in the ground, tree trunks and roots.

Both species of genet are fairly common in bush country and acacia woodland. They are inquisitive and seemingly unafraid of human presence, and may sometimes be seen around camps or lodges at night.

The African civet (which occurs in most types of country from forest to open bush) and the palm civet (heavily wooded and forest areas) are less frequently seen. They are both strictly nocturnal and somewhat secretive.

Vocalisations are used for contact (genets: "uff-uff-uff"; civets: "tsa-tsa-tsa"), as well as for alarm, excitement or threat, when they growl, spit and hiss.

Their enemies include medium-sized predators such as African wild cats and large owls. When threatened they rely on stealth and early warning. Genets have very good eyesight, especially at dusk.

Genets and civets are generally solitary and only occasionally seen in pairs. Their striking black and white markings on faces, body and tail are undoubtedly used in sexual and social signalling. They are largely opportunistic feeders but also function as quick and efficient predators. Their diet includes all vertebrates and invertebrates – up to the size of domestic cats and antelope calves in the case of the African civet.

## Weasels and their relatives

There are a number of weasel-like carnivores active in Kenya, but it's a fortunate tourist who gets to see one. They are either rare, or shy, or strictly nocturnal – or all three.

The zorilla is a skunk-like creature that hunts only at night and sleeps during the day. Its close relative, the African striped weasel, is similarly nocturnal and, although it is found all over Kenya, it is rare and infrequently seen. Both species are capable hunters, feeding on insects, small mammals and birds.

The ratel or honey badger, a thick-set, ferocious, badger-like animal, ventures out in the morning and evening as well as at night, but it is so uncommon that sightings are rare. Rodents are the main item in the ratel's diet, although it may catch small antelopes.

The clawless otter is an aquatic animal that lives in family groups by rivers, streams and swamps. It has a typical otter's short legs and flattened tail, but, unlike most otters, its toes are not webbed and it has no claws. This handicap does not prevent it from taking crabs, fish, frogs, molluscs and insects, which it catches during dives that can last over a minute. Its relative, the spotted-necked otter, a slightly smaller species, is found in Lake Victoria. ❑

**LEFT:** the African civet is normally nocturnal...
**RIGHT:** ...and so is the large-spotted genet.

# GRAZERS AND BROWSERS

*Kenya contains a huge diversity of vegetarians, ranging from the world's tallest animal to antelopes the size of a small dog*

The grasslands and bushlands of East Africa support the most splendid variety of herbivores in the world. In Kenya alone, there are more than 30 different species of antelope, ranging in size from the majestic eland – the world's largest antelope – to the tiny Zanzibar duiker, standing about 30 cm (12 ins) tall at the shoulder. Some of them graze (eat grass) indiscriminately; others graze very selectively, choosing their habitat according to their diet; others both graze and browse (eat the shoots and leaves of trees and shrubs); and a few are almost exclusively browsers.

Whatever they eat, all antelopes are ruminants – that is, they have several stomachs for fodder in varying stages of digestion and they reprocess already swallowed fodder by chewing the cud, like buffalos and domestic cattle.

All species are diurnal (active in the day), with preference for the cooler mornings and evening for feeding. Except for impala and some of the very small antelopes, most breed in a very narrow period, usually dropping their calves just before the rains. Antelopes rely on alertness and flight to escape their enemies – predators such as lions, leopards, cheetahs and hyenas.

## Wildebeests and their relatives

The size of an antelope is no guide to its zoological classification. The *Alcelaphinae* family, for instance, includes the largish wildebeest or white-bearded gnu, the hartebeest and the topi, but also the much smaller impala, which looks more like a gazelle.

They favour mostly open and wooded grassland, and generally avoid bushland and thickets where grass growth is relatively weak and there is more cover for predators. Impalas, however, prefer woodlands, riverine strips and zones between vegetation types (transition zones).

You are likely to see the lugubrious-looking wildebeest (*Connochaetes taurinus*) in large numbers – possibly hundreds of thousands – if you visit the Maasai Mara when they are passing through on their annual migration between August and October. (*See the Maasai Mara chapter on page 197 for more on the migration.*)

The kongoni or Coke's hartebeest (*Alcelaphus buselaphus*) is the most common of the

hartebeests in Kenya, a long-faced, fawn-coloured antelope with coat-hanger horns and a whitish rump. It is widespread on the grassy plains of southern Kenya, from sea level to around 2,000 metres (6,500 ft).

The topi (*Damaliscus korrigum*) is similar in build to the hartebeest, but is easily distinguished by its rich rufous colour and black or purplish patches on its flanks. Topi are sometimes seen alone in areas such as the Mara – where they are fond of standing on termite mounds as a lookout point – but also sometimes join up with the wildebeest in the migration.

The smallest and most delicate of this group is the impala (*Aepyceros melampus*), a reddish-

**LEFT:** migrating wildebeest crossing the Mara River.
**RIGHT:** a gerenuk reaches for sparse greenery.

fawn antelope that's common in the southern half of Kenya. They are graceful, nimble and capable of prodigious leaps when threatened by a predator. Only the male impala sports the elegant lyre-shaped horns.

Close relatives of the *Alcelaphinae* are the *Reduncini* – medium-sized antelopes whose males have somewhat lyre-shaped horns. In Kenya they are represented by two species of waterbuck (*Kobus ellipsiprymnus* and *K. defassa*) and two reedbucks (*Redunca redunca* and *R. fulvorufula*).

The waterbucks are robust, thick-set antelopes with a shaggy grey-brown coat and

heavily-ringed, backwards-curving horns. As their name implies, they are happiest near water, and live in small groups in riverine woodland and well-watered grassland.

Reedbucks are smaller and more spritely, with shorter, forward-pointing horns. The Bohor reedbuck is found singly or in small groups, in marshy surroundings or areas of lush grass, throughout southern Kenya. Chandler's mountain reedbuck prefers higher country and is found on grassy hillsides up to 3,600 metres (12,000 ft) in central and western districts.

## Dainty gazelles

There are some 20 species and subspecies of gazelle in the *Antilopini* family. All have long legs, slender bodies that are fawn on top and whitish underneath, a white rump and a black-tipped, constantly wagging tail. Males are larger than females and have better developed S-shaped horns. The species you are most likely to see in Kenya are Grant's gazelle (*Gazella granti*), Thomson's gazelle (*G. thomsoni*), distinguished by the black stripe along its side, and the gerenuk (*Litocranius walleri*).

The gazelles both graze and browse, but prefer well-watered grasslands where there is plenty of grazing. The gerenuk, however, is a specialist browser, with a distinctive long slender neck that enables it to reach high up on bushes and small trees.

## Antelopes like horses

The *Hippotraginae* tribe includes the larger, thick-necked, "horse-like" antelopes that sport impressively long, swept-back or straight horns. In Kenya this means the oryx (*Oryx gazella*), the roan (*Hippotragus equinus*) and the sable (*H. niger*).

The oryx is happy in extremely arid habitat, and is able to survive in near-desert conditions. Roan and sable, by contrast, prefer grasslands with good bush and tree cover, and they both frequent well-watered grasslands and wooded valleys. There are two distinct races of oryx in Kenya: the beisa oryx, which lives north of the Tana River, westwards to Uganda, and the fringe-eared oryx (very similar but with a tuft of black hair at the tips of its ears), which is found southeast of the Tana River and to the south of the Aberdare Mountains.

The sable and the roan are considerably less common in Kenya. In fact, their very existence

---

### RESPONSIBILITIES OF LEADERSHIP

Impalas generally live in two sorts of herds. A breeding herd (sometimes called a "harem") consists of females and their young, with just one adult male in charge. A "bachelor herd" is one which all the other males travel around together, each waiting for a chance to challenge a ram for the right to lead his harem.

After a successful challenge, the loser retires to a bachelor herd, and it is the new ram's responsibility to fend off future challengers, to direct the harem to sources of food and to service any female in season. It's small wonder that his tenure as herd leader rarely lasts more than a few weeks.

in the country is so precarious that sanctuaries have been established specifically to protect the last breeding herds – namely, in the Shimba Hills National Reserve, to the south of Mombasa, for the beautiful black sable; and in the Ruma National Park, near Lake Victoria, for the roan.

## Spiralling horns

The *Tragelaphinae* are a group of slender, longish-necked antelopes characterised by well-developed spiralling horns on the males. In Kenya the group is represented by the eland (*Taurotragus oryx*), the bushbuck (*Tragelaphus*

in sub-humid areas, in regions of thick cover, such as forest (bongo), bushland (bushbuck, lesser kudu) and hill thickets (greater kudu). They are all diurnal creatures, although bushbucks will sometimes become nocturnal in areas of persecution.

The magnificent eland is an exception to most of the *Tragelaphinae* rules. For one thing, it is much larger than all the others; for another, both the male and the female eland have thick spiralled horns. And it is the only real plains grazer in the group, frequenting open grasslands and often roaming as high as 4,500 metres (14,850 ft).

*scriptus*), the lesser kudu (*Tragelaphus imberbis*), the greater kudu (*T. strepsiceros*) – and possibly the bongo (*T. euryceros*), though this is now extremely rare.

They are all russet to grey-brown in colour, often with vertical white stripes or lines of dots on their sides and flanks. Males are larger and often darker or greyer than the females. They all share a delicate, high-stepping gait, even the 2-metre (6-ft) tall eland.

Most of these antelopes live in small groups

**LEFT:** the oryx, with its straight horns and distinctive facial markings.
**ABOVE:** a clash between impala bucks.

## Smaller antelopes

At the other end of the size scale from the mighty eland are the *Antelopinae* family: dainty, round-backed antelopes that include duikers, dikdiks, the oribi and the klipspringer. They all look more or less similar and are all less than 80 cm (31 ins) high; males have horns, females are either hornless or have small, poorly-formed horns. They inhabit areas of dense cover, are territorial and live in very small groups centred around lifelong pairs; all mark their territories with secretions from conspicuous glands in front of their eyes.

The duikers' and dikdiks' short-necked, arched-back profile assists in rapid movement through thick bush. Oribis, which inhabit open grasslands, have a more upright posture, as do klipspringers, which must balance upright as they spring nimbly from rock to rock.

There are several species of duiker, the rarest (and one of the smallest) being the Zanzibar or Aders' duiker (*Cephalophus adersi*). This tiny antelope, bright chestnut in colour and standing only 30 cm (12 ins) high at the shoulder, is now extinct in Zanzibar, but still flourishes in the Sokoke-Arabuko For-

**WARNING WHISTLE**

Most antelopes whistle urgently as an alarm call, to warn of predators. The exceptions include the smallest antelopes, which use a high-pitched "zick-zick" sound, hence the name dikdik.

## Top-level browser

There are two species of giraffe and one sub-species, all of which are found in Kenya: the Maasai giraffe (*Giraffa camelopardalis*) and its subspecies Rothschild's giraffe, and the reticulated giraffe (*Giraffa reticulata*). These three differ only in their blotch pattern, and their distribution. All other characteristics are the same.

The pattern of their coats is fixed for life, making it possible for human observers to distinguish one animal from

est on Kenya's coast. It is elusive, shy and partly nocturnal – so you will need a lot of patience to spot one.

The small antelopes are generally active all day, with peaks in early morning and evening. Their enemies are all the large predators, plus an array of medium and small predators, including cats, snakes, birds of prey, ratels and baboons. Their only defence is to take flight.

Dwarf and small antelopes are almost exclusively browsers and nibblers on fine-structured vegetation. They eat the most nutritious plants and parts that provide a high degree of nutrition. They are not normally seen drinking: moisture comes mainly from food plants.

another. Animals tend to get darker with age. It is not easy to distinguish males from females, although males tend to be a little bigger and seem to spend more time feeding from tree canopies than females, which prefer to feed on low-lying vegetation.

Giraffes weigh up to 1,000 kg (2,200 lb). Their high centre of gravity accounts for their strange and distinctive gait: both legs on one side appear to move at the same time, which gives the impression that the giraffe is actually rolling. When galloping, the hindlegs swing forward together to plant in front of the forefeet. Giraffes can reach a maximum speed of 60 kph (37 mph).

They inhabit open woodland and wooded grassland, but may also be seen in bushed grassland and occasionally at a forest edge.

Giraffes are diurnal, but also move about at night. They sometimes utter snorts and grunts, but are normally silent animals. These long-legged creatures have few enemies. They are most vulnerable when drinking – when they splay their front legs and lower their heads – often in the vicinity of thick, waterside vegetation. Animals will only drink after carefully looking around.

### LINGUAL LENGTH

The giraffe's black tongue is the longest of any mammal's – 45 cm (18 ins) – and mobile enough to curl round the tips of branches.

A ritualised form of fighting, known as "necking", is carried out by young males, normally between three and four years old. The animals intertwine necks, often accompanied by light blows with the head. The "winner" of the bout often climbs on the back of the "loser" – which quite frequently leads to the erroneous conclusion that necking is a courtship ritual.

Feeding occurs generally between six and nine in the morning and three to six in the afternoon. Giraffes are ruminants and spend a

Young animals may be taken by lions if the adults are not around. Females will defend their young against any attacker by kicking with their front legs.

Giraffes are loosely gregarious, with a usual group size of between two and 12 (usually six or less). The composition of herds changes constantly as adults come and go. The home range of a female may be 120 sq. km (48 sq. miles), but they spend most of their time in the central part of this range, where they feed. Males wander in and out of female home ranges.

**LEFT:** the Maasai giraffe, the tallest animal on earth.
**ABOVE:** a Burchell's zebra mare suckles a foal.

good portion of the day resting and chewing the cud. They are exclusively browsers, with 95 percent of their feeding confined to the foliage of bushes and trees, mainly acacias. All parts are taken – leaves, buds, shoots, fruits. Normally, giraffes drink once a week, taking up 30–50 litres (8–13 gallons) at a go. If vegetation is particularly dry, they may need to drink every two days.

### "Striped donkeys"

*Punda milia,* the Swahili name for zebra, means "striped donkey". There is some controversy as to the functions of the stripes, but the general opinion is that they serve as a form of visual anti-predator device, either as a camouflage or to break up form when seen from a distance.

Two species are found in Kenya: Grevy's and Burchell's zebra. Grevy's zebras (*Equus grevyi*) are found only in northern Kenya. There are about 10,000 left, but their numbers were seriously reduced by humans hunting them for their skins. They have narrower stripes and larger ears than Burchell's zebra (*Equus burchelli*), also called the common or plains zebra, which are found throughout East and Central Africa.

Zebras are animals of open and wooded grasslands. Grevy's can inhabit more arid areas and are much more drought-resistant than Bur-

the Serengeti join the wildebeest to participate in the great annual migration that passes through the Maasai Mara.

Grevy's zebra have temporary associations that rarely last more than a few months. Territorial males defend large areas during the breeding season and attempt to keep female groups within their boundaries. Outside the breeding season, they mix with other male groups.

Zebras have evolved stomachs which allow them to feed on coarse, stemmy grass largely passed over by other members of the grazing community. This enables them to survive when other grazers cannot.

chell's, which are rarely found far from a source of water. Both species are active round the clock but will look for shade at midday, resting periodically at night.

Among their enemies are lions, spotted hyenas and, of course, man. Zebras make a typical horse-like neighing sound and a high-pitched bark when alarmed. A common response to alarm is bunching. Stallions are fierce fighters and kick back with great ferocity. Mares are equally brave when their foals are threatened.

Burchell's zebra live in groups with permanent membership and usually consisting of a lead stallion and a number of females with their offspring. Many thousands of Burchell's from

## The hippopotamus

Hippos (*Hippopotamus amphibius*) are the world's second largest terrestrial mammal, weighing up to 2,000 kg (4,400 lb), with barrel-shaped bodies and short legs. Their heads are adapted for life in water, with eyes, ears and nose all on the upper side. Hippo jaws can open up to 150 degrees wide, which makes a very impressive sight when this is all that can be seen of the semi-submerged animal.

Hippos live in still or slow-running water, and spend the whole day totally or partially

**ABOVE:** hippos spend all day in the water.
**RIGHT:** mating warthogs, Kenya's commonest pig.

submerged, floating beneath the surface and bouncing from the bottom to come up for air every few minutes. Dives generally last less than 5 minutes but can be as long as 15. They do not feed on aquatic vegetation, but come out of the water at night to feed on the shore, following well-worn trails to their nocturnal grazing. During the rainy season when grass is abundant they feed near the water. In the dry season they may walk up to 10 km (6 miles) inland in search of food. Their half-metre wide mouths allow them to eat very short grass.

The total amount of food taken by an adult hippo is less than other cloven-hoofed animals need (only 1 to 1.5 percent of its body weight each day). This is possible only because of the hippo's undemanding lifestyle: floating around the pool all day does not take much effort.

## Pig tales

There are three wild pigs in Kenya, all medium-sized herbivores with compact bodies, large heads and short necks. They all have coarse, bristly coats, small eyes, long ears, prominent snouts and tusks (elongated canines). The flattened face and broad snout, ending in the characteristic naked pig nose, are related to both the search for food and fighting style. Despite their

### A DANGEROUS GIANT

Man is the hippo's only real threat, although a pride of lions will attack a solitary hippo on land, and crocodiles undoubtedly take the occasional baby hippo in the water. Females defend their young by making use of their long tusks (actually canine teeth).

Despite their benign look, hippos probably account for more wildlife-induced human deaths than any other animal, including lions and snakes. They specialise in capsizing boats which get too near, either drowning or biting the people inside. Hippos are also dangerous on land at night, since they will run over anybody standing between them and the water.

heavy bodies, pigs can swim and they are agile and quick. All male pigs are larger than females and have larger tusks and warts. Sight is, in general, the poorest of the pig senses.

The three species are: the giant forest hog (*Hylochoerus meinertzhageni*), covered with shaggy, dark, coarse hair; the bush pig (*Potamochoerus porcus*), varying in colour from reddish-brown in the forests to blackish-brown in the drier bushland; and the warthog (*Phacochoerus aethiopicus*), which is less hairy but is covered with sparse bristles and hairs along the neck and back that can be raised like a crest and serve as a signal during social interactions.

Of the three, you are less likely to encounter

either the giant forest hog or the bush pig. The former lives in small numbers in the forests of Mount Kenya and the Aberdares, and in some high forests in western Kenya. It is largely nocturnal. The bush pig is more widely distributed, in highlands and rainforests, riverine woodlands and dense bush. Though it may be common in many areas, it is seldom seen owing to its nocturnal habits.

The diurnal warthog is a more common sight, usually in family groups on the open plains, feeding mainly on grass. While feeding, they

walk from tuft to tuft, or move slowly forward in a characteristic "kneeling" or "bowing" posture, by lowering their short-necked front end and settling on their "wrists". They use their tusks only occasionally to root out food: most digging is done with the rough upper and leading edge of the nose.

The bush pig spends more time rooting by digging with its nose. It can dig several centimetres deeper than warthogs by taking full advantage of its more flexible snout. Giant forest hogs feed predominantly in grassy forest clearings where they eat mainly grass. In the denser forest, however, they eat a variety of herbs and plant parts. They rarely root with

their snouts, and the combined length of their head and neck allows them to reach the grass without kneeling.

The most important pig predators are lions and cheetahs, and the nocturnal pigs are also susceptible to leopards. Pigs will defend themselves from predators by using their tusks, which are pointed and very sharp. Nevertheless, their main line of defence is to retreat at speed, usually towards the nearest hole. Warthogs characteristically raise their tails erect when on the move.

## Monkey business

Though not strictly vegetarian, East Africa's monkeys should be mentioned here. Several species live in Kenya, but most of them are very localised in their distribution – the blue monkey, for instance, in small pockets in the west of the country; the De Brazza's monkey in forests on Mount Elgon and the Cherengani Range; the patas monkey in savannah country around Nanyuki, Rumuruti and Eldoret-Kitale; and the black and white colobus in highland forests.

One versatile monkey that is found throughout the country is the vervet (*Cercopithecus aethiops*), also known as green monkey, grivet, guenon and tantalus monkey. It is an archetypal monkey – slight of build, agile and long-tailed, and always seen in noisy, bickering, family troops with lots of young animals. Both sexes are similar, although males are about 40 percent heavier, with conspicuous red, white and blue genital colouration.

Vervets generally inhabit well-wooded and well-watered grasslands but can also be found from semi-arid regions (usually near rivers or swamps) to evergreen forest edges at altitudes from sea-level to 4,000 metres (13,000 ft). They are strictly diurnal animals, although they may feed on moonlit nights.

They have acute eyesight and excellent hearing, but a poor sense of smell. As well as vocal calls (*see box, above*), they have a wide range of facial expressions – such as lowering their eyebrows, baring their teeth, raising or jerking their heads – with which to communicate.

Vervets are prey to large raptors, snakes and cats ranging from servals to leopards. Their basic form of defence is alertness and flight. They are very gregarious and live in troops of between six and 60 animals, sometimes reaching as many as 100. Troops comprise one or more adult males, adult females and young of all ages and sizes. Troops are territorial and defend their range against neighbouring troops with noisy group displays at the territory boundary.

Vervets are omnivorous with a predilection for vegetable matter. Their preferred tastes include fruits, flowers, grass seeds, shoots and bark, as well as insects, reptiles, small mammals, young birds and eggs.

### PRIMATE RIVALRY

Baboons' main enemy is man, with whom they compete for agricultural crops. They are also prone to human diseases, such as tuberculosis and yellow fever.

more widespread elsewhere in Kenya, in a variety of habitats from rocky bush and acacia woodland to open plains (provided there are trees or rocky outcrops nearby).

Baboons are strictly diurnal and sleep in trees at night. They also take to the trees for defence purposes, but otherwise spend most of their waking time on the ground, foraging for shoots, roots, seeds, flowers and insects, and making an occasional kill – hares or young gazelles being common prey.

Baboons are very gregarious and live in

## Baboons

Baboons are heavily-built monkeys with rounded heads, protruding, dog-like muzzles and long arms. Their coat is shaggy and varies in colour from the yellow baboon's light sandy yellow to the almost olive green of the olive baboon.

There are five main species of baboon, but only two are found in Kenya. The yellow baboon (*Papio cynocephalus*) lives in bush country and woodland in the east of the country; the slightly larger olive baboon (*Papio anubis*) is

family troops from 10 to 150 strong, with a mixture of all ages and sexes. At the centre of the groups is a dominant male, which assumes authority by force and stays in command until he is usurped by a younger, more aggressive male. Surrounding him are females and daughters who stay with the family group as long as they live. Young males leave the family group on reaching sexual maturity.

They exhibit a wide vocal repertoire, from sharp barks in alarm or warning, to squeals and titterings when siblings play together, through screams as subordinant animals are chased off by superiors, to murmuring between mother and young. ❏

**LEFT:** portrait of a vervet monkey.
**ABOVE:** a female olive baboon with her offspring.

# EAST AFRICAN BIRDS

*The extravagant diversity of Kenya's landscape, with habitats from alpine*
*to desert, supports a corresponding abundance of bird life*

The enormous variety and concentration of bird life in East Africa has been sadly neglected. So far 1,293 bird species have been recorded in the region and scientists believe that many unrecognised birds are yet to be discovered, especially in remote areas. Compare this figure with the 250 or so recorded bird species in Great Britain or the 850 in Canada, Mexico and the United States and you will understand why Kenya, with over 1,100 different birds, is an ornithologist's delight.

Nature has provided East Africa with a tropical environment with every conceivable type of habitat. Equatorial snow on volcanic mountain ranges, cool lush forests on their slopes, vast open temperate plains, harsh dry deserts and lowland equatorial forests, sea-shores and mangrove swamps providing perpetual food supplies, all contribute to this unique region. The vast majority of birds live and breed here year round, but several hundred species come from northern latitudes, when harsh winters destroy their food sources.

It is estimated that up to 6,000 million birds make the annual journey to Africa from as far east as the Bering Straits and as far west as northern Scandinavia, with some birds flying as far as the southern tip of the continent. Those that survive make the return journey each spring to breed in their chosen latitudes.

## Age-old migrations

In East Africa there are only wet and dry seasons and even these vary dramatically from place to place and year to year. Driven by some ancient instinct, birds know when to leave their breeding areas to seek a better place to live.

This is instinctive, not learned behaviour. Many species that breed in the northern latitudes and migrate to Africa each year actually leave their young to find their own way south, or perish in the attempt. A perfect example of this is the Eurasian cuckoo (*Cuculus canorus*)

which lays its eggs in the nests of foster parents. The young cuckoo, even when totally blind, instinctively and forcibly ejects any other egg or even young chick from its nest. Foster parents spend the next 20 or so days feeding this voracious monster until it can fly and feed itself. By now its parents have long since left

for Africa, often weeks before the European weather turns miserable. The young cuckoo starts the long journey south with no guidance, following its instinct to fly or die.

Many ducks and geese exhibit similar behaviour. Once breeding is over adult birds go into "eclipse", when they moult their flight feathers and cannot fly until new feathers have grown. In the meantime their new brood has learned to fly very well and they disappear south, well ahead of their parents.

Those that survive the long journey over harsh deserts, flying mostly at night, find rest and feeding grounds in the amenable climate of Kenya. There is a sudden influx of

**LEFT:** a huge flock of young ostriches.
**RIGHT:** the bateleur has the shortest tail of any eagle.

birds almost overnight as huge numbers appear in the bush country, forests and even surburban gardens.

Bird migration has fascinated man for centuries. Their ability to navigate over thousands of miles with none of man's sophisticated technology, and to return repeatedly to the same nest site to breed is a remarkable achievement.

Bird enthusiasts throughout the world have cooperated to study this extraordinary phenomenon. They trap birds in nets, identify and weigh them, and record wing length and other data. Then a small numbered ring is attached to one leg and the bird is released. By making

ringing details available to all, it's possible to build up a picture of migration patterns.

The sophistication of the migratory phenomenon is just beginning to be understood. We know why birds migrate, but much work needs to be done before we understand the complexities of birds' highly-tuned navigation systems.

## Conservation

Birds play an important role in the lives of man, not least for their aesthetic value. We all know how much pleasure can be derived from watching them in our gardens, but birds also perform an essential function in keeping the number of insects under control. Perhaps most important, though, is the way birds serve as an indication of man's destructive activities on the environment.

The classic example is the effect of DDT (dichlorodiphenyltrichloroethane) on the eggs of birds of prey. This was widely publicised in the 1960s, and alerted governments throughout the world to the perils of using long-term insecticides. Birds of prey are at the end of a food-chain. Their prey, be it mice, rats, lizards or other birds, all feed on grains or insects which, in this case, had been treated with DDT. The compound built up in their bodies, without serious effect, to very high levels. But the effect on the birds of prey was to weaken their egg shells, effectively destroying their ability to reproduce. Once this was realised and conclusively proven, DDT was banned.

## The water birds

The East African climate is controlled by two major factors: a meteorological phenomenon known as the intertropical convergence zone, which produces the two main rainy seasons with specific wind directions, and the various ranges and altitudes of mountains in relation to these winds, at different times of the year.

On the coast the climate is tropical all year round, and the beaches, with wide tide differentials (up to 4 metres/13 ft), provide massive food supplies for migrating waders or shore birds. At low tide from September to March, thousands of these birds can be seen feeding along the beaches, coral pools and mud flats.

Sanderlings (*Calidris alba*), whimbrels (*Numenius phaeopus*), ringed plovers (*Charadrius hiaticula*), turnstones (*Arenaria interpres*), greenshanks (*Tringa nebularia*),

### TRANSCONTINENTAL FLIGHTS

Ringing migratory birds, and recording the time and place of the encounter, means that if ever a bird is recovered or seen again, its migration route, flight pattern and the time taken to cover the distance can be roughly estimated.

The number of ringed birds recovered is very small, but these studies add to the sum of man's knowledge and some startling data has come to light. A ringed shore bird was once picked up dead in Kenya's Rift Valley. Investigations showed that it had been ringed by Russian enthusiasts just west of the Bering Straits – only 18 days before.

oystercatchers (*Haemantopus ostralegus*), and other migrants live and feed here, storing up energy for the long flight back to their northern breeding grounds in the spring.

Resident birds are also much in evidence. Grey herons (*Ardea cinerea*) feed in the shallow pools, gulls of several species are ever-present, and in the evening large flocks of terns come to roost on the coral cliffs. Breeding colonies of the roseate tern (*Sterna dougallii*) establish themselves on offshore islands, and there is a confusing variety and large numbers of egrets.

> **ANVIL CHORUS**
>
> The blacksmith plover is so named because its repetitive "tink-tink" call sounds like a hammer being struck on metal.

In shallow water without coral cliffs, mangrove swamps develop. Here the mud attracts mangrove kingfishers (*Halcyon senegaloides*), night herons (*Nycticorax nycticorax*) and other species of heron, including the strange black heron (*Ardea melanocephala*), with its unique feeding behaviour. It paddles in the mud with bright yellow feet and then brings its wings up over its head in umbrella fashion to shade the water underneath.

There are also crab plovers (*Dronius ardeola*), and yellow-billed storks (*Ibis ibis*), which feed by sticking their partly opened, long bills into shallow water and, with a sweeping action, snap them shut the moment they touch something edible.

## Along the rivers

The great rivers flowing east from the mountains, across semi-desert country down to the sea, create a third environment, known as riverine forests. Birds take advantage of this narrow strip of permanent water where food supplies are always available. Weaver birds of all kinds nest in the overhanging trees.

Tawny eagles (*Aquila rapax*), martial eagles (*Polemaetus bellicosus*), Wahlberg's eagles (*Aquila wahlbergi*) and others nest in the tree-tops and feed off small mammals, dry-country game and birds such as guinea fowl and francolin which come to the water to drink. Blacksmith plovers (*Vanellus armatus*) nest on the sand bars and huge flocks of sand grouse come to quench their thirst and bathe.

On each side of these rivers stretch vast

areas of semi-desert and scrub. This is harsh land at relatively low altitude, with scarce and erratic rainfall. For most of the year it is extremely dry. When rain does fall, however, the land blooms: every living thing from plants to elephants takes advantage of the vast increase in food supply. Insects flourish, plants flower and seed madly, and the bird life erupts to match.

Every tree is suddenly full of nesting birds: buffalo weavers (*Bubalornis niger* and *albirostris*), white-headed weavers (*Dinemelalia dinemelli*), thousands of queleas

(*Quelea cardinalis*), yellow-necked francolin (*Francolinus leucoscepus*), hornbills of many types, and those that prey on this new abundance. Secretary birds (*Sagittarius serpentarius*) nest on the top of flat trees, while black-crested snake eagles (*Circaetus gallicus pectoralis*) wait to snatch lizards or snakes.

## Arid regions

In the north of Kenya lie vast areas of almost true desert, most of it uninhabited by man. Here are the true dry-country birds which have evolved to take advantage of their enivronment: large Heuglin's bustard (*Neotis henglinii*), sand grouse which fly 30 to 50 km (18–30 miles)

**LEFT:** a family of white-necked cormorants.
**RIGHT:** an Egyptian vulture uses stones to crack eggs.

each day to scarce water holes, and the tiny, short-crested lark (*Galerida cristata*).

Vast areas of Kenya are covered by savannah – great open grass-covered plains, where rainfall is erratic, but usually good when it does fall. Watercourses, some permanent, others only seasonal, create tree-lined valleys which slice through the plains where larks (*Alaudidae*) and pipits (*Motacillidae*) of all types, plovers (*Charadriidae*), longclaws (*Macronyx*) and a vast variety of so-called grass warblers (*Cisticola*) breed

and live. The ugly scavenging marabou stork (*Leptoptilos crumeniferus*) is often seen. Overhead soars almost every species of vulture.

Along the valleys cutting through this region, heavier growth of trees and scrub provide shelter and nest sites for other birds, who feed on the plains: colourful barbets (*Captonidae*), fruit- and seed-eating birds, bush shrikes (*Malaconotus*), francolins (*Francolinus*), guinea fowl and doves of all kinds.

Birds of prey, notably the chanting goshawks (*Melierax poliopterus, M. metabates*), find this environment much to their liking, and bateleur eagles (*Terathopius ecaudatus*) effortlessly soar for hours at a time.

## FAR-FLUNG FEEDING

Vultures gather with astonishing speed at the scene of a kill. But their nests are in treetops or on rocky cliffs many miles from the open plains that supply their food.

## Birds of the mountains

Mount Kenya lies on the equator. Here, altitudes of up to 5,000 metres (16,400 ft), coupled with latitude, create a peculiar habitat – an environment described by scientists as afro-alpine, or equatorial alpine.

Permanent glaciers predominate above a height of 4,700 metres (15,400 ft) above sea level, but regular and heavy snowfalls usually melt fairly rapidly in the tropical sun, making it seem like winter every night and summer every day.

From one of Africa's great birds of prey, Mackinder's eagle owl (*Bubo capensis*), down to the tiny scarlet-tufted malachite sunbird (*Nectarinia johnstoni*) or the hill chat (*Pinarochroa sordida*), the birds confined to this alpine zone could probably not survive elsewhere. There are many other species of birds, but the environment tends to keep numbers and variety down. Of great interest, however, is the way birds have evolved to survive in any environment: vultures have been recorded on the snowline of several East African mountains, although there is no good explanation for their choice of habitat.

The lower slopes of Mount Kenya are covered with dense tropical rainforest. The winds are predominantly easterly, blowing from the Indian Ocean, so east-facing slopes tend to have a higher rainfall and more morning mist. The forests grow all year round so they are always green, lush and cool, and provide a permament home for bird life.

In the treetops, insect-loving shrikes (*Laniidae* and *Prionopidae*) feed in noisy family parties, often accompanied by starlings (*Strunidae*) of various different species.

At lower levels, nearer the moist, cool earth, plant and insect life are abundant. Robin chats (*Pycnonotidae*) of several kinds find this perfect. So do bulbuls (*Pycnonotus barbatus*) and several species of greenbul. From the forest floor to the treetops, turacos, with their long tails, brilliant scarlet wings and raucous calls, feed on the abundant seeds and fruit.

On the forest floor, scaly francolins (*Francolinus squamatus*) busily scratch and worry the earth, while overhead the great crowned eagle (*Stephanoaetus coronatus*), possibly Africa's most powerful bird of prey, soars in display – sometimes appearing as only a speck in the sky, its piercing call drawing attention long before it is seen.

This is a place to sit quietly and watch. If the wild fig trees are fruiting, sit under one because the ripe fruit attracts green pigeons (*Treon australis*), more turacos (*Musophagidae*), olive thrushes (*Turdus oli-vaceus*), starlings and barbets of many kinds. When the fruit becomes overripe, it attracts insects, which are followed by a huge influx of insect-eating birds.

**NEST MYSTERY**

In the Arabuku-Sokoke Forest, Clarke's weavers occur in flocks of 100 or more – but their nests have never been found.

Much of this forest has now been destroyed by man, but in the Arabuku-Sokoke Forest Reserve, near Malindi, live three bird species that exist nowhere else in the world. The Sokoke scops owl (*Otus irenae*), the Sokoke pipit (*Anthus sokokensis*) and Clarke's weaver (*Ploceus golandi*) can all be seen with a little effort.

Swamps appear in deserts in years of unusual rainfall and immediately attract the attention of birds not generally found there. Since the swamp holds water long after the surrounding

## Low forest and swamp

True African jungle does not really exist in Kenya – Kakamega Forest in the west, at an altitude of over 1,500 metres (4,920 feet), cannot properly be called lowland forest. But along the coastline are the sparse remains of a once vast forest, created by unique local conditions. Situated 5 km (3 miles) inland from the sea, this forest evolved to take advantage of fertile coral-based soils, an erratic but heavy annual rainfall and zero altitude.

**LEFT:** the striking red and yellow barbet.
**ABOVE:** a black-headed weaver and elaborately woven nests.

country has returned to normal, the birds will stay. Other swamps are more permanent. Water-loving birds always appear where there is food and disappear when the water dries up.

## When to visit

The rainy season in East Africa is the equivalent of spring elsewhere. Rain triggers food, which in turn triggers breeding. So if you want to see bird-nesting sequences and mating behaviour, you should plan to visit between April and May or in November and December. If you are more interested in seeing local birds rather than migrants, then come between March and September. ❏

# HEAVYWEIGHT FLYING MACHINES

*Among Kenya's 1,000-plus bird species are some of the largest and most dramatic avians in the world – and most of them are easy to spot*

Many of Kenya's biggest birds are rarely seen on the wing, although only one species is truly flightless (*see panel, right*). Others simply prefer to spend their days on the ground, such as the ground hornbill (*above*), a bird the size of a turkey that can be seen lumbering around in small family groups, rooting for grubs and insects.

Other large ground feeders include the secretary bird (whose head feathers allegedly resemble the quill pens of old clerical workers), the guinea-fowls (helmeted, crested and vulturine), cranes and bustards, francolins and spurfowl. These are all capable fliers, and usually roost in trees at night, but you will most often see them at ground level.

The same goes for the large birds associated with water – the great white heron, the yellow-billed and open-billed storks, and their even bigger relative the saddlebill, with its massive yellow, red and black beak. Another large stork, the marabou, sometimes feeds on frogs, but is also happy to abandon the water to scavenge along with vultures at carrion or lion kills.

Vultures – there are seven species in Kenya – always feed on the ground, where they sometimes seem ungainly and clumsy. But they spend most of the day gliding elegantly and effortlessly above the plains, employing thermals to reach altitudes of up to 900 metres (3,000 ft). Even at this height, their astonishing eyesight can discern a likely kill kilometres away.

▷ **TEAM WORK**
White pelicans breed in vast colonies around the Rift Valley lakes. They catch fish by hunting as a team and use their beak pouches as dip-nets.

△ **WHITE-TOPPED KILLER**
Unlike most of its kind, the white-headed vulture sometimes kills its own prey, including smaller birds and monitor lizards.

▷ **SHOWING OFF**
The crowned crane, with its crest of bristly feathers, is common. This male is putting on a mating display.

◁ **ALL PUFFED UP**
The kori bustard is the world's heaviest flying creature. During its extraordinary mating display, the male stands erect, flattens its tail along its back and inflates its throat.

## THE BIGGEST BIRD ON EARTH

Ostriches are the biggest birds in the world, measuring up to 2.5 metres (8 ft) in height and weighing up to 135 kg (300 lb). Though they still have flight feathers, ostriches cannot fly and have evolved long, powerful legs as their main form of defence. One kick from their two-toed foot is enough to kill a man. They can also run at up to 70 kph (45 mph) and can maintain speeds of 50 kph (30 mph) for up to 30 minutes. Their long necks allow them to spot enemies from a great distance and ostriches often serve as an early warning systems for other animals. True to myth, they may flatten their heads to the ground if approached.

An ostrich egg is 15 cm (6 ins) long and weighs as much as 36 hen's eggs.

△ **FILTER FEEDERS**
The greater (white and red) and lesser flamingo (pink) sometimes number up to 2 million on Lake Nakuru. They feed on tiny organisms by sieving water through their bills.

▽ **LONG-RANGE FLIER**
The white-backed vulture soars on thermals for up to six hours a day looking for food, often returning 100 miles (160 km) to roost. Its nest can measure 2 metres (6 ft) across.

△ **STANDING TALL**
The goliath heron, 150 cm (5 ft) tall, is the largest of all the world's herons. It is common on Lake Baringo.

◁ **PEDESTRIAN PREDATOR**
The secretary bird is the only bird of prey that walks to work. It kills snakes, lizards, rodents and insects by stamping them to death. Its scaly legs protect it against snake bites.

▷ **BROWN RAPTOR**
The tawny eagle, the commonest of Kenya's large birds of prey, is often seen alongside vultures at a lion kill, but also hunts for itself.

# KENYA'S REPTILES

*From ferocious giants that can kill and consume a zebra to tiny fly-eating lizards, Kenya has a wild abundance of scaly, cold-blooded beasts*

The richness of reptile fauna in East Africa compares favourably with any other part of the world. Fortunately, reptiles have no significant commercial value in Kenya, so poaching is not a major problem. A few crocodiles are killed for their skins and smuggled out individually, but there is very little trade in snakes and lizards. However, many reptiles are killed on sight by local people as a matter of principle. Sadly, the numbers of individual animals and even entire species are being rapidly reduced by habitat devastation and by the expanding human population.

## Crocodiles

The Nile crocodile (*Crocodylus niloticus*) is a ferocious inhabitant of rivers and lakes, which grows to 5 metres (16½ ft) and more. Where there was enough water, crocs used to be fairly ubiquitous at middle and lower altitudes. Although their range has been substantially reduced through uncontrolled trapping and shooting, they are still common in many areas.

There is often a spectacular concentration at Crocodile Point, below the Lugard Falls of the Galana River (Tsavo East), and they are also easily seen at Lake Baringo. During the last few years crocodiles have been on the increase in the Ewaso Ngiro River (Samburu); and a few can usually be seen at Mzima Springs, at the Hippo Pools of Nairobi National Park, and on the Mara and Tana rivers. One of the last great sanctuaries of crocodiles is Lake Turkana.

The creature has a voracious appetite and, in spite of its reduced numbers, the crocodile takes many human lives every year, particularly among local people using the rivers.

## Secretive snakes

Visitors to Kenya are usually surprised at the apparent scarcity of snakes. But these reptiles are shy and secretive, and some have predominantly nocturnal habits. Only on rare occasions

**LEFT:** crocodiles congregate to share their body heat.
**RIGHT:** a spitting cobra usually aims for the eyes.

will the tourist travelling around the country by car catch a short glimpse of one slithering across the road. A person living in the country and often moving about on foot soon comes to realise that snakes are by no means uncommon. But most of them – including the venomous species – have a marked tendency to get out of

the way of any human being, warned of his approach by the vibration of the ground.

There are three species of mamba, the largest being the black mamba (*Dendroaspis polylepis*), which can grow to more than 5 metres (16½ ft) and is not black but a silvery olive colour. It has a nasty reputation for aggressive attacks but, in fact, unless it is pursued or otherwise aggravated, it behaves with the utmost discretion. This is just as well since black mambas can inflict a lightning bite, injecting immense quantities of exceedingly powerful venom. In Kenya this species is not at all common.

The other two mambas rarely reach over 2 metres (6 ft) in length. The common green mamba (*Dendroaspis angusticeps*) is seen along the coast; Jameson's mamba (*Dendroaspis jamesoni*) lives in the west. Both are a brilliant green colour, though the Jameson's has a velvet black tail. They are quite deadly, but their venom is only about one-fifth as toxic as that of the black mamba.

The puff adder (*Bitis arietans*) is widespread and fairly numerous, and must be considered as the most dangerous of Kenya's snakes. Relying on its wonderful mottled brown camouflage, it does

### MEET THE SNAKES

The National Museum in Nairobi runs an informative and entertaining snake park opposite the main building, with additional satellites in Kisumu and Kitale.

not generally take evasive action but remains motionless, so a person walking through scrub or high grass can easily step close enough to make it strike with lightning speed.

When it's cornered, the spitting cobra (*Naja nigricollis*) ejaculates its venom, aiming at the face of its presumed enemy. If the eyes are washed out quickly the effect is only temporary but acutely painful; if neglected, permanent damage to the eyesight can result.

The green tree snake or boomslang (*Dispholidus typus*) may be seen slithering along a branch. It carries its poison fangs so far back in its jaws that a human being, in order to be bitten, would have to put a finger into its mouth.

The rock python (*Python sebae*) is a truly magnificent snake that often attains up to 5 metres (16½ ft) in length. There are records of pythons over 11 metres (37 ft) long. As they are heavy-bodied, even one of medium length is quite massive. While they prefer to be near water, they can be found anywhere except at very high altitudes. A large python can be a dangerous adversary for humans if disturbed but will not attack unless provoked. Although widely distributed and not uncommon in some places, this impressive creature is not often seen.

There are a number of small vipers of which three merit special mention. The Worthington's viper (*Bitis worthingtoni*) is an attractive little snake with black, brown, lilac and white markings, horns over its eyes, a saturnine face and an irascible disposition. It lives only in the hills around Lake Naivasha. The mountain or Hind's viper (*Vipera hindii*) is a diminutive snake resembling a tiny melanotic European viper. It can be found only well above the treeline in moorland on top of the Aberdare mountains.

The last of the trio is the Mount Kenya bush viper (*Atheris desaixi*), which was discovered only in 1967. This snake belongs to a West African genus and nobody suspected that a species existed this side of the Great Rift Valley.

There are too many harmless snakes to mention in detail, including specialist feeders such as centipede eaters, slug eaters, egg eaters and even a little shovel-nosed snake which lives off gecko eggs. Others are more general feeders, such as the sand snakes (*Psammophis*) which, despite their name, never live in sand.

## Tortoises and turtles

Only three species of tortoise are found in Kenya. The leopard tortoise (*Geochelone pardalis*) is the largest and can grow to well over 45 cm (18 ins). This rotund animal of benign disposition is a dull yellow colour with black flecks and lives in the savannah.

The forest or hinge-backed tortoise (*Kinixys belliana*) is quite carnivorous and has a hinged arrangement on its carapace which enables it to close up the back opening in its shell to protect the tucked-in hind limbs and tail.

From the rocky areas comes the strangest of the three: the pancake tortoise (*Malachochersus torneiri*), so called because it is quite flat, and has a flexible papery shell. Unlike most tortoises, which retire into their shells when threatened, these fellows gallop off at a good speed and hide among the rocks like a lizard. Even when you find their hiding place they usually wedge themselves in so tightly that they are difficult to extricate.

The only freshwater turtle found in Kenya has a flattish, rubbery shell and a narrow pointed head. This, the widely distributed Nile soft-shelled turtle (*Trionyx triunguis*), grows to a very large size. Be careful when handling them as they have little sense of humour and bite like weasels.

## Lizards

Over 180 different species of lizard exist in East Africa, varying in size from the 2-metre (6-ft) monitors to the tiny cat-eyed coralrag skink (*Ablepharus boutonii*) which lives on outcrops of coralrag (petrified coral in limestone) and maintains an osmotic balance by having very saline blood.

The Nile monitor (*Varanus niloticus*), mainly found along rivers, is known to dig up crocodile's nests and to eat the eggs. The spotted monitor (*Varanus exanthamaticus*) can be found in dry bush and savannah country, at a considerable distance from any water.

There are many kinds of agama lizard, some with bright red or orange heads, others with steely purplish blue or shiny green heads. The agama, which can be seen around many lodges and camps, is also known as the rainbow lizard for its dazzling colour changes. The males have coloured heads, and it is fascinating to watch their colours intensify or fade away, according to their state of emotional agitation.

Geckos are widespread in Kenya, and are quite harmless. In fact, their taste for household bugs often makes them a welcome sight. Of the 40 or so species found in the country, two are transplants from Madagascar, which probably arrived many generations ago with the dhow trade. These are both brilliant emerald green, while native geckos are neither very large nor strikingly coloured. They all share the adhesive pads on their toes that allow them to run up and down walls and walk on ceilings.

Giant plated lizards (*Gerrhosaurus major*) are handsome and have a reddish-brown skin that looks like chain mail. They are largely fruit-eaters but will eat insects and mice if they get the chance. These lizards can become very tame and sometimes will hang around campsites begging for scraps.

Of Kenya's multitude of lizards there is one other that deserves a special mention: the serrated toed lizard (*Holaspis guentheri*). These are small lizards of the high primary forest, conspicuously marked with bright yellow longitudinal bars. They can glide from tree to tree like the Asiatic dracos. ❑

### A KALEIDOSCOPE OF CHAMELEONS

Kenya's chameleons come in many sizes and shapes, from the cat-sized Meller's chameleon (*Chamaeleo melleri*), which sometimes catches birds, to the tiny pygmy chameleon (*Rhampholeon kerstenii*), the size of a small mouse, which lives on tiny insects.

There are chameleons with three horns on the nose such as Jackson's chameleon (*Chamaeleo jacksonii*). Others, such as Fischer's chameleon (*Chamaeleo fischeri*), have two side-by-side protuberances that resemble small pineapples. Still others have a single little spike on the nose – and some even have plain, unadorned noses.

**LEFT:** the leopard tortoise, easy to spot.
**RIGHT:** the monitor, the largest of Africa's lizards.

# PLANT LIFE

*Kenya contains an astonishing variety of plants, each perfectly adapted
to its habitat, from alpine peaks to humid coastal swamps*

The diversity of flora in Kenya reflects the country's wide range of ecological and climatic conditions. Rainfall and altitude are the two major factors affecting the distribution and growth of different species of flora – and this is a country that rises from sea-level to nearly 5,200 metres (17,000 ft), and varies in rainfall from 125 mm (5 ins) to 2,500 mm (100 ins) a year.

Above 3,650 metres (12,000 ft) lies the alpine zone with its own species of flora adapted to the extreme conditions. Below that, between 1,800 and 3,650 metres (5,900–12,000 ft), the highland areas contain moorland, upland grassy plains and forests that flourish in areas of high rainfall (though there is very little true rainforest in Kenya).

Areas with medium to high rainfall at altitudes of 1,100 to 2,000 metres (3,600–6,560 ft) are usually covered with wooded grasslands with *Acacia, Albizzia* and *Combretum* trees. Grasslands are medium to low-rainfall areas at altitudes of 760–1,800 metres (2,500–5,900 ft). Bushland is generally found below 1,650 metres (5,450 ft) and is sometimes interspersed with grasslands. Finally, Kenya's semi-desert areas, where rainfall is generally below 250 mm (10 ins), is often covered with arid bushland or dwarf shrub grasslands.

## Plant families

Many families of plants – such as the mallows (*Malvaceae*), composites (*Compositae*) and orchids (*Orchidaceae*) – have a wide tolerance of different ecological conditions and can be found throughout the region.

For example, orchids, both terrestrial and epiphytic (growing on another plant), can be found from sea level to altitudes of around 3,600 metres (11,800 ft) in conditions ranging from warm and humid to dry and cold.

LEFT: tussock grass and a type of "red hot poker" high in the Aberdares.
RIGHT: bright flowers attract birds, which play an important role in pollination.

Where ecological zones have marked characteristics, flora has adapted itself to meet them. For example, in East Africa's vast grassland areas, the thorn tree (genus *Acacia*) has evolved to cope with both fire and drought. In many species the seed actually germinates more easily after fire; and leaves are thin, often turning

their narrower margins towards the sun to limit transpiration (loss of water vapour).

In all drier areas the grasses (*Gramineae*) produce an unusually large quantity of seed to enable them to survive long periods when no rain falls and when germination is either doubtful or impossible. Similarly, the flowers of many plants have a higher than average nectar content to attract bees to stimulate fertilisation. Others, such as *Loranthaceae* and *Aloes*, have bright orange or red flowers to attract birds, since the dry conditions inhibit much of the insect life that normally performs the pollination. Many plants in semi-desert and bushland regions have grey and aromatic foliage: the colour limits transpiration and the scents attract pollinating insects.

In the medium-altitude zones of grassland and wooded grassland there are 14 genera and 137 species of *Malvaceae*. Notable among them are *Hibiscus*, *Abutilon* and *Pavonia*, which are found mainly in grassy plains and, strangely enough, in rocky terrain and lava flows.

*Papilionoideae,* the pea family, is also prominent in open and wooded grasslands and highlands. Represented strongly by the genus *Crotalaria*, of which there are probably more than 200 species in the region, they are widely distributed and can often be seen in consider-

able drifts of colour, mainly with yellow or yellow and orange flowers, though there are one or two species which are predominantly blue.

## The carpet flowers

A notable feature from sea-level to more than 3,350 metres (11,000 ft) is the convolvulus family (*Convolvulaceae*), which have no less than 22 genera and 170 species in the region. Prominent everywhere is the genus *Ipomoea,* whose myriad flowers scramble over coral at the coast and also thrive in semi-desert scrub, in wooded grasslands, forest glades and even on the moorlands.

*Cycnium tubulosum tubulosum*, a member of *Scrophuliaraceae* with white "pocket handkerchief" flowers, is dotted all over the grassland plains, especially on black cotton soils. A near relative, *C. tubulosum montanum*, has large pink flowers and extends to slightly higher altitudes. Both are parasitic on the roots of grasses and speckle the countryside for huge areas where grasses have been burnt or grazed heavily.

In dry, open bushland is another parasitic plant from the *Orobanchaceae* or broomrape family, *Cistanche tubulosa*. An erect, unbranched spike of yellow flowers like a large hyacinth springs out of a bare patch of soil, drawing its nourishment from the roots of neighbouring shrubs or trees.

Throughout shady and damp places in Kenya's higher rainfall regions, nestling in banks or decorating the sides of streams, you can find members of the *Balsaminaceae* family, allied to the "Busy Lizzies" or impatiens of gardens in temperate zones.

The desert rose (*Adenium obesum*) is found in semi-arid areas, often among inhospitable rocks. From the family *Apocynaceae,* this plant has magnificent long red to pink tubular flowers and fat fleshy branches: it appears a glowing mass of colour in a semi-lunar landscape.

## Lilies of the field

Among the *Liliaceae* (lily family) are three outstanding species. *Gloriosa superba*, sometimes known as "the flame lily", is a particularly beautiful plant with a red, red and yellow or red and green striped flower whose outside petals bend abruptly backwards. It is widespread in the area below an altitude of 2,500 metres (8,200 ft). There is a singularly fine variant at lower altitudes with lemon-coloured seg-

---

### HIGH ACHIEVERS

In high montane and alpine areas there are three curious evolutions, all growing to extraordinary heights. The tree groundsel (*Dendro senecio*) reaches up to 10 metres (33 ft), with a flower 1 metre (3ft) long. The giant lobelia grows to 4 metres (13 ft) or more, with an inflorescence (cluster of flowers) 3 metres (10 ft) long and an exaggerated deep calyx in which the blue flower is almost hidden, as protection against the dramatic variations in temperature at these altitudes. The giant heather (*Erica arborea*) has evolved into a veritable tree, up to 8 metres (26 ft) tall and with white flowers clustered at the end of its many branches.

ments and a deeper violet meridian stripe. The plant grows from a V-shaped tuber and can reach 5 metres (16½ ft).

*Albuca abyssinica* is the most common of all the lilies in East Africa. This robust plant, up to 1 metre (3ft) tall, has bell-shaped flowers rather widely spaced on the stalk. Though they never open fully, these flowers are yellowish-green in colour with a darkish stripe down the middle of each petal and off-yellow on the margins.

### HOW MANY PLANTS?

No-one knows just how many plants exist in Kenya, but when botanists complete their survey into the flora of East Africa, it's probable that more than 11,000 species will have been noted.

trees or on the side of termite mounds, the flower spike arises before the leaves and is crowned with up to 150 small flowers-making a single magnificent red to pink head that looks like a gigantic shaving brush. Crinums often flower at the same time, notably *C. macowanii*, named the "pyjama lily" after the pink stripes marking the long tubular flowers. It grows throughout East Africa and is often seen at the sides of roads and in ditches.

In the iris family (*Iridaceae*) the genus *Gladi-*

Aloes are among the *Liliaceae* most widespread in the middle and lower altitudes. Red, orange or yellow with green spotted or striped leaves, they form dense groups of beautiful colour, especially in grassland areas where grazing has reduced competition. Elephants are particularly fond of the aloe.

In the amaryllis family (*Amaryllidaceae*) are two beautiful species. *Scadoxus multiflorus*, the fireball lily, is an arresting sight. Growing from a deep rooted bulb in rocky places, riverine forest and open grassland, often in the shade of

*olus* has three beautiful species. *G. natalensis* is found up to an altitude of 3,000 metres (10,000 ft), has yellowish-brown to orange flowers and is a relative of the garden varieties derived from *G. primulinus*. Above that altitude, the finest species of them all, *G. watsonioides,* with bright red flowers, grows in stony soils only in alpine and sub-alpine regions on Mount Kenya. *G. ukambanensis* is a delightful species with white, delicately scented flowers, produced copiously but capriciously in wet years. It is restricted to stony soils in the Machakos district and in the Maasai Mara. ❑

**LEFT:** this delicate orchid is found at higher altitudes.
**ABOVE:** golden flowers cover the *Cassia didimobotrya*.

◆ *For a comprehensive photo-feature on Kenya's trees, please turn to pages 260–61.*

# THE SAFARI EXPERIENCE

*The beaches are great and the people fascinating, but for most visitors*
*Kenya's main attraction is its wild places and the creatures that live there*

For more than a century, visitors from Europe and America have been turning up to track Kenya's game – and originally to slaughter it in great quantities to provide trophies. Since hunting was banned in 1977, photographs and videos are the only legal trophies that visitors can take away with them, but not much else has changed. The most popular areas to visit are the same (except that these days most of them are designated national parks or reserves), the animals are the same (except where poaching has affected populations), and the best safaris, as ever, are organised and led by local residents who know the country well.

Any visitor to Kenya can be sure that whatever mode of transport, and whatever their budget, the thrill of the first sight of wildlife will be a moment to remember. No matter how many television programmes on African wildlife you watch or how many zoos you visit, the vastness of the landscape and the freedom of these majestic animals in their own habitat is an overwhelming experience.

## Ready-made packages

For first-time visitors, the easiest way to become acquainted with Kenya's natural riches is on a package safari. The package includes transport around the country, game drives with an experienced guide, accommodation in hotels, game lodges or tented camps, and all meals. The most popular tourist transport is the ubiquitous minibus – the seven- or nine-seaters most tour operators use for rattling around the country on various permutations of the main safari circuits. For small parties (four tourists or fewer), some operators use customised 4x4 vehicles such as Land-Rovers or Landcruisers.

Some firms run regular or even scheduled minibus safaris – such as the United Touring Company's "Safaritrail" programme. One exceptional all-in rustic safari is the "Turkana Bus", an enterprise of an experienced local "bush-whacker", Dick Hedges. This takes all comers, but mostly youths, on an inexpensive ride up to Lake Turkana, with camp accommodation and food included.

## Luxury safaris

Some large firms provide deluxe safaris, but perhaps the best old-style safari is still provided by ex-hunters who operate as family concerns. The success of a safari was and is determined by the personal relationship and rapport built up between client and guide, and this is something that cannot easily be duplicated by commercial firms.

Before any safari, the guide will have mapped out a rough itinerary to suit the client's needs. Applying local knowledge, he or she will try to ensure that, as far as possible, the client will be kept off the beaten tracks and regular circuits. Even in the parks and reserves, the

**PRECEDING PAGES:** elephants in the warm evening light in Tsavo West; a camel safari in northern Kenya.
**LEFT:** an early 20th-century illustration satirises the Great White Hunter.
**RIGHT:** hunting plains game.

guide will try to keep the tour private and, knowing the country well, will often be able to take the visitor to rewarding places on private land or elsewhere – far from the formal sanctuaries. The campsites will be private, too.

The private guide will cost around US$500 per person per day for a party of six, or around $1,000 a day for a single client. A comfortable cruising vehicle (more than one if necessary) will be provided, backed up with a seven-ton truck which carries the staff and camping equipment. Each client or couple will have an insect-proof sleeping tent, a bath or shower tent, and the camp will have a large dining tent.

calm anxieties. Any good guide is sensitive to the needs of the visitors, particularly those on safari for the first time. After dinner, congenial company and a nightcap around the embers of the campfire is a reassuring and deeply satisfying experience.

## Four-legged safaris

If you're an experienced rider, it's possible to view the plains game from the back of a horse. On a typical horseback safari, the tents, camp gear, groceries, horse grain and safari staff are carried by truck along bush tracks while riders go cross country, led by an experienced guide,

Refrigerators are part of the equipment and cold drinks and ice are always available.

Usually the lorry and camp staff will have preceded the clients to the appointed destination, so that it's all ready for them – cold drinks, hot showers, whatever – when they arrive after a long, dusty drive. The camp chefs turn out exquisite meals in the roughest of surroundings. (Put them in well-appointed kitchens and they would be utterly lost.) Whatever the food, the evening meal is always an event in the bush.

Visitors may be perfectly at ease with wild Africa during the day, but as night falls and the unfamiliar sounds come through the darkness some reassurance of civilisation is required to

covering between 25 and 40 km (15–25 miles) a day. Picnic lunch and water bottles, together with a few personal effects, are carried in saddle bags strapped to cavalry saddles.

After a substantial English breakfast, you head out in the African wilds on a cross-country trek that takes you through mountains, forests, grassy plains, rivers or escarpments filled with a variety of wildlife. There are no fences, telegraph poles or tarmac roads, and the sense of space and freedom is quite overwhelming. You ride among huge herds of plains game,

**ABOVE:** a thrilling photo-opportunity for safari visitors.
**RIGHT:** a camel train loaded up and ready to roll.

sometimes canter with giraffe or wade across muddy rivers, observed by families of hippo.

While you explore the wild blue yonder, staff pull down the tents, drive round on bush tracks and then re-erect the whole camp at the next waterhole. After six or seven hours in the saddle (broken by a lunch stop) the party ride into the camp at about 4 pm for tea or cold drinks and hot showers before dinner.

It's an extraordinary way to experience some of Africa's most beautiful countryside: the vast open spaces are quite breathtaking, and without a vehicle you really feel on even terms with the wild animals – no other sounds or smells except those of the bush. It should be emphasised that to enjoy the experience, clients must be fit, mentally tuned in, able to face unpredictable situations and confident on horseback at all paces.

It's also possible to ride for a few hours a day at some of the private ranches that offer homestays. See the Travel Tips section for more information.

## Luxury camel safaris

An even more exotic way of traversing the bush is to ride on – or walk along with – a camel train, on a safari operated by ex-hunters or

ranchers on the fringe of the northern deserts around such places as Rumuruti.

These are marvellous expeditions, the best of them with a great retinue of Samburu staff, liveried in red loincloths and carrying spears. There may be a dozen camels, carrying everything from the morning coffee to the evening bath; plus the ex-white hunter, who knows the Latin name for every blade of grass, and a *cordon bleu* chef in the background organising the bush lunch and a three-course campfire dinner in the evening.

A normal day begins with an early rise, around dawn, after a pot of tea has been served. There's no need for bed-making or tent-tidying,

---

### RESERVE YOUR HORSE

There are a couple of companies that offer horseback safaris, including the original pioneer of this sort of adventure, Tony Church of Safaris Unlimited. He offers seven itineraries from five to 16 days exploring Maasailand, incorporating the Loita Hills and the Maasai Mara, the Great Rift Valley, Laikipia, Mount Kenya and north towards Samburu.

Because so few horseback safaris are available, there's often a waiting-list and it's necessary to book well in advance. Contact Safaris Unlimited, PO Box 24181, Nairobi; tel: 891168, fax: 891113, email: safunlim@users.africaonline.co.ke.

as all the chores are taken care of by the retinue. Those who wish can take a warm shower before sitting down to a full English breakfast served under an umbrella acacia. Down below in the wide sandy *luggas* (dry river beds), the camels are loaded up, some of them saddled, and finally they get up, rear ends first, making excruciating bleats and grunts of protest.

The camels carry a fly-camp, a canvas "Hilton" complete with such basic necessities as cans of Naivasha asparagus and red wine. The white wine will probably have gone

is a couple of hours' siesta, afternoon tea, and then maybe an expedition on foot off the river course into the bush.

It could be that the hunter has spotted kudu tracks, or signs of some other wildlife, possibly elephant. In that event it turns into something like an old-fashioned hunt: two or three hours following the spoor, the African trackers leading and the gun-bearers following. It could lead up to discovering the animals – in which case, of course, the climactic shot has to be with a camera.

### MOBILE BAR

Refreshments during the day's camel trek consist of bottled beer or soda kept cool in canvas bags, stuffed with wet straw, swinging from the camels.

ahead in the fridges, which are transported in the main camp's trucks heading 25–30 km (15–20 miles) up river, ready for the trekkers to arrive before nightfall.

Most people walk, plodding along the hard sand in the middle of the dry river beds or on the flat banks, where bright green grass is cropped short into lawns by Samburu goats and cattle. Alternatively, the camels can be ridden. First comes a back-arching balletic movement as the animal gets up, followed by a sensuous gentle swaying movement – almost a glide along. It's easy even for novices.

The day's trek normally pauses around lunch-time. And afterwards, almost certainly,

### ADVICE FOR DRIVERS

Driving around Kenya is a risky business if you are new to the country. Even the major circuit roads are in a bad state of repair, potholes abound and places to repair breakdowns are very scarce. If you are determined to go it alone, you should first seek local advice about road conditions and any predictable hazards.

The Automobile Association of Kenya can tell you all you need to know for driving on the main roads – tel: (02) 720382. If you plan to enter national parks or reserves, it's also wise to consult the nearest Kenya Wildlife Service (KWS) post for local information. For the KWS headquarters in Nairobi, tel: 574145.

## Do-it-yourself

It is possible, of course, to spurn the many safari companies and organise your own game-watching trip. Unless you're very experienced – or very lucky – you're unlikely to see as much as you would with a knowledgeable guide. But there's a certain satisfaction to be had from travelling quite independently.

Cross-country vehicles are available for hire, at least in Nairobi, but they're expensive. Usually the rentals are sedans or small station wagons from scores of car hire firms, ranging from the multinationals like Avis and Hertz down to street-corner garages. At the coast, the open and

If you plan to camp out in the bush, take advice from locals or perhaps one of the tour firms which offer this more adventurous safari option. It's safe in established sites in the national parks and reserves, since most of them provide water, cooking fuel and other basic facilities. It can be all right elsewhere in the country, as long as you keep well away from centres of population, but take advice from the local Kenya Wildlife Service post. There are occasional reports of attacks on camps. While locals with knowledge of the area and language may camp out in the wilds, it's not recommended for anyone unfamiliar with Africa.

airy Minimoke is a popular hire for short trips.

It's also possible to hire minibuses, which are in fact ideal for independent safari purposes – high clearance, reliable air-cooled engines (if they're Volkswagens), with elevated, all-round vision for game spotting. They're good for almost all itineraries, except the rough and gullied eastern side of Lake Turkana.

It's advisable to book your accommodation in advance, rather than turning up at lodges or camps unannounced. (*See the accommodation listings in the Travel Tips section.*)

**LEFT:** a motorised safari in the 1930s.
**ABOVE:** camping in the highlands near Mount Kenya.

## Other forms of transport

Outside the safari experience, it's not difficult to get around on regular transport, starting at the budget end of the options: the country buses. Cheap and cheerful, these can be an experience in themselves, with squawking chickens, maybe a goat on the roof-rack, and at least a houseful of possessions piled up to staggering heights. For some expatriates who have been in the country for years, the cranking, diesel-belching rural bus system is unthinkable, but the easy-going and patient visitor may be happy with public transport. There are severable useful routes, such as the one from Malindi up to Lamu – straightforward, but long, hot, crowded and bumpy depending on the state of the roads. Because of security concerns, the Malindi–Lamu bus usually carries an armed guard these days. Bus passengers should always be alert for pickpockets.

Then there are the *matatus*. These can be anything from a short, squat bus to a moving chassis and superstructure with seats. There is only one common denominator for this extraordinarily motley collection of vehicles – they're always crammed. Eight-seaters carry 20; the *manamba* (conductor) swings from the

rear door, and, as in the Nigerian cartoons, bodies fly off round every bend.

Where they're going is an enigma for the uninitiated but wherever it is, it's almost always too fast. Most drivers suffer a total amnesia of the rules of the road – notably the speed limit – and operate with the guidance system of a suicidal bat. Sometimes the scenario is amusing but, too often, it's tragic. The hideous pile-ups of these *matatus* are legion. As you may gather, they're not exactly recommended to visitors.

But the train is good for some routes. The overnight service from Nairobi to Mombasa, at around 55 kph (35 mph) for much of the way, is as sedate as in the old days of steam. You

**FLY YOURSELF**

Visitors with a valid pilot's licence can hire light aircraft from the Aero Club of East Africa at Wilson Airport, Nairobi (tel: 501772).

should pre-book a first-class (two-bed) or second-class (four-bed) *couchette*, since the journey from the capital runs overnight, departing at 6 or 7pm and arriving at the coast at about 8am the next day. A *couchette* has a small hand basin and a fan, but the facilities are far from luxurious. The fare includes dinner, breakfast and a bedroll. The rail journey to the coast is certainly an experience, but not recommended to anyone in a hurry.

Kenya Railways operates 2,650 km (1,645 miles) of track, mostly up-country – to Kisumu and Malaba on the Ugandan border – in much the same leisurely style as the coast trip. The route runs down and across the Rift Valley, then up the western scarp to the highest railhead in the Commonwealth, at around 2,750 metres (9,000 ft), near Timboroa. Then it's a gentle run down to Lake Victoria.

## Travelling by air

Light aircraft provide an up-market, but affordable, option for travelling around Kenya. Landing strips are littered about the country. They exist in all the main parks and reserves, normally close to the lodges or luxury tented camps, which send transport to meet the tourist air delivery. There are also strips close to townships, villages, ranches and large farms.

The hub of the network is the national Wilson Airport in the southern suburbs of Nairobi. In the early 1970s, before the bite of world recession, this was the busiest airport in Africa, averaging 15,000 movements a month. Since most of these were during daylight hours, the momentum of take-off and landings built up to one every 1½ minutes. The flow of traffic is still frenetic, and includes all kinds of plane – from what look like toy aircraft to executive jets.

At least half a dozen companies charter chauffeured planes out of Wilson, some with branch operations in Mombasa and some running scheduled departures for places like Mombasa, Malindi, Lamu, Amboseli, Samburu, Nanyuki, Nyeri and the Maasai Mara. A further limited air option is with Kenya Airways' internal services to and from Nairobi, Mombasa, Malindi and Kisumu. ❏

**LEFT:** a close look at the local wildlife from a horse.
**RIGHT:** camping in Amboseli.

# ACTIVE PURSUITS

*A holiday in Kenya need not involve just looking at animals or lying on a beach. There's plenty to do for the more energetically inclined*

**M**ount Kenya provides a variety of challenges to mountaineers, trekkers and rock-climbers. The main summit peaks of Batian and Nelion should be undertaken only by mountaineers experienced at climbing steep ice and rock at altitude. But many trek to the summit of the third highest peak, Point Lenana. It's worth the effort as it gives a good idea of the atmosphere of this beautiful mountain.

The base for climbing Mount Kenya is at Naro Moru, 171 km (106 miles) from Nairobi on the main road to Nanyuki. The track from here is the shortest way up (allow three days), and most tourists ascend the mountain this way, neglecting the more involved routes, of which there are seven. Naro Moru River Lodge will arrange fully packaged climbs of Point Lenana.

It's also possible to climb Point Lenana from the east, by way of the Chogoria Track. The town of Chogoria is 228 km (141 miles) from Nairobi, on the road to Meru. There are no hotels in town that offer fully equipped climbs, but porters can be arranged through Livingstone Barine (send him a telegram at PO Box 7, Chogoria, and he will contact you). Three days should be allowed to reach Point Lenana. A good trek is to climb the Chogoria track to Lenana then descend the Naro Moru track, so completing a full traverse of the mountain.

(For more on climbing in Kenya, see *The Mountain National Parks* on page 231.)

## Freshwater fishing

The world's freshwater angler may not give Kenya a passing thought in his search for productive waters. Yet the country offers the expert ample and varied reward for his skills. Even a beginner has a sporting chance of landing a fish he needn't lie about.

In the Central Highlands there are innumerable trout streams of a quality that would command formidable fees if they were in Europe. In Kenya, however, they are available for locals

and visitors for no more than the nominal cost of a sports fishing licence.

Fly-fishing came to Kenya just before World War I, when the European settlers became nostalgic for their native lochs and moorland streams. The rainbow trout they imported from South Africa are doing exceptionally well in

the parasite- and predator-free streams of Mount Kenya and the Aberdares. Up in the forests, it's an unlucky angler who fails to capture his limit of six fish per day per river.

Below the forests, the rivers are larger, deeper and no longer crystal-clear. They're milky with sediment, but still offer an occasional heavyweight trout. By this stage, the fish are wise in the ways of the world and choosy in what they will eat. They're not easily lured, but when they are, they may make a good meal – surprisingly fine fleshed for their size.

Below the highlands in the Central Rift, Lake Naivasha contains plenty of small tilapia for a good day's sport, but the angler's favourite

---

**LEFT:** Mount Kenya is a challenge for rock-climbers.
**RIGHT:** fishing for Nile Perch in Lake Turkana.

quarry is the largemouth or black bass, a native of the southern United States introduced to Naivasha in 1930, which ranges from a modest 500 g (1 lb) to 3 kg (6 lb) or more. Few anglers have a blank day, and bags of 20 or more of good-size bass would be considered average.

## Deep sea fishing

The abundance and variety of game fish, together with well-equipped boats and professional crews, make the coast of East Africa a paradise for sports fishermen. From Pemba Channel on the Tanzanian border all the way north to Kiwayu, there are efficient charter operators available during the eight-month fishing season (August to March). The high winds of the *kusi* (southeast monsoon) make waters unfishable between late March and late July.

The most challenging sport fish of the ocean – black, blue and striped marlin, broadbill swordfish and Pacific sailfish – all abound in these waters, as do the powerful yellowfin tuna and a wide variety of game fish including barracuda, dolphinfish, kingfish and Pacific bonito.

Fishing tackle and boats run by Kenya's dedicated professional operators – about 20 in all – are based at points along the 400-km (250-mile) coastline. At Malindi there are charter

operators who have become especially skilled at light tackle and fly casting for sailfish, marlin, broadbill and other smaller species of game fish. For more information write to the Kenya Association of Sea Angling Clubs, PO Box 267, Watamu, Kenya.

## Other watersports

Windsurfing has not bypassed the shores of the Indian Ocean. Already the venue for international windsurfing competitions, the Kenyan coast, with its constant breeze and comparatively placid and warm waters, is ideal for the sport. The sheltered lagoons are interlaced with sailboards tacking, beating and running before

### THE BIG ONE

The ultimate freshwater fishing adventure in Kenya is arguably the search for the giant Nile perch on lakes Turkana or Victoria. The largest freshwater fish anywhere, growing to well over 100 kg (220 lb), it's underrated as a fighter by the heavy-tackle brigade, but it will fight a rare battle on a light line. The catch is not returned, except for the 13-kg (30-lb) infants, since these huge fish are excellent for eating. Choicest cuts like the cheeks are grilled and taste like rock-lobster. Part of the catch may be salted and sun-dried and the larger fillets packed in ice for eventual transport home. The debris is abandoned for the crocodiles.

the wind – a brilliant array of colour splashed across the blue water. Tuition and board hire are available at virtually every hotel and beach resort, and a nucleus of wind-surfing enthusiasts also ply their hobby on the lakes and dams in up-country Kenya.

The ability to swim a little, or simply to float, permits the less athletic to snorkel. Simply by donning a glass mask, the wonders beneath the crystal-clear waters are revealed in all their brilliance. The shark-free coral gardens and inner reefs are a paradise of colour and movement – brilliant coral, fish and plant life combine in a spectacle no photograph can adequately reproduce.

The more experienced can scuba-dive, spending longer periods underwater, but this is a pastime that requires training. Scuba schools abound, all professionally run and offering first-rate equipment for hire. The Kenyan coast has achieved a reputation in scuba circles for the quality of its diving, and the sport competes with windsurfing for popularity.

There is an opportunity for sailors to tack, reach and run with the wind on lakes Naivasha and Victoria. Water-skiers can enjoy jumping the waves at the coast and at lakes Naivasha and Baringo. For the intrepid adventurer, one, two- or three-day white-water rafting trips on the Tana, Mathioya or Athi Rivers are organised by Mark Savage of White Water Adventures – tel/fax: (02) 521590.

## Scenic golf

The golfer who brings his clubs to Kenya will find some superb scenic courses to choose from – from sea-level all the way up to a course which boasts the highest tee in the Commonwealth, at over (2,400 metres) 7,800 ft. New arrivals in Nairobi, driving in from the airport, are often startled to see a golf course nestling within a nine-iron lob of the Parliament Buildings in the city centre. This is the Railway Course, the junior of three within the city limits. Royal Nairobi, built in 1906, claims seniority (the "Royal" was bestowed on the Nairobi Golf Club in 1935 by King George V).

Muthaiga Golf Club – which hosts the Kenya

---

**WINGS OVER WILDLIFE**

You can get an aerial view of the wildlife in the Aberdares by taking a breathtaking flight in a glider with a qualified pilot. Contact the Gliding Club of Kenya in Mweiga, tel/fax: (0171) 2748.

---

Open every year – is also within a 10-minute taxi ride of Nairobi's central hotels. To the north of the city is the Windsor Golf and Country Club, which is home to one of the top courses on the continent and certainly the best in Kenya. In the suburb of Karen is the Karen Country Club course on land that was once part of Karen Blixen's coffee estate.

Visitors are welcome at all Kenya golf clubs. Green fees are moderate and caddies are always available. At the more popular and crowded courses, there

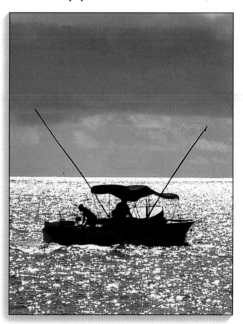

are restrictions on visitors at weekends, but it's usually possible to play with members.

A round of golf on a Kenyan course can have diversions beyond the vagaries of directing the ball in the right direction. Exotic and sometimes noisy bird life is profuse, and a number of clubs have local rules which may appear strange to players from overseas. The course at Kisumu, on the shores of Lake Victoria, has a rule which always intrigues a visitor: "If a ball comes to rest in dangerous proximity to a hippopotamus or crocodile, another ball may be dropped at a safe distance, but no nearer the hole, without penalty." This rule is no joke – it has been invoked.  ❏

---

**LEFT:** water-skiing on Lake Naivasha.
**RIGHT:** heading for offshore fishing grounds.

# SPORTING KENYA

*Kenyan runners are internationally known in the athletics stadium, but there are many other fields in which the country performs with vigour*

With fine and usually predictable weather, Kenya affords endless opportunities for the sports spectator. The country's enthusiasm for varied sporting activity is indicated by the existence of more than 40 different associations and management bodies which control a diversity of sports and pastimes, ranging from athletics to windsurfing. Sport is an important part of the Kenyan way of life, and newspapers devote many pages to local and overseas sporting events.

Although facilities for some sports are below international expectations, there are no doubts that improvement in this area is a major feature of development planning. On a social level, which embraces the vast majority of sports played, facilities are good and the standards high. The club is the focus of much sport; in Nairobi alone, there are more than 20 clubs which cater for one or more sporting activity.

## The Safari Rally

Every year, around the end of February or early March, some of the world's finest rally drivers converge on Nairobi to face the multiple challenges of dust, mud, fatigue and diabolical roads in one of the world's greatest motoring events, the Safari Rally. Along with the rally crews come top mechanics, team managers, journalists, photographers and ordinary rally watchers who cannot resist the magic of the Safari.

The event began simply enough in 1953, when 57 local drivers, in ordinary cars, struggled round Kenya, Uganda and Tanganyika (then still under British rule). The instigators were keen to keep it an amateur event: no winner was declared for the first rally, no service crews were allowed and repairs had to be done by the participants themselves (although it was permitted to use a dealer's workshop en route). Route surveys were also virtually unknown in

those early days; so it was a case of "slam the door and the first one back is the winner". The glamour of the event, however, brought professional interest, and soon the Safari attracted the attention of the overseas motoring press. A handful of drivers from outside East Africa tackled the rally on a purely amateur basis – particularly after the Safari Rally was granted international status in 1957.

Today it is an important event, with works teams and professional drivers competing for points in the World Rally Championship. It has a reputation as an event that overseas drivers find extremely difficult to win, and it's true that experience of driving in East African conditions counts for a great deal. To date the rally has been won by local drivers on all but 19 occasions. Despite that, the world's top rally teams spend a small fortune to try to win the event and thereby reap international publicity.

Aside from the Safari Rally, Kenya has a full calendar of motorsport events, including the

**PRECEDING PAGES:** heavy going in the Safari Rally.
**LEFT:** soccer is the national sport.
**RIGHT:** Mahmoud Abbas, Kenya's best-known international goalkeeper.

Kenya National Rally, Clubman Rally and Motocross Championships, all organised by recognised motor clubs around the country.

## Football frenzy

While Kenya's athletes make sports headlines abroad, it is Association Football, or soccer, that commands the attention within Kenya. Though it never reaches the fervent support that accompanies the game in South America or Europe, soccer is played by thousands on any level ground with anything that reasonably represents a ball. Thousands of supporters cram the stadiums for the weekend league and cup often acquit themselves with distinction against visiting professionals.

The Kenyan national team – the Harambee Stars – proved themselves in international competition within Africa by winning the East and Central Africa Challenge Cup three years in succession. Recently, Kenya was the beaten finalist in the All Africa Games.

## Fast and furious rugby

Kenyan rugby players favour a fast, open game, with plenty of running and handling, which makes for excellent spectator entertainment. The Kenya Rugby Football Union comprises

matches – although (as elsewhere) over-exuberance from the crowds occasionally requires police intervention.

Domestically, Kenyan football now has two fully fledged leagues, each containing 18 clubs, with promotion and relegation for three teams each season. The major tournament of the year is the Moi Golden Cup, a knockout competition played by all 36 clubs. The two top clubs, Gor Mahia and AFC Leopards, have each won African cup competitions – for instance, Gor Mahia won the Nelson Mandela Cup in the Africa Cup Winners Tournament.

Kenya is a popular tour destination for European football clubs, and local amateur teams

### THE SEVEN-MAN GAME

Kenya is developing a growing reputation in seven-a-side rugby. The national sevens squad has competed in international tournaments in Britain, Dubai, Singapore and Holland, and in 1998 was one of the 20 countries competing in the first Commonwealth Games Rugby Tournament in Kuala Lumpur, Malaysia.

At home in Kenya, the last weekend in June sees the staging of the International Safari Sevens, the premier sevens competition on the continent, which attracts teams from Europe, Asia and Africa. In 1997, Kenya thrilled the home crowd when they lifted the Tusker Trophy by beating Cumbria in the final.

20 teams in two divisions. The majority of the clubs are based around the Nairobi area, but the game is played as far afield as Nakuru, Kisumu and Mombasa. The season runs from late March until early September.

As well as the leagues, the club sides also compete in the end of season Enterprise and Mwamba Knockout Cups, regional East African tournaments which also include teams from Uganda and Tanzania. Seven-a-side rugby is growing in popularity and prestige (*see below, left*).

### CRICKETING EXPORTS

Several Kenyan-born cricketers have gone on to play at the top level abroad: Derek Pringle for England, Qasim Omar for Pakistan and Dilip Patel for New Zealand.

beat India – in India. Kenya was one of only three non-Test-playing countries (the others being Bangladesh and Scotland) to qualify for the 1999 Cricket World Cup.

At club level, Kenyan cricket is fiercely competitive, with volatile temperaments sometimes gaining the upper hand of reason. Watching a league match, the result of which may decide the destination of the trophy, is not for the faint-hearted. The Kenyan umpire is as unfortunate as his counterparts elsewhere – seldom right, often friendless.

## Competitive cricket

Cricket has a strong place in the country's sporting calendar. Although Kenya has some way to go before the national team is admitted into the elite circle of Test Match-playing countries, it has competed in the World Cricket Cup since 1975 – memorably beating the mighty West Indies side in an early round in 1996.

In 1997, the international authorities granted Kenya official "one-day" status, entitling them to compete regularly in limited-overs internationals. In one such game, in May 1998, Kenya

The domestic cricket season is between June and March. There are a large number of league matches, and also international club games against visiting overseas sides, such as provincial teams from South Africa.

An afternoon spent watching cricket in the sylvan surroundings of Nairobi Club can be entertaining and rewarding. Should the cricket pall, a short stroll allows the visitor to view tennis, bowls or squash before returning to catch the last few overs, then it's time to retire to the bar for a review of the day's events. Cricketers are social folk, and the services of any useful player will be keenly sought to play for this or that side in a competitive environment.

**LEFT:** rugby union played under the East African sun.
**ABOVE:** a game of cricket at the Nairobi Club.

## Sticks and rackets

The City Park Hockey Stadium – the only hockey stadium in the whole of Kenya – now has an all-weather Astroturf pitch, where teams can compete and practise on the surface used in international competition. Kenya's hockey players, both men and women, have won gold medals at the All Africa Games, and also compete in the Commonwealth Games and the Olympics. Hockey is enthusiastically played by men and women at a social level, mainly on murram or grass pitches.

Three major tennis competitions, including the Kenya Open, are held at the beginning of the year, and many smaller tournaments around the country throughout the year. Kenya has hosted Davis Cup group competitions on a number of occasions.

Squash is a rapidly growing sport and one in which Kenyan teams have done remarkably well in international competitions, including the World Junior Championships and the Commonwealth Games.

A select number of sports clubs cater for lawn bowls and croquet, with top-class facilities and standards. Kenyan teams regularly compete in international tournaments such as the Commonwealth Games.

## The sport of kings

Kenya's climate and open spaces provide limitless scope for a range of equestrian activities, the envy of those who dwell in more constricted surroundings. Throughout the year, apart from a short break in August, horse racing is held every Sunday and on most public holidays at the Ngong Road Racecourse, just outside Nairobi. The picturesque course is well patronised on racing days, and the standard of racing is high.

During the British winter, several professional jockeys enjoy a working holiday by riding in Nairobi. The legendary Lester Pigott has ridden the course – inevitably on a winner with his first ride – and has commented most favourably on the course and its facilities.

Run right-handed, the entire course is visible from the stands. With an eight-race card, the entrance fee also gives access to the stands and clubhouse. Catering and other facilities are splendid, and with both tote and bookmakers on hand to take care of the gambling urge, there can be few more enjoyable ways of spending a Sunday afternoon. Racing is run professionally, with stipendiary stewards and a qualified handicapper, and Kenya racing has rid itself of its slightly unsavoury reputation of years gone by.

Good quality breeding stock has been imported into Kenya over many years and there is a flourishing bloodstock industry, with horses exported to other African countries. There is a tendency for horses to grow rather more "leggy" than their northern counterparts, but there is remarkable quality to be seen throughout the 300 or so horses in training. ❑

### COMPETING ON HORSES

Polo has a small following in Kenya but is played regularly at weekends in Jamhuri Park, Nairobi, and up-country at Gilgil and Timau. Standards vary, with a few good players and a remarkable number of new players taking to the game. An annual international tournament attracts well-known high-handicap players from overseas.

A number of equestrian events – including dressage, show jumping and cross-country jumping – are held throughout the year at various venues around the country, culminating in the Horse of the Year Show held at Nairobi's Jamhuri Park in August.

**LEFT:** traditional attire for bowls at the Nairobi Club.

# Running for Gold

**K**enyan athletes – especially long and middle-distance runners – have been a powerful presence in world athletics for more than three decades. Yet Kenya did not appear in any international athletics meeting until 1952 and did not win any medals until the 1958 Commonwealth Games. It was in the 1960s that Kenyan runners began to attract worldwide attention – particularly two outstanding athletes, Kipchoge Keino and Naftali Temu.

"Kip" Keino won the first of many gold medals in the 1,500 metres at the first All Africa Games in Brazzaville in 1965. The next year he picked up two golds at the Commonwealth Games, where Temu also won the 6-mile race, and followed that with the 5,000 metres title at the World Games in Helsinki. Then the world was stunned by a dazzling team performance at the Mexico Olympics of 1968. Represented by only 18 athletes, Kenya still collected more medals than any other nation except the USA: one bronze, four silver and three golds – Keino in the 1,500 metres, Temu in the 10,000 and Amos Biwott in the 3,000 metres steeplechase. The Kenyans returned home to a heroes' welcome.

Some critics claimed that their unexpected success was due to the altitude of Mexico City – similar to that of their Kenyan homeland. But at the 1972 Munich Olympics they proved that height had nothing to do with it. Kip Keino picked up a gold and a silver, Benjamin Jipcho a silver, the Kenyan team won the 4 x 400 relay, and there were two bronze medals into the bargain.

In all, Kenyan runners have collected more than 40 Olympic track medals since 1968, a feat all the more remarkable as Kenya did not compete in the Games in Montreal (1976) and Moscow (1980) because of political boycotts.

By the time Kip Keino retired in 1978, his relaxed style and devastating finish had won him a host of admirers and emulators on the tracks of Europe and America. His mantle fell upon Henry Rono, who burst on to the scene setting world records in the 3,000, 5,000 and 10,000 metres and, for good measure, the 3,000 metres steeplechase. Rono was at his peak at the time of the Moscow Olympics, and will go down in history as the finest world record holder who never competed in the Games.

And so it has gone on thoughout the 1980s and 1990s, Kenyan athletes consistently beating the world at long and middle distance events...gold medals for the 800, 1,500, 5,000 and 3,000 steeplechase at the Seoul Olympics...two gold, four silver and two bronze at Barcelona...but only a handful of medals, with no golds, in Atlanta in 1996. By then, other African nations such as Ethiopia and Morocco had started to follow Kenya's lead and were producing world-class distance runners.

Even so, at the end of the 1998 athletics season, Kenyans held no less than seven world records – that is, if you include one Kenyan-born athlete who has settled in Europe: Wilson Kipketer, the outstanding 800-metre runner of the late '90s, is now a Danish cit-

izen and competes for Denmark. The other world-beaters – still staunchly Kenyan – include Daniel Komen over 3,000 and 5,000 metres, Paul Tergat and Moses Tanui over longer distances (including marathons) and Bernard Barmasai in the 3,000 metres steeplechase.

Is the Kenyan landscape, climate or altitude an explanation for this seemingly endless stream of distance runners? That's for sports physiologists to argue over, but it is interesting to note that all Kenya's world-beating stars have come from a small number of tribes, the Gusii and three Kalenjin groups – the Nandi, the Sabaot and especially the Kipsigis. And, perhaps significantly, all of these have their homeland in the Great Rift Valley in western Kenya.    ❏

**RIGHT:** Kenya's Daniel Komen breaks the 5,000 metres World Record in Brussels in 1997.

# EATING AND ENTERTAINMENT

*There's no shortage of restaurants in Nairobi and on the coast – and the cuisine*

*has a richness and variety that reflects Kenya's cospmopolitan culture*

Before you visit any Nairobi restaurant, try to take a quick trip to the City Market. The quality and variety of vegetables and fruits in Kenya is usually a wonderful discovery for the first-time visitor. The market will prepare you for the country's limitless choice of foods – from asparagus to tree tomato – and is an ideal shopping place for picnics.

Your next task is to pick a place for lunch as you explore the city. The Norfolk Hotel is an obvious choice. The veranda has an *à la carte* menu of simple "international cuisine", but it is the scenery, not the food, that draws the crowds. Nairobi walks by as it has since 1904, when the mock-Tudor hotel was first built. The historic watering-hole has collected its tales of drunken settlers, writers and movie stars – a history surpassed only by the notorious Muthaiga Club. (The Muthaiga and other clubs in Nairobi and Mombasa are private, although tour operators can sometimes get clients in on the sly.)

Lunchtime alternatives include the Trattoria, offering pasta favourites; African Heritage, a boutique and restaurant combination that serves good local cuisine; and the Thorn Tree Café at the New Stanley Hotel. The huge old thorn tree here was recently cut down as it had outgrown the limited space. But a replacement has been planted and the famous bulletin board restored, carrying requests for everything from overland ride sharing to camel stud services.

## International influences

It was the Arabs who started the cosmopolitan trend in local cuisine, sailing in with their dried fruits, rice and spices and expanding the diet of the coastal Swahilis. But it took centuries for this influence to spread inland, where people subsisted on a diet heavy in sorghum and millet, supplemented only by whatever fruits, roots and seeds they could find.

---

**PRECEDING PAGES:** spit-roasting meat in a country of carnivores.
**LEFT:** seafood specialities on the coast.
**RIGHT:** traditional Kenyan fare.

The arrival of the Portuguese in 1496 changed all that, with the introduction of foods from newly discovered Brazil. Maize, bananas, pineapples, chillies, peppers, sweet potatoes and manioc were all brought in, most of them destined to become local staples. The Portuguese – clearly evangelical gardeners – also

brought oranges, lemons and limes from China and India, as well as domestic pigs.

The British were next to influence eating and drinking habits in Kenya, importing new breeds of sheep, goats and cattle, together with the essentials of life like strawberries and asparagus. They planted high-quality coffee and taught their cooks how to make lumpy custard, as well as which way to serve the port with up-country "Njoro Stilton".

They also imported thousands of Indians to build the railway to Uganda, and with these immigrants came the curries, chapatis and chutneys that are now as traditional a Sunday lunch in Kenya as roast beef is in Yorkshire.

Later, between and after the wars, the Continentals arrived with their spicy sausages and pastas. More recently, global fast foods from hamburgers to pizzas have appeared in Nairobi.

## Superb seafood

One justly famous restaurant is the Tamarind, with its sea-blue decor and consistently superb food. A visit here is more an evening out than a meal, starting in the upstairs bar with "nibbles" of maybe tiny fried prawns, coconut strips and banana crisps. For a more substantial starter, try smoked trout with horseradish sauce, a mound of the minuscule Mombasa oysters, fish

tartare or perhaps dried impala. For the main cause, there are spiny lobsters, king crab claws, Malindi sole, or a mixture of the lot in a superb seafood casserole.

A restaurant which claims to "absolutely ooze good taste" is Alan Bobbé's Bistro, run by the eponymous owner, for years the doyen of Kenyan restaurateurs. The bistro is small and intimate, with music to match – soft Debussy and Chopin. The menu is handwritten, inscribed with Mr Bobbé's droll comments on the dishes and his fairly high prices. Much more reasonable is the lunchtime tariff for plates of seafish *meunière* or salads.

## Spicy hot restaurants

Indian curry houses of varying quality are scattered all over the city. The most distinctive of them are perhaps the two Minar restaurants, which serve delicate Mughal cuisine. Originally created for the appetites of the rich and pampered Mughal rulers of northern India, the food here is unbelievably subtle, made from expensive ingredients like almonds, cashews, cream and exotic spices.

Even at the first try, Mughal food is highly acceptable to Western taste. Start with poppadoms and move on to chicken kebabs (first marinated in spiced yoghurt and grilled), followed by saucy dishes – mutton rogon gosh, chicken makhan wallah – and then kulfi, a rich, dense saffron-flavoured ice cream. It's easy to overdo it, so be careful with the sauces.

Another popular Indian restaurant is the Haandi in The Mall at Westlands, which specialises in Punjabi and Rajasthani cuisine. The dishes are served in small clay pots kept warm at the table by traditional *jikos* (burners).

The grill rooms of the major hotels are not always very popular, but the Norfolk's Ibis Grill is as good as most of the top restaurants in the

**READ ALL ABOUT IT**

In all, there are now more than 300 restaurants listed in the *Eating Out Guide to Kenya*, which is worth the investment for identifying the best of them.

One of Nairobi's newest restaurants, the Lord Errol in the suburb of Runda, has also quickly become recognised as one of Kenya's finest. The grand entrance and decor reflect the Happy Valley era of the late 1930s, the Highlander Bar is all mahogany, brass and memorabilia, and there are two restaurants: the Conservatory and the more formal Claremont, with Victorian-style panelling and stained glass. The cuisine is classical French.

The cosy RaceCourse Restaurant at Ngong

city. In cool, understated surrounding, diners (many of them locals) select from a fairly original menu of *nouvelle cuisine* dishes.

Le Restaurant, the main dining room of the Hotel Inter-Continental, offers elegant dining options from a varied menu of Mediterranean food, unusual seafood dishes and some tempting and imaginative desserts. Nairobi's newest hotel, the Grand Regency, has five restaurants and a wide range of cuisine, with the Atrium Brasserie featuring a different themed menu every night.

Race Course serves rich French cuisine and seafood. For more subtle romance, try the Horseman in the suburb of Karen, where candlelight glints on the crystal and strawberries are dipped in chilled champagne. Rolf Schmidt, the polo-playing proprietor, is middle-European – and so is the cuisine, which is pricey but reliably excellent.

The International Casino complex on Museum Hill has two good Italian restaurants: the semi-alfresco Toona Tree (casual with live bands) and the Galleria (expensive).

There are many excellent Chinese restaurants in Nairobi, serving food that is good, fresh and authentic. The best include the Dragon Pearl,

**LEFT:** lobster is plentiful in Mombasa.
**ABOVE:** the Kirinyaga restaurant at Nairobi Safari Club.

the Pagoda, the Rickshaw, the China Plate and the Hong Kong. Japanese restaurants now include the Akasaka, the Shogun and the Misono. The Bangkok in Westlands offers spicy Thai food, while Korean cooking is available at the Koreana in the Yaya Centre.

## Nairobi nightlife

The Carnivore, vast and immensely successful, is famous for a set menu of one great roast of meat after another – as much as you can eat of Molo lamb, skewered chickens, beef, impala, Thomson's gazelle and ostrich. The Carnivore's Simba Saloon is almost as famous for its

Gypsy's (a tapas bar) in Westlands, ZanzeBar in the Kenya Cinema Plaza, Psy's Bar at the Langata Shopping Centre, The Barn at the Ngong Race Course, plus a few others that operate only on Friday and Saturday nights.

Other nightclubs include the Florida and New Florida. These feature disco music in smoke-filled rooms with many young girls who can give you a lot more than a good time. Men should beware.

Nairobi now has a number of casinos, the most famous being the International Casino, followed by the Mayfair Casino Club at the Holiday Inn Mayfair Court, the Four Aces, and

extravagant entertainment – rock music every Wednesday; African Night on Friday, with African food, drink and music; all-night disco on Saturday and soul music on Sunday. The Carnivore attracts big-name performers from all over Africa.

The Safari Park Hotel complex on the Thika road has six restaurants encompassing African, Japanese, Chinese, Italian, Indian and Continental food. The main restaurant, the Nyama Choma Ranch, serves up grilled meats and a nightly floor show by the "Safari Cats", presenting modern and traditional African dance with marvellous costumes and choreography.

There are a number of bars with small discos:

the casino at the Hotel Inter-Continental.

## Up-country style

Out of Nairobi on safari, the restaurant choices are few but, fortunately, the lodges offer bountiful food, even if the quality is variable. One of the best is the millionaires' holiday camp, the Mount Kenya Safari Club, which is widely known for its lunchtime buffets and for the seven-course evening extravaganzas.

Appetites sharpened in the mountain air will be satisfied by a sumptuous free service lunch at the Aberdare Country Club. The Outspan also features a good lunchtime buffet, while dinners at the three Aberdare game lodges –

Mountain Lodge, the Ark and Treetops – are remarkably good, taking into consideration the difficulties of supply and preparation. Kentrout, at the base of the northern side of Mount Kenya, is a bit off the beaten track but worth the effort. Their name says it all and the fish is very fresh.

Package safari tours afford travellers limited choice of menu in such remote areas as the Maasai Mara. It's a question of whether or not the chef's on form the day you arrive at the camp. However, it's reliably haute cuisine at Governor's Camp, where the lunchtime buffet, eaten alfresco surrounded by the magnificent Mara, is enjoyed by all who stay there.

## A varied menu in Mombasa

In striking contrast to the dry warmth of a Mara afternoon is the sticky and steamy air of Mombasa. Arriving at lunchtime at the airport is like stepping fully-clothed into a sauna. Food may be the last thing you will want until you've had a wash in the ocean or taken a nap on the beach. Then the choices for dining in and around Old Mombasa are legion: Chinese and Indian restaurants abound in town and some of the beach hotels offer unexpectedly ritzy grill rooms.

The elegant Capri, a well-chilled, dimly-lit restaurant in Ambalal House, specialises in fresh seafood. Downstairs, the international crowd mingles with well-heeled locals in the Arcade Cafe, which serves an inviting variety of Continental pastries, homemade ice-cream and ice-cold coffee.

The Shehnai Restaurant on Maungaro Street serves what could be described as "Mughal *nouvelle cuisine*", light northern Indian dishes eminently suited to the climate. The decor is elegantly Asiatic, with tall handcarved wooden chairs set around small tables topped with stiffly starched cloths. Ask for help with the menu, as most dishes will be unfamiliar. Two other good Indian restaurants are Chetna's and Singh's, both on Haile Selassie Avenue.

After a stroll around the Old Town or Mombasa's bustling city market, you might step into Stephen's Bar, a simple back-street dive which attracts just about everyone: backpackers,

---

**LEFT:** showtime at the Carnivore restaurant, Nairobi.
**RIGHT:** chicken in the Mughal style.

**MOMBASA AT NIGHT**

You can dine in ancient Fort Jesus, following a dhow trip and a spectacular sound-and-light presentation in the fort. Contact Jahazi Marine, tel: (011) 472213.

locals, up-market tourists and itinerant critics. They all go there for the home-cooked Goan food prepared by the manager's wife. Try the whole fish stuffed with the lady's blend of masalas and grilled over charcoal.

Even if dining is all "packaged" in your hotel holiday, you should try to escape for just one meal out at the Tamarind, a superb restaurant which can scarcely be equalled anywhere in the world. Moorish-styled, it is set on a hill overlooking the old harbour, with the tables set out on the

flower-filled terrace. It is basically a seafood restaurant, with the menu much the same as its namesake in Nairobi except, for some reason, the food always seems to taste better in Mombasa. The specialities of the house are many and varied: try lobster Tamarind, fish tartare, prawns piri piri and coupe bahari, or just order oysters and champagne and enjoy being alive.

If you feel lucky, the Golden Key Casino is upstairs. Or, if you feel nautical, take the Tamarind Dhow and enjoy a romantic evening of seafood and light music while floating under the stars.

Good value eating can be had in the Mombasa "suburb" of Bamburi, at Yules Beach Bar and Restaurant and at the Chameleon. Also along this stretch of beach are Pirates, with its waterslide, and the famous Bora-Bora Night Club and Restaurant.

Much less well-known, but good, is the Seahaven Restaurant on the North Coast. Watch for its signs before Mtwapa Creek, off the main road on a mile of sandy track to a flower-covered inn.

## Seafood by the seaside

The Imani Dhow at the Severin Sea Lodge has good seafood, and is equally memorable for the enormous 20-ton boat set inside the restaurant.

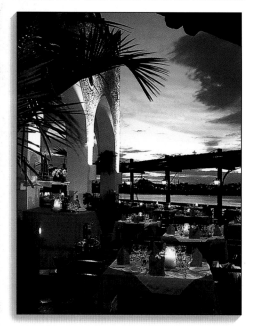

Il Duetto at the Nyali Golf Club offers good Italian food, and the nearby Minar Restaurant has equally good Mughal cuisine. On Mtwapa Creek is the Kenya Marineland restaurant – expensive but very good.

Sun-bleached Diani Beach on the South Coast has a few restaurants worth mentioning, in particular the classy Ali Barbour's, set in a natural cave and offering a menu of interesting, if pricey, dishes. Don't expect quantity, but you will get quality. The luxurious air-conditioned Swahili Grill in the Diani Reef Hotel is usually good; ask for flambé dishes here, or for the lobster and seafood fondue.

The atmosphere in the Makaa Grill at the Africana Sea Lodge is much more laid-back. So is the menu, which has a selection of highly original dishes mixing ideas from around the world with the best of local ingredients. The food is stunningly presented, and the experience of dining in the grill room is likely to be memorable – also, a little pricey.

If you're passing through Kilifi, there's a wonderful little Italian trattoria just on the north side of the Kilifi Bridge on the left. Once you reach Malindi, the Old Man of the Sea offers excellent seafood and La Malindina serves an impressive seven-course Italian seafood meal. There are a number of pizzerias with good pasta and pizzas, notably Putipu and I Love Pizza. At the north end of town, in a pink shopping complex, is Lorenzo's, with a pergola-covered verandah that catches the sea breeze, and probably the best à la carte menu in town.

## A last supper in Lamu

Finally, Lamu, the most exotic place in Kenya, is an island where the ancient Swahili culture is mostly uncorrupted by incursions from the West or anywhere else. Unfortunately the restaurants aren't fantastic, though sometimes the Bush Garden can produce a really excellent Swahili seafood dishes or delicious "tree" oysters, prised off half-submerged mangroves. Other small restaurants to mention are the Hapa Hapa and the Olympic, both serving Swahili food. It's worth noting that, in this very Muslim town, most restaurants do not serve alcohol.

Peponi's, the one up-market hotel on the island at the village of Shela, is now getting a reputation for excellent food, and surprises clients with some really imaginative dishes. Actually, when the food supply and erratic water problems are considered, just getting a decent meal at all on Lamu is more than appreciated.

It's probably best to just wander through the streets, stopping for ice-cream or yoghurt as the heat starts to shimmer on the dusty streets. Fresh juices are marvellous, notably the lip-puckering tamarind. Later in the day is the time for a thimbleful of black coffee topped with a pinch of ground ginger. Ask for a *kaimati*, a Swahili-style doughnut flavoured with cardamon, or a hunk of sticky *halva*, an Arab sweetmeat made with almonds and ghee.

**LEFT:** the terrace of the Tamarind restaurant, Mombasa.
**RIGHT:** a lavish old-style buffet.

# PLACES

*A detailed guide to the entire country, with principal sites
clearly cross-referenced by number to the maps*

The state-of-the-art airport outside Nairobi, and the capital city itself, can claim to have fairly advanced systems of living, working and taking care of visitors. But from there on, a safari in Kenya backtracks in time, following the spoor of millennia down to the origins of man around Lake Turkana.

The remains of times long past are evident all over the country. Immediately north of the capital, for instance, massive volcanoes that appeared after ancient geological upheavals have fallen in on themselves to form the Great Rift Valley. The sentinel Mount Kenya, with a small conceit of snow on the top, stands over the agricultural heartland of the country. The Age of the Mammals is in evidence all over Kenya, but exemplified in more than 40 national parks and game reserves, where the animals and pristine landscapes are entirely conserved.

This section of the book travels in detail from the cosmopolitan modern capital to the ancient Arab towns of the coast, and in between takes a close look at all the principal wildlife areas. Of these, the major spectacles are in the Maasai Mara National Reserve, seasonally inundated by the Serengeti migration of 2 million plains game; in Amboseli, under Kilimanjaro; and in Tsavo, immense and untrammelled wilderness reaching almost to the coast.

In the north, high-forested parkland is lit at night by the artificial moons of celebrated lodges such as Treetops, and beyond are more sanctuaries in Samburu country and remote Meru and Kora. Again north, but in the Rift itself, is a skein of wild lakes: Naivasha, Elmenteita, Nakuru (home of what is rated the "greatest bird spectacle on earth"), Bogoria, Baringo, and ultimately the fabled "Jade Sea" of Turkana. In the west, through Maasailand, are Lake Victoria and the sub-tropical homeland of the people of the Nile.

And finally, the 480 km (300 miles) of superb coastline. We explore Mombasa, the modern port where the eastern dhow trading ambience persists; the exquisite white-sand beaches, whose five-star resorts can compete with any in the world; ancient places like Lamu that seem to exist almost entirely in the 18th-century Arab world; and the offshore national parks where stunning marine wildlife can be viewed in the clear waters of the the Indian Ocean. ❏

**PRECEDING PAGES:** impala seem oblivious to a hot-air balloon in the Maasai Mara; anti-poaching patrols in Kenya's northern wilderness; Mount Kenya seen from the lounge of the famous Safari Club.
**LEFT:** an Amboseli vulture gazes on Kilimanjaro.

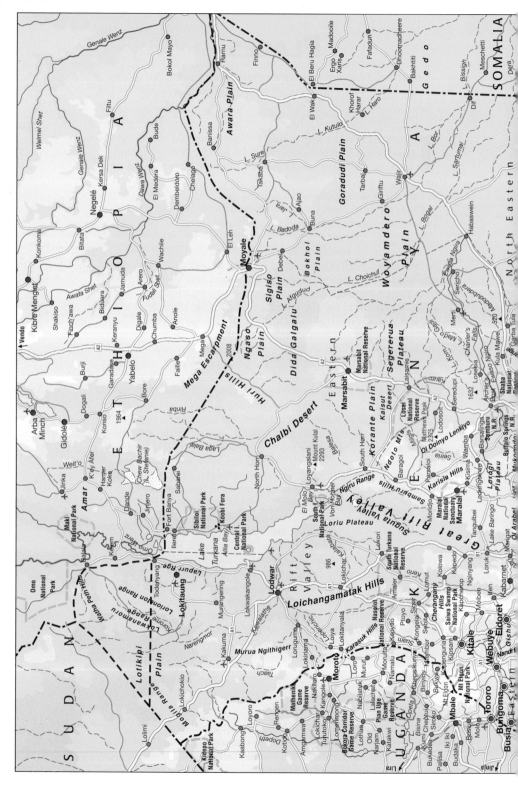

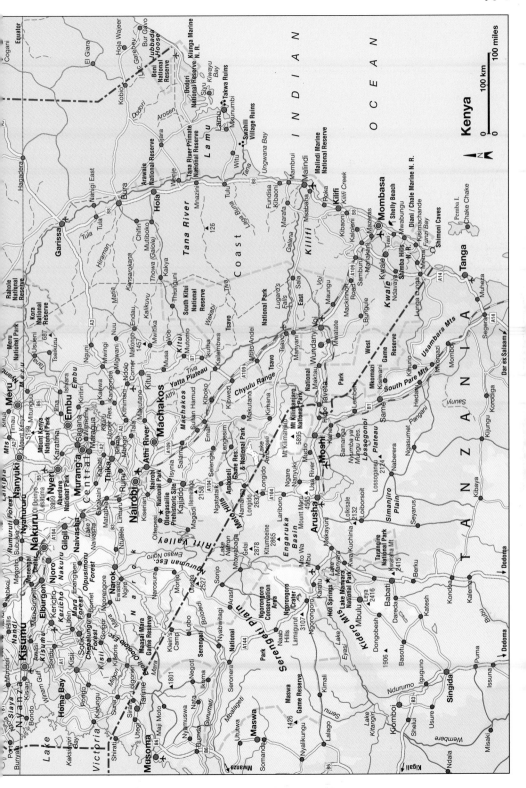

**Kenya**

100 miles
100 km

# NAIROBI

*A sprawling modern city barely 100 years old, the capital of Kenya is a vigorous tumult of cultures, drawn together and driven by fierce commercial instincts*

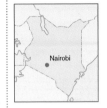

Map on page 174

Kenya's capital city started life as a railway station, built in 1899 at the point that the great Mombasa–Lake Victoria railway had just reached – the flat-land where the Maasai grazed their cattle, close to a swamp and a small river they called Enkare Nyrobi for its "cool" water. The station built there took up the Maasai name, ellipsed to "Nairobi".

The government seat was soon moved up to the Nairobi rail centre; commercial enterprise followed and, within a short time, a sprawling shanty town had sprung up, which rapidly displaced Mombasa as the country's centre of business. Indians – some of them ex-railway coolies – helped establish Nairobi's economic pre-eminence, providing financial services to the fledgling East African governments and railway authorities. The city also attracted wealthy international sportsmen from all over the western world to hunt in Kenya's much vaunted game lands.

The essential nature of Nairobi has remained cosmopolitan. Somalis, Arabs, Goans, Comoros islanders, Nubians, Indians, Pakistanis, Japanese and many European and North American nationals – all live fairly easily among the majority Kenyan communities. By far the most numerous of the city Africans are the Kikuyu, which is hardly surprising since Nairobi stands on the fringe of their traditional homelands. To a substantial degree, the city depends on them. Convoys of trucks and pick-ups stream in nightly from the rich farmlands in Kikuyu country, providing the bulk of the fresh produce that sustains the city.

Nairobi's population has grown at a phenomenal rate in the century since the tented labour lines of the founding railway. The city is now crowded with more than 2 million people, with a projected figure of 2,243,000 by the year 2000. This rocketing population growth is obviously a major concern to the government, with its tide of people leaving the land and pouring into the city in the hope of finding the streets paved with gold. For most of them, there is nothing but poverty, since neither employment opportunities nor accommodation could possibly grow fast enough.

## A green city

If anything, the city's trees and gardens are more a distinctive feature than its towering skyline. Yet when the railway arrived, the land had very few trees – as is clearly shown in early photographs. The transformation was thanks to Administrator John Ainsworth, who immediately set about making shaded avenues out of Nairobi's dusty tracks, often planting trees that were not native to Kenya. Even so, there is some indigenous forest within the city limits, preserved within the **City Park**, bounded by the Limuru and Forest

**LEFT:** sprawling Nairobi is a green city.
**BELOW:** curios and crafts for sale.

*Almost all the trees that decorate Nairobi are immigrants: the blue gums, wattles and grevilleas come from Australia. The jacaranda clouding the western suburbs in a lilac-mauve haze every October and the brilliant bougainvillea both came from Brazil.*

roads just north of the centre. The **Nairobi Arboretum**, just off State House Road, is another significant forest within the close bounds of the city that is being preserved for future generations. The vast recreational **Uhuru Park** Ⓐ is adjacent to the city centre – a distinction for Nairobi in an era of sprawling concrete jungles.

## Hard cash from tourism

Visitors are well looked after in Nairobi. The city has had long experience of hospitality, way back to the first station café and the Norfolk Hotel in 1904. It has long been recognised that Kenya's wildlife attracts tourists and their hard currency. It was from this early concept of tourism that Kenya – and Nairobi in particular – developed a special style in catering for visitors. First this was exclusive, with professional "white hunters" providing luxury (as well as sport) in the bush. In due course, the hunters were succeeded by photographers, with a safari system adapted to motorised game-viewing around the country's parks.

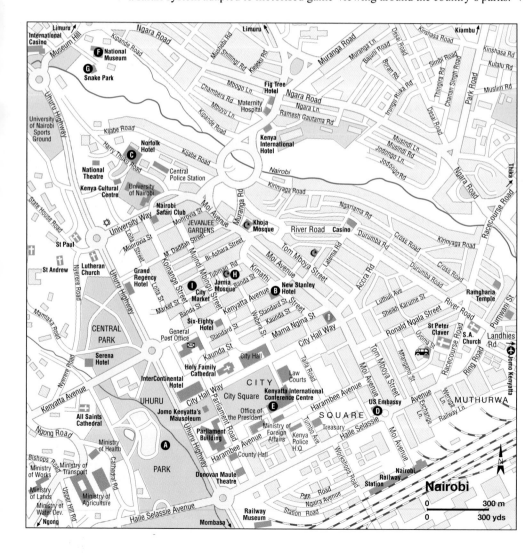

This long evolution in Kenyan tourism has made Nairobi one of the most traveller-oriented cities in Africa. **Jomo Kenyatta International Airport**, 13 km (8 miles) from the city centre, is among the world's most modern in design.

Visitors' accommodation in the city covers a near-complete range of prices and standards, from do-it-yourself hostels and camping grounds to multinational (and some local) 5-star hotels. For years, the outdoor Thorn Tree café at the **New Stanley Hotel B** has been the epicentre of safari-base Nairobi. (The famous acacia tree which gave the café its name was recently cut down as it had grown too big, but a new one has been planted.) The hotel itself has been built and rebuilt since its origins above a shop on the shanty town main street.

The other old-timer of the industry is the **Norfolk Hotel C**, the scene of a 1980 bomb outrage after the Israeli rescue of hostages at Entebbe Airport in Uganda. The bomb exploded in the middle of a New Year's Eve party, and many people were killed or maimed. The damaged section has since been rebuilt, preserving its Tudor-style black beams and white stucco. The devastation, loss of life and utter trauma of this bomb attack was tragically repeated in August 1998, when terrorists detonated a car-bomb behind the **American Embassy D**, killing over 240 and injuring thousands more.

Both the Norfolk and the New Stanley are international class hotels, as are the **Hilton**, **Inter-Continental**, **Serena** and the **Nairobi Safari Club**. The **Grand Regency** is one of the most recent of the capital's prestigious hostelries, providing palatial suites for its clientele of royalty, film stars and other celebrities. The **Panafric**, **Six-Eighty**, **Landmark**, **Holiday Inn Mayfair** and the **Fairview Hotel** also offer good accommodation. The Fairview, although it's a short distance from the centre of Nairobi, is located in quiet leafy grounds.

*Nairobi's airport is served by more than 30 international airlines providing connections with all continents except South America.*

## City-centre sights

In line with its evolution as an international centre in Africa, Nairobi offers some of the best major conference facilities on the continent. The **Kenyatta International Conference Centre E** is the city landmark, a 27-storey round tower (which, sadly, no longer has a restaurant on top). The building style is sober and modern, but "Africanised" with a tumbling riot of flowers and shrubs, and an amphitheatre supposedly designed in the shape of a traditional hut. The conference centre's architectural disparity reflects the city's own sharply contrasting facets – East and West, but essentially African.

Except for business, stopovers in Nairobi are normally short – the city is essentially the point of departure for safaris. However, there are a few places worth visiting. The **National Museum F** is one of them (daily, 9.30am–6pm). This houses one of the world's great zoological collections and, mainly through its connection with the Leakey family of palaeontologists, it has become a major international centre for the study of human evolution. A morning spent wandering through its halls, or in the adjacent **Snake Park G** (daily, 9.30am–6pm), is well worthwhile. Various groups work from here, such as the East African Natural History Society, the Kenya section of Birdlife International and the Kenya Horticultural Society.

Map on page 174

**BELOW:** the historic Norfolk Hotel, partly rebuilt after a 1980 bomb blast.

*A guided tour of the historic Parliament Building (any day of the week) can be arranged by telephoning the office of the Chief Sergeant-at-Arms, on (02) 221291.*

**BELOW:** Nairobi's modern skyline.

There are many places of worship, of all religions, in the city. Perhaps the most beautiful is the **Jamia Mosque ❶**, designed in the Indian style in 1925. Nearby is the **City Market ❶**, between Muindi Mbingu and Koinange Streets. The main building contains a colourful jumble of exotic fuit and vegetables, while outside around 150 stalls sell curios and craftwork – including some genuine bargains if you are prepared to haggle.

## Outside the centre

Spectator sports in Nairobi include polo, show-jumping, rugby, soccer, hockey, athletics, boxing and cricket. Horse-racing at the **Ngong Racetrack ❶** is meticulously organised by the Jockey Club of Kenya (there's a meeting most Sundays of the year) and even if you are down with the bookies, the superb garden setting of the course more than compensates. As for participant sports, there are numerous swimming pools, facilities to play tennis or squash, and nine 18-hole golf courses in and around the city. Special interests are also catered for, from skin-diving, go-carting, water sliding, sailing and tenpin bowling to Scottish country dancing.

Heading 5 to 10 minutes (depending on the traffic) west of the city centre you reach the suburb of **Westlands ❷**, which includes three main shopping malls and a large assortment of shops and restaurants of all different nationalities. Towards the Limuru Road is **Gigiri ❸**, a US$30 million complex which houses the United Nations Environmental Programme and other UN organisations – the first world headquarters of the United Nations to be established in a developing country.

Further north is the **Village Market ❹**, Nairobi's newest shopping centre, approximately 15 minutes from the city. It contains attractions such as water-

slides, mini golf and a cinema, as well as a post office, a great variety of food stalls, restaurants and, of course, shops and a supermarket. Every Friday, the very popular open-air **Maasai Market** is held in one of the parking areas near the children's playground.

Heading north out of Nairobi on the Thika Road, at Kasarani, is the **Safari Park Hotel ❺**, about a 15-minute drive from the city centre. It offers diverse bars and restaurants, houses a casino and is located in beautiful grounds. Across from this hotel is the new, ultra-modern **Moi International Stadium ❻**, accommodating up to 80,000 people, where many international sporting events take place. This is a reflection of the internationally acclaimed sporting prowess of Kenya's middle- and long-distance runners. Between the Thika Road and the Kiambu Road, about 20 minutes' drive from the centre, is the **Windsor Golf and Country Club ❼**, a peaceful resort recently built in beautifully laid-out grounds, with one of the finest golf courses in East Africa.

Going south of the city, just outside town on the Langata Road past the domestic Wilson Airport, is the famous **Carnivore Restaurant ❽** and, next door, the **Splash water park** with its great water slides and vast swimming pools. Around the corner a new **go-cart track** provides more thrills and spills. Five minutes further up Langata Road, through the main entrance to Nairobi National Park (see below), is the **Kenya Wildlife Services Headquarters ❾**, which has a collection of animals originally set up as a wildlife orphanage, but these days more of a zoo. The new "Safari Walk" here is a good representation of different Kenyan habitats and environments (daily, 9am–4pm).

A more genuine orphanage is the the one run by the **David Sheldrick Conservation Foundation ❿** in a compound in the west corner of the park

Maps on pages 174 & 177

*At the Carnivore Restaurant, you can eat every imaginable meat, from zebra and crocodile to impala and eland steaks.*

**BELOW:** Nairobi's Kenyatta International Conference Centre.

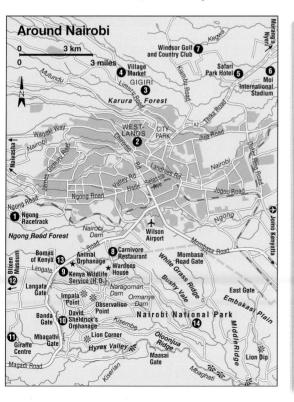

**Around Nairobi**

**Map
on page
177**

*The museum in the
former home of
Karen Blixen (above)
does not contain
much that belonged
to the author, but
does have some of
the props from the
film "Out of Africa".*

**BELOW:** meet the
tallest mammal at
the Giraffe Centre.

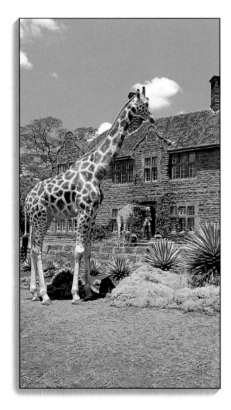

(entrance through the Banda Gate, open to the public daily 4–6pm). Sheldrick
was the founder-warden of the Tsavo National Park, and here his widow Daphne
cares for orphaned elephants and rhinos.

Off the Langata South Road, situated near the Gogo Falls about 30 minutes
southwest of town, is the **Giraffe Centre ⓫**. Here you can offer food pellets to
the giraffes at eye-level, take in some bird-watching, enjoy a wildlife video or
lecture in the auditorium, do some shopping and take refreshments (open
Mon–Fri 4–5.30pm, school holidays 11am–5.30pm, Sat–Sun 10am–5.30pm).

Returning to Langata South Road, turn left and continue for another 5 minutes or so, until you get to Karen Road, where you turn left and go past **Karen
Country Club** for about 3 km (1˘ miles) to the **Karen Blixen Museum ⓬** on
your right (daily, 9am–6pm). Karen Blixen's house commands a lovely view of
the Ngong Hills and is set within a charming garden. The museum staff take the
visitors on guided tours of the house and grounds, and explain how Blixen man-
aged the coffee plantation.

Near the entrance to the Nairobi National Park is the **Bomas of Kenya ⓭**, a
permanent exhibition of African dancing and culture, including a number of
tribal village (or *boma*) building styles. Troupes of professional dancers perform
"traditional" dances every day (from 2.30pm) in this popular cultural centre.

## Kenya's first national park

The capital's most visited tourist attraction is the **Nairobi National Park ⓮**, in
the south-eastern sector of the city – 113 sq. km (44 sq. miles) of "wilderness
suburb" populated exclusively by free-ranging wild animals. It happened
because Nairobi was sited at the western edge of the Athi Plains which, together
with the contiguous Kapiti Plains to the south and
southeast, used to be inundated with fauna almost as
numerous as in the Mara-Serengeti. The animals were
all over the place in the early days, so that night-
watchmen in Nairobi's main thoroughfare, Station
Road (now Moi Avenue), were supplied with lock-up
sentry boxes. A soldier of the time, Col. Richard
Meinertzhagen, recalled at least two race meetings
being disrupted by rhinos.

The populace may not have wholly welcomed the
presence of wild animals in the centre of town, but
they seem to have recognised the cachet of having the
wildlife around. Most of the Athi Plains were sold
and settled, but a large area to the southwest of town
was reserved as Nairobi Commonage. Only a few of
the Somali herdsmen and their families were allowed
to live there (as a reward for military service rendered
to the Crown), but otherwise the land was left wild.

During both world wars the Commonage was taken
over as a weapons range, and the wildlife accordingly
took a hammering. But in 1945 the land was gazetted
a national park – the first in Kenya. Buffalo and rhino
were reintroduced so that the full range of the original
Athi fauna was reassembled. Today, a browsing rhino
or sprinting cheetah is photographed against the backdrop of a modern city skyline; or a lion kills a gazelle
in the wild no more than a 15-minute drive from the
portico of the Hilton. ❑

# The Kikuyu

About 40 percent of the population of Nairobi are Kikuyu, a Bantu people who number 4.6 million in total, the largest of all Kenya's ethnic groups. They migrated to their present homeland in Kenya's Central Province from Meru and Tharaka some 400 years ago. The Kikuyu burned and cleared the dense forests of their new home by purchase, blood-brotherhood and intermarriage with the original hunter-gatherer inhabitants.

Tribal organisation is based on the family, with several families living together to form a homestead. A Kikuyu community is traditionally governed by a council of elders (*kiama*), a select few of whom compose the secret council known as *njama*.

Cattle, formerly a symbol of social status and wealth, also provided hides for bedding, sandals and carrying straps. Sheep and goats are still used for religious sacrifices. Permanent crops such as bananas, sugar cane, cassava and yams, together with beans, millet, maize, sweet potatoes, a variety of vegetables and black beans form the staple diet.

Kikuyu crafts include making pots for cooking, carrying and storage. Pots were also a major item of barter. The Kikuyu weave baskets from a variety of fibres, originally obtained from the bark of shrubs, now of sisal or synthetic thread. Arrowheads, spears, swords, cowbells and rattles were made by blacksmiths, who were believed to have magical abilities.

The Kikuyu traded livestock, agricultural produce and iron implements, tobacco, salt and ochre at regular local markets, and also maintained trading contacts with the neighbouring Maasai, Kamba and Okiek. A caravan of women transporting goods for barter was protected by a middleman related to the group with whom they traded.

A confrontation occurred in the late 1920s between Kikuyu tribal leaders and the European missionaries over the socio-religious rite of clitoridectomy of girls. (Male youths are also circumcised when they join the ranks of the warriors.) Disaffection with the missionaries led to the establishment of the Kikuyu Independent Schools Association and the Kikuyu Karing'a (Pure) Educational Association, out of which evolved the African Pentecostal Church and African Orthodox Church – both based on the Old Testament, which nowhere condemns female circumcision.

The Kikuyu adapted to the challenge of Western culture, perhaps better than any other tribe. They displayed a political awareness that resulted, in 1920, in the formation of the Kikuyu Association, which was soon drawing up a petition of grievances to present to the Chief Native Commissioner. Forced labour, land expropriation and the lack of public services and educational opportunities were to remain the main unresolved grievances until the end of the colonial era.

Today, progressive Kikuyu farmers have bought most of the former White Highlands farmlands and adopted modern agricultural practices, benefiting from the upgrading of their livestock, the accessible markets of Nairobi and a growing export trade. They have emerged as Kenya's major farming community, and are also very active in business and commerce throughout the country. ❑

**RIGHT:** traditional beads adorn a Kikuyu.

# AMBOSELI NATIONAL PARK

Map on page 184

*Amboseli is everyone's picture of Kenya: open plains, woodlands and swamps, with an abundance of wildlife, all set against the spectacular backdrop of Mount Kilimanjaro*

Nairobi

**A**mboseli National Park is normally best viewed around dawn. The animals are up and Mount Kilimanjaro, across the border in Tanzania, is exposed for an hour or so before pulling up a blanket of cloud. Alternatively, Amboseli at sundown can be as unreal as a pantomime set. On the vast stage, the mammals are lit by strong pink and amber gels, with the mountain a gradually darkening cycloramic backdrop. Looming above that is perhaps a necklet ruff of cloud, the black hump of high moorlands and the speckled edge of the well-known snows of Kibo summit at 5,895 metres (19,340 ft).

Amboseli is one of the oldest national parks in East Africa, having enjoyed more or less protected status for over 40 years. It was originally part of the Southern Maasai Reserve, which also encompassed the **Kajiado** and **Narok** area where several clans of the nomadic Maasai people lived. The park became the Amboseli Reserve in 1948, when the right of the Maasai people to live there was recognised and a special area for wildlife was set aside. In 1961 the Amboseli Reserve was handed over to Maasai Tribal Control and became a Maasai Game Reserve, together with the much larger Maasai Mara Reserve.

However, competition for grazing became such a problem that in 1970 a sanctuary around the swamp was preserved for game only and the Maasai were not allowed to enter. This aggrieved them so much that they killed many of the rhino population without even taking their horns. Consequently, a ring of bore holes around the park and a portion of the swamp was given back to the Maasai in exchange for an area to the north. Eventually, in 1977, Amboseli achieved full national park status, a comparatively small protected area of 392 sq. km (160 sq. miles).

**PRECEDING PAGES:** there are around 600 elephants in Amboseli. **LEFT:** a lioness keeps watch. **BELOW:** a marabou stork.

## Elephant tales

The national park is famous for its tranquil beauty and easily approachable wildlife. The Amboseli elephant population, only about 600 strong, is one of the few in all of Africa which has not been ravaged by poachers. It is also one of the longest studied and best researched by Cynthia Moss and her colleagues, who know every elephant by face and name and have written about them in the book, *Elephant Memories*. The **Amboseli Elephant Research Project ❶** can be visited by arrangement (staff sometimes give lectures): enquire at the lodges in the park.

**Lake Amboseli ❷**, from which the park takes its name, is a dry lake, some 10x16 km (6x10 miles), and is flooded only during the rare occasions when there are heavy rains. The maximum depth in the wettest years is about half a metre (18 ins), but the surface is more usually a dry, caked expanse of volcanic soil – boring to look at, if it were not for the

*The bateleur has a much shorter tail than most eagles, so to keep its balance when soaring it rocks from side to side with wings outstretched. This is the origin of its unusual name: bateleur is French for "tightrope-walker".*

frequent appearance of a phantom lake in a genuinely spectacular mirage. The entire horizon seems liquid, with perhaps a file of wildebeest reflected on itself in a shimmering mirror image. Mirages aside, the lake's fine, alkaline dust has a habit of creeping into every crevice, so photographic equipment should be protected in plastic bags.

The clouds of dust which blow up from the perennially dry bed of the lake provide a stark contrast to the lush vegetation of the marshy areas such as Enkongo Narok, which form the heart of the ecosystem. These swamps are fed by the melting snows of Kilimanjaro, which percolate through porous volcanic soils, forming underground streams which rise close to the surface in the ancient lake basin.

Where the water reaches the surface, the desert is suddenly green, sprouting with wild palms and enough grass cover to attract the fauna for miles around. Forests of towering yellow-barked acacias ("fever trees") used to surround the Amboseli swamps, but their numbers were gradually reduced by the elephant population, which stripped off and ate the bark and were initially blamed for all the damage.

However, it was then discovered that the naturally rising water table, induced by a period of good rains, was bringing toxic salts to the surface, which were "pickling" the tree roots. This caused physiological drought because the trees could not absorb enough water through their roots to compensate for the moisture lost from the leaves through transpiration. Even today you can see moribund fever trees which appear to be dying from the top down. Overall, however, the park has a varied habitat with open plains, umbrella acacia woodland, swamps and surrounding marsh areas.

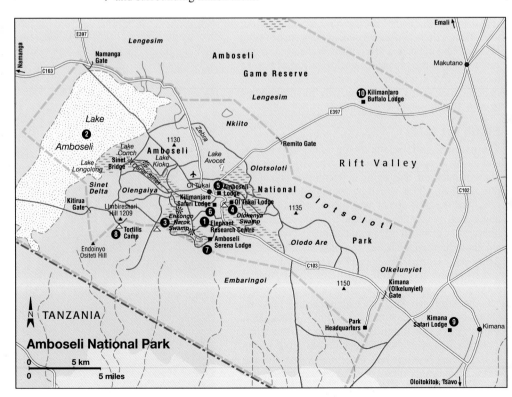

Amboseli National Park

Map on page 184

## Park life

Due to the open nature of most of Amboseli, lions are easily found and can occasionally be watched stalking their prey. Buffalo numbers have increased and plains game such as zebra, giraffe and gazelle abound. Small groups of gerenuk can occasionally be found in the arid bush standing on their hind legs to browse upon more succulent leaves on the higher branches. Hippos live in the open waters and swamp channels formed by seeping waters from Kilimanjaro. Buffalos feed in the shore line swamps and elephants penetrate deeper, often emerging with a high tide mark on their flanks.

For years ecological and behavioural studies of these beasts have been carried out in the park, so animals are accustomed to cars and visitors will be able to observe these large mammals at close range from inside their vehicles. However, encounters with Maasai warriors have left the animals wary of people on foot. An elephant feeding peacefully 3 metres (10 ft) from your car will run off in alarm – or attack in a rage – if someone suddenly gets out.

The density of visitors has had negative impacts on wildlife. Cheetahs, for example, have been so harassed by crowding vehicles that they have abandoned their usual habit of hunting in the early morning and late afternoon, and have taken to hunting at midday, when most tourists are back at the lodge having lunch and a siesta. Since this is not the best time of day to hunt, the result has been a reduction in the cheetahs' reproductive success.

*How can such enormous numbers of game live in this extraordinary desert?*

— JOSEPH THOMSON ON AMBOSELI, 1883

## Vultures and weavers

The film *Where No Vultures Fly* was shot in Amboseli, which seems somewhat at odds with the location since six species of vultures – often airborne on hot updrafts from the desert – are recorded in the park's checklist of over 420 bird species. Of these, the kingfishers are perhaps the most photogenic, especially when caught making a strike. The Taveta golden weaver is the most distinctive, or emblematic, as it occurs only in this general region. The swamps and marshy areas support a wide variety of water fowl, with no less than 12 species of heron. Birds of prey are also represented with over 10 varieties of eagle, as well as kites, buzzards, goshawks and harriers.

The most productive game runs are normally around the main swamps of **Enkongo Narok ❸** ("black and benevolent"), where icy water bubbles out of fissures in black lava. Another favourite run is up the solitary **Observation Hill**, up which one may be chased all the way – as has happened – by a mad, rogue elephant with ants up its trunk. Otherwise, the hill is for long-range lion spotting.

## Practical facts

Amboseli can be reached from Nairobi by two main routes, the most common one being along the main Kajiado-Namanga road, turning left at **Namanga**, entering the park through the main gate nearby and following the road to **Ol Tukai Lodge ❹**. The distance from Nairobi to the lodge is 240 km (150 miles). The second access point is along the main Mombasa road, turning right just beyond the railway bridge past

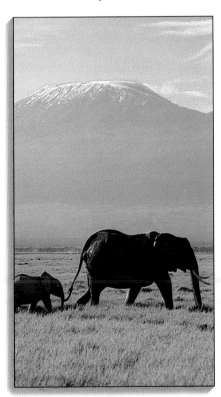

**BELOW:** elephants amble across Amboseli.

Map on page 184

*The self-help bandas (rondavels) at Ol Tukai, opened to the public in 1950, were among the first accommodation for guests in any Kenyan National Park.*

**Emali** and then following the Oloitokitok road for approximately 65 km (40 miles), taking another right turn near the flat-top **Lemeiboti hill** and following this road for 32 km (20 miles) before reaching the lodge. This route is shorter, but the Namanga road is in better condition. Flights from Nairobi are also available.

The original camp at Ol Tukai was built as a film-set amenity in 1948 for *The Snows of Kilimanjaro*, and used the following year by the crew of *Where No Vultures Fly*. The original huts have now been demolished and replaced by the new **Ol Tukai Lodge**, informal buildings of wood, stone and slate offering first-class accommodation and panoramic views of Kilimanjaro. Nearby **Amboseli Lodge ❺** offers international standards of accommodation and cuisine. Other lodges include **Kilimanjaro Safari Lodge ❻**, by a seasonal swamp where game congregate, and **Amboseli Serena Lodge ❼**, built in the style of a Maasai *manyatta* (village) near one of the springs feeding Enkongo Narok swamp. The three campsites within the park have only very basic amenities.

Just outside the bounds of the park, on the south side, lies the luxury **Tortilis Camp ❽**, which has beautiful tents, excellent food and a swimming pool. Also outside the park are **Kimana Lodge ❾**, to the east of the boundary about 15 km (9 miles) from the **Kimana Gate** on the Oloitokitok road, and, to the northeast, **Kilimanjaro Buffalo Lodge ❿**, through the Remito gate on the road to Emali. The idyllic **Ziwani Tented Camp** is situated further east, between Amboseli and Tsavo West National Park.

There are advantages to staying in accommodation outside the national park itself: visitors are not restricted by game park regulations, and so you are allowed to take game walks and night drives (both of which are forbidden within national parks and reserves). ❑

**BELOW:** zebra and wildebeest are often companions.

# The Kamba

Occupying the Machakos and Kitui districts of Eastern Province, the Kamba are a people of the plains. Numbering around 2,200,000, they constitute the fourth largest ethnic group in Kenya. They account for their presence in the region with the myth that Mulungu (the Supreme Being) planted the first Kamba man and woman on Mount Nzaui. In reality, the Kamba probably migrated north to their present homeland from Kilimanjaro.

Hunters, who also kept some livestock and cultivated millets and sorghums, the Kamba probably settled four centuries ago at Mbuni, taking advantage of the higher rainfall and fertile soils to adopt a more sedentary life as agriculturalists. From Mbuni they colonised the whole area.

At first they traded in arrow poisons and iron implements with the neighbouring Kikuyu, Embu, Tharaka and Mijikenda. Then came a second stage in the growth of the Kamba economy. By 1840, Kamba caravans loaded with ivory were reported almost weekly at the coast. In return they traded glass beads, copper, blue calico and salt for barter in the interior.

But late in the 19th century rinderpest seriously attacked the Kamba's herds, and with the building of the Uganda Railway and the ban on further expansion, the Kamba were soon in economic trouble. Their land was no longer fertile. Their refusal to reduce their herds and the erosion of the impoverished soil led to periods of famine.

Skilled craftsmen, the Kamba use iron and copper wire to make bracelets, necklets, arrowheads and spears. The same skills serve to create inlaid stools of exceptional beauty: their traditional art of woodcarving is the basis of a major handicraft industry. Clay cooking pots are made by the women, as are the finely plaited baskets made from fibres of the baobab and wild fig trees.

The basic unit of Kamba life, economic, political, religious and social, is the extended family. Both sexes undergo circumcision. In some parts there are two stages: the "small" ceremony at four or five, and the "big" ceremony at puberty with a long initiation and scarifying of the chest and abdomen for purposes of ornamentation.

Traditional Kamba weapons are the bow and arrow, the long fighting sword and the throwing club. Kamba arrows are usually poisoned, with the iron point wrapped in a pliable piece of thin leather to keep the poison moist and to ensure optimum effectiveness as well as protection against accidental injury.

Unlike the Kikuyu, the Kamba were slow to adopt progressive agricultural methods, preferring to serve in the police and King's African Rifles. Drought and famine still plague the Kamba, especially in Kitui. There are government and *harambee* (self-help) water schemes and integrated development projects. But the further desiccation of Kamba country (Ukambani) as a result of poor agricultural practices, and deforestation arising from charcoal production, continues to militate against successful economic development in the area. ❑

**RIGHT:** Kamba men trading arrows.

# TSAVO EAST AND WEST

*Tsavo is one of the largest wildlife sanctuaries anywhere in the world. Once famous for its man-eating lions, it now provides luxury accommodation for viewing wildlife of all kinds*

Map on page 190

Nairobi

The route to Tsavo from Amboseli (about 130km/80 miles) is out through Kimana village on a straightish southeasterly line of dirt roads and tracks to Tsavo West and on to **Kilaguni**, the traditional centre of the park. As a useful point of reference, a high-folded range of green hills – an unusually vivid, velvety green – stays on the left but gets gradually closer. This is the **Chyulu Range ❶**, which is incorporated within the **Chyulu Hills National Park** and may be among the world's youngest mountains, finally formed perhaps not more than a few hundred years ago. It's obviously a comparatively recent happening since one of the spur ridges is still black, cauterised pumice.

Overall, the range is approximately 80 km (50 miles) long, 7 km (4 miles) wide and just over 2,200 metres (7,000 feet) at its highest point. A track on the crest is scenic over the expanse of Tsavo Park but is seldom used and becomes downright dangerous when the mists descend. In among the hills is **Ol Donyo Wuas ❷**, a small luxury camp with superb views of Mt Kilimanjaro, and another small camp, **Kampi ya Kanzi ❸**, the dream of a young Italian boy come true. Here you enjoy Africa with an Italian touch and your days are not predetermined by a set programme.

**LEFT:** a buffalo in the morning mist.
**BELOW:** an ornate termite mound.

## Tsavo West National Park

Much of Tsavo West is of recent volcanic origin and is therefore very hilly. Entering from the Tsavo Gate, you come across the palm-fringed Tsavo River, from where the country rises through dense shrub to the steep, rocky **Ngulia Hills** which dominate the area. Of the volcanic cones, rock outcrops and lava flows that you can see, the most famous is Shaitani ("devil" in Swahili) – the black scar of lava that looks as if it has only just cooled, near Kilaguni Lodge.

The Ngulia range peaks at close to 1,800 metres (6,000 ft) and on the southern side drops a sheer 600 metres (2,000 ft) to the Tsavo River valley. Apart from the permanent spectacle, the Ngulias stage a special nocturnal show towards the end of the year. Thousands of birds appear out of the nightly mountain mists. They are palearctic migrants, flying out from the European winter, and about 40 species have been recorded. More than 60,000 birds have been netted and ringed – some subsequently tracked back as far north as St Petersburg.

The famous **Mzima Springs ❹** are found in this volcanic zone. The springs gush out 225 million litres (50 million gallons) of water a day, of which 30 million litres (7 million gallons) are piped down to provide Mombasa with water. The rest of the water flows into the Tsavo and Galana rivers. The water originates on the snowcap of Kilimanjaro and in the Chyulu

*The "king of beasts" feeds almost exclusively on meat, but is not averse to enjoying an ostrich egg for breakfast.*

**BELOW:** a view of cloud-covered Kilimanjaro from Tsavo West.

Hills as rain which percolates rapidly through the porous volcanic soils to form underground rivers.

Hippos followed by shoals of barbels and crocodiles can be watched from an underwater **observation chamber** at Mzima Springs. The best time for viewing is early in the morning; during the day hippos move to the shade of the papyrus stand and remain out of sight. East of the springs (downstream) is a stand of wild date and raphia palms, the latter with fronds of up to 9 metres (30 ft).

North of the Mzima Springs are numerous extinct volcanoes, rising cone-shaped from the plains. Mount Kilimanjaro dominates the western horizon. To the south is a beautiful picnic site at **Poacher's Lookout** on the top of a hill. The view across the plains to Kilimanjaro is worth the trip.

Tsavo West stretches further south to the **Serengeti Plains** which, despite their name, have nothing to do with the Serengeti National Park, although the landscape is similar. This part of the park, lying at the foot of Kilimanjaro, is crossed by the road and railway from Voi to Taveta.

## Birds and baobabs

Tsavo West has spectacular baobab trees, which used to be far more numerous. In the mid-1970s, there was an enormous and as yet unexplained attack by elephants on baobabs. Some claim it was because of the drought, others claim that there were "too many" elephants. Whatever the reason, the remaining baobabs are quite safe today.

The variety and sheer numbers of birds in Tsavo are incredible. **Lake Jipe** ❺, at the southwest tip of the park, is surrounded by tall reeds and is one of the most important wetlands in Kenya, providing a sanctuary for a number of water and

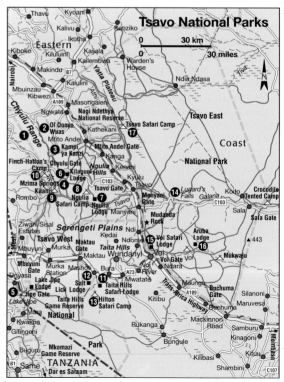

Map on page 190

marsh birds, including migrants from Europe. Some of the birds commonly seen at the lake are knob-billed geese, pied kingfishers, white-backed night herons, black herons, palm-nut vultures and the African skimmer. You can stay at the **Lake Jipe Safari Lodge** to experience this beautiful wetland to the full.

If you take an early morning game drive accompanied by a park ranger you might catch a glimpse of another endangered species. The few rhino left in Tsavo are protected in a fenced sanctuary at the foot of the Ngulia Hills. Other wildlife in the park includes lion, cheetah, leopard, buffalo, spotted hyena, warthog, Maasai giraffe, kongoni, duiker, waterbuck, klipspringer, impala, Grant's gazelle, oryx, eland and zebra. The lions of Tsavo are legendary but after the rains, when the grass grows very long, they are difficult to spot.

*Kilaguni Lodge was the first wildlife lodge built in a Kenyan national park. It was opened in 1962 by the Duke of Gloucester.*

Among the rarer fauna are caracal, kudu and Hunter's hartebeest, relocated from Tsavo East a few years ago from the Tana River area, where they were in danger of extinction. Also in the park is a herd of the bat-eared, pinstriped Grevy's zebra, which was brought in as a refugee group to escape poachers in Samburu. They seem to have confounded the dismal prognosis of zoologists by surviving out of their normal desert habitat.

Accommodation is available at a series of lodges within the park. The flood-lit waterhole at luxurious **Kilaguni Lodge** ⑥ attracts an incredible variety of animals, especially in the dry season. All the rooms have splendid views and the food is first class. **Ngulia Lodge** ⑦, sited on the edge of a great escarpment, is frequently visited by leopards, some of which have been carefully studied by scientists, who put radio collars on them to track their movements. Only 5 metres (16 ft) from the veranda there is a water-hole and salt lick where elephants converge to within touching distance and dig at the salt-bearing earth with their tusks. **Ngulia Safari Camp** ⑧, not far from Ngulia Lodge, has six *bandas* on the side of a hill overlooking a small dam that's visited by elephants. There is another self-catering camp at **Kitani** ⑨, not far from Mzima Springs. At minimal cost these self-help camps provide lamps, gas, bedrolls and mosquito nets, although you may prefer to bring your own.

**BELOW:** Hilton's Salt Lick Lodge is elevated for better game viewing.

By contrast, **Finch-Hatton's** ⑩ is a luxurious tented camp, situated at the foot of the Chyulu Hills near a series of hippo pools and natural springs. The dining area, bar and terrace overlook the hippo pool, with views of Kilimanjaro. The **Taita Hills Safari Lodge** ⑪, at the foot of the Taita Hills, offers full hotel amenities and has the only golf course in that region. **Salt Lick Lodge** ⑫, 7 km (4 miles) away, is elevated for viewing animals at the Salt Lick water-holes. The **Hilton Safari Camp** ⑬, on the bank of the River Bura in a dense riverine forest, is based around a house that was originally built for the film *A Tale of Africa*. These three units, all within the Taita Hills Hilton Wildlife Sanctuary on the outskirts of Tsavo West, offer excellent wildlife viewing with a luxury resort atmosphere.

## Tsavo East

The outstanding physical feature in Tsavo East is the **Yatta Plateau**, which runs almost parallel to, and is easily seen from, the Nairobi–Mombasa road. The

*Lugard's Falls are named after the first British proconsul, Lord Lugard, who volunteered for diplomatic service in East Africa to forget an unrequited love in England.*

**BELOW:** a tawny eagle soars.

plateau, which is between 5 and 10 km (3–6 miles) wide and about 305 metres (1,000 ft) high, originated as a lava flow from Ol Doinyo Sabuk east of Nairobi. Natural erosion over the millenia has exposed the flow to form the striking plateau seen today.

Around Voi, close to the road boundary, extends flat, dry, semi-desert thorn-bush country stretching as far as the eye can see. Running east from Voi is the Voi River, which is partly swamp and does not flow all year round. It meanders slowly to **Aruba,** where a large man-made dam, the remains of a defunct fish-farming scheme, makes an oasis for both animals and birds. Along the banks of the river is the dependent riverine woodland and numerous wildlife paths leading down to water-holes. The road between Aruba dam and Buchuma Gate on the Mombasa road is heavily populated with weavers, starlings and lilac-breasted rollers with iridescent wings.

One of the most spectacular sights in the park is the **Lugard's Falls ⑭**, 40 km (25 miles) north of Voi. Here the Galana river, which in its early stages borders Nairobi National Park, rushes through water-worn coloured rock. It is said that you can step across it at its narrowest point; perhaps the crocodiles downstream look forward to meeting those who try. A good spot to see them is **Crocodile Point** further along the river. Lesser kudu hide in the dry bush-land along the river banks.

**Mudanda Rock**, a 1.5-km-long (2-mile) rock between Voi and Manyani Gate, is a water catchment area which supplies a natural dam at its base. It is a vital watering point during the dry season and therefore one of the best wild-life viewing areas in the park. Large numbers of elephants used to congregate there before Tsavo's elephant population was drastically reduced by ivory poachers. Visitors can leave their cars at the rock and climb up to overlook the dam.

### Feasting beasts

Tsavo's lions were made famous by Colonel Patterson in his book, *The Maneaters of Tsavo*, which records the havoc caused by marauding man-eating lions to the imported Indian labour brought in to build the Mombasa–Nairobi railway during the early part of the 20th century.

Grant's gazelles, zebra, impala, kongoni, giraffe and lion have replaced elephants as the most common animals in Tsavo East. Large herds of buffalo can also be found. Buffalo have enjoyed a well deserved reputation in the past as being extremely dangerous when wounded or hunted. But since the banning of hunting, buffalo no longer associate danger with man or vehicles so they are generally quite docile.

Some of the more rare and unusual animals include oryx, lesser kudu and klipspringers; the latter can be seen standing motionless on rocky outcrops. Rock hyraxes, the improbable first cousins of elephants, can be seen sunning on rocks and chasing one another in and out of rocky crevices.

Conspicuous white-headed buffalo weavers (the most striking characteristic of which is arguably the red rump and not the white head) and red and yellow bishop birds are found everywhere. Some of the more

unusual local birds include pale chanting goshawks, carmine bee-eaters, red and yellow barbets, palm-nut vultures, African skimmers, yellow-throated long-claws and rosy-patched shrikes.

The roads north of the Galana River and east of the Yatta Plateau are closed to the public, except when special permits are granted by the park warden. The country is wild and woolly, and spotted with outcrops such as Jimetunda and seasonal rivers such as Lag Tiva.

Various accommodation is available. **Voi Safari Lodge** ⓯ clings to the side of a hill overlooking the vast expanse of Tsavo and is literally built into the rock – many of the floors are natural rock. There are two water-holes and even during the hottest times of day various wildlife, such as impala and warthog, come to drink.

Other accommodation can be found at the self-service **Aruba Lodge** ⓰, near the Aruba dam, and a number of tented camps such as Epiya Chapeyu Tented Camp, Galdessa, Satao Camp and Tiva River Camp. There is also Crocodile Tented Camp on the road to Malindi, just outside the park beyond the **Sala Gate**. Every night, there is a ritual in which huge crocodiles are "called" out of the Galana river with chants and drums, up to the veranda to be fed on offal.

A dirt road from Mtito Andei runs to the west bank of the Athi River opposite **Tsavo Safari Camp** ⓱, which is reached by boat. Don't miss the incredible view at sunset from Yatta Plateau. Plans are under way to re-open **Sheldrick Blind**, an overnight hideaway on the eastern wall of the plateau from where leopard and other nocturnal animals can be watched. It is named after David Sheldrick, the most famous of Tsavo park wardens. Public campsites with minimal facilities are available throughout both Tsavo East and West. ❑

Map
on page
190

*Just inside the Voi Gate is the former home of David Sheldrick, Tsavo's first warden. It is here that the orphaned animals from Daphne Sheldrick's home in Nairobi are first released back into the wild.*

**BELOW:** a lioness gets to grips with one of her cubs.

# THE MAASAI MARA

*The Mara is a natural continuation of the famous Serengeti Plain: undulating grassland, dramatic escarpments, beautiful acacia forests – and the greatest wildlife show on earth*

Map on page 198

Nairobi

The Mara Game Reserve was established in 1961 and covers an area of some 1,800 square kilometres (720 square miles). The southern boundary lies on the border with Tanzania's Serengeti National Park. The Loita Hills mark the eastern boundary; to the west lies the splendid Esoit Oloololo (Siria) Escarpment, while the north is bordered by the Itong Hills. The Mara's wide horizons are unforgettable and game are clearly visible. It is also the scene of the greatest animal show on earth, known simply as The Migration.

In terms of statistics, Barnum & Bailey were never close to the show provided by the Serengeti-Mara: a company of 3 million animals, an arena 2,000 miles (3,200 km) round and a non-stop year-long spectacle – every year for hundreds of thousands of years. At the last count, there were 1.4 million wildebeests in the main cavalcade, 550,000 gazelles, 200,000 zebras, 64,000 impalas – and so on down the checklist of East African grazers and browsers. These are the moving herds of The Migration.

In this extraordinary natural circus, the wildebeest (or white-bearded gnu) is regarded as the clown, largely because of the way it looks: a head far too big for a spindly torso and legs. An over-long snout, a pair of over-small horns and a wispy white Mandarin beard complete the assembly. Wildebeests also play the fool much of the time. Arching their backs, they buck up and down in a straight take-off of the Maasai *ipid* dance, or then spin and fall, or generally charge about for what looks like the sheer fun of it. But there is also something of the Pagliacci about the gnu, some off-stage worry which is serious and often tragic. An animal endlessly pirouetting on itself may be a terminal casualty of a botfly embedded in its brain. A hundred may die in a crazy nose-dive into a ravine.

The word *mara* means "spotted". Why the Maasai applied it to this area is anyone's guess, although one theory is that it relates to the landscape, which is patched or mottled with groves of acacia and thickets of lesser whistling thorn. More likely, however, the Mara was named for the spotty, speckled inundation of the wildebeest and a million other herbivores that occurs any time between the end of June and the middle of September.

PRECEDING PAGES: a topi stands sentinel in the Maasai Mara. LEFT: sundown in the savannah. BELOW: a nimble klipspringer.

## The Grand Tour

Given the option, the wildebeest would probably never come up to the Mara. They would stay down south, on the vast alluvial short-grass plains of the Serengeti, which they prefer because there is virtually no cover for the predators. But they soon mow the grazing to stubble, the land dries up and they are forced to move out following the northwesterly bearing of the "long rains".

*The ungainly wildebeest is clearly a survivor as a species. At Olduvai Gorge, where Louis and Mary Leakey dug early man out of the sediment, they also unearthed remains of early wildebeest, carbon-dating the bones back 2 million years.*

The great journey generally has a disorderly start. None of the animals seems to know what's happening, except for a few individuals in the 1.4 million who must sniff the air, decide it's time and amble off towards Lake Victoria. The others follow, straggling individuals and small groups, but eventually bunching in broad lines of march which look like columns of safari ants. They wheel before the lake, moving due north to cross the Mara, Sand and Talek rivers at exactly the same places each year. This brings them into Kenya, where there will be good grazing in the best-watered section of the ring from the Mara and the dozen other rivers that flow off the western wall of the Rift.

The herds tend to break up and scatter across the hills, but also on valley fields of "golden grass" – actually russet red *Themeda triandra* – which contributes to the Mara motley. The wildebeest are highly vulnerable to predators launching out of the thickets, so whenever they smell the October "short rains" moving up from the south, the hordes reform and restart the migration. This time, for some unknown reason, the lines are narrower and more dispersed for the southeasterly arc, back to where it all started.

## Resident game

The lush grasslands interspersed with silver- and russet-leaved croton thickets, hillocks and forested river banks provide a good variety of habitats for wildlife. There are many buffalo and quite a few rhino in the Mara, as well as herds of Thomson's and Grant's gazelles, topi and impala. Predators include large prides of lions (the largest population to be found in Kenya), a fair number of cheetahs and leopards, spotted hyenas and silver- or black-backed jackals. There are over 450 recorded species of birds in this reserve, including the rare Verreaux's

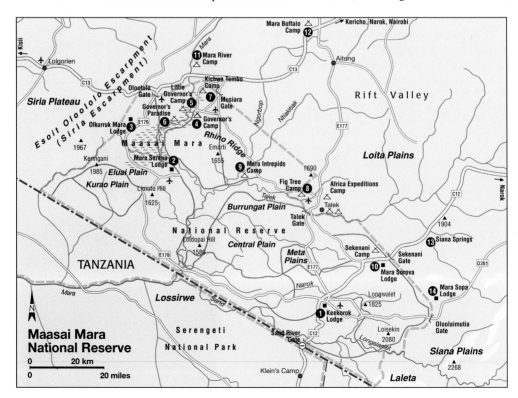

Maasai Mara National Reserve

TANZANIA

Serengeti National Park

Siria Plateau

Rift Valley

Loita Plains

Siana Plains

0    20 km
0    20 miles

Map on page 198

eagle owl. Other common birds include ostrich, kori bustards, martial eagles and various other birds of prey.

The Mara is the archetypal arena of conflicts between man and nature in modern Africa. Wheat schemes and livestock improvement programmes to the north meet the greatest remaining wildlife migration to the south. At the interface, conservationists and ecologists strive to reconcile the needs and aspirations of the Maasai landowners. Although fraught with problems, many of the results have been encouraging – apart from elephant and rhino poaching, which is a blight throughout Africa. Many tourism-based enterprises, such as tented camps, are run by local landowners who recognise that wildlife can be a resource worth husbanding.

## Bloodshed at "Blood Valley"

There are two ways to reach the Maasai Mara from Nairobi, either the high or the low road west towards Nakuru. "Up" is a reasonable tarmac highway across the top of the Rift escarpment; "down", formerly a minefield of potholes, has recently been resurfaced and is a pleasure to drive on. Either way, the route leads to the northern end of the **Kedong Valley** about 50 km (30 miles) from Nairobi. In the old days, this was "Blood Valley", where Maasai massacred 550 caravan porters and, later, "Trader Dick" came after them in a reprisal raid.

These days, at nearby **Mayer's Farm**, the *moran* (warriors) dance for tourists over afternoon tea. A left turn is signposted to **Narok**, the town that administers the northern half of Maasailand. It is full of strolling *moran* buying very little from shanty *dukas* (stores). Sixteen km (10 miles) out, on a good tarmac road, is a Game Department barrier at **Ewaso Ngiro** ("brown river" in Maa). At this

*The original road across the Rift escarpment to the Maasai Mara was built by Italian prisoners of war. A tiny chapel at the foot of the rift is a memento of their Catholic presence.*

**BELOW:** a cheetah and her cub.

Map
on page
198

**TIP**

At certain times of
year, several of the
camps organise
rafting trips on the
lazy, meandering
Mara River.

**BELOW:** a pair
of reedbuck.

point, there is a confusion of tracks, especially if the signpost is missing, which it frequently is. Take the left turn to **Sekenani Gate**, then straight ahead to **Aitong**, for Governor's Camp and the western end of the Mara.

However, to **Keekorok**, the traditional centre of Mara Reserve, the compass bearing is southwest on the centre track for about 72 km (45 miles) of bumpy, all-weather dirt. Altogether, the drive from Nairobi is a rough 231 km (145 miles), so that charter or light-aircraft scheduled services to Keekorok or another Mara airstrip are worthwhile – if you can afford it.

### Staying in the Mara

**Keekorok Lodge ❶**, in the east, was a traditional resting place on the long - safari from the Serengeti to Nairobi. These days, it is well laid out with cottages and good facilities including car mechanics – sometimes essential after the rough and bumpy roads. **Mara Serena Lodge ❷**, in the west, is set high on a saddle overlooking rolling grasslands and the far-off Esoit Oloololo escarpment. Bedrooms are stylised mud *manyattas* grouped in outward-looking rings. **Olkurruk Mara Lodge ❸** lies just inside the reserve's western boundary, overshadowed by the escarpment.

The Mara area has numerous tented camps, including **Governor's Camp ❹** on the Mara River, where old colonial governors used to pitch their tents; it is now a very up-market retreat. The same company also owns **Governor's Paradise ❻** private camp and **Little Governor's ❺**. Right on the boundaries of the reserve are **Kichwa Tembo Camp ❼** (*kichwa tembo* means "elephant's head" in Swahili) and **Fig Tree Camp ❽**, both offering romantic settings where you can lose yourself in the true safari atmosphere. **Mara Intrepids Camp ❾** is situated in the centre of the reserve, and thus offers great views of the Migration when it comes through. **Mara Sarova Lodge ❿** is about 5 km (3 miles) into the reserve from the Sekenani Gate.

Outside the reserve, the **Mara River Camp ⓫** lies about 8 km (5 miles) north of the Oloololo Gate, on the Mara River. Further to the northeast, on the road to Ngorengore, **Mara Buffalo Camp ⓬** consists of thatched *bandas* situated near a hippo pool that's supposedly one of the best popuated in Kenya. Also outside the reserve is **Siana Springs ⓭**, a lodge about 20 km (12 miles) from Sekenani Gate. **Mara Sopa Lodge ⓮**, just outside the reserve's eastern boundary, blends in with its surroundings in the Oloolaimutia Valley, and puts the accent on the Maasai people as well as the flora and fauna.

There are a number of semi-permanent camps and homestays around the reserve – for example, the Cheli & Peacock Mara Camp, a seasonal camp in the protected Koyiaki wilderness area. Africa Expeditions has two private camps, one just outside the reserve, on the Talek River, and the other in the Loita Hills to the east of the reserve. The Out of Africa Camp is a semi-permanent camp on private Maasai ranch land, tucked away in a large copse of indigenous trees north of the Mara on the Aitong Plain. Rekero Ranch, in the wheatlands that border the Mara, caters for eight guests in thatched bungalows. ❑

# Up, Up and Away

Jules Verne's novel *Five Weeks in a Balloon*, published in 1862, was the first to mention ballooning in Africa and was the inspiration for English gas balloonist Anthony Smith's visit 100 years later. Using a hydrogen-filled balloon, he successfully crossed from Zanzibar to Tanzania, and also completed flights over the Serengeti and the Great Rift Valley.

Accompanying Smith as cameraman during these early flights was Alan Root, now a renowned wildlife film maker. He realised that, if problems of expense and manoeuvrability could be overcome, a balloon basket was the perfect place from which to appreciate the majesty of the African landscape.

Root had a hot-air balloon delivered to Kenya and, with the aid of a trained pilot, set about learning to fly it. Early flights were hazardous until European flying techniques were adapted to African conditions. The result of Root's efforts was one of his most popular films, *Safari by Balloon*.

While on location Root was several times asked by passing travellers for rides over the savannah. It was these visitors to Kenya, wanting to see the game from a different perspective, who prompted him to set up Kenya's first balloon company, Balloon Safaris. Based at Keekorok Lodge in the Maasai Mara Game Reserve, the company has flown 35,000 passengers since its inaugural flight in 1976. The original five-passenger balloons with their cramped baskets have now been superseded by balloons three times bigger, with baskets containing seats for 12 passengers.

Since those first flights, balloon safaris have now become a major attraction for many visitors in Kenya. Other balloon companies have sprung up in the Mara based at Governor's Camp, Sarova Camp and Fig Tree Camp. Wherever you stay in the Mara, you're close to a balloon base if you wish to fly. Although open year-round, the optimum time to balloon in the Mara is from July to October during the annual wildebeest migration, when over one million animals cross the plains.

The daily flights lift off with the rising sun for an hour-long journey over an average distance of about 12 km (8 miles). Being highly manoeuvrable, the balloons can skim treetops or rise to over 300 metres (1,000 feet) for panoramic views of the rolling Mara plains. All balloon companies serve a champagne breakfast wherever they land in the park, something as memorable as the flight itself.

Because balloons are moved by the prevailing winds they cannot return to their take-off point. After breakfast passengers are driven slowly back to the lodge by retriever vehicles. All companies return passengers to their respective lodges by mid-morning after presenting them with a certificate to mark the occasion.

In 1988, balloon companies started flying in two other game parks. In Samburu Game Reserve balloonists have the chance to enjoy the magnificent scenery with Mount Kenya in the distance. Ballooning in the privately-owned Taita Hills Game Sanctuary near Tsavo West offers views of Kilimanjaro as well as a variety of game. ❑

**RIGHT:** floating over the Mara in the dawn light.

# WARRIOR NOMADS OF THE PLAINS

*East Africa's most famous tribe has a long history of nomadic pastoralism and warlike aggression. But today their unique lifestyle is under threat*

Around 1,000 years ago, a group of nomadic pastoralists moved south from Lake Turkana, spreading across the fertile lands of the Rift Valley. By the 19th century, the Maasai had established a reputation as powerful and ferocious people: their warrior bands raided deep into neighbouring territories, stealing cattle and demanding tribute from the trade caravans.

Even since the colonial British moved the Maasai out of their northern grazing lands into the less fertile savannah region in the south, they have largely maintained their traditional nomadic way of life, grazing their cattle over vast areas, living in temporary villages (*manyattas*) of huts ringed by a thorn fence as defence against wild animals. Their diet consists mainly of milk, blood drawn from their cattle, and occasionally millet and maize. Possession of land means nothing to them: their wealth is measured in cattle, which are rarely slaughtered, and then only for ceremonial purposes. The flesh of wild beasts is forbidden, except for eland and buffalo.

At the time of their circumcision, around age 12 to 15, Maasai males are initiated as *moran* (young warriors). For about 15 years their duty is to keep watch over the livestock and defend the clan against enemies. Strict taboos apply to this age-group, including a prohibition on marriage and alcohol. At around age 30, another set of rituals, *eunoto*, translates the warriors into elders, who can then marry.

△ **GREASY LOCKS**
Appearance is important to the *moran*, whose long hair is braided with animal fat and coloured red with ochre.

▷ **PLAY TIME**
This ancient board game is played throughout Africa. The Maasai call it *enkeshui*.

▽ **RITE OF PASSAGE**
After serving his time as a *moran*, the young warrior has his head shaved and his body decorated for the ceremony of *eunoto*.

▷ **ABOUT TO BE WARRIORS**
Before they become *moran*, Maasai boys have an initiation period, during which they wear these distinctive tunics.

## MAINTENANCE WORK
It is the women's task to look after the *manyatta*. This woman is waterproofing the roof of a hut with mud and cow dung.

▷ **HIGH JUMP**
The Maasai's traditional *ipid* dance, which involves leaping high in the air, demonstrates the vigour and virility of a *moran*.

△ **BLOOD-LETTING**
Maasai are skilled at drawing blood from cattle without killing the beast. From top: an arrow is shot at the cow's jugular vein; a disc on the arrowhead limits the depth it penetrates; blood spurts into a gourd and the wound is sealed with a mixture of dung and grass; later, clotted blood is eaten from the gourd.

## THE MAASAI AND TOURISM

Maasai are excluded from the national parks and reserves, though they may have seasonally grazed their cattle in these areas for generations. The government claims that conservation areas attract lucrative tourism, which in turn benefits local people. But the Maasai are rarely the beneficiaries. In effect they have been denied access to vital grazing grounds in the name of tourism. The results have been dramatic. Some Maasai now charge tourists an admission fee to their villages, to take photographs and buy souvenirs. Even on the coast, far from their traditional homelands, Maasai are seen selling trinkets to tourists. Elswhere they have created permanent group ranches, where they herd their cattle and grow food. But the land is often unsuitable for intensive grazing or agriculture. Whatever their future, a radical change to the Maasai's nomadic lifestyle seems inevitable.

# NORTHERN GAME COUNTRY

Map on page 208

*North of Mount Kenya is a vast area of desert and semi-desert that stretches all the way to Sudan and Ethiopia. It's a magnificent and largely unexplored wilderness*

Nairobi

The region that used to be called the Northern Frontier District is a stark, rugged landscape where nomads, who have changed little over centuries, still drive their herds chasing the ephemeral growth of grass. It is the emptiness and wildness that makes a visit to the Samburu, Buffalo Springs and Shaba National Reserves such an unforgettable experience.

To reach this wilderness area, drive northward from Nanyuki on a rather rough tarmac road; Mount Kenya lies on your right, with vast stretches of open bush country ahead of you. Not far from Timau is the turning to Borana Ranch, which takes you (after about an hour's drive) through the wildlife area to **Borana Lodge**. The lodge offers first-class accommodation in six unique cottages built of cedar and glass, with fine views of Mount Kenya. This retreat (where the writers of *The Lion King* supposedly got their inspiration) sits on a private game ranch in a valley running from the Laikipia Plateau down to the Samburu plains.

Back on the main road to Isiolo, about 2 km (1 mile) from the Meru junction is the entrance to the **Lewa Wildlife Conservancy**. This encompasses both the Ngare Sergoi Rhino Sanctuary for endangered black rhinos and the **Lewa Downs Ranch**, where visitors can stay at Wilderness Trails, the home of the Craig family since 1924, which offers a relaxed understated homestay in the ranch house. The Craigs and their staff offer game walks, horseback rides and game drives by day and by night.

Northwest of Lewa Downs is the **Il Ngwesi** group ranch, home of the famed Il Ngwesi self-catering lodge, which recently won a British Airways Ecotourism Award. It is constructed out of local driftwood and clay, and has no windows. There is a full contingent of staff who will do your cooking. The furnishings are in keeping with the theme of the lodge – simple but elegant. Income from the lodge goes to community projects. Just north of Wamba is **Sarara Camp**, located in the Namunyak Wildlife Conservation Trust, which is also promoted and supported by the Lewa Wildlife Conservancy. You can either self-cater or pay for a fully-catered stay.

## Samburu and Buffalo Springs

The two reserves, Samburu to the north of the Ewaso Ngiro ("brown water") River and Buffalo Springs to the south, are usually treated as one unit by both tour companies and local wildlife. A bridge across the Ewaso Ngiro a little way upstream of Samburu Lodge connects the two areas.

From Nairobi to the reserves, it is approximately 300 km (186 miles) on tarmac up to **Isiolo**, then on a dirt road for about another 50 km (30 miles). The most

**PRECEDING PAGES:** Kenya's northern deserts seen from the Lorogi Plateau. **LEFT:** a wary female leopard. **BELOW:** a pair of shy dikdik.

*Grevy's zebra used to be hunted for its fine, narrow-striped skin, and was also exported in great numbers to European zoos. It is only slowly re-establishing a viable population in northern Kenya.*

convenient entrance to the reserves is the **Ngare Mara Gate**, 20 km (12 miles) north of Isiolo, through the Buffalo Springs Reserve. Another entrance, 3 km (2 miles) before reaching Archer's Post, is called **Buffalo Springs Gate**. The road directly into Samburu National Reserve, reached from the township of Archer's Post, is fairly rough, and should be attempted only in a four-wheel-drive vehicle, but the journey is made more interesting by the several Samburu *manyattas* (enclosed villages) passed on the way. There's also a tarmac airstrip for tourists who do not wish to endure the long drive.

Physically dramatic, with a great table mountain called **Ololokwe** in the background, the 100-sq. km (40-sq. mile) Samburu National Reserve is baked red-brown for most of the year. A permanent relief is in the broad green ribbon of trees along the Ewaso Ngiro, which originates on the Laikipia Plateau in the west, is fed by the runoff from the Aberdares and Mount Kenya, and vanishes beyond Samburu in the recesses of the Lorian Swamp in the east towards Somalia. The river is a permanent source of water for animals and is lined by acacias, tamarind and doum palms. The major, central part of both reserves is dry, open, thorn-bush country, which becomes green only during the rains.

A variety of animals can be found, including diminishing numbers of elephant and numerous buffalo and waterbuck that feed on the vegetation around the river and in the adjoining swamps. Impala herds, with one male guarding up to 50 females and young, graze along the riverine vegetation. Grevy's zebra, beisa oryx, reticulated giraffe and gerenuk are found only in this sort of dry semi-arid country. Oryx are very shy, relatively scarce animals with beautifully marked heads and long, straight horns. Dikdik are far more common and particularly like the rocky hills and dry acacia woodland to be found here.

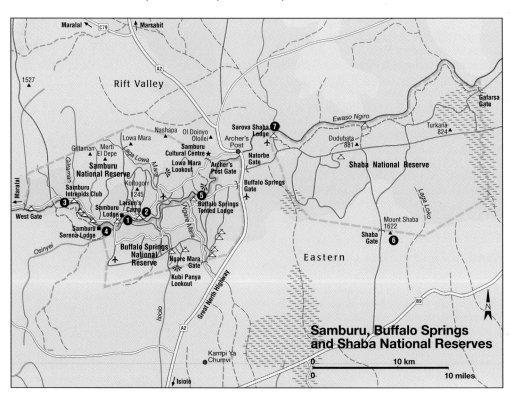

Samburu, Buffalo Springs and Shaba National Reserves

## Dinner guests

Crocodiles sun themselves on the banks of the river. Lion, cheetah and leopard are also fairly easy to see, thanks to the sparse grass cover. Smaller mammals include ground squirrels, which are common around the lodges, and dwarf mongooses, frequently seen scampering across the open ground looking for food.

Birds are abundant, with more than 365 species recorded, including the Somali race of ostrich, which has blue legs that are particularly conspicuous during the breeding season. Numerous flocks of helmeted and vulturine guineafowls can be seen, especially in the afternoon as they go to the river to drink. Martial eagles, one of the largest aerial predators, are often seen perching on a vantage point scanning for movements in the grass indicating potential prey. Other birds of prey, such as bateleur and pygmy falcon, are also common. Along the banks of the rivers, kingfishers and Layard's black weavers are found. The rare Narina's trogon, a bird with a bright green and red breast, related to the parrot, is also seen in the riverine woodland.

The comfortable **Samburu Lodge ❶** is on the north side of the river near the western boundary. You can watch crocodiles being fed on leftovers, and there is a platform where goat carcasses are hung from trees to attract the big cats, especially leopards. Downstream from Samburu Lodge is **Larsen's ❷**, the ultimate in luxury tented camps. This is a small 17-tent camp, situated on the bank of the Ewaso Ngiro, offering high style with colonial elegance, game viewing from a tree platform over the vast Samburu plain, game drives in the late afternoon, dinner by candlelight and coffee around the campfire.

In the northwestern section of the reserve is **Samburu Intrepids Club ❸**, a luxury lodge that's reminiscent of a fantasy tree house set on stilts with its

Map on page 208

**TIP**

Although Samburu and Buffalo Springs are usually regarded as a single reserve, separate entrance fees are payable for each. Tickets are sold at the connecting bridge, as well as at the boundary gates.

**BELOW:** Samburu sights – a termite mound and weaver birds' nests.

Map on page 208

*Inquisitive ground squirrels are frequent visitors to Samburu lodges. They live in underground warrens and do not climb trees.*

**BELOW:** the beast that gave Buffalo Springs its name.

vaulted thatched roofs, sprawling wooden terraces and 25 tents elevated on individual decks overlooking the river. **Samburu Serena Lodge ④** is situated outside the reserve to the west. This lodge has recently undergone major renovations, replacing all old facilities with new, all under canvas and in keeping with the environment.

The equally well-appointed **Buffalo Springs Tented Lodge ⑤** is on the south bank, not far from the eastern gate. A short distance away are the clear pools of Buffalo Springs. The story goes that during World War II an Italian bomb, dropped by a plane from occupied Somalia, missed Isiolo township and formed the pool.

## Shaba National Reserve

The third and largest of the reserves in this region lies to the east of Buffalo Springs and Samburu, across the Isiolo-Moyale road, and on the south bank of the Ewaso Ngiro. **Shaba National Reserve** (240 sq. km/96 sq. miles) is reached by a turn-off 2 km (1 mile) short of Archer's Post through the **Natorbe Gate**. Shaba has a particular place in the history of Kenyan game conservation. It was there that author Joy Adamson was murdered early in 1980, leaving behind her unfinished trilogy of books on the rehabilitation of leopard to the wild.

The reserve's central attraction is again the wide, sauntering Ewaso Ngiro on its way to the Lorian Swamp, as well as the tall trees of the stark riverine forest that provide a sharp contrast to the rugged and pitted tracts which make up much of the sanctuary. Many small hills diversify Shaba and, with four springs, the reserve is better watered than its neighbours.

Heavy downpours often render the already rough tracks accessible only for

four-wheel-drive vehicles. All this serves only to enhance the traveller's sense of the reserve's isolation, which is the essence of Shaba – a place for the connoisseur, where an authentic African experience is the objective.

Shaba National Reserve takes its name from **Mount Shaba ⑥**, a copper-coloured sandstone hill which lies partially in the reserve and is famous for its lava flows that oozed down from the **Nyambeni Hills** only 5,000 years ago. The western side of the reserve is bushed grassland savannah, dotted with thorn bushes, gradually becoming acacia woodland nearer Mount Shaba. Beyond the mountain the vegetation becomes grassland plains. A series of springs bubble up in the river in the northeastern side of the reserve. One spring, **Penny's Drop**, was named after Joy Adamson's leopard Penny, which she released back into the wild in Shaba Reserve.

Although heavy poaching in Shaba has made animals very shy, you might be lucky enough to see elephant, lion, cheetah, leopard, waterbuck, as well as all the animals specially adapted to the dry region: beisa oryx, gerenuk, Grevy's zebra, reticulated giraffe and Somali ostrich.

The only accommodation in the reserve is the **Sarova Shaba Lodge ⑦**, which has 80 thatched-roof bedrooms, a restaurant, two bars, a swimming pool and conference facilities. ❑

# The Samburu

A nomadic Maa-speaking people, the Samburu (73,400 of them) live mainly in northern Kenya between Lake Turkana and the Ewaso Ngiro river. Known long ago as the *Loibor Kineji* (people of the white goats), the Samburu sometimes refer to themselves as *il-Oikop*. Baragoi, Maralal and Wamba are the main centres of administration.

As with other pastoralists of the north, their lifestyle has changed little over the last hundred years. They live in low huts carefully crafted with interwoven sticks and plastered with mud and cattle dung. Samburu homes are windowless and dark so as to keep out flies. They also keep in smoke, which probably accounts for the existence of chronic chest infections and trachoma, which can eventually result in blindness.

An extended family of brothers, wives and parents live in a circular formation of huts surrounded by a high thorn branch fence called a *boma*. Livestock is herded inside at night where the thorn forms an effective barrier against marauding predators. The smallest animals are brought into the huts.

The Samburu live on the livestock – more specifically, on a thick curdled milk which tastes like smoke-flavoured yoghurt. Sometimes this is mixed with cattle blood and, on special occasions only, they eat meat. Their entire lifestyle is centred on cows, camels and goats, which they refer to as their wealth and only sometimes slaughter for ritual events. Money doesn't mean much to them and the little they have is carried by the warriors in socks, knotted and hung from their belts.

The tribe is divided into eight clans: four belong to the "white cows" and four to the "black cows", with these further divided into series of sub-clans. Greetings between strangers always include a who's-who breakdown of clan, sub-clan and age-group, which usually results in the satisfying discovery of a distant relationship of some sort.

As a child, a boy tends his father's herds. Then, when he reaches puberty, he is circumcised and becomes a warrior, known as a *murrani* or a *moran*. The warrior years are halcyon for the young men, whose role is comparable to the knights of the Middle Ages. But they also undertake tough and sometimes dangerous assignments to ensure the safety and well-being of their community. On the ochre plains of El Barta, you may encounter caravans of cattle herded by these warriors carrying twin spears. During droughts, they may drive their herds hundreds of miles from one patch of sparse grazing to another.

Unlike the warlike Maasai, whose language and cultural heritage they share, the Samburu do not adopt an aggressive and dominant cultural stance towards other tribes. Instead they place a high social value on a mature sense of respect. Today group and individual ranching schemes and improved educational facilities are bringing about long-resisted change. Many Samburu *il-murran* enlisted in the British Forces during World War II, and many Samburu still serve in the Kenya armed forces and police. ❏

**RIGHT:** a young Samburu warrior.

# MERU AND KORA

*In an area formerly popular with hunters, these reserves were established for the rehabilitation of wildlife. Though they are off the beaten safari trail, they offer spectacular game viewing*

**M**eru National Park achieved world recognition with Joy Adamson's *Born Free*, the story of Elsa the lioness that was rehabilitated to the wild. The similar tale of Pippa, her cheetah, was told in *The Spotted Sphinx*. After her release, Pippa eventually gave birth to two litters of fine cubs. Despite being one of the major national parks in Kenya, and a very beautiful one, Meru is off the mainstream circuit for the majority of visitors. But it is well worth a visit. The park covers an area of 800 sq. km (320 sq. miles), lying to the west of Mount Kenya in the semi-arid area of the country. It straddles the equator and ranges from an altitude of 1,000 metres (3,300 ft) in the foothills of the Nyambeni Range (the northern boundary) to less than 300 metres (990 ft) on the Tana River in the south.

Two routes lead from Nairobi to Meru National Park: one around Mount Kenya, through **Nanyuki**, and the other one through **Embu**. Both roads go to **Meru** town, from where it is 78 km (48 miles) to the park. If you go via Nanyuki, you can enter the park from the west using the **Murera Gate**. Some visitors prefer to fly in to avoid the slow and winding road.

The main tourist roads are in the western part, with only a few roads in the remote east. The eastern park boundary is bordered by the Bisanadi National Reserve; to the southeast are the North Kitui and Kora National Reserves; while to the north of Kora is the Rahole National Reserve. Together with Meru, they create a wildlife sanctuary that encompasses 4,670 sq. km (1,868 sq. miles).

Vegetation is mainly bushland, with combretum bush prevailing in the north and commiphora in the south. The northeast is dominated by grassland with borassus palms and acacia woodland. There is plenty of water, the main perennial river being the Tana, which is the longest in Kenya. Many other small streams occur in the park. Most are bordered by riverine forest. Some valleys are partially flooded during the rainy season, providing a swampy grassland habitat favoured by buffalo and waterbuck.

**LEFT:** a lion relaxes.
**BELOW:** a Chuka drummer from the Meru district.

## Reviving stock

Animal life is now plentiful, but game had virtually vanished by 1959, when the local council of the Wameru tribe seized the initiative from the colonial government and designated the area for conservation and rehabilitation. Large numbers of buffalo can usually be found around the swamps and the Tana River, and the river provides a sanctuary for hippopotamus and crocodile. Big herds of elephant often used to be seen in the swamp area near the Meru Mulika Lodge, but their numbers were drastically reduced by poaching. Black rhinos used to be abundant in the park, but

*Over the years, many leopards have been brought to Meru from other parts of Kenya, in an attempt to build a viable population of the cats here.*

sadly they too have been heavily poached, as was the small protected herd of white rhinos introduced here from South Africa in the hope that they would breed. In 1988 the five remaining animals were killed by poachers, aided, it is alleged, by a disgruntled park ranger who used to protect them.

Meru supports a range of species more usually found in northern areas, including the Grevy's zebra, the beisa oryx and the reticulated giraffe, which is rust-red coloured with distinctive thin white lines creating a "crazy paving" effect. Dikdik, gerenuk (which supposedly do not need water and survive on dew) and the big cats are abundant, but sometimes difficult to see because of the tall grass cover and thick bush. Eland and kongoni prefer the wetter grassland areas. Lesser kudu, either alone or in pairs, can be found in thickets or in valley bottoms in the evening.

Bird-watchers should look out for the relatively uncommon palm-nut vulture, which feeds on a mixture of palm nuts and carrion. In addition, the palm swift can be seen building its nest on the underside of palm fronds. Pel's fishing owl and the rare Peter's finfoot live near the Tana River. Peter's finfoots resemble long-necked slender ducks or small cormorants. They are very secretive and are usually seen swimming under overhanging trees close to the bank. Helmeted and vulturine (with slender, striped necks) guinea-fowl are common.

## Wilderness area

The backdrops at Meru are picturesque, sometimes abstract; at **Adamson's Falls ❶** on the Tana River, blocks of granite have been weathered and watered into weird shapes, like modern sculptures. On clear mornings, the snow peaks of Mount Kenya appear in the southwest, but perhaps the definitive skyscape for

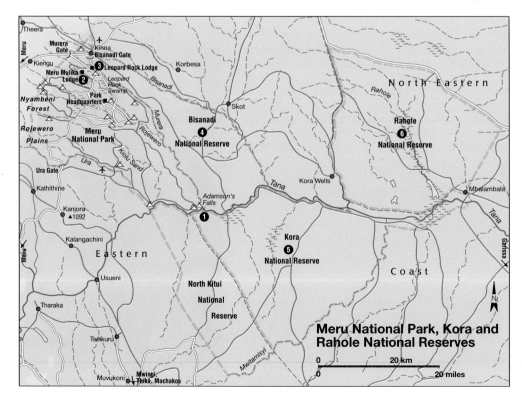

Meru National Park, Kora and Rahole National Reserves

0                    20 km
0                    20 miles

the park is with the sun directly behind the high bordering Nyambeni Range, the light shafting through the summits for an impression of a romanticised religious painting.

Geologically the park is extremely interesting. Most of the land surface is olivine basalt lava flows from the Nyambenis, overlaid with rich brown and gray volcanic or black cotton soils strewn with small pumice boulders. The basement rock occasionally outcrops as low inselbergs or *kopjes* (rocky outcrops) to relieve the monotony of the dry bush country.

The park is roughly bisected by the **Rojewero River**, which marks an abrupt change of landscape. On one side, open grasslands stretch out of the Nyambeni foothills; on the other is thick Commiphora bush which spreads north and eastwards 480 km (300 miles) to the coast. This is arid, broken country cut by innumerable sand *luggas* (dry river beds).

There are 19 rivers and streams in the park, 15 of them permanent. In addition, numerous swamps and springs occur where the lava is spread thin on the basement system and in the line of a fault running southwestwards from Kinna to Kilimakieru. The main feeder springs and swamps are the Kithima ya Mugumu ("Fig Tree Springs"), Murera Springs, Bisanadi and Buguma Swamps, and Mulika Swamp, where the park's only fully serviced lodge is situated. The **Meru Mulika Lodge ❷** has numerous thatched huts in an attractive setting overlooking the swamp, where herds of elephant come to drink. Unfortunately, at the time of going to press, the lodge was not operational, although negotiations were proceeding for another hotel group to come in and revamp it. Any experienced safari company should be able to tell you if the lodge is back in business.

Not far away, on the banks of Murera River, is **Leopard Rock ❸**, a self-

Map on page 214

**TIP**

If you plan to drive through Meru, it is wise to check with the Park HQ (southwest of Meru Mulika Lodge) on the condition of tracks, especially along the rivers.

**BELOW:** a pale chanting goshawk stops for directions.

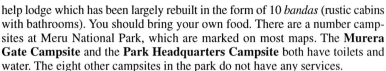

Map on page 214

*The Tana River is the habitat boundary between two species. The reticulated giraffe (above), lives north of the Tana, its cousin the Maasai giraffe to the south.*

**BELOW:** a Maasai giraffe at sunset.

help lodge which has been largely rebuilt in the form of 10 *bandas* (rustic cabins with bathrooms). You should bring your own food. There are a number campsites at Meru National Park, which are marked on most maps. The **Murera Gate Campsite** and the **Park Headquarters Campsite** both have toilets and water. The eight other campsites in the park do not have any services.

One section of the park has been designated a wilderness area, in which there are no roads. This area can only be reached by four-wheel drive vehicles, accompanied by an experienced ranger. Similarly, the 600 sq. km (240 sq. miles) of the **Bisanadi National Reserve ❹**, which adjoins Meru National Park, is undeveloped for tourism. Access is difficult even with four-wheel drive vehicles. The habitat, flora and fauna are similar to Meru, with more spectacular elongated rocky outcrops.

### Kora and Rahole

Bordering on the middle reaches of the Tana River, the 1,790 sq. km (700 sq. miles) of the **Kora National Reserve ❺** were made famous by George Adamson and Tony Fitzjohn, who for years engaged in the dangerous business of re-introducing captive lions and leopards to the wild. Tragically, Adamson was ambushed and killed by bandits in August 1989.

The remote Kora region is adjoined to Rahole National Reserve, and is composed of riverine woodland along the Tana River and miles of bushland in the interior. It is also renowned for rocky outcrops with their own unique habitats and fauna. You will not see wildlife in great numbers, but there are occasional sightings of lion, lesser kudu, elephant and waterbuck. The river is beautiful in this section and is well stocked with hippos and crocodiles.

Kora was the site of a major ecological survey in 1983 carried out by the National Museums of Kenya and the Royal Geographical Society, with support from the US National Aeronautic and Space Administration and the United Nations Environment Programme. The results gave valuable insights and management information for a wild part of Africa increasingly encroached by Somali pastoralists.

Kora is about 130 km (80 miles) from the township of **Garissa**. There are no tourist facilities in what is essentially an area set aside for scientific research, although there are plans for an 80-bed "ecolodge" to be built. A bridge is being built over the Tana, to link Kora to Bisanadi National Reserve.

North across the Tana River from Kora is the **Rahole National Reserve ❻**. This remote reserve of 1,270 sq. km (508 sq. miles) was developed to illustrate the potential for local wildlife to co-exist with tribes that live in the area. However, the experiment seems to have failed, as poaching is rife and settlements abound. Until it can be developed to ensure a tourism industry with revenues for local pastoralists, the area will remain undistinguished and unremarkable, although there is plenty of splendid scenery.

There are no tourist facilities except those mentioned at Meru, 40 km (25 miles) upstream. In addition, in the dry season Rahole is really only accessible from the east, via the Garsen-Garissa road. ❑

# Freedom Fighters

Joy-Friederike Gessner was born in 1910 in Troppau – which was then part of Austria-Hungary and is now Oppava in the Czech Republic. After an education in Vienna followed by two divorces, she came to Kenya in 1939.

George Adamson was born in Etwah in India in 1906, and at the age of 18 travelled to Kenya to seek his fortune. After working as a gold prospector, goat trader and big game hunter, he landed temporary work as an assistant game warden in 1938.

The couple met at Christmas 1942, and married in 1944. It was the beginning of a partnership that became world-famous in the field of animal conservation. For over 30 years Joy and George Adamson, together and apart, devoted their lives to rearing orphaned big cats and preparing them for re-introduction to the wild.

The story began in 1956, when George was forced to shoot a lioness that was attacking him. She left three cubs, which the Adamsons "adopted" and raised. One of them, Elsa, became internationally famous through Joy's trilogy of books, *Born Free: A Lioness of Two Worlds, Living Free: The Story of Elsa and her Cubs,* and *Forever Free: Elsa's Pride.* They were all best-sellers, and adapted into successful films, starting with *Born Free* in 1966.

By then, Joy Adamson had founded the Elsa Wild Animal Appeal and George had left his job as a game warden to devote all his considerable energies to the task of rearing and releasing lions – not only Elsa and her family but many other orphaned cubs that were brought to the Adamsons as their fame spread. Joy also trained a young cheetah, Pippa, back to her wild ways, and even found time to write an illuminating book, *The Peoples of Kenya,* in 1967.

In 1970 the couple separated. George moved to Kora, rented an area from the Meru Council and established *Kampi ya Simba* (Lion Camp) to continue his work. By 1978 he had released more than 23 orphaned or captive lions into the wild. Meanwhile Joy moved

to Shaba, where she began to concern herself with leopards. Her last book, *Queen of Shaba: The Story of an African Leopard,* was published posthumously, for in 1980 she was murdered in her Shaba camp by a disgruntled employee.

Although they had lived apart for nine years, the death of his wife deeply affected George Adamson. He withdrew from all public activity and rarely left Kora. There he worked devotedly with his beloved lions with an associate, Tony Fitzjohn, and a small team of equally dedicated workers.

Unhappily, the Kora area (not yet a national reserve) had been invaded by *shifta,* nomadic Somali pastoralists, with their goats and camels, to the great detriment of the wildlife. By 1988, they had poached all the remaining elephant and rhino in the area, and killed three game rangers.

In August 1989 poachers ambushed some of George Adamson's camp staff. He drove out to help, and was shot dead. He was 83. He is buried at Kampi ya Simba, beside his favourite lion, Elsa's son "Boy".    ❑

**RIGHT:** George Adamason in remote Kora.

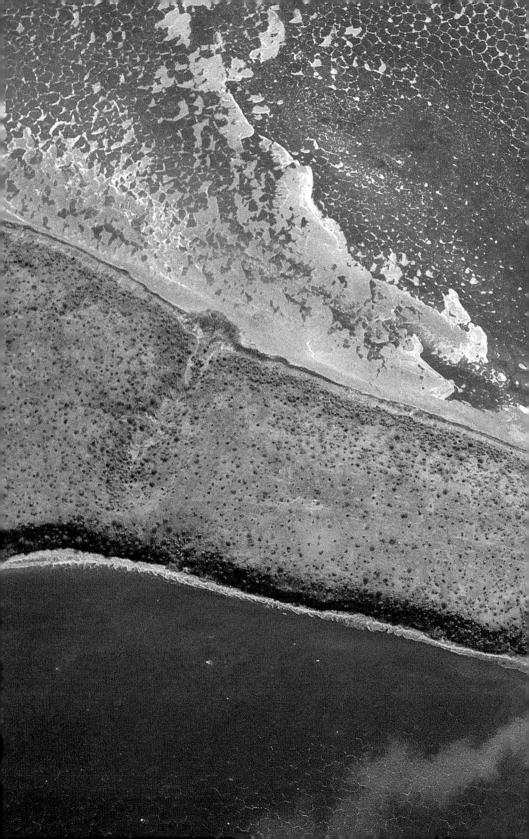

# THE LAKES OF THE GREAT RIFT VALLEY

*The largest split in the earth's crust runs through Kenya, making a mighty valley characterised by volcanoes and lakes that are full (and sometimes empty) of undrinkable water*

Map on page 222

Tectonic theory has it that the earth's crust is a set of plates floating on liquid magma deep down below. Sometimes the plates break up and the parts drift away from one another. These breaks are usually below the ocean surface, but one of them splits the earth. It runs from the Jordan Valley in the north, takes in the whole of the Red Sea, sheers through Ethiopia, Kenya, Tanzania and Mozambique and finally reaches the sea near the Zambezi delta.

This **Great Rift Valley** is more than 8,700 km (5,400 miles) long – a crack in the African plate that, in length, exceeds one-quarter of the earth's circumference. An arm of it runs through much of the Nile Valley, scours across western Uganda and Tanzania and joins the main Rift in southern Tanzania. In places, the walls of the Rift rise little more than 30 metres (100 ft) above the valley floor. Elsewhere, there are steep, often sheer cliffs to above 1,200 metres (4,000 ft), but nowhere is the Rift more sharply defined than where it cuts through the highlands of Kenya. In addition to the towering walls, the whole length of valley in Kenya is studded with volcanoes.

Also scattered along the length of the Kenya Rift is a chain of seven lakes. These are unusual in that not a single one of them has an obvious outflow. Water pours in from the rainfall on the surrounding land and more or less stays there in the shallow pans. While a high rate of evaporation keeps the levels fairly constant, it also causes an accumulation of salts and minerals in the waters of the lake. As a result, all but two of the Rift Valley lakes are so saline that they are virtually undrinkable.

## Hot spot

The most alkaline of all these lakes is **Magadi ❶**, in the extreme south of the country, but easily accessible from Nairobi. The drive on a good road, which climbs up to the southern shoulder of the Ngong Hills before dropping precipitously into the Rift, takes little over an hour.

The descent to the valley close to Magadi occurs in stages, down scarp after steep scarp through a harsh, stark landscape that is increasingly dry and hot as the altitude falls. At the end of the road, shimmering in temperatures above 38°C (100°F) in the shade, is Lake Magadi itself. At first glance, the term "lake" seems a misnomer since there is little water evident. The lake bed appears white; in fact, it's an enormous pan of trona – an agglomeration of mixed salts – over 100 sq. km (40 sq. miles) in extent.

Around the periphery is a series of hot springs, highly charged with salts and bubbling out of the

Nairobi

**PRECEDING PAGES:** Magadi's trona deposits glow red. **LEFT:** soda washed up on Magadi's shores. **BELOW:** a pelican on Lake Naivasha.

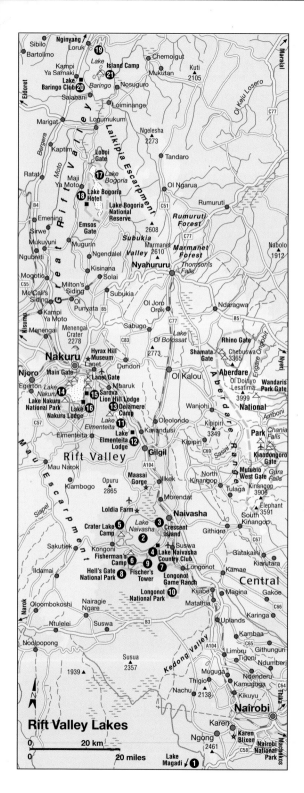

**Rift Valley Lakes**

ground at temperatures of about 45°C (113°F). They flow into the huge evaporation pan, where the sun and searing winds leave nothing but the thick white deposits of sludge. But in this is an almost endless source of potash, salt and related chemicals which have been exploited by the Magadi Soda Company since before World War I – Kenya's oldest mining venture, with a company township built up on a peninsula into the lake.

At the far southern end of Lake Magadi, where the largest springs occur, is an area of open water. Although undrinkable, it produces a wealth of microscopic aquatic life which, in turn, attracts many water birds and bird-watchers. Many African species are permanently on show, including flamingos, and the lake also hosts waders and many others escaping the winter in Europe.

## A freshwater exception

Going north from Magadi, the next lake along the Rift is **Naivasha 2**, which is easily accessible from Nairobi (80 km/50 miles) on the main Nairobi-Kisumu road. The old road, snaking down the eastern Rift Valley wall as it follows an ancient elephant trail, has recently been resurfaced and much improved. As you descend, there is a magnificent view of the lake and the extinct volcanoes, Suswa and Longonot, in the valley bottom. The lake lies on the valley floor at about 1,890 metres (6,200 ft) above sea-level.

Its area has fluctuated a great deal over the centuries, but currently covers about 170 sq. km (60 sq. miles). Fence posts stand forlornly way out from the shore as mementos of the days before 1961 when farmers and ranchers grazed their cattle far beyond the present shore.

An oddity characterises Lake Naivasha: although it has no visible outlet, it is one of the two freshwater lakes (Baringo is the other) in the Rift. Many theories have been forwarded to explain the phenomenon, but none is entirely satisfactory. The most obvious is that there must be massive underground seepage through the lake flow – a diffused outflow that takes the place of a conventional discharging river. Whatever the reason, Naivasha water is indeed fresh, potable, abundant and excellent for irrigating the surrounding fertile volcanic soils. Not surprisingly, it is also ringed by agricultural land, from which spring many tons of vegetables and flowers harvested for both Nairobi and overseas markets.

On the eastern end of **Crescent Island** ❸ sailing is possible at a private boating club. Sunday regattas are an incongruous sight on the bottom of the Rift Valley and the view of the valley walls from the lake is an altogether exhilarating experience.

Among the resident birds are fish eagles, ospreys, lily-trotters, black crakes and a variety of herons. Hippo also live in the lake. A number of mammals can be seen grazing in the surrounding lake environs, such as zebra, impala, buffalo, giraffe, kongoni and, at night, hippos.

Accommodation is available at **Lake Naivasha Country Club** ❹, where the resplendent traditional Kenya Sunday lunch is recommended, even if you are not staying there. The view over the lake, from the well-manicured lawn, in the shade of yellow-barked fever trees, will not be soon forgotten. For an experience in the bush, stay at the well appointed **Crater Lake Tented Camp** ❺, enclosed by the walls of the crater and its own game sanctuary. There are a series of campsites on the southern side of the lake, probably the best known being **Fisherman's Camp** ❻, where you can rent a *banda* or pitch your own tent. There are also a number of excellent homestays around the lake, including **Longonot Game Ranch** ❼, offering horseback riding over the plains.

Map on page 222

*In the 1940s, Lake Naivasha Country Club was Kenya's international air terminal: British Overseas Airways flying boats landed on the lake on their way from Cairo to Cape Town.*

**BELOW:** hippos abound in Lake Naivasha.

## Going to Hell

**Hell's Gate National Park** ❽, a dramatically beautiful slice through the volcanic ridge south of Lake Naivasha, was created in 1984. It lies some 13 km (8 miles) south-east of Naivasha and is about 68 sq. km (27 sq. miles) in area.

The park is an impressive gorge with towering cliffs. Close to the entrance is **Fischer's Tower** ❾, a lone 25-metre (82-ft) high rock. Powerful geysers, which gave the park its name, have been harnessed with foreign aid to generate electricity. The geothermal electricity project has been carefully executed so that it does not affect the beauty of the park.

*Hell's Gate is one of only a few national parks in Kenya where it is permitted to explore on foot; hence the area is a favourite with picnickers, hikers and rock-climbers.*

Among the birds to be seen are a colony of Ruppell's vultures and a pair of resident lammergeyers that breed on the cliffs. The lammergeyers have developed the habit of scavenging bones, flying them to considerable heights and dropping them onto rocks to crack them and reveal the bone marrow. There are several "dropping points" in Hell's Gate. There are also Verreaux's eagles, invariably seen soaring in pairs, and many other notable birds of prey. Mammals found in the park include Thomson's gazelle, zebra, hyrax, cheetah and leopard.

Camping is the only available accommodation in the park. It might be wise to enter into a private arrangement with a local Maasai warrior to guard your vehicle for the night.

To the southeast of Hell's Gate is the **Longonot National Park** ❿, to which access is from the bottom road to Naivasha. The young volcano rises to 2,776 meters (9,105 ft) above sea-level. Mount Longonot offers a wide range of attractions for those who are keen on activity holidays, including hiking, rock climbing, biking and bird-watching. There is no accommodation at Longonot, but Kenya Wildlife Service rangers are available as guides.

**BELOW:** white pelicans on a fishing expedition.

## Dry lakes, swirling dust

You have only to drive a further 80 km (50 miles) up the Trans-Africa Highway from Naivasha to view two more lakes also situated in the highland part of the Rift, at about the same altitude. Both are highly saline. Like Naivasha, they vary enormously in size and sometimes disappear altogether, during which time they are reduced to white salt flats, swirling with dust-devils.

The first, **Lake Elmenteita ⓫**, about 40 km (25 miles) from Naivasha, is one of the stop-off points for millions of flamingos en route to Magadi, Nakuru or Lake Natron in Tanzania. The new **Lake Elmenteita Lodge ⓬** overlooks the lake and offers horse riding and game walks. Situated within the vast estate of the current Lord Delamere is **Delamere Camp ⓭**, a small tented camp within the bounds of the Soysambu Wildlife Sanctuary offering game drives, walks and wonderful bird-watching. A homestay can be arranged at River House just outside nearby Gilgil.

Then, another 40 km (25 miles) to the north, comes **Lake Nakuru ⓮**. When this lake regularly dried up in the mid-1950s, strong daily winds swept up the dust into a dense white soda smog which blew 65 km (40 miles) away up the Rift Valley. But when heavy rains fell in 1961, the lake filled to its brim and the soda smogs were soon forgotten. However, 1997 saw Lake Nakuru dry up again, with the same strong winds and daily soda smog blowing around the agricultural town of **Nakuru** and the surrounding area.

The alkaline constitution of Lake Nakuru supports a vast flowering of the blue-green algae and diatoms on which flamingos live. The waters are so rich that the birds assemble there in their millions. The roseate mass they create along the shorelines is a spectacle of immense beauty. Over 400 varieties of

Map on page 222

*Although up to 2 million flamingos regularly feed in Lake Nakuru, they do not breed here. Their favourite nesting site is Lake Natron, just over the border in Tanzania.*

**BELOW:** greater flamingos on Lake Nakuru.

*Lake Nakuru National Park has one of Kenya's largest populations of black rhinos, brought to the sanctuary from all over Kenya.*

birds can be seen altogether, although not at the same time since many are migrant visitors from the northern hemisphere. Great numbers of pelicans can be seen at the southern and eastern shores.

**Lake Nakuru National Park** was created in 1961 as a bird sanctuary. Originally, it comprised only the lake and its immediate surroundings, including the escarpment at its western side known as **Baboon Cliffs**. It was expanded in 1974 with help from WWF, and now includes an extensive area of savannah to the south. Now the park – total area about 200 sq. km (80 sq. miles) – has been fenced in to make a rhino sanctuary. Other species of mammal include lion, leopard and hyena. It is the best place in Kenya to see Bohor reedbuck and Defassa waterbuck. A herd of Rothschild giraffes was introduced in 1977.

**Sarova Lion Hill Lodge** ⓰ is perched on high ground by the eastern boundary overlooking the lake. It is also adjacent to Kenya's finest euphorbia forest, filled with the grotesque, giant cactus-like trees. On cold evenings a fire is lit by the bar. **Lake Nakuru Lodge** ⓰ used to be part of Lord Delamere's estate and, apart from the main manor house, there are new *bandas* for visitors. Safari vehicles are available for hire and an airstrip is close by. There are also two well-maintained campsites with good water supplies, a self-help *banda* site and four picnic sites within the park.

## Bogoria and Baringo

To the north of Nakuru, the land falls away from the highlands. At this point, the Trans-Africa Highway veers to the west to break out of the Rift, whereas the way to the next valley lake is straight on. **Bogoria** ⓱ was formerly known as Lake Hannington in Kenya's colonial era, after the missionary bishop who was

Map on page 222

murdered in Uganda. It's a slender stretch of blue water under towering cliffs, like a splinter sticking into the northern foot of the highlands. Also saline charged, this body of water has an added attraction of shoreline hot geysers spouting up from the bowels of the earth.

**Lake Bogoria National Reserve** was gazetted to protect the herds of greater kudu which live mainly on the western slopes of the Laikipia Escarpment, which towers over the lake to the east. The reserve covers approximately 110 sq. km (44 sq. miles) and includes the shallow soda lake, which attracts huge flocks of flamingos.

Accommodation is available at the **Lake Bogoria Hotel** ⓲ which has the only spa in Kenya. There are three campsites at the southern end of the lake near Emos Gate. No facilities are available, so all necessary water has to be brought along, since the water in the lake is not drinkable. There is also a campsite (with water available) just outside the northern entrance to the reserve, as well as a picnic site at the hot springs.

No one who travels a few more kilometres north from here misses **Baringo** ⓳, the second freshwater lake in the Rift. It is twice the size of Naivasha, and poses the same question: why, with no outlet, does it stay fresh? Baringo is home to great numbers of birds and hippos, which can be seen in the evenings grazing at the shoreside.

First-class accommodation is available either at the **Lake Baringo Club** ⓴, which offers guided bird-watching walks, boat trips, water-skiing and camel rides, or at **Island Camp** ㉑, on Ol Kokwa Island, a luxury tented lodge with swimming pool and water sports. Camping facilities, as well as *bandas* are available at Robert's Camp on the lake shore. ❑

*You will rarely see pelicans at Lake Bogoria, for one simple reason – the water is so alkaline that the fish on which the birds depend cannot live there.*

**BELOW:** curious flamingo nests on Lake Bogoria.

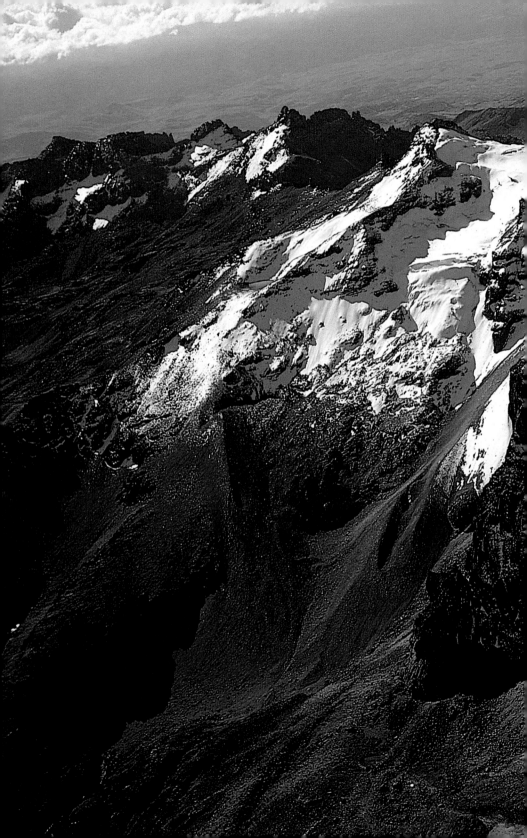

# THE MOUNTAIN NATIONAL PARKS

*Kenya's highest region climbs from savannah through rainforest and bamboo jungle to moorland heath and finally snow-capped peaks. It's a unique part of the country*

Map on page 233

The Mount Kenya and the Aberdare national parks are about 80 km (50 miles) apart and comprise the highest reaches of the country's central highlands. The Mount Kenya park covers an area of roughly 490 sq. km (190 sq. miles) above the 3,470-metre (11,375-ft) contour line, with two salients stretching down the western slopes. The Aberdare park is about the same size and comprises high plateau, moorlands and peaks, with a forested ridge on the eastern flank known as the Treetops Salient, after the world-famous lodge.

Both parks – the country's main watersheds – are surrounded by forest reserves and are home to a wide range of wildlife. They were set up principally as recreation areas for walking treks in the moorland-heath zones and for climbing Mount Kenya, whose highest point, the **Batian ❶** peak, is 5,199 metres (17,058 ft) above sea-level.

Just over 100 years ago, the mountain was barely known to the outside world. Early travellers' tales of snow on the Equator were generally disbelieved. In 1887, Count Samuel Teleki von Szek and his Austrian companion, Ludwig von Höhnel, climbed to within 900 metres (3,000 ft) of the summit of Mount Kenya. Twelve years later, an Englishman, Sir Halford Mackinder, finally made it to the top, but even this failed to rouse much international interest.

Thirty years elapsed before the distinguished mountaineer Eric Shipton made the second recorded ascent. Thereafter the climb became popular, and there are now many well-established main routes to the summit and scores of minor ascents for the skilful alpine mountaineer (*see page 232*).

The two salients excepted, **Mount Kenya National Park ❷** begins where the upper forest merges with the heath zones of mostly *Erica arborea,* a weirdly shaped bush often as large as a tree and covered with moss and lichen. At just over 3,300 metres (11,000 ft), this giant heather is replaced by open moorland covered in tussock grass and studded with many species of giant lobelia and groundsel growing to a height of about 4 metres (15 ft). The ground is a rich profusion of everlasting helichrysums and alchemillas, interspersed with gladioli, delphiniums and "red-hot pokers".

The many mountain ridges resemble the spokes of a wheel meeting at a central hub formed by the gigantic spikes of Batian and Nelion (the second highest peak at 5,188 metres/17,022 ft). These are surrounded by many other smaller peaks, snow fields and glaciers, tarns, lakes, waterfalls and imposing scree slopes. The peaks are the remnants of a central core of an ancient volcanic crater, the rim of which has long since eroded

**PRECEDING PAGES:** snow on Mt Kenya's Batian peak.
**LEFT:** Queen's Cave waterfall.
**BELOW:** giant groundsel in the Aberdares.

# Climbing Kenya

The prime attraction for rock climbers and mountaineers in Kenya is Mount Kenya, with its twin peaks of **Batian** and **Nelion**, both over 5,000 metres (16,400 ft). Below these, jutting upwards abruptly from fields of scree and ice, is a complex of ridges, walls and couloirs, which offers high-standard technical rock and ice routes of about 650–1,200 metres (700–1,300 yards) in length, at an altitude of more than 4,400 metres (14,500 ft).

Climbs here are graded – though definitive grading is impossible because of variable seasonal and meteorological conditions. About half of the climbs are alpine Grade V, and the remainder are equally Grades VI and IV. Under prime conditions, some routes may be easier while under bad conditions a route may be a grade or more harder.

Climbing is generally attempted only during the two dry seasons: late December to early March, and July to early October. It is still possible during the off-seasons, but the accumulations of ice and snow make approach conditions very difficult, and the climbs are usually at least one grade harder and take several hours longer.

Mount Kenya is on the Equator, which means seasonal variations in climbing routes. In January and February, when the sun is in the southern hemisphere, the south faces of the mountain receive direct sunlight, making them suitable for rock climbing, while the north faces remain iced-up and inaccessible. From July to September, the situation is reversed.

Steep rock and technical ice routes are usually climbed on two 9mm ropes for greater security and a smoother descent, while easier rock and snow may be negotiated on a single 11mm rope. Most rock routes can be climbed with a selection of nuts and slings, although a few blade and angle pitons are usually carried for safety on unfamiliar routes. Tabular screws, wart-hogs, front-point unhinged crampons and ice hammers or axes with a good drooping pick are necessary for ice routes.

A tent is not normally required, as all routes can be approached from established huts, but bivouac equipment should be carried on all climbs and is particularly essential for the longer, harder routes. Tourist lodges around the mountain provide everything you will need: guides, porters, cooks, pack animals, tentage, climbing and camping equipment, food and transport to roadheads.

Altitude problems remain the most serious limitation to good performance on the mountain. Conditioning is important, technical competence essential, and acclimatisation at high altitude for a few days before the ascent is required to prevent pulmonary oedema and other altitude illnesses.

Technical climbing on the main peaks is not for everyone. **Point Lenana**, the third peak at 4,985 metres (16,355 ft), offers spectacular ridge walks, and some of the outlying peaks are accessible to non-technical climbers. The mountain can be traversed over several days by keen walkers or climbers wishing to acclimatise gently before attempting a summit ascent. ❑

**LEFT:** looking towards the main peaks.

away. Below these jagged summits are intersecting glacier routes up 4,985 metres (16,355 ft) to **Point Lenana ❸**, which are suitable for visitors with little or no climbing experience.

The mountain has a wide variety of avifauna, ranging from the huge eagles to the delicate multicoloured sunbirds. Among the most distinctive species are crowned eagle, mountain buzzard, Mackinder's owl, Jackson's francolin, golden-winged and scarlet-tufted malachite sunbirds, and mountain chat.

The forests below the moorlands contain a rich abundance of game animals including elephant, rhino, buffalo, leopard, bushbuck, several species of duiker, giant forest hog, and colobus and Sykes monkeys. The remains of an elephant and several buffaloes have been found in the peak region above 4,300 metres (14,000 ft) but no one knows why they ventured into these high zones. Tracks of leopards and wild dogs have occasionally been recorded in the snow at around 4,600 metres (15,000 ft) above sea-level.

The attractive features of the mountain are 32 small lakes and colourful tarns. **Hall Tarn** is superbly situated, overlooking a valley and **Lake Michaelson**, well over 300 metres (1,000 ft) below. At the **Curling Pond**, beneath the **Lewis Glacier**, it's possible to skate and the game of curling has been played there.

Dense rainforests cover the lower salients and slopes of the mountain and the main tree species are the cedar, olive and podo (*podocarpus*). Above this lies a bamboo zone at approximately 2,400 metres (7,800 ft), which in turn gives way to a belt of glorious rosewood (*hagenia*) trees and giant St John's wort (*hypericum*) before dying out at the heath zone at 3,200 metres (10,400 ft).

Several vehicle tracks wind their way up the forested ridges. The quickest access to the peaks is via the Naro Moru track, which reaches just over 3,020

Map on page 233

*The rock hyrax is a rabbit-sized creature found on the cliffs and rock faces of the mountain national parks. Incredibly, the hyrax is the closest living relative to the elephant and the dugong (sea cow).*

**BELOW:** the national flag flies on Mount Kenya.

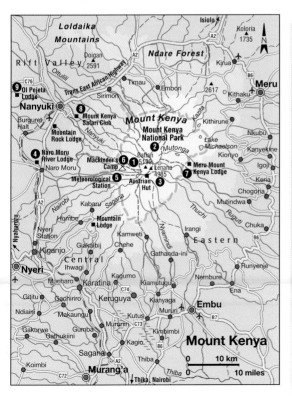

**TIP**

To enjoy the beauty of Mount Kenya without the arduous trials of climbing, contact Tropic Air at Nanyuki airfield (tel: 0176 32890) for a breath-taking one-hour flight around the peaks.

metres (9,900 ft) and stops immediately below the moorlands. All visitors must sign in at the park entrance gate. You are not permitted through the gates unaccompanied – except on a day trip, which must end at 4pm. For longer stays on the mountain, there must be at least two people, guides and porters included. These, together with all climbing equipment, can be hired at the **Naro Moru River Lodge ❹**, a delightful spot in beautiful gardens through which the Naro Moru flows (regularly restocked with trout for fishermen). There is also accommodation at the **Met Station Lodge ❺** (at 3,000 metres/10,000 ft) and at Mackinder's Camp, also known as **Teleki Lodge ❻** (4,330 metres /14,200 ft), which is warm and staffed by qualified guides.

Another approach to the mountain is from **Chogoria** on the eastern side – perhaps the toughest and most demanding route, as it goes through thick forest. You can stay at the **Meru Mount Kenya Lodge ❼**, which is just inside the park and offers self-service *bandas*.

## Views of Mount Kenya

You don't need to camp at altitude to enjoy the spectacle of the mountain's snow-capped peaks gleaming in the sun. Near **Nanyuki** to the west is the famous **Mount Kenya Safari Club ❽**, established by a Texan oil baron, a Swiss millionaire and film star William Holden. There are superb views of the mountain from its beautifully manicured gardens, which have flowerbeds, bowling greens and ornamental ponds. There's also a nine-hole golf course and the only heated swimming pool on the Equator. Surrounding the club is the Mount Kenya Game Ranch, a wildlife sanctuary which incorporates the William Holden Wildlife Education Centre. Another exceptional place to stay within sight of Mount Kenya is

**BELOW:** the Gura waterfall in the Aberdares is Kenya's tallest.

**Ol Pejeta Lodge 9**, on the Laikipia Plateau on the way to Nanyuki. The ranch, formerly owned by millionaire Adnan Kashoggi, is now owned by Lonrho Hotels, who run both the lodge and the neighbouring Sweetwaters Camp.

Maps on pages 233 & 235

## Aberdare National Park

The mountain range in Aberdare National Park has in fact been renamed the Nyandarua but the old name – Aberdares – persists. The mountains rise in the north to the highest moorland peak of **Ol Doinyo Lesatima 10** at 3,999 metres (13,120 ft), and some 40 km (25 miles) to the south stands the well-known summit of **Kinangop 11** at 3,906 metres (12,816 ft). Between these two peaks is a plateau of moorland – gently undulating country covered in tussock grass and large areas of mixed giant heath. Ice-cold streams, well stocked with trout, thread their way across the moorlands and cascade over a series of waterfalls to form the headwaters of several of the major rivers.

The Aberdares are well-endowed with a great variety and quantity of wild animals despite the occurrence of periodic cold and mist. The western slopes of the range are principally part of the Rift wall, and are therefore relatively steep and generally not as attractive to game as are the more gentle slopes of the eastern side. Elephant, buffalo, rhino, eland, waterbuck, bushbuck, reedbuck, several species of duikers, suni, bushpig, warthog, serval cat, lion, Sykes' monkey and hyena occur in varying numbers and most of them are easily seen. Rhinos are sparse here, as everywhere else in the country, but they can be seen on the moors and particularly on the **Treetops Salient**.

Herds of elephant and buffalo migrate with the rain, occupying the bamboo and rainforest zones during the dry seasons. When the rain begins, the game

**TIP**

During the rainy seasons, the roads through the Aberdare Park are barely passable. Take advice from rangers at the the park gates, or at any hotel or lodge.

**BELOW:** a leopard drinks from a mountain stream.

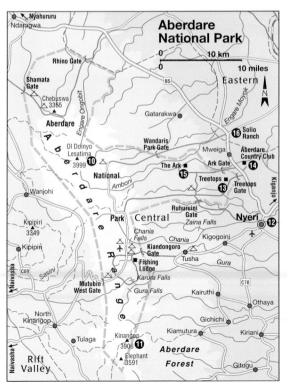

Map
on page
235

*The Ark is built
entirely of wood in a
vague imitation of
Noah's vessel.*

**BELOW:** elephants
at the water-hole
by The Ark.

migrates to the plateau moorlands and the lower areas of the Treetops Salient, where the forest is not so dense and the ridges are less steep.

The Park is criss-crossed with tracks, many of which were made by British troops during the Mau Mau rebellion in the 1950s. The most important of these is the road from **Nyeri** ⓬, which climbs the eastern slopes and across the moorlands, reaching a height of 3,170 metres (10,400 ft), and finally descends the western slopes and crosses the Kinangop farmlands to Naivasha.

The Outspan Hotel in Nyeri offers distant views of Mount Kenya, has tasteful guest rooms with fireplaces and serves meals in a baronial style dining room. Lord Baden Powell, the founder of the scouting movement, spent the last three years of his life in a cottage here. This is now a small museum.

Visitors to **Treetops** ⓭ meet at the Outspan and are transported by the hotel through the coffee plantations, to the famous lodge overlooking a waterhole and saltlick. This is where, in February 1952, Princess Elizabeth learned of her accession to the throne of Britain.

On the road northwest from Nyeri is the **Aberdare Country Club** ⓮. Set on the side of a hill, it affords great views of Mount Kenya and the Laikipia plains. The club grounds are attractive with a golf course and horse riding among other outdoor activities. Visitors to **The Ark** ⓯, another forest lodge, assemble and board transport here. The trip is 18 km (11 miles) from the club into the Aberdare National Park through the Ark Gate. The Ark is situated over a natural water-hole, illuminated at night so that nocturnal visitors can be viewed.

Back on the main road, heading north, is **Solio Ranch** ⓰, a private sanctuary that has been successful in breeding both white and black rhino. Patrick's Camp in Solio is modelled on a turn-of-the-century hunting camp. ❑

# Picture This

**E**ast Africa attracts photographers the way a zebra carcass attracts vultures. Nowhere else in the world is it possible to find such diversity and concentrations of photogenic creatures, not to mention such a variety of dramatic scenery.

Early cameras were too big to carry in the field. A turn-of-the-century picture shows an earnest photographer pursuing a rhino with a camera the size of a microwave oven. It weighed 7 kg (16 lb). Exposure took minutes – too long to capture an unrestrained creature on film.

Since then, cameras and wildlife photography have changed dramatically. Faster film, telephoto lenses and motordrives give photographers additional flexibility.

Safari-goers will find that the most suitable cameras is a 35mm SLR (single lens reflex) model with interchangeable lenses.

Lenses are a wildlife photographer's most important accessories. A 600mm telephoto lens is the practical upper size limit for work in the field. But zoom lenses in the 80mm to 200mm range are more versatile and offer better value for money. An economical way of extending your focal length is with a "doubler" or 2x converter.

Telephoto lenses are prone to camera shake since they magnify image movement. Shoulder supports help to reduce camera shake; so do sand or bean bags. These look like small pillows filled with dried beans or sand. Lay the bag down on the roof of your open safari vehicle and mould the lens on to it. Tripods provide the best stability but are very cumbersome when used in vehicles. A monopod is a practical compromise.

Recent years have seen the introduction of very fast colour film, which is capable of producing perfectly acceptable results. Even so, to capture an animal on the move you should shoot at fast shutter speeds. (Camera film in Kenya, when available, is very expensive, so you should always bring more film than you expect to shoot.)

The best times to take pictures in the Kenyan bush are before 9am and after 4pm, when the sun is low and not too fierce. In the middle of the day, unless it is overcast, the light is simply too bright, "bleaching out" colours, and shadows are impenetrably black. A polarising filter can help to diffuse the worst of the sun's rays; a "warm" amber filter such as an 81A is useful, too, to correct the "bleaching out" of colour. At the very least, you should always have an ultraviolet filter fitted. Not only does it correct the blue blur you sometimes see on the distant horizon, but it also protects your lens.

Most safari pictures are taken from the roof-hatch of a vehicle, but shooting everything from above can create stereotyped images. Shooting from a lower angle out of a side window frequently results in more striking and dramatic pictures.

During dry times of the year, dust can be a serious hazard to your photographic equipment. It is particularly important to protect the camera from wind-blown dust when you are loading and unloading film. Keep all your cameras, lenses and film in sealed polythene bags when not in use. ❏

**RIGHT:** remote control for a low-angle close-up.

# NORTH TO LAKE TURKANA

*The journey to Kenya's northernmost regions by road is a gruelling trek across rugged but fascinating terrain. And the journey's end, the "Jade Sea", is a place of spellbinding beauty*

Map on page 242

Nairobi

The term "Northern Kenya" in the safari lexicon covers thousands of square kilometres of dusty plains, relieved by daunting volcanic formations and whimsical dry rivers known as *luggas* – lazy avenues of sand for most of the time, but filled by sudden torrents of rushing water in a flash flood. The general area – once called the "Northern Frontier District" (NFD) – extends west from Lake Baringo and the fabled Lake Turkana to Sudan. On the eastern side, it spreads from the Lorogi Plateau up to Ethiopia and east to Somalia. Like much of Kenya, the approaches are delineated by the few main roads which lead to district centres, such as Lodwar, Maralal, Marsabit and Isiolo.

To a great extent the tribesmen who live in the area (all of them nomadic pastoralists), have been lost in the folds of time. They are hardy people born of a warrior tradition, including the Samburu, Turkana, Rendille and Boran. Cattle raiding among tribes is as much a sport as soccer elsewhere in Kenya. To this day, disputes are settled by gun and spear without formal law and order.

During colonial days, the British recognised this spirited independence of action and closed the area to all but civil service officials and professional hunting parties in pursuit of elephant or other game. Today, travel is unrestricted, but not necessarily easy. There are bone-shaking kilometres of corrugated track, which make a safari an endurance test. But it is well worth it for the stunning scenery, colourful people and herds of wild animals. So long as you stick to the more conventional routes, you will be able to find accommodation at lodges. But if you intend to camp, you are faced with the dilemma of what food and equipment to pack into a limited space, bearing in mind the need to carry plenty of fuel and water. Local advice on tactical problems of the northern safari is essential.

## The traveller's challenge

The roads – beyond the realm of comparison with standard thoroughfares – pose a challenge to both man and machine. In the dry season, it's a bit like driving on an old-fashioned washboard and, after rain, on a river of mud. Always take a high-rise "Tanganyika" jack with you, plus a shovel, and two planks for getting out of a bog or soft sand drifts.

Disregard distances on maps when it comes to planning schedules and seek local advice instead. Depending on weather and road conditions, it may take a whole day to drive 80 km (50 miles). In fact, schedules should be discarded entirely, so far as this can be reconciled with pre-arranged bookings at lodges. Part of the allure of the north is to succumb to its gentle pace.

One of the best ways to experience the trip to Turkana and the north, if you don't mind roughing it

**PRECEDING PAGES:** El-Molo fishermen in Lake Turkana. **LEFT:** a large croc beside the lake. **BELOW:** Rendille women in Kaisut Desert.

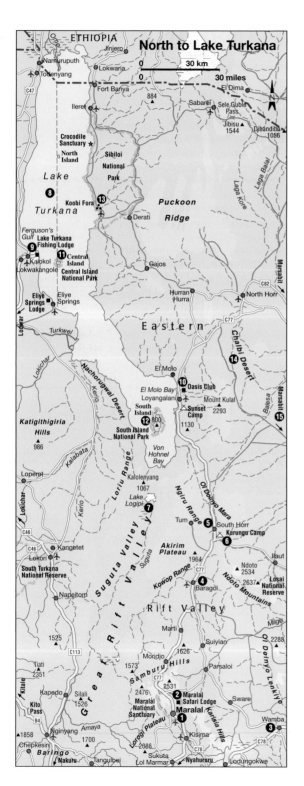

North to Lake Turkana

a bit, is to take the "Turkana Bus", a very well organised safari which can be booked through most travel agents, and also from Safari Camp Services – Tel: Nairobi (02) 330130.

## The glittering town

Perched on the edge of forested hills, is **Maralal ❶**, the administrative centre for Samburu District. The town's name – Samburu for "glittering" – was inspired by the first building, erected in 1934: a shack with a corrugated iron roof that gleamed in the sun. Since then the place has grown, but it still has all the aspects of a frontier town. Pepper trees line (but do not shade) the dusty main street. So do a colourful cross-section of people: indolent warriors leaning on the walls of flaky *dukas* (stores) are a preview of what is ahead on the route. Maralal's most precious amenity is a fuel station, almost the last between there and the Ethiopian border farther north.

Just out of town, left at the main roundabout and a mile or so down the road, is the **Maralal Safari Lodge ❷**, the only comfortable accommodation in the area. Overlooking a water-hole where zebra, impala and buffalo gather, the spacious rooms have high-pitched cedar ceilings and fireplaces (evenings are always chilly). The lodge arranges trips to a hide on a nearby hill, from where you can silently watch a leopard approach goat bait hung in a tree. (Take advantage of this: these shy cats are difficult to view close at hand.)

Also ask at the lodge for a guide to take you to a look-out point farther north along the road where the **Lorogi Plateau** drops steeply to the rugged country below. The best time is during the hazy hours of early morning, when layer upon layer of volcanic ranges can be seen stretching northwards to the southern shore of Lake Turkana. It is an incredible sight, and not for nothing is it also known as World's End.

East of Maralal lies the small outpost of **Wamba ❸**, with its mission hospital and a few *dukas* to serve the nomadic tribesmen. Just to the north of Wamba is **Sarara Camp**, located in the Namunyak Wildlife Conservation Trust, which is promoted and supported by Lewa Wildlife Conservancy (*see page 207*). You can either self-cater or pay for a fully-catered stay in this camp, which lies in a little-known and beautiful region.

## Tribesmen's lifestyle

From Maralal, the Samburu tribe spreads over an area of about 28,500 sq. km (11,000 sq. miles). This includes the higher Lorogi Plateau, rimmed with cedar forests, as well as the arid scrubland to the north where thorn trees mark the course of river beds and people dig in the sand for water. The tribe, considered to be related to the better-known Maasai, is a splinter group which broke away from the other East Nilotic tribes and migrated south down the Nile in the 16th century. They refer to themselves not as Samburu but *il-Oikop* (*see page 211*).

This dusty landscape, speckled with cattle, ostrich and zebra, may seem monotonous. But it has its tales to tell. The road passes through the town of **Baragoi ❹** and winds on, flanked by Koitokol Mountain on the right and the saw-toothed Kowop Range on the left. Here, the Turkana trespassed and clashed with the Samburu as recently as 1980. Only one man was wounded in the skirmish, a warrior who was speared in the back. But it seems that a friend gripped the spear shaft and pulled it out from the front. The wound was packed with herbs and the injured man survived. Deeds such as this accord these young men their heroic reputations.

From there, it's on to **South Horr ❺**, sandwiched between Ol Doinyo Mara mountains to the right and the Ngiru Range on the left. This lush valley grows

Map on page 242

*In Maralal a simple bungalow has been turned into a national monument. This is where Mzee Jomo Kenyatta was detained by the British in 1961.*

**LEFT:** a heavily decorated Borana woman.
**BELOW:** drying fish at Ferguson's Gulf.

bananas and paw-paws (papaya), which are brought in to the towns. The Catholic mission also sells lemons to thirsty travellers. Towering above the village, on Ngiru's flank, is **Kosikosi**, a brown, fissured outcrop of rock gleaming in the sun.

On the southeast side of South Horr is **Kurungu Camp ❻**, a welcome stopover with double cabins and cold beer. Kurungu puts on spectacular dances where warriors and young girls move in a snorting, yelling throng, as spears twirl in the air. Men and women each have their special songs that must be sung separately. Once, when a priest asked his congregation to raise their voices in unison in a hymn of thanks for the onset of the rains, the request also gave rise to much anxiety. The churchgoers feared this social violation would induce yet another drought.

Before reaching South Horr, there is a road to the left that leads to **Tum**, a seldom visited village nestling against Ngiru's western slopes. This is the home of Lesepen, the aged astrologer and oracle of the Samburu, who foretells the future by gazing at Mars and Venus – the morning and evening star.

Tum is also the gateway to the **Suguta Valley**, an alien moonscape originally moulded by erupting volcanoes on the approach to the southern end of Lake Turkana. A track from the village leads down to the tiny settlement of **Parkati**, "the place of no water", on the valley's edge. Halfway down the track is a roadside cross, fashioned from orange pipes. Its inscription in Turkana says: "Rest in peace. We will see you again." This simple monument commemorates a Catholic priest who was murdered nearby in 1981 by Turkana bandits known as Ng'oroko.

They have since been subdued by the army and no longer present a menace to travellers. Even so, the Suguta's jagged scarps of black lava (the height of

*In legend, Kosikosi is the home of the Samburu god Enkai (or Ngei). A bull is sacrificed on this natural altar at the start of circumcision ceremonies.*

**BELOW:** the Suguta Valley, stretching west from the Ngiru Range.

Map on page 242

office blocks) impede a vehicle's progress and inspire visions of ambush. The Turkana live here, tending their goats and camels, alongside silver-backed jackals and Grant's gazelle.

On the floor of the valley is **Lake Logipi** ❼, framed by an amphitheatre of rust-red hills. Logipi Hill, ringed by silver, rises from its centre like a shining Excalibur. This shallow soda pan is visited seasonally by thousands of flamingos, which form a shimmering cerise carpet as they sift the waters with upside-down beaks.

## Lake Turkana, the "Jade Sea"

Logipi's northern neighbour, **Lake Turkana** ❽, is the final destination for every safari in this area – after a journey of at least two days from Nairobi. The lake, which is about 300 km (185 miles) long and 50 km (30 miles) wide, has its northern tip in Ethiopia. It is a place of spellbinding beauty. The algae that abound in the lake change their colour from charcoal grey to Delft blue as clouds scud overhead. But most often its surface dances deep green in the sunlight, giving it the nickname "Jade Sea".

With temperatures touching 63°C (145°F), Lake Turkana's cool depths look tempting. But note that the bitter alkaline waters can never quench your thirst, and swimming is a pastime to be treated with a certain amount of caution. There are plenty of crocodiles here, and they can be seen basking along the shore, seldom venturing far from the beaches. For the most part they are fish-eaters, hence the belief that the saurians in Turkana *never* eat humans. However, when a scientist, Alistair Graham, conducted a study of crocodile behaviour at the lake in 1965–67, and in the process lost his colleague to one of the reptiles, it

*The 3,000-strong El-Molo who live on the shores of Lake Turkana are the smallest of Kenya's ethnic groups. They once numbered fewer than 500 people.*

**BELOW:** Central Island, in vast Lake Turkana, is a national park.

# The Turkana

The Turkana (280,000 in number) inhabit the whole northwest of Kenya between Lake Turkana to the east and the escarpment marking the Uganda boundary on the west. They originated from the area further west. Turkana belong either to the forest people (Nimonia) or the people of the plains (Nocuro), into which all territorial districts are irrationally divided. There are 20 or so clans but the effective Turkana community is a neighbourhood.

Milk and blood are their main diet, and cattle provide hides to make sleeping mats and sandals, and to cover the huts against rain. Their horns are used for snuff containers. Camels are also important in the Turkana economy, while goats and sheep are killed for guests, minor rituals or meat. Donkeys are used solely as pack animals, with hides cut into strips for panniers.

Dried milk is made by boiling large quantities of fresh milk and drying it on skins. Wild berries are crushed and made into cakes with blood or ground into a dried meal. Women cultivate their homelands near watercourses in the rainy season where they grow millet and gourds. Fishing in Lake Turkana is especially practised in the dry season or famines.

A Turkana homestead (*awi*) comprises a man and his wife and their children. Sons remain within the family group, while daughters leave their homestead as soon as they get married. A family *awi* usually consists of the principal enclosure for the head of the family and a secondary enclosure where additional wives and their children and married sons live.

For the Turkana, marriage is a three-year ceremonial process designed to ensure the ritual, spiritual and social well-being of those involved. Not until the first child has been weaned and has reached walking age can the marriage process be completed. Considerable numbers of stock (cattle or camels) are required to meet the bride price, and these the suitor obtains from his own herds and those of his father, his uncles and bond-friends. The important position of the wife in the *awi* is reflected in the close ties that will be perpetuated between her husband on one hand and her father and brothers on the other.

The Turkana have evolved a material culture peculiar to themselves. They carve water troughs and containers from wood and decorate them with poker work; fat, butter and milk containers are made from hides (particularly camel) decorated with beadwork and cowries. Traditional weapons are a 2.5-metre (8-ft) leaf-shaped spear, knobkerrie fighting stick, wrist knife, finger hook and, for defence, a shield of buffalo, giraffe or hippo hide. The women wear enormous quantities of beads around the neck and a neck-ring of brass or aluminium.

Improved communications are slowly eroding the Turkana's traditional insularity in their desert homeland. Settlement schemes based on irrigated plots along the Turkwel and Kerio rivers, and fishing cooperatives along the western shore of Lake Turkana, are being encouraged by the government. ❑

**LEFT:** a Turkana women wearing an abundance of elaborate necklaces.

Map on page 242

was accepted that the crocodiles of Lake Turkana *do* eat large mammals, albeit rarely. Indeed, such is the infrequency of attacks on humans that Turkana can be considered relatively safe to swim in.

Sportsmen appreciate the lake for its fishing possibilities and almost invariably have this in mind when they head for either the **Lake Turkana Fishing Lodge ⑨**, at Ferguson's Gulf on the western side, or the **Oasis Club ⑩** at Loyangalani on the eastern shore. For campers, the **Sunset Camp**, southeast of the village, has drinking water and showers. For keen anglers who don't want to endure a two-day overland trip for a spot of fishing, there is a kilometre-long airstrip nearby.

Anglers in search of sport try for the great Nile perch (*Lates niloticus*), a melancholy but enormous fish that can tip the scales at 100 kg (220 lb). As an angling challenge, however, it is a disappointment, providing about as much fight as an outsized goldfish. Less spectacular but more exciting are the tiger-fish that can be reeled in from the shore.

**Central Island ⑪**, in the middle of Lake Turkana, can be reached by boat from Ferguson's Gulf. The island's main crater lake is a nesting point for an extremely large number of crocodiles and many water birds. Once you're on the island, the rest of the trip has to be undertaken on foot, which can be very strenuous in the heat of the day. Until recently, the island was populated more by immigrant Luo fishermen from Lake Victoria than by crocodiles.

**South Island ⑫** is the bird-watcher's and Nile perch fisherman's paradise of Lake Turkana. Care must be exercised if you are camping rough since the large population of crocodiles can be dangerous. The airstrip on the island is a twisted, rock-strewn horror – a challenge for every bush pilot in Kenya.

**TIP**

Since Lake Turkana Fishing Lodge caters mainly for weekend visitors who fly from Nairobi, short-notice accommodation is usually available midweek.

**BELOW:** the remains of a petrified forest on Sibiloi Mountain.

Map
on page
242

*There in the sand beside a thorny bush lay a domed greyish-white object. For years I had dreamed of such a prize and now I had found it – a nearly complete skull of an early hominid.*

– RICHARD LEAKEY

**BELOW:** Chalbi Desert.
**RIGHT:** a giant Nile perch, Lake Turkana.

## The first human?

It is ironic that Lake Turkana, where today men and animals struggle for survival, may actually have been the birthplace of mankind itself. Kenyan paleontologist Richard Leakey and a team of international scientists have spent many years carefully brushing away sand and dust from a treasure trove of hominid bones and stone tools. These finds prove that man-like creatures with a relatively high level of intelligence inhabited the lake shores as far back as 2 million years ago.

**Koobi Fora** ⓭, the name given to the heart of this palaeontological site that fans out over 2,500 sq. km (1,000 sq. miles), burst into the public arena in 1972. This was when Bernard Ng'eneo, a member of the Leakey team who was passing through a gully he had often walked before, caught a glimpse of a tiny fragment of skull. Eventually more than 300 segments were sifted from the sand.

When reconstructed, the skull – simply known by its archaeologists' index number of "1470" – was recognised as the earliest firm evidence of human's evolution from apes, replanting our ancestral roots by half a million years. Visitors can reach the site by a chartered plane or on a track from Loyangalani, although this is rough even by northern standards. There are self-help cabins at Koobi Fora, which can be booked through the National Museums of Kenya in Nairobi.

Koobi Fora is a part of **Sibiloi National Park**, a little used wildlife sanctuary where visitors can watch lion, cheetah, oryx, zebra and topi in almost guaranteed solitude. Just before the park's entrance, on the right, is **Sibiloi Mountain**, where giant petrified trees 125 cm (4 ft) in girth are strewn like building blocks of the gods. Seven million years ago, these junipers stood at 15 metres (50 ft) and could have flourished because of high rainfall.

## Mirages in the Chalbi

To vary the return journey to Nairobi, turn right at North Horr and then take the track to the left, to drive southeast across the **Chalbi Desert** ⓮. Here, in this stretch of true desert, mirages play tricks on the traveller. Dark triangular blobs drifting effortlessly through ribbons of water evaporate as you approach. In their place are a string of several hundred dusky camels in the care of Gabbra tribesmen who will raise their rifles in friendly salute.

On the far side of the Chalbi is **Marsabit** ⓯, perhaps the most fascinating of the myriad volcanic mountains in the north. Long extinct, it is capped with mist forests where elephant and greater kudu live. Just 4 km (2½ miles) from the town, in **Marsabit National Park**, is Marsabit Lodge overlooking a crater lake. Farther up the mountain is an enchanting water-filled crater, known appropriately as **Lake Paradise**. This tranquil setting, which provides a breathtaking view over several hundred miles, is a place that travel writers of less generous spirit are tempted to keep to themselves.

The road south from Marsabit to **Isiolo**, at the foot of the Mount Kenya massif, is best driven in convoy. This may not allow the traveller to linger by the Mathews Range on the right. But, at this stage, it won't matter too much. The rest of the northern safari will have been more than enough. ❏

# WESTERN KENYA: A SCENIC CIRCUIT

*A circular tour of the west takes in tea and coffee plantations, farmlands with a very British character, Kenya's second highest mountain and the largest lake in Africa*

Map on page 254

he Trans-Africa Highway climbs the western wall of the Rift Valley by a less spectacular route than its descent on the eastern side. It is a steep climb nonetheless since **Nakuru ❶**, lying on the valley floor, is around 1,800 metres (6,000 ft) above sea-level, while the highest point the road reaches above the western wall is well over 2,700 metres (9,000 ft).

At that point, 8 km (5 miles) off the main trunk route, is the small farming town of **Molo ❷**. The town is set in high-altitude open downs which are more reminiscent of Scotland than Africa – more so with the chill and mists of the morning. It's not surprising that the Molo area attracted the early white settlers, who saw it as prime sheep country. It wasn't quite like that, however, since the pests and blights were distinctly African. But the settlers won out in the end and the result is the superb "Molo" lamb as a staple on many dinner tables in Kenya. Now the white settlers have all gone, with their large farms subdivided and given out to the local African community.

It is here on the lower slopes of Londiani that you can sample some of the pioneer history by staying at **Deloraine**, the former home of Lord Francis Scott, built in 1920 and one of the grandest examples of colonial architecture in the country. It features a magnificent garden, a croquet lawn and tennis court. There are plenty of horses to ride around the farm.

Close by Molo, near **Mau Summit ❸**, the trunk route splits. The Trans-Africa Highway heads northwest across the highland plateau west of the Rift to Eldoret, eventually reaching the Uganda border at Malaba. The other heads southwest as the main route to Lake Victoria.

**PRECEDING PAGES:** a *kopje* in Mount Elgon National Park. **LEFT:** Luo fishermen on Lake Victoria. **BELOW:** an ostrich on the western plains at sunset.

## Eldoret and Elgon

Not far from the fork, the highway crosses the equator and the wide level plain of the Uasin Gishu Plateau to the town of **Eldoret ❹** – or "64" as it's sometimes called, since it was set up by milepost 64 of the ox-wagon route from Londiani once used by the local "voertrekker" South Africans.

When they arrived before World War I, the plateau was teeming with wildlife, rather like the Athi Plains around Nairobi or the Mara-Serengeti. The game soon disappeared, however, since the settlers turned the Uasin Gishu into Kenya's main granary. Maize and wheat fields stretched from horizon to horizon, and still do in parts.

Eldoret is now a major farming town, with an airport of international standards. Accommodation is available at the Eldoret Club or at the Hotel Sirikwa.

*Until recently the Molo Hunt – hounds, horns, hunting pinks, the works – used to roam the farmlands west of Nakuru.*

To the northeast of Eldoret is the breathtaking **Kerio Valley/Kamnarok National Reserve ❺**, reached via Iten and Tambach.

Beyond Eldoret, filling much of the western horizon, is the massive extinct volcano of **Mount Elgon ❻**. It is around 880 metres (3,000 ft) short of Mount Kenya, but the circumference of its base makes it a bigger massif. At its foot stands **Kitale ❼**, the northernmost of the agricultural towns built by the settlers in the colonial era. With Elgon's slopes to the west and the high Cherangani Hills to the east, the agriculture about Kitale is as diverse as it can get in Kenya. Beef and dairy farms, coffee estates, wheat and maize fields surround the town, and on the higher slopes are orchards of temperate European fruits, like apples.

In its upper, forested reaches, Mount Elgon is also a national park, but one of the least developed. Dense, tall forest and a lack of roads inhibit game viewing, but it is possible to hike up to the summit, across moorlands of giant heather. **Mount Elgon Lodge**, a converted farmhouse with wonderful views, midway between Kitale and the peak, makes a good base.

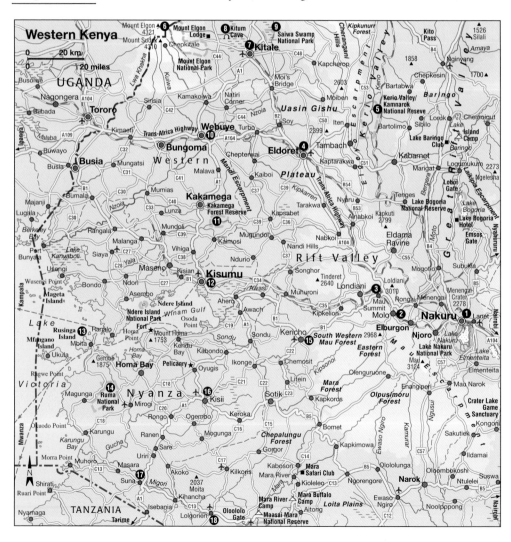

While the volcanic soils of Kenya's mountain ranges are fertile, they don't seem to yield the minerals the elephant crave – except at rare salt-licks, one of them in the distinctive **Kitum Cave** ❽, which has attracted the big mammals for centuries. Quite literally, the elephant mine the cave, gouging out the walls and extending the shafts hundreds of feet into the mountain.

**Saiwa Swamp National Park** ❾, to the east of Kitale, is Kenya's smallest, at only 3 sq. km (740 acres). It opened in 1974 to protect the semi-aquatic sitatunga antelope, notable for its wide-splayed hooves which allow it to walk on the soggy surface of the swamp. Saiwa is also home to the endangered De Brazza's monkey and a variety of otter, giant forest squirrel, black-and-white colobus monkeys, bushbuck and grey duiker. There are three nature trails, bridges for walking, three sitatunga viewing platforms and two campsites within the park.

From Elgon, the country to the south falls away fairly gently towards Lake Victoria and the Nile Valley. The highway passes **Webuye** ❿, where Kenya's fledgling paper industry is located in an area of dense settlement, principally of the Luhya peoples. Their headquarters are in the township of **Kakamega**, which is 42 km (26 miles) to the south of the highway.

Not far from the town is the **Kakamega Forest Reserve** ⓫, a centre of significant conservationist interest since it is a relic of the Equatorial rainforest which once spread from West Africa to the East African coast. Zaire is not easy to get to for tourists, so the Kakamega "jungle" is increasingly popular for specialists looking for Central African species of animals, birds and plants – although the future of this rare habitat is insecure because of the massive population increase in the area. Accommodation is available in the reserve in the

Map on page 254

**TIP**

It is possible to climb Mount Elgon at any time of year, though December–March are the best months. For more information, contact the Mountain Club of Kenya, tel: Nairobi (02) 501747.

**BELOW:** comfortable Mount Elgon Lodge.

*Arab slave traders brought the dhow to Lake Victoria, and the style was copied by Luo shipwrights.*

form of a guesthouse, self-help *bandas*, two campsites and the Rondo Retreat, as well as at the Golf Hotel in Kakamega town.

About 48 km (30 miles) south of Kakamega is the town of **Kisumu** ⑫, on the shores of Lake Victoria. Ranked third in size after Nairobi and Mombasa, Kisumu was the original terminus for the Uganda Railway, when it was known as Port Florence (after the wife of a railway engineer). The town has since developed not only as the major administrative centre for most of western Kenya, but also as a port with shipbuilding and repair facilities. Its atmosphere is distinctly nautical, which is not surprising given the vast size of Lake Victoria – its area of 63,000 sq. km (26,500 sq. miles) makes it the largest lake in Africa and the world's second largest freshwater lake.

Kisumu's fortunes were reversed in 1977 after the disruption of the East African Community, a political and economic arrangement whereby Kenya, Uganda and Tanzania shared steamer and general communications services. The town is now recovering through diversification into light industry and is once more a regional centre of economic activity for 2 million Luo people of the lake and **Winam Gulf** region. Many of them are still fishermen – indeed, the Luo are found around many fish-bearing lakes and rivers in Kenya, in Uganda and down to south Tanzania. There's accommodation at the **Imperial Hotel** and the **Sunset Hotel**, in town, and at the **Nyanza Club** on the shore of the lake.

## Arab sails on Lake Victoria

**BELOW:** a large tea plantation near Kericho.

The fishing fleets of Lake Victoria, with their white lateen sails against a deep blue background, appear to be out of the romantic myths of the Sindbad coast. There is, in fact, a connection, dating back to the time when the Arab slavers were

marauding around Victoria, building boats for the lake in the same style as their dhows on the ocean. The Luo shipwrights promptly adopted the lateen sail.

If you want the (somewhat limited) challenge of tackling a giant Nile perch, the place to stay is the **Rusinga Island Camp** ⓭, which has comfortable accommodation for fishermen in idyllic surroundings. When the huge fish were first introduced into the lake in the 1950s, the experiment was unsuccessful. A decade later, scientists of the East African Freshwater Fisheries Organization at Jinja gave the matter more thought and repeated the introduction. This time it worked and there was an explosion of Nile perch throughout the lake, and particularly in the Winam Gulf. As usual, man's intervention in the natural environment had unforeseen results. The two indigenous species of tilapia have since disappeared, much to the Luo's dismay, since they don't much like the taste of the now dominant perch.

Kenya's main sugar-growing area lies close to Kisumu, in the **Nyando Valley** at the head of the Winam Gulf. Production is from both large estates as well as from smallholders in a policy unusual in Africa for its tolerant flexibility.

On the north side of the gulf, about 30 km (19 miles) from Kisumu, is one of Kenya's smaller national parks, the 4 sq. km (1½ sq. miles) **Ndere Island**, which has been a sanctuary since 1986.

On the far side of the gulf from Kisumu, in the lee of **Homa Bay** town, lies the **Ruma National Park** ⓮. This is mostly uninhabited because of tsetse fly and the sleeping sickness it carries, which is no worry to in-and-out tourists. At some stage, this refuge for Kenya's remaining roan antelope will be integrated into the country's wildlife circuits. For the moment, however, it's something of a backwater for the specialist.

Map on page 254

*Ruma National Park was created as a sanctuary for the roan antelope, which is found nowhere else in Kenya.*

**BELOW:** tea-pickers are traditionally paid by the basket.

Map on page 254

*Soapstone carvings made by the Gusii people around Tabaka, south of Kisii, are sold in curio shops all over the country.*

**BELOW:** irrigation schemes have brought prosperity to the west.

## Tea plantations at Kericho

Back to the fork at Mau Summit, the southern highway runs some 50 km (30 miles) through forest reserve and plantations before reaching the "tea capital" of **Kericho** ⓯. High ground, temperate climate and high rainfall off Lake Victoria make the district ideal for the production of tea.

When the Europeans first arrived, much of the area was under tall montane forest. With a massive import of capital, the land was cleared and planted so that ridge after ridge is now patterned a bright, almost apple-green as one of the most productive tea areas on earth. As a consolation for the conservation purists, who regret the loss of natural forest, there is no erosion. The tea plants retain the soil and anyway have an attraction of their own in a distinctive greening of the hills. The place to stay in Kericho is, appropriately, the **Tea Hotel**.

From Kericho a major road descends to Kisumu, while another holds to the high ground through Sotik, **Kisii** ⓰ and eventually to the Tanzanian border.

The Kisii highlands, the home of the Gusii people, are exceptionally rich, although very little of their land is now left fallow. As in other areas of the western highlands, the population growth is exceptionally high and causes a constant migration of people to other parts of the country in search of employment or new land to cultivate.

Hidden away in southwest Kenya, the agricultural contribution that the Gusii people make to the country's economy is often overlooked. Yet they produce tea, coffee and pyrethrum – major foreign exchange earners – in considerable quantity. Unlike in Kericho, where the tea plantations are owned and run by large commercial concerns backed by international capital, production by the Gusii and their neighbours is mainly from smallholdings. For a century or more, conventional wisdom held that tea could only be efficiently grown on large plantations. This was challenged by Leslie Brown, famous as an authority on birds of prey, but also Kenya's senior agriculturalist at the close of the colonial era.

He was right; Kenya is now the world's third largest tea producer after India and Sri Lanka, and more than half the output is being collected from thousands of individual African planters on small plots of tea-growing land. As a result, the local tea economy is particularly robust and the same policy is now being applied to the country's sugar production.

Because Kisii and the southwest of Kenya generally are so densely populated, it's not wildlife country and thus off the main tourist circuits. The visitor is unlikely to have any contact with the Gusii or their culture, except through their soapstone carvings, attractive if somewhat stereotyped artifacts, mostly animal figurines dyed black or left in the natural pinks, whites and greys of the soft stone.

From Kisii, it is possible to travel south to the Tanzanian border, which is 98 km (61 miles) away at Isebania. From there, you can continue down to the lakeside town of Musoma. However, most visitors turn off east on the way – at **Suna** ⓱, 77 km (48 miles) from Kisii – and then head through **Lolgorien** ⓲ (the scene of a minor gold rush in the inter-war years), down the Siria escarpment and into the Maasai Mara. ❑

# The Luo

The second-largest of the non-Bantu ethnic groups in Kenya after the Kikuyu, the 2.7 million-strong Luo of the Central and South Nyanza districts, around the Winam Gulf of Lake Victoria, represent the most vigorous of southward drives of Nilotes from the Sudan.

The first wave of Luo immigrants probably arrived in Nyanza about five centuries ago. The arrival of the last of the Luo groups in the 18th century coincided with the thrust into South Nyanza, which caused the Gusii, Kuria and Suba to retreat and also brought the Luo people into contact with the Maasai and the Kipsigis.

Cattle and constant migrations in search of pastures for their herds dominated the life of the first Luo immigrants. But they adjusted to growing population pressures by adopting a sedentary way of life in relatively isolated homesteads. Although cattle continued to dominate ritual and economic activities, agriculture and fishing became increasingly important for subsistence. Sorghum, *sim-sim* (sesame) and finger millet were the traditional crops grown, and now vegetables, groundnuts, coffee and sugar-cane are valuable additions in a cash economy. These people still maintain their migratory instincts – tens of thousands seeking employment have flooded the major towns, especially Nairobi and Mombasa.

Foremost among Kenya's people in their fishing skills, the Luo today mainly use gill nets and long-line fishing to catch tilapia and other fish. Extensive use is still made of basket traps, either on their own or in conjunction with the *osageru* fish maze and the *kek* river fence at the mouths of rivers. The Luo formerly used crude log and bundle rafts of papyrus or saplings on Lake Victoria. In deeper water, hollowed-out log canoes or plank-built craft of considerable complexity and size are employed.

The dhow-type fishing boats used in offshore fishing were first constructed on the Winam Gulf by Asians and later adapted and built by the Luo people themselves. They have also adopted the more advanced *ssesse* canoe of the Baganda, and many are now moulded in glass-fibre and often powered by outboard motors.

The head of a homestead has his own hut (*duol*) built near the cattle enclosure. Here, important matters relating to the household and community are discussed among the clan elders. Wives have their individual huts and may not sleep in the *duol*. Traditionally, a young woman whose suitor had given her parents enough cattle would be carried off by force by the bridegroom and his friends. Today, bride prices are often paid in cash in lieu of cattle and marriages are formalised by Christian rite.

The Luo are an articulate, community-conscious people, and were prominent in Kenya's struggle for independence, providing many leading trade unionists and politicians, including the late Tom Mboya and the former Vice-President of Kenya, Oginga Odinga. Luo folklore has been imaginatively captured in the modern fiction of Grace Ogot and Tom Okoya.                     ❑

**RIGHT:** drying fish in the sun by Lake Victoria.

# UMBRELLAS AND CANDELABRAS

*Kenya's varied landscape is adorned by a great variety of trees – some dramatic, some beautiful, and some downright eccentric*

As well as hundreds of indigenous African trees, Kenya also contains a remarkable number of "exotics" – trees originally from tropical zones elsewhere in the world. There are several palm trees, for instance, but only one species is truly indigenous to Kenya – the doum palm (*above*), the only member of its family to grow branches. The long, slender stems repeatedly divide into two, giving the doum its distinctive appearance.

The wild date palm, on the other hand, was introduced to these parts by Arab traders, presumably so that its fruit could be cultivated, but it has spread wild along rivers and around swamps. Some authorities believe the coconut palm originally came from Polynesia, others from South America. But sea-borne coconuts were washed up on African shores so long ago that this versatile tree has provided food and manufacturing materials here for centuries.

There are more than 40 species of indigenous acacia in Kenya – plus several more, such as the golden wattle, introduced by Europeans from Australia. There are Australian eucalypts, too, including the blue gum and the red-flowering gum, both first brought to Nairobi to beautify the streets of the scruffy little frontier town.

Australian flame trees grow alongside the native Nandi flame tree – both with spectacular fiery blooms. And there are imports from Asia, the South Seas and Central and South America. The countryside, especially after the rains, is a colourful riot of botanical glories.

▷ **FAMILIAR ACACIA**
The umbrella thorn (*Acacia tortilis*) is a distinctive feature of the savannah. Giraffes browse its leaves, and its fallen seed pods are a favourite of impalas.

▽ **VIVID BLOSSOMS**
*Erythrina abyssinica* is one of many flowering trees that depend on birds to distribute their seed: hence the colourful flowers.

△ **YELLOW FEVER**
The yellow-barked acacia is known as the fever tree because early explorers who camped beneath it blamed it (wrongly) for their bouts of malaria.

◁ **SWEET SCENTED**
The beautiful frangipani, originally from Central America, is named after an Italian nobleman who made perfume from it.

## THE TREE WHERE MAN WAS BORN

The baobab (*Adansonia digitata*) is central to many African legends, and it is not hard to see why. It is a bizarre tree.

Its trunk can grow up to 9 metres (30 ft) in diameter, yet its thick branches do not grow in proportion, and being bare of leaves for most of the year, they look more like roots. The Kamba tribe say that God planted the baobab upside-down as punishment for its not growing where he wanted.

Then there is its remarkable longevity. There are baobabs growing today that were young trees at the time of Christ. The creation myths of several tribes tell of the first humans descending from a baobab – the tree where man was born.

Ancient baobabs have survived centuries of ravages by elephants, which tear off the bark, possibly for the calcium it stores. The trees' trunks are riddled with hollows and crevices, which serve as a home for nocturnal creatures such as bushbabies, owls and bats – and, according to many tribes, to nocturnal spirits as well.

◁ **FALLEN FLOWERS**
When jacaranda blooms (Sep–Nov), its petals form a thick carpet in Nairobi and other towns.

▽ **VALUABLE TREE**
The coconut palm provides food, drink, cooking oil, fibre for rope and matting, and leaves for thatching.

▽ **STRANGE SUCCULENT**
The "candelabra tree" is a cactus-like euphorbia. Its candlestick branches reach up to 15 metres (50 ft).

△ **AERIAL ROOTS**
Mangrove forests, with their long, aerial roots, thrive in coastal estuaries. The wood is used for poles, the bark for tanning.

# MOMBASA

*The final few chapters explore Kenya's coast – with its beautiful beaches, spectacular coral reefs and fascinating towns with an Arabic flavour. We start with the vibrant city of Mombasa*

Map on page 266

A Swahili proverb sums up the pervasive atmosphere of the Kenya coast: *Haraka haraka haina baraka* – "Haste, haste brings no blessing". Here, the gentle philosophy of the Swahili people spawns a leisurely pace of life, as might be expected at zero altitude on the Equator. It's hot, humid and yet tempered all the time by the northeast or southeast monsoon, the trade winds of the Indian Ocean determining the seasons.

The northeasterly *kaskazi* blows from October until March, with its rainfall peak in November. This is the warmer of the two monsoon seasons with the hottest months occurring on the coast in January and February. The dhows sail south on this wind from the Middle East and Gulf ports, down to East Africa and across to India. The southeasterly *kusi* blows from April until September, and its rainfall peak is from May until July. It's the stronger of the two winds, the cooler and the less comfortable, but this is relative since the climate stays mostly benign. Ancient dhows returned north on the *kusi*, carrying ivory, frankincense, gum arabic and slaves. Cargo nowadays is mostly mangrove poles from Kenya's tidal flats which are used for building throughout the Arabian Gulf.

Facing winds that have blown across several thousand miles of ocean, Kenya's beaches might be expected to be constantly battered by surf – wild, dangerous playgrounds. But they are not; for almost the entire length of the coast, the shallows and sands are protected by a coral reef about a mile off shore and stretching from Vanga in the south to Lamu in the north. The only breaks found are facing the creeks of Mombasa, Mtwapa and Kilifi – the outlets of now extinct rivers – and at the Sabaki and Tana rivers (north of Malindi), which also cut through the reef with their outpouring of fresh water and millions of tons of silt.

Between the fringing coral reefs and the shoreline are shallow, safe waters. There are few or no sharks, only scores of species of spectacular coral fish easily observed in the clear, warm ocean. As for the beaches, they're often miles on end of fine white sand, edged in dunes and serried ranks of coconut palms and wispy casuarina trees.

**PRECEDING PAGES:** Mombasa Island from the north, with Makupa Causeway in the foreground. **LEFT:** cannon and shot at Fort Jesus. **BELOW:** the terrace of a luxury Mombasa hotel.

## Mombasa Island

This exceptional coastline effectively runs out north and south from Mombasa, which is the largest port on the eastern littoral of the continent with the exception of Durban in South Africa. The town-port is the commercial gateway to a vast "interior", stretching west into Zaire, northwest into Sudan and southwest into Zambia. Countries without a seaport, such as Rwanda and Uganda, depend to a large extent on Mombasa for imports and exports of their cash crop commodities.

In the days before Christ, Mombasa was apparently called "Tonika", which is a fit description for Kenya's main seaside town and the major centre for rest and relaxation. Just the sight of it, from an escarpment above the island, is instant relief for the weekender from Nairobi and the up-country interior. It is just as attractive to arrivals from further afield – a quarter of a million European visitors fly in every year from Germany, Britain and Scandinavia.

Incidentally, the sea route to Mombasa today is almost impossible. Cargo ships sail out of a dozen North Sea and Mediterranean ports, but the chances of a passenger berth are slim to non-existent. The only possibility is aboard a dhow down from the Gulf, on a world cruise liner, or on a local scheduled cruise. Cruises on the *Royal Star*, which sails between Lamu, Mombasa and Zanzibar, can be booked through the African Safari Club; tel: Mombasa (011) 472021.

Mombasa is often described as a "melting pot", with all its coastal cultures – indigenous, colonial and transient – and increasingly its migrants from mainland Africa. They all steam together in Mombasa like the classic curry of

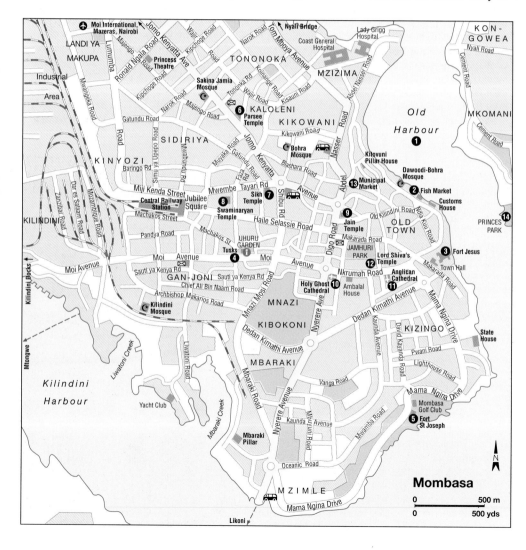

Mombasa

the region which, as it happens, is not a bad simile, appropriate down to the condiments on the side: mangoes, pineapples, paw-paw (papaya) and coconut, all of which are grown locally.

Mombasa is pungent, tangy, spicy – essentially a sailor's town. It's also hot, at least when the sun assumes the perpendicular from mid-morning to mid-afternoon, when Mombasa dozes off. It's also impossible to determine the separate ingredients or how much of what went into the stew.

## The Old Town

Joined to the mainland by a wide causeway, Mombasa town is mostly spread over a small coral island, flanked by two creeks, Tudor and Kilindini ("deep water"), which provide its natural harbours. The **Old Harbour ❶** grew up beside the eastern Tudor inlet, but as trade grew in the early part of this century and when the harbour capacity became overstretched, a new port was built at Kilindini on the western side of the island.

Thus the traditional and interesting waterfront of the Old Town was spared demolition and redevelopment; nowadays, it remains as a "period piece" attraction. Characteristically, it has an Arab-Indian mix and consists of a maze of narrow streets and passages (many of which are impassable to motor traffic), with overhanging "Juliet" balconies and carved doorways. Goldsmiths and silversmiths are traditional craftsmen in the Old Town, but other traders conduct a substantial import-export business despite the quaint and unpretentious appearance of their storefronts.

At the old harbour is an open square containing the **Customs House**, the **Fish Market ❷** and several shops specialising in carpets, chests and brass-

Map on page 266

*The buildings of the Old Town are constructed mainly of coral rock.*

**BELOW:** Mombasa Old Town.

*Fort Jesus was used as a prison by the British until 1958, when the Gulbenkian Foundation provided £30,000 for its restoration and the establishment of a museum.*

ware brought by dhows from the Persian Gulf. A short distance away is a shop selling "non-alcohol-based perfumes", presumably for the teetotal Muslims.

Usually in the harbour are small coastal dhows from Lamu and Somalia at anchor, trading in fruit, dried fish and similar commodities. It's only during the December to April season of the *kusi* monsoon that the large ocean-going booms and sambuks from farther afield can be seen. Nowadays, these amount to little more than a picturesque remnant of the dhow fleets of the heyday of slaves and ivory. Even these – or most of them – have diesel engines to supplement the traditional lateen sailing power.

Still, there is lots to see at the old harbour during the relatively quieter months – fishermen, stevedores and sailors unconsciously photogenic, and perhaps a *Nakhoda* (a dhow captain) offering cups of sweet black coffee during a drawn-out discussion over the purchase of a Persian carpet or a Zanzibar sea-chest.

Nearby is the brooding bulk of **Fort Jesus ❸**, constructed by the Portuguese in 1593 as the ultimate in indestructible fortresses. Its walls are 15 metres (50 ft) high and 2.5 metres (8 ft) thick. Now a museum of coastal antiquities, it has fine exhibits of ceramics and carved doors. The fort (open daily, 8am–6.30pm) is administered by the National Museums of Kenya, which charges a small entrance fee.

## A colourful sprawl

The 20th century has seen the rapid expansion of Mombasa beyond the Old Town. Today's city contains administrative buildings dating from the early colonial days; street markets for souvenirs, fruits and colourful cloth; a jostle of pavement vendors selling coffee, coconut milk, roasted maize and cassava;

**BELOW:** Mombasa's best-known landmark, the tusks spanning Moi Avenue.

Map on page 266

and, in sharp contrast, new office blocks, the smart Post Office and modern shops stocking goods from all over the world.

**Moi Avenue** links the old and new port areas and supports most of the travel and shipping agencies, local tour operators, curio shops, and the better hotels, bars and restaurants. The dual carriageway is spanned by the city landmark – four crossed elephant **Tusks** ❹, made of aluminium and erected to commemorate Queen Elizabeth's visit in 1952. They locate the efficient Mombasa and Coast Visitor Information Bureau and nearby Uhuru Garden, with the National Freedom Monument.

Enthusiasts may continue on to visit **Kilindini Docks**, which are modern, efficient and still expanding. A distant view will suffice for most visitors, however, and this is particularly attractive at night, as the ship and shore lights reflect on the waters of Kilindini Creek. A walk at dusk along Mama Ngina Drive, past **Fort St Joseph** ❺ and through the course of the Mombasa Golf Club, also provides a chance to breathe the cool sea air and join the colourful promenade of the city's cosmopolitan populace.

Mombasa is notable for its great variety of churches, mosques and temples. Travelling south from Makupa Causeway on Jomo Kenyatta Avenue, you'll see the **Parsee Temple** ❻ on your left, then, on Mwembe Tayari Road to the right, the **Sikh Temple** ❼ and **Swaminaryan Temple** ❽. If you continue to the main thoroughfare, Digo Road, you'll find the Khunzi Mosque and, nearby on Langoni Road, the beautiful **Jain Temple** ❾, with its marble pillars, elephants flanking the solid silver doors, and domes and pyramids on the roof. South along Digo Road is the Roman Catholic **Holy Ghost Cathedral** ❿ and, on Nkrumah Road, the curiously Moorish-looking **Anglican Cathedral** ⓫, which was erected as a memorial to Archbishop Hannington, who was killed in Uganda in 1885. It lies virtually opposite **Lord Shiva's Temple** ⓬, the religious centre for the city's Hindus, with the tallest spire in town, topped by a crown of solid gold. The Baluchi Mosque on Makadara Road is the successor to the original built by the Baluchis who migrated here from the Makran coast (now Pakistan). The oldest place of worship is the Mandhry Mosque on Bachaway Road, which dates back to 1570.

## Delightful diversions

Mombasa is essentially a casual place and visitors will soon be as relaxed as the residents. The right clothes are cool cotton prints, such as the *kikoi* sarong, the strikingly patterned *kanga* or white full-length *khanzu*, bought perhaps after a happy haggle with the laconic (and experienced) shopkeepers of Biashara (Bazaar) Street. Nearby is the famous **Municipal Market** ⓭ (formerly Mackinnon Market), selling vegetables, fruits, spices and baskets.

At night the city shakes off its languorous daytime air and offers its visitors a lively nightlife, ranging from sophisticated dining and dancing at smart beach hotels to the uninhibited atmosphere of cabaret clubs and sailors' bars. There are a number of casinos, four cinemas and the Little Theatre Club, which regularly puts on amateur productions.

*On Mama Ngina Drive (named after the wife of Jomo Kenyatta) are two ritzy gambling establishments: the casino in the Hotel Oceanic and the Florida Nightclub, with roulette and blackjack as well as a vibrant disco.*

**BELOW:** Mombasa's municipal market.

A wide variety of good food is available in Arab, Chinese, Indian, Pakistani and European styles. In addition, seafood is inexpensive as well as plentiful. One *touristique* but enjoyable diversion is the Dhow Sundowner Cruise along the shores of Mombasa Island. As darkness falls, the dhow docks and visitors proceed to Fort Jesus, its main entrance "guarded" by "Arab and Portugese" men with blazing torches. Inside, a sound and light presentation of the turbulent history of the East African Coast is followed by a candalabra-lit dinner. (Book with Jahazi Marine, PO Box 89357, Mombasa, tel: 472213.)

There is plenty of tourist accommodation in Mombasa, from luxury to basic. See the listings in the Travel Tips section of this book.

## Centuries of trade

Trade is essential to life in Mombasa, as it has been for at least two millennia. Exports of tea, coffee, pyrethrum, potash and many other commodities pour out of the interior, through acres of warehouses and on to the quays. Tankers discharge crude oil into Kenya's refinery, almost the sole source of processed fuel for the East African region. Bulk cement carriers load cargo from the Bamburi silos north of Mombasa, Africa's largest cement works. Apart from the vast array of export and import operations, Mombasa has its own industrial complex which manufactures anything from pins to hull plates for ocean-going ships.

An indicator of the importance of Mombasa to the Kenya economy is **Moi International Airport**, a few miles to the west of the island. Fully equipped and big enough for the intercontinental jets, the airport brings tourists directly to the coast from Europe. Kenya Airways and a number of private charter companies operate flights to Kenya's main tourist attractions, including the coastal resorts up to Lamu. For the old-fashioned up-country safari, the railway terminus is in the centre of the town, as are bus and taxi stops for departures to the beaches and beyond, north and south of Mombasa Island.

The town is not without its problems. Mombasa's thriving commerce draws in the poor, the displaced and the ambitious from all over the countryside; and the price it pays is the strain in attempting to match the pace of population growth with the provision of accommodation, services and facilities. Overwhelmed by the problems of essential maintenance and development, the Town Council was temporarily replaced by an administrative Governing Commission appointed by the central government.

But recently a new mayor was appointed and improvements are already visible: street cleaning and rubbish collection have reappeared, roads have been resurfaced, new trees planted. The problems of power and water have yet to be resolved, and most hotels and restaurants still have their own generators.

## Around Mombasa

This century Mombasa has spilled beyond the island on to the mainland in all directions. To the south, the link between suburbs is the Likoni ferry, which plies across the mouth of the deep-water Kilindini Port. To the northwest, Makupa Causeway carries road, rail and fuel arteries to Nairobi and up-country Kenya. To

the east, the connection is via the Nyali toll bridge, which spans the upper reaches of Tudor Creek.

Just over Nyali Bridge, towards the north coast, is **Freretown**, the site of one of the oldest churches in East Africa. Sir Bartle Frere founded this settlement in the 1870s for freed slaves, and many of their descendants still live there.

A right turn off Nyali Bridge leads to a memorial to Dr Johann L. Krapf, the first Christian missionary (after the Portuguese), and the graves of his young family who died "of the fever" there in 1844. Nearby is **Princes Park ⑭** extending round to Mackenzie Point. This was land donated to Mombasa for the recreation of its people by the British Dukes of Gloucester and Windsor. Today it is the venue for the annual Mombasa Agricultural Show. Just to the north is **Nyali**, the town's finest garden suburb, offering a good beach, a sports club, an 18-hole golf course, and three of the finest hotels on the coast.

Another excursion is to the workshop of the Wakamba carvers situated along the airport road where it branches from the main Nairobi road at Changamwe. Many of the stereotyped wooden wildlife on sale in the middle of the town are produced at this workshop, whose showroom also displays some unusual pieces.

At **Mazeras**, about 19 km (12 miles) along the Nairobi road, are the small municipal Botanical Gardens, which contain a wide range of tropical shrubs, flowers and trees – many of which are eventually used to beautify the city streets, parks and public places.

The mission stations of **Rabai** and **Ribe**, established by Lutheran pastors in the mid-19th century, are situated a few kilometres inland, and near **Mariakani**, 16 km (10 miles) farther on, you can visit a traditional *kaya* or stockaded settlement of the Giriama tribe. ❑

Map on page 266

*The Tamarind Restaurant in Nyali is probably the most famous eating place on the coast. It has Moorish architecture, a flower-filled terrace overlooking the Old Harbour and superb seafood specialities.*

**BELOW:** women selling *kangas* on a Mombasa beach.

# THE SOUTH COAST

*Palm-fringed beaches stretch south from Mombasa like a string of pearls. The resorts range from glamorous Diani Beach to laid-back Wasini Island*

Map on page 274

The "coasts" north and south of Mombasa compete vigorously for the tourist trade. There are endless debates about which has more to offer but, in fact, there's not a lot of difference between the two sectors. The South Coast has a longer unbroken stretch of reef and, debatably, a larger and more varied lagoon area between the reef and beaches. Across the Likoni ferry, the major road from Mombasa south to Tanzania runs parallel to the shore, about 2 km (1 mile) inland. The best beaches are found between the townships of Tiwi and Diani – a 21-km (13-mile) stretch starting about 20 km (12 miles) south of Mombasa. In this sector, hotels, campsites and private properties line the entire length of the shore.

To reach **Tiwi Beach** ❶, turn left 6 km (4 miles) after the turning to Kwale. Tiwi has many quiet beaches and self-catering bungalows. If you're heading for **Diani Beach** ❷, cross the Mwachema River estuary and turn left at **Ukunda**, a few kilometres further south. Ukunda has a large number of small shops, a couple of petrol stations, and small local bars and hotels. It is impossible to miss the Diani Beach turning, as all the hotels are heavily advertised here.

Diani is a ribbon of flawless tropical beach, straight for over 13 km (8 miles) and probably 75 metres (80 yards) wide at low tide. The sand is white, fine-grained, gently cambered to the ocean and shaded on the spectator side with palms and casuarina. The ocean at Diani, or rather the inshore shallows, are entirely protected by the fringing reef, massive and solid like a sea-wall. Nothing gets in – no sharks, no other large marine life, no pollution and not even sea-weed. The ocean scenery also seems on a larger scale than anywhere else on the Kenya coast, subtle and infinitely varied. When the tide goes out, a half-mile stretch of coral and sand between the reef and shore is exposed as a mosaic of rock pools.

A narrow lagoon at the outlet of the Mwachema River, at the northern end of the beach, is a decorative pattern of islands. At high tide it's all covered, but to no great depth. The coral formations show on the mirror-flat surface as a vast abstract colour wash, with changing warmer tints around dawn and in the early evening. Occasionally the coral is scoured out into deep caves, some with black felt ceilings of countless bats. They peel off and erupt in the evenings, great clouds of them against the sunset.

The land immediately behind the beach is scenic and only partially developed, mostly with coconut, banana and citrus cultivation. Elsewhere there are patches of original forest.

In a grove of flat boababs at **Kongo**, between Tiwi and Diani on the Mwachema estuary, is the **Mwana Mosque** ❸, built by 16th-century pilgrims. The

**LEFT:** Diani has some of Kenya's best beaches.
**BELOW:** Nomad's at Diani – the only beach bar along the whole coast.

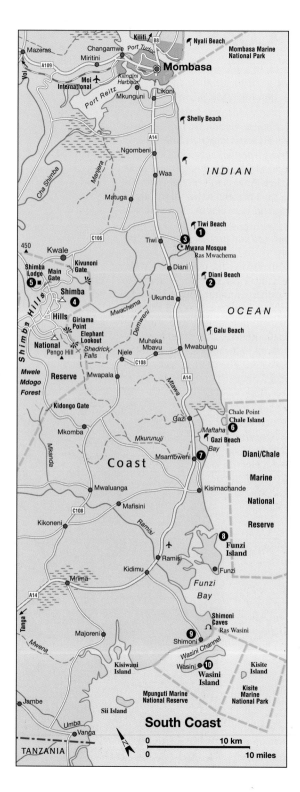

vaulted prayer room is intact and still used by worshippers.

Development on the Diani Strip has been fairly intense, not only in tourist accommodation, but in a whole range of ancillary services. There's a shopping centre, restaurants, hairdressing salons, vehicle hire, training facilities and equipment for scuba-diving, windsurfing, glass-bottomed boating and deep-sea fishing. Hotels here range from air-conditioned concrete and glass to vintage, open villa-style fanned by breezes off the ocean. All offer assorted watersports and deep-sea fishing, and all have small but good restaurants. Worthy of note are the **Jadini Beach Hotel**, one of the oldest on the South Coast, and the **Indian Ocean Beach Club**, one of the newest and best, designed in Swahili style with thatched roofs and whitewashed rooms amid ancient baobab trees.

A few miles inland, running parallel to the Tiwi-Diani beaches, are the Shimba Hills – a set of gentle, rolling downs rising to 450 metres (1,500 ft) from the coastal plain. The upper reaches make up the **Shimba Hills National Reserve ❹**, 192 sq. km (74 sq. miles) of parkland reserved for Kenya's last breeding herd of sable antelope. The park also has buffalo, a resident herd of elephant, and a few lions and leopards. The birds are profuse and sometimes rare, such as the Fischer's turaco and the palm nut vulture. The spurfowl is the local emblem.

An easy car drive from any of the beach resorts, the Shimba Hills reserve not only gives the visitor a chance to see distinctive wildlife but also provides a cool change from the humid coastal strip. In addition, there are long-range views from the hills over the ocean or, to the south, the Usambara and Pare mountains of Tanzania. **Shimba Lodge ❺**, overlooking a water-hole in the middle of the forest, is a spectacular tree lodge particularly noted for night-time game viewing.

Officially, the immediate ambit of the Tiwi-Diani holiday comes to an end at **Chale Island ❻**. This speck of coral is a stopover for boat trips at the south extreme of the beach. Beyond that, down to the Tanzanian border at Vanga, is what the Diani planners describe as a "remote area" for longer excursions out of the beach hotels. In 1995, the Diani/Chale Marine National Reserve was created to protect these fragile coral reefs.

Near Chale Island are two time-lapsed fishing villages, **Kinondo** and **Gazi**, and, just to the south, **Msambweni ❼**, which has a fine, empty beach, a large hole in the ground reputed to be an old slave pen, no restaurants or shops save for a few *dukas*, and Seascape Beach Villas – for a get-away-from-it-all stay. Further south is **Funzi Island ❽**, home of a fishing resort. You can also camp on the island, which is reached by walking across the channel at low tide.

At the far end of the South Coast, about 70 km (45 miles) from Mombasa, is the Pemba Channel Fishing Club at **Shimoni ❾**. The deep trench of this channel between the Kenya coast and the Tanzanian island of Pemba is the main run for the big marlin. It's therefore also a popular base for serious deep-sea fishermen in Kenya. It is said, in the bar of the fishing club, that world record marlin are out there – somewhere. One of them, well over 450 kg (1,000 lb), was once hooked but slipped the line.

Shimoni, now a village, was once headquarters of the Imperial British East Africa Company (*see page 34*). Now it's the HQ of Mpunguti Marine National Reserve and Kisite Marine National Park, scientifically important habitats. Across a narrow sound, on **Wasini Island ❿**, is an Arab settlement almost as ancient as Lamu. From Wasini you can take a dhow cruise which incorporates a snorkeling trip to the reefs around Kisite Island and a seafood lunch at the Wasini Island Restaurant. ❑

Map on page 274

*Shimba Hills National Reserve is the only places in Kenya where you can see the beautiful sable antelope.*

**BELOW:** Mwana Mosque, amid ancient baobabs.

# NORTH TO MALINDI

*There are more delicious beaches on the coast north of
Mombasa – not to mention Arabic ruins, wildlife reserves and a
sultry town that was a favourite with Ernest Hemingway*

Map
on page
280

L eaving Mombasa by the Nyali Bridge you will soon reach **Nyali Beach ❶**,
a coastal strip that's dense with private properties and hotels, of which the
doyen is the Nyali Beach Hotel – for many years the trend-setter for standards of excellence. Perhaps the coast's most up-market restaurant is the
Tamarind, with a reputation for excellent seafood. It also organises an evening
dhow trip with food and music.

The Links Road from Nyali Beach leads to the **Nyali Golf Club** (with a
superb 18-hole course and a fine Indian restaurant in the clubhouse) and also to
**Mamba Crocodile Village**. This claims to be the largest crocodile farm in
Africa, containing over 10,000 crocs, from enormous man-eaters to tiny hatch-
lings the size of your hand (open daily, 8am–6pm).

About 7 km (4 miles) north of Nyali Bridge is the **Bombolulu Workshop**,
which was set up by a German philanthropist for homeless and handicapped
people to give them an opportunity to work and support themselves. This
they do by producing handicrafts, jewellery, furniture and clothing for sale
(open daily, 8am–6pm).

Next, the road passes the Bamburi cement factory. This is the largest of its
kind in Africa, producing upwards of a million tons of cement a year. Its raw
material is the coral limestone that underlies much of
Kenya's coastal plain, and the vast amount quarried
over three decades left an enormous unsightly depression. The experts said nothing could be done, that the
ground was too saline to support trees or even grass.
It would have to be left as an inevitable wound
inflicted on the environment in the interest of profit.
But the factory owners turned to an agronomist, René
Haller, a Swiss of considerable optimism, who said
that he might be able to do something with the quarry.

**PRECEDING PAGES:**
a fishing vessel
heads for home.
**LEFT:** palm trees
and the Indian
Ocean, Malindi.
**BELOW:** tourists
take a trip in
a dhow.

## Environmental wonder

The result of Haller's work is the **Bamburi Quarry
Nature Park ❷**, which ranks as one of the most remarkable environmental rehabilitation projects anywhere in the world. He planted trees in what they said
was sterile lime and, within two decades, has built up
a forest producing commercial timber. Where the experts said grass wouldn't grow, there are now the
green meadows of a small wildlife park. The quarry
area also features fish and crocodile farms, an exper-
imental banana plantation and even a vineyard. All
this is open to visitors (daily, 7am–6pm).

A mile further on is **Kenyatta Beach**, where the
late president had his coastal home, and **Bamburi
Beach**, which has a number of excellent hotels and
restaurants, plus the famous Bora Bora Night Club
(nightly live show and disco).

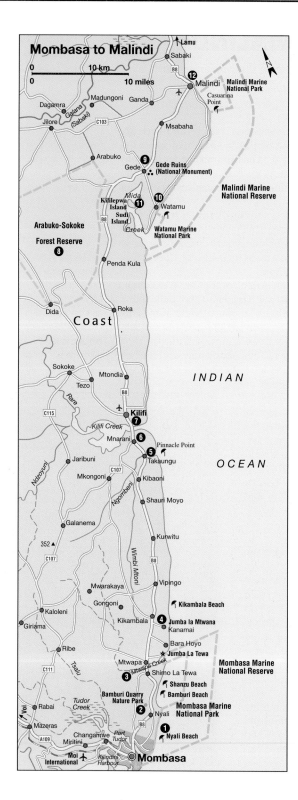

Mombasa to Malindi

Beyond Bamburi, 19 km (12 miles) north of Mombasa, a single-span suspension bridge crosses **Mtwapa Creek ❸**, an old river course cut deeply into the coral limestone. In this area, only relatively short lengths of beach are developed for tourism, but some of them – especially at **Shanzu** – have exceptionally fine hotels, including the Mombasa Inter-Continental and the Serena Beach Hotel, the latter built to resemble a small Arabic village. Watersports centres and marinas line both sides of the creek.

For the most part, the road north to Kilifi runs through the vast **Vipingo Sisal Estate**, one of the largest and best run in Africa. Lines of the sharp-pointed plants stretch to the horizon, their leaves eventually cut and the fibre extracted for manufacture into coarse string.

### Ancient ruins

About 16 km (10 miles) north of Mtwapa lies the lost city of **Jumba la Mtwana ❹**, a slave-traders' outpost which was abandoned at least 400 years ago and quickly engulfed by jungle. A further 20 km (12 miles) up the road is the sandy track leading to **Takaungu ❺**, a quaint Arabic village which contains the forgotten grave of an Omani sultan who died there in the 19th century. You can stay at Takaungu House, an old slave trader's home situated on the sweeping curve of a deserted beach.

Ten km (6 miles) beyond the Takaungu turn-off is **Mnarani ❻**, on the south side of Kilifi Creek, where there are several hotels, with watersports facilities, and also some 17th-century ruins including a mosque and some pillar tombs. A new bridge across Kilifi Creek has replaced the unreliable ferries and has removed the necessity of taking the long dirt road detour many miles inland.

On the creek's north shore stands the township of **Kilifi ❼**, administrative centre of a district that stretches to the borders of the Tsavo National Parks.

Of all the coastal centres, Kilifi has held out most strongly against the uncontrolled development of tourism. Most of the sea-front land is privately owned, much of it in the hands of retired farmers from the highlands. But the presence of sleek, ocean-going yachts and powerful fishing cruisers attests the attractions of Kilifi to up-market visitors – notably deep-sea fishing.

Map on page 280

## Rare mammals

Some 20 km (12 miles) after the Kilifi ferry crossing, the **Arabuku-Sokoke Forest Reserve ❽** can be seen on the left. There are several access routes, most of which require four-wheel-drive vehicles. The reserve runs parallel to the coastline for a stretch of about 400 sq. km (155 sq. miles). Tightly surrounded by farmland, it is the last remaining extensive patch of *brachestygia* woodland and lowland coastal rainforest of azaleas left in Kenya.

The forest is home to a number of interesting and rare mammals including the Zanzibar or Ader's duiker and the yellow-rumped elephant shrew. Both are difficult to see because of their shy nature and small size. Elephant shrews, with their elephantine snouts, are the largest members of this peculiar African family, measuring 50 cm (20 ins) long.

A number of rare and common local birds are also found here, including the Sokoke scops owl, thick-billed cuckoo, Retz's helmet shrike, Amani sunbird, Fischer's turaco, Sokoke pipit and southern-banded harrier eagle. Clarke's weavers occur in flocks of 100 or more but their nests have never been found. Another memorable sight is the thousands of butterflies that drink along the pools near the forest tracks. There's a nature trail you can walk from near the Visitors' Centre.

*Millions of carmine bee-eaters nest in the mangrove swamps at Kilifi Creek. At dusk huge flocks of the graceful red-bodied, long-tailed bird swoop around in search of insects.*

**LEFT:** woodcarvings for the tourist market.
**BELOW:** chilling out on Bamburi Beach.

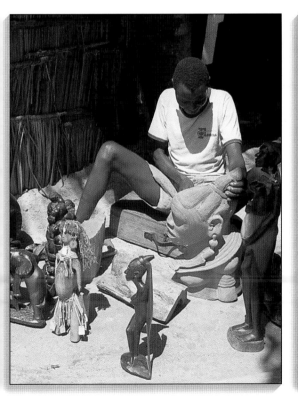

*Vasco da Gama called in at Malindi on his way to India in 1498. Before he left, he raised a memorial cross beside the Sultan of Malindi's palace. It was moved to its present location in the 16th century.*

**BELOW:** a ruined mosque at Gede.

## Lost city

On the outer reaches of the forest, about 40 km (25 miles) from Kilifi, lies the lost city of **Gede** ❾. This was clearly an early Islamic port which was suddenly and inexplicably abandoned, probably in the 17th or 18th century. Although an invasion of trees and bush has reduced the town to a ruin, there are many well-preserved relics of a mosque and some houses in the traditional Swahili style. It is something of a mystery how, presumably, the sea receded to leave the port high and dry. It is curious, too, why there is barely a mention of Gede in any of the ancient maritime literature, although there are full Arab and Portuguese logs on all the other coastal ports from Lamu to Vanga. Excavations continue and there's also a small museum (open daily, 7am–6pm).

On today's coast near Gede is the popular beach resort of **Watamu** ❿, another strip lined with beach bungalows and hotels, most of them providing facilities and equipment for deep-sea fishing and water sports. Watamu is a favourite watering place for locals, and provides perhaps the most frantic New Year's Eve party in the country, drawing up to as many as 2,000 young people who disco till sun-up at Ocean Sports. This is on **Turtle Bay**, the best beach section, which takes its name from a turtle-shaped coral outcrop just offshore.

Inland from Watamu lies **Mida Creek** ⓫, a series of tidal mudflats surrounded by mangrove trees. It is known for the numbers of waders that break their journey here between March and May on their way north during the annual migration. Ospreys, several species of terns and the rare, non-migrant crab plover also inhabit the creek. In the mangroves flocks of the brilliant carmine bee-eaters flash in the sunlight.

Snorkelling is possible for the more experienced – but only on the advice of a local expert who knows when the time and tide is right. You can enter the creek at park headquarters and float with the current in the dark, murky water. Look out for the rock cod (*tewa*), weighing up to 180 kg (400 lb), that lurk in the caves.

## Malindi

About 19 km (12 miles) north of Gede is the sultry town and sweeping beaches of **Malindi** ⓬, the last of the coast's main tourist resorts. It has been developed to cater for both local and foreign tourism from Europe, especially Italy and Germany, and with its lively hotels, nightclubs and bars, it is well set up for the hedonist on holiday.

Daily flights from Nairobi, Mombasa, Lamu and the game parks arrive at the small airport situated 2 km (1 mile) outside town on the Mombasa Road. The main road forks at a roundabout – turn right for the south end of Malindi and its beautiful beaches and hotels, left for the main town on the Lamu Road. Where this meets the sea, you're in Malindi's main shopping area – four shopping plazas each with its own open-air bar/restaurant. On the seaward side of the road is the **Blue Marlin Hotel**, Ernest Hemingway's favourite hangout when he came here big-game fishing in the 1930s. Southwards along the seafront is **Lawson's Hotel**, another period piece established in 1934 by a retired District Officer, and the **District**

**Commissioner's Office**, originally built by the Imperial British East Africa Company in 1890. This is a gazetted building and it is hoped that it will be turned into a museum sometime soon.

You are now on the outskirts of the **old town**, an interesting Swahili quarter dating from 1930–50, with a large and busy market. Keep to the left past the **Juma'a Mosque** (on the site where slaves were auctioned weekly until 1873) and the 15th-century pillar tomb of Sheikh Abdul Hassan. Along here is the **Malindi Sea Fishing Club**, where onlookers can view the day's catch at the weighing station by the fish market. Further on stands what is possibly East Africa's oldest church, the small Portugese **Chapel of St Francis Xavier**, where two sailors were buried. Opposite ,on the headland, is the Vasco da Gama Pillar, a cross carved from Lisbon stone marking the navigator's visit in 1498.

The road south leads to the beach strip of **Silversands**, which includes the vast Coral Keys Hotel and a campsite just beyond, terminating with the Driftwood Beach Club. Further south (take the signposted turning to the Malindi Marine National Park at Casuarina Point) is a **Crocodile Farm and Snake Park**, then the entrance to the **Marine Park** itself and its offices. Here you barter with the boatboys for your trip on the glass-bottomed boats that take you snorkelling in the park.

Malindi Bay suffers from the seasonal dumping of brown silt, caused by up-country flooding, from the Sabaki River which has its outlet at the north end of the bay. However, the beaches south of Vasco da Gama Point are protected by coral reefs and are largely unaffected by this. The bay, on the other hand, is not protected by reefs, and so produces remarkably big waves for stand-up surfing, especially when the *kusi* monsoon comes in May and June. ❑

*Malindi is the big-game fishing centre of the Kenya coast and hosts a number of large fishing competitions between September and April.*

**BELOW:** Giriama women at Malindi's busy market.

# TO LAMU AND BEYOND

*It is possible to fly to the fascinating Arab-flavoured town of Lamu – but the overland journey is an exotic treat for the adventurous. Either way, the journey's end is a delight*

Map on page 288

Nairobi

F rom Malindi, the 225-km (140-mile) road to Lamu first crosses the Sabaki River over a suspension bridge. This was constructed after the previous more flimsy structure was swept away by a massive flood of the river in 1961–62. Five km (3 miles) further on is the turning to **Mambrui**  , which is strongly Muslim in character. It has a fine mosque and pillar tomb, as well as access to a vast expanse of beach stretching up a spit of sand dunes. The town has recently been subjected to large-scale tourist development, and there are a number of hotels and restaurants situated on Sheshale Beach.

About 6 km (3 miles) beyond Mambrui is a turning which leads to **Ngomeni**, facing the Italians' San Marco satellite launching pad a kilometre (½-mile) or so out to sea. A worthwhile deviation in the area is to **Marafa**, about 32 km (20 miles) on a rough road left out of Mambrui. From the village, a track runs down to "Hell's Kitchen" ❷, a spectacular gorge of eroded rock pinnacles and cliffs in striking colours.

Back on the main route, the road continues through the village of **Gongoni**, where there are several extensive salt works that stretch nearly all the way to Garsen. Beyond this, cultivated areas are gradually left behind and the road passes through a belt of coastal thicket for about 40 km (25 miles) to a possible detour to **Karawa** ❸, a government holding ground for cattle. The only reason for a visit – strictly for the adventurous – would probably be to see the sand dunes of **Ungwana Bay**, the largest beach on the whole East Africa coast, entirely waterless, undeveloped and deserted.

At 80 km (50 miles) from Malindi is the landing stage for the **Tana Delta Camp** ❹. Transport is organised by the camp from Malindi, including the 20-km (12-mile) boat ride on the *African Queen*, a replica of Humphrey Bogart's vessel. The tented camp sits on the dunes, in the shade of the thick riverine forest, a remote, undiscovered and totally unspoilt area. A stay at the camp usually includes canoe rides in and out of the mangroves, therapeutic mud-baths in the river, bird-watching on the mudbanks of the delta, watching zebra, topi, waterbuck and buffalo coming in for their evening drink, and shore line fishing at the village of **Kipini**, where the Tana River reaches the sea.

Back on the main road, a few kilometres before Garsen, at **Minjila** ❺, there is a new bridge and a new road to Lamu. At this junction there is a small hill affording the only view in the entire lower Tana basin – a hazy vista of endless dry bush country, broken only by the green ribbon of the riverine strip. Down below, on a 5-km (3-mile) track towards the river is **Idsowe**, a typical village of the lower Pokomo,

**PRECEDING PAGES:** a ritual sword fight at the Maulidi festival. **LEFT:** a Lamu elder. **BELOW:** Muslim women wearing *bui buis*.

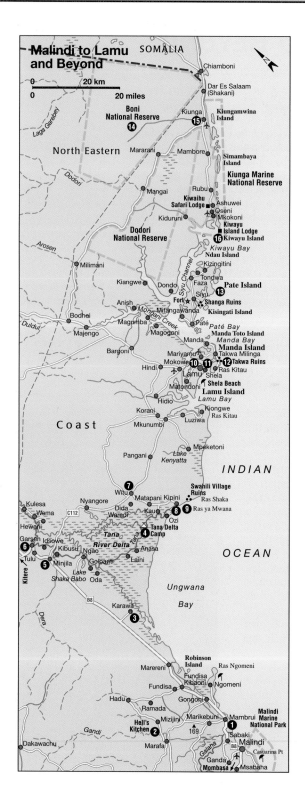

Malindi to Lamu and Beyond

or "Malachini", who are all Christian converts. It's otherwise unremarkable except for a famous heron breeding ground on a nearby lake. If the river floods in May, the whole delta supports a huge number of water birds and many species of heron breed on this lake in June–July.

## Road closed

The old route to Lamu from Garsen used to take you across the Tana by ferry and then across the flood-plain of the Tana Delta on a raised road. This route was treacherous at the best of times, and when the Tana river was in flood it disappeared completely. Finally, after the heavy rains of 1997–98, the river breached the embankment in several places and forced the authorities to build the new bridge at Minjila as well as a new embankment across the swamps, with a road that is tarmacked as far as Witu.

So now the route to Lamu bypasses **Garsen ❻**, but the town is worth a side-trip. It is an important local trading centre, and Waldei Gabbra (Somalis), Orma and Pokomo people crowd the street on any morning. It's a good place to buy a soda and sit and watch the scene.

The new road from Minjila leaves the flood-plain at a bridge called **Lango la Simba** (Lion's Gate), and enters a woodland thicket zone before **Witu ❼**, the next place of interest. Before you reach Witu there is a very large rice scheme, with a factory. This is home to the spectacular indigenous Borassus palm. The now deserted and overgrown mango plantations of the area give a hint of Witu's prosperous past, but few would guess that this sleepy village was once the centre of an important sultanate and, briefly, the capital of the short-lived state of "Swahililand" (see page 34).

Just beyond Witu is a turn-off to the beach, about 19 km (12 miles) away at the village of **Kipini ❽**. This is at the present mouth of the Tana and was the district headquarters until this was subsequently moved well up river to Hola. Like Witu, the village is Swahili in character with stone-walled houses and *makuti* (palm leaf) thatched roofs.

The river outlet to the sea has been there only since the 1860s, when the Sultan of Witu had a canal dug between the old course of the river and a small stream called the Ozi, which flowed into the sea at Kipini. During a big flood in 1892 the river adopted the canal as its main course and the old flow has largely silted up.

Map on page 288

## Haunted house

As a district headquarters, Kipini acquired notoriety through the suicides of three administrators, and the old District Commissioner's house is supposedly haunted. The village still has a sultry, jaded and a very romantic atmosphere. The DC's launch, the *Pelican,* which used to patrol upstream as far as Garissa, is still here, though in a sad state of disrepair. A track leads along the coast to the east and there are several old Swahili ruins, the best being at **Ras ya Mwana ❾**, 11 km (7 miles) from Kipini.

Beyond Witu the road passes through the edge of **Witu Forest**, once much more extensive than it is now. The surrounding area is largely a parkland of doum palm and bush interspersed with grassy *ziwas* – shallow depressions which flood during the rains. Baboons, topi and elephants can be seen in this area, which is now gazetted the **Pandanguo Game Reserve**.

At the village of Mkunumbi, the road turns inland for some distance to go around the creeks and mangrove swamps that lace the area. Eventually, the sea is reached again at the village of **Mokowe**. At this point, travellers must take a boat across to the island of Lamu. Cars may be left at the jetty, where a night

*Kenya's first postage stamp was issued in the 1860s by the Sultan of Witu.*

**BELOW:** a solitary heron in the Tana Delta.

# The Bajun, Swahili and Shirazi

The Swahili-speaking people of the Kenya coast share a common language, religion (Islam) and culture. Of Bantu origin, Swahili has become the national language of Kenya and is widely spoken throughout East Africa and Zaire.

The **Bajun**, who number around 37,000 and inhabit the Lamu archipelago and coastal strip to the north, speak a Swahili dialect of their own known as Kitikuu. They are thought to have originated from an undetermined location to the north. Arabian settlement from the Persian Gulf brought about a further evolution of the Bajun people, as did the later incursions of the Oromo-speaking people.

Centuries of immigration and conquest, transmigration and miscegenation, resulted in the Bantu-speaking **Swahili** absorbing immigrants of Arab and Persian descent. Loosely applied, the term Swahili has come to

mean almost any Muslim from the coast.

The **Shirazi** (numbering, together with the Swahili, 5,500) are a scattered maritime and agricultural people. They claim to have originated from a homeland in Persia in the 10th to 12th centuries and once made up the aristocratic dynasties of Shaka, Malindi and Mombasa. The modern view places no credence in the legend of their origins and today little remains to set them apart from the Swahili other than pride in a shady past.

Fishing and agriculture feature prominently in the economy of the Bajun, Swahili and Shirazi. Fish spears, handlines and different types of basket traps made of palm rib or bamboo are all commonly used to catch fish. Fine-meshed cast nets, drift nets employed in surface fishing from boats and long seine nets positioned from boats and then hand-hauled up on the beach are all employed in communal fishing.

From recorded time, the peoples of the Kenya coast have engaged in shifting agriculture. Of considerable importance in the economy is the ubiquitous coconut, which provides food, drink, oil and the raw material for building, thatching, rope-making and plaited basketwork. The coastal people cultivate numerous root crops, including cassava, sweet potato, yam and taro, cereals such as millet, rice and maize, and a wide variety of fruit trees including banana, mango, orange, lime and papaya. Cashews, cotton and mangrove-cutting provide important cash incomes in the Lamu area.

The fleet of ocean-going dhows once upon a time numbered several hundred; today, a few individual, motorised dhows maintain the trading links with Arabia and the Persian Gulf. In creeks and harbours a dug-out canoe is often used; occasionally a double-outrigger canoe may be seen. The graceful *jahazi* with a billowing triangular sail is common in the Lamu archipelago, along with the all-purpose, keel-less *dau la mwao*.

Many people who live by the coast are skilled craftsmen. Here, ship-building and woodworking, the plaiting of baskets, mats and other items, rope-making from coir, and metal- and leather-work remain traditional occupations of the villagers.  ❑

**LEFT:** music is important to the Bajun.

watchman guards them (for a tip). Alternatively, they can be left at a car-park behind the garage in Mokowe or sometimes at the police station. Both of these car-parks are more than a couple of kilometres (1 mile) from the jetty, so you'll have to hitch a ride if you have too much baggage to carry. There are daily bus services to and from Lamu, but be warned that the prevalence of bandits has led to buses being accompanied by an armed escort.

Map on page 288

## The Lamu Archipelago

Lamu and neighbouring islands on the far north of Kenya's coastline have become a fashionable destination for discerning tourists. The port of **Lamu** ❿ is the only substantial survivor of an urban civilisation that has existed for at least 1,000 years on this part of the coast. It retains an almost entirely unspoiled 19th-century appearance and lifestyle and, since access is now fully developed, has become one of Kenya's premier visitor attractions.

*The first British proconsul in Lamu was Rider Haggard's brother, Capt. Jack Haggard, whose letters home about African life inspired the author.*

Settlements in the archipelago were first noted in the 2nd century AD although no evidence of habitation earlier than 9th century has yet been excavated. The settlements of Weyuni and Hedabu date back at least to the 13th century. Hedabu, once a principal township, was finally engulfed by sand dunes probably 500 years ago and these shifting sands are now threatening **Shela**, a picturesque village and fabulous tourist beach at the southern tip of the island.

Lamu itself was a thriving port by 1505, though there were frequent troubles between it and the sultanates of Mombasa, Zanzibar and Pate (pronounced *pâté*), the dominant island port to the north. At this time, the Lamu economy was slave-based. Like most other states in the archipelago, its production was mainly grains and fruits, and its exports included ambergris, mangrove poles, turtle shells, rhino horn and ivory. These highly profitable commodities were sent on dhows to Yemen, Arabia, the Persian Gulf and on the reverse trade winds to India.

**BELOW:** a Muslim studies the Koran.

During the 17th century, the nomadic Oromo tribes invaded from the north and sacked most of the coast settlements, except on the islands. The effect was migration to Lamu, Pate, Siyu and Faza, all of which developed rapidly, with Pate becoming pre-eminent by the 18th century.

Culture flourished at this time; a great tradition of poetry was developed and architecturally ambitious houses were built, some with hot-and-cold plumbing systems which made European ablutions primitive by comparison. Clothing was elegant and jewellery ornate, with gold and silver cloth woven in Lamu and furniture inlaid with silver and ivory.

But paradise was not complete. The island states warred with each other until 1813, when the people of Lamu trounced an army from Pate at the battle of Shela. From then on, Lamu began its golden age, which lasted more or less until 1873 when Britain forced Zanzibar to sign an anti-slaving pact. The Royal Navy patrolled the coast and prevented the Sultan's attempt at slipping slave dhows past the blockade. By 1897, there were fewer than 10,000 slaves on the island and 10 years later slavery was abolished for all time.

*The Dodori National Reserve, just north of Lamu, was set up in 1976 to protect the breeding grounds of the local population of topi.*

## The first tourists

The cheap labour on which Lamu's prosperity depended was gone and the island plunged into decline. An American visitor at the time wrote: "The freeing of the slaves has reduced most of the free-born inhabitants to a state of poverty and, moreover, those with property and coconut *shambas* find it difficult or impossible nowadays to find sufficient labour. I fear there is, then, little hope of their ancient prosperity returning to them, for they have no arts, large industries or resources on which to fall back."

He was among the island's first "tourists", who also included Henry Morton Stanley. A few years later, the Germans moved in to establish the short-lived "Protectorate" around Witu on the mainland and opened the Lamu Post Office, the first established outside Germany. For 70 years, Lamu merely jogged along, half comatose – isolated from developments within the new British East African Protectorate and later the Kenya Colony. The technology of Europe's industrial revolution was not imported, nor was the competitive ambition and materialism of the 20th century. The island is still largely untouched by "civilisation", which accounts for its unique charm.

Then, in 1962, shortly before Kenya's Independence, Lamu's economy began to rally, principally from a new role as shipper of Somali cattle to Mombasa. Tourism arrived in 1967 with an initial eight beds at the Peponi Hotel in Shela Village. Since then a number of hotels have been built, and scores of lodging houses opened by the local people. Communication with the island is also being improved, with the upgrading of the Malindi-Mokowe road and of airstrips on Manda Island and mainland Mokowe. There are daily scheduled air services from Nairobi, Mombasa and Malindi to Lamu.

**BELOW:** ocean-front houses at Lamu.

## Old world intact

For the moment, Lamu's old-world ambience remains a major visitor attraction. The approach to the town is still exclusively by sea – usually by creaking diesel-powered launches from the road-head at Mokowe or a jetty close to the airstrip on Manda Island. A strong sea wall runs the length of the town, decorated in places with black, defunct cannon. Many buildings facing the sea have Arab/Swahili-style pillars, castellations or verandas, and behind them is a maze of narrow streets no wider than the span of a donkey cart (the only haulage vehicle in Lamu). The oldest of Lamu's 22 mosques is the **Pwani**. Its *qibla* (dome) dates back to 1370. The **Juma'a** (Friday) **Mosque** was started in 1511, but almost all other buildings date from the late 18th century.

Very little architectural development has taken place since, and the narrow cloistered town plan is intact. Inset in the unbroken lines of tall buildings are heavy, ornately carved timbered doors and shuttered windows precluding a glimpse of often attractive courtyard gardens inside. There are tiny shops in alleyways, always thronged with strollers – the men in white full-length *khanzu* and *kofia* caps, the woman in black cover-all dresses, called *bui bui* in Swahili.

Close to the Boma (District Commissioner's Office) is the excellent **Lamu Museum** (open daily, 8am–6pm), and behind here is the main town square and market, dominated by a fort (1821) that now houses a public library. Behind this, on rising ground, are some of the larger houses of the town, many of which span the streets and create mysterious cloisters of light and dark. They give way to a mosaic of Swahili mud-and-wattle houses, thatched with *makuti*, leading to the viewpoint summit of the hill. On the high ground is the old town hospital.

The beach tourism sector of Lamu is at **Shela ⑪** village on the east side of the

Map on page 288

**TIP**

Lamu is pleasant at any time of year, but the tourist class hotels are closed May–June for renovation and holidays.

**BELOW:** sand dunes on Shela Beach.

Map on page 288

*The beach beyond Shela is unprotected by a reef, and one of the few places on the coast where waves are consistently big enough for surfing.*

**BELOW:** a stroll along Shela's 13-km (8-mile) beach.
**RIGHT:** showing off an ivory *siwa*, used for wedding fanfares.

island, where the Peponi Hotel marks the beginning of a 13-km (8-mile) beach of uninterrupted, empty sand flanked by high dunes. At the end of Shela Beach is the village of **Kipungani**, noted for its mango orchards and two old mosques. On the west side of the island, the nearest settlement to the mainland is **Matondoni**, whose people are friendly and addicted to music and dance festivals.

These celebrations or *ziaras* give special eminence to Lamu in the Muslim world. The most important of them is the *Maulidi al Nebi* (birthday of the Prophet). This is a week of religious festivals, feasting and dancing that draws thousands of pilgrims from East and North Africa, Arabia and the Arabian Gulf to inundate the town for the event. They sing and dance in the square before the principal **Riyadha Mosque** and there is an impressive evening worship in the open air under the stars.

Among the many visitor attractions of Lamu are the typical souvenirs of Arab silver jewellery, carved chests, model dhows and Swahili furniture.

## Excursions from Lamu

On Manda Island are the ruins of a 16th/17th-century village called **Takwa** ⓬, which compares in interest and state of preservation to Gede (*see page 282*). The Manda town ruins at the island's north end are completely overgrown and buried, but recent archaeological work has determined them to date from the 9th-century – making them the oldest on the Kenyan coast. Manda Island can be reached only by dhow, from either Lamu or Shela.

About 32 km (20 miles) northeast of Lamu is **Pate Island** ⓭. The ruined towns of **Faza** and **Siyu** (which also has a well-preserved fort) can both be visited at any tide. The town of Pate itself is more difficult to reach, but on the right tide it is possible to land there. Otherwise it's a long but fascinating hike from a landing stage on the southern end of the island.

To the northeast, **Boni National Reserve** ⓮ has been established, but only on the map. It is otherwise undeveloped, largely because of its proximity to the border of Somalia and fears for security. It lies in the heart of wildlife-rich primeval forest, but observation of the animals is hampered by the thick vegetation.

The road eventually climbs over the Mundane Range, a low ridge of ancient sand dunes, and on down to the ocean at **Kiunga** ⓯. The village itself is attractively set, with a beautiful old district officer's house perched on a coral headland. Kiunga harbour is protected by a string of raised coral islands 1 km (˘ mile) off the present coastline. These are important breeding grounds for seabirds which nest there between July and October. It is also the site of **Kiunga Marine National Reserve**.

North of the village, a track goes up to the international boundary with Somalia, just beyond Shakani. To the south, the track follows the coast, past ruins at Omwe and Ashuwel, ending at the bay of Mkokoni opposite **Kiwayu Island** ⓰ – a marvellous spot for reef snorkelling or castaway beachcombing. **Kiwayu Safari Village**, situated in a remote hideaway on the island, has eight palm-thatched cottages with every conceivable comfort. ❑

# OFFSHORE ASSETS

*Much of Kenya's underwater wildlife is now protected by marine parks and reserves – and you don't need to be an experienced diver to explore the colourful creatures of the reef*

Map on pages 280 & 288

**K**enya took the lead in Africa by establishing national parks and reserves in the richest sections of its Indian Ocean reef. In these areas, it is forbidden to spear-fish, to remove shells or coral, or to disturb the occupants of a balanced but highly sensitive ecosystem. For a small fee, though, it's possible to snorkel or scuba-dive among gardens of coral which, for attraction and diversity, challenge the fêted reef of the Red Sea.

Not that the protected areas are the only places for underwater safaris; there are many others, some of which may also become sanctuaries in due course. These are all along the fringing reef which parallels the entire coastline, apart from breaks at *mlangos* (Swahili for "doors") at the outlets of extinct or extant rivers. The shallows and lagoons between the reef and the beach vary in width and depth. In places, it's possible to wade out in ankle-deep water half a mile to the reef; in others, you have to swim or take a boat. Incidentally, it's perfectly safe in these inshore waters, since in the small minds of the sharks there's an awareness that, inside the reef, they could be trapped and possibly beached by the receding tide, so they stay outside.

Parks and reserves were set up essentially as a conservation measure; one of the main concerns is to combat the serious threat of over-exploitation of shells on the reef by thoughtless souvenir-hunters. Efforts have been made to control the number of shell dealers, who must obtain a costly licence, but sadly it's still common to see illegal collectors on the beach with sackfuls of cowrie shells, conches, helmets and tritons.

Corals and starfish obviously belong underwater and, once removed, lose their brilliant colours, become brittle and give off an unattractive stench. Neither are the reef fish of much use – most of them are bony and unpalatable – and yet they were once taken out indiscriminately. The same goes for small crabs and other shellfish, which should be allowed to grow to a respectable size before they are removed.

## First reserve

The first reserve to be established was the **Malindi-Watamu Marine Reserve**, stretching from just south of Malindi town to below Watamu at Mida Creek. It extends out to sea for 5.5 km (3 nautical miles) and the landward boundary is 30 metres (100 ft) from the high-water mark.

Inside the reserve are two national parks; the first, Malindi, extends about a mile out from the shore between Chanoni Point and Leopard Point, with the park base between the two at Casuarina Point. In this, the main area of interest is known as **North Reef**, which lies roughly parallel to the shore. Low tide exposes much of this reef, leaving numerous shallow

**PRECEDING PAGES:** scuba-diving on Kenya's reef. **LEFT:** vast shoals of small fry swarm in the tropical waters. **BELOW:** the vibrant coral trout.

**BELOW:** a diver heads for the surface.
**RIGHT:** extravagant coral shapes on the Shimoni reef.

pools. The southern part comprises the coral gardens, which slope off on the seaward side into **Stork Passage**, some 15 metres (50 ft) deep. On the shore side, the coral is flanked by the slightly shallower **Barracuda Channel**. Fish in these gardens are marvellously colourful, perhaps the most common being the blue surgeon fish with its built-in "scalpel" at the base of the tail. This is a defence mechanism – the fish extends the very sharp spine when it feels threatened. Although it's not poisonous, the scalpel can inflict a severe wound, and the fish is generally treated with caution by fishermen emptying their nets.

Many varieties of butterfly fish occur, including the coachman with its long trailing dorsal fin. This fish is often mistaken for the similar Moorish Idol, which is also very common. Angel fish abound, their immature coloration being so different from the adult that identification is not easy for the beginner.

Holes and crevices in the coral are hiding places for the shy reef residents, including moray eels, soldier fish, barbel eels and octopus. Turtles are frequently seen and may allow the occasional lightweight snorkeller to hold on to their shells for a short but extremely exhilarating ride. Needless to say, it is an offence to collect turtles' eggs, of which many hundreds at a time are laid and buried in the sand above the high-water mark.

## Coral gardens

The **Watamu Marine National Park**, some 24 km (15 miles) south of Malindi, is the second park in the reserve waters, with the outside of the reef wall forming its eastern boundary. A channel runs inside the lagoon for the length of the bay, on the eastern edge of which are the scattered coral heads of much-visited coral gardens. Buoys mark the boundaries, so that the boats moor outside with-

out damaging the coral. The most exciting area of the Watamu Park is the **Big Three Caves**, at the entrance to Mida Creek on the southern boundary. This is named after a trio of resident giant grouper, or rock cod (*tewa* in Swahili). They are as big as a hammerhead shark and arguably just as ugly, for which reason one of them was called "Edward G".

Few people, apart from experienced divers, get to see these 200-kg (450-lb) giants. The caves are all about 4 metres (13 ft) below the level of high tide and stay covered when the tide is out. Park wardens protect the area possessively and they tend to limit the number of visitors to the caves. In fact access is not easy – only by boat and only during a very short period of slack tide which moderates a current that can run at up to 9 kph (5 knots).

There's a soft and colourful carpet of corals around and inside the caves. The fish are somewhat confused by it all and swim upside down on the roof of the caves, picking up particles of food, entirely unconcerned by the disorientating effect they have on watching divers.

Inland of the creek, the tidal flats have their own claim for attention, particularly for ornithologists. Surrounded by mangroves, this estuarine area is home to half a dozen species of heron and egret. During November to March, migrant waders such as curlews, whimbrels, sanderlings, turnstones, sandpipers and plovers appear in large numbers, many roosting at the northern end of the creek at low tide. The hotels will arrange boat trips to the creek, but it's also possible to approach on foot.

## Whale Island and Blue Lagoon

Another location for birds is **Whale Island**, particularly terns which breed there in August and September. This is just outside Mida Creek at the southern end of the park. It appears inhospitable, but in fact can be explored on foot at low tide. The rock pools are alive with crabs and other nautical small fry.

To the north of Turtle Bay is the shallow, sheltered **Blue Lagoon**, sandy bottomed and free of currents. At low tide, woolly-necked storks can often be seen foraging for food, and the cliffs at the southern end are heavily populated with multicoloured crabs, skittering over the sharp terrain.

Most of the hotels have facilities for visitors to explore the marine parks, and glass-bottomed boats are available for hire at reasonable rates. Masks and snorkels can usually be hired by those who feel restricted by the confines of a square viewing window in the bottom of the boat. For those who have their own equipment, it's often possible to persuade the local fishermen to transport passengers to the reef in their *ngalawas*. These simple dug-out craft are fashioned from a single tree trunk, but with outriggers which make them surprisingly stable.

There are also commercial operators in the Malindi-Watamu areas who will hire diving equipment – tanks, weight-belts, regulators, life-jackets and even underwater cameras – so long as divers can produce the required certificates of competence and proof of fitness. In Malindi, the **Driftwood Club**'s resident

Map on pages 280 & 288

*The black-and-white damsel fish in Watamu Marine Park are almost tame. They associate the arrival of glass-bottomed boats with a free meal and will jostle in a shoal for titbits of food.*

**BELOW:** the aptly named imperial angel fish.

*Conditions are best for snorkelling or diving at low tide. If this is in the early morning, the water surface will not be too disturbed by wind. In between tides, currents can be strong and the water tends to be murky.*

instructor takes divers to accessible sites in the Park. In Watamu, the Ocean Sports, Seafarers, Turtle Bay and Watamu Beach hotels have boats and equipment for hire, and a diving centre operated by Lorenz Riedl offers self-catering accommodation as well.

It's always worth seeking out these operators, whose local knowledge can save you valuable time in locating the prime dive sites. These are often named after their "discoverers" – "Hancock's Hole" or "Ed's Caves" – known by the local diving fraternity, but not marked on any maps.

In the far north beyond Lamu is the **Kiunga Marine National Park**. Its reefs are interspersed with 50 limestone islands which are vital nesting areas for migratory birds. This marine park provides an important shelter for rare sea turtles and dugongs.

Another turtle haven is just north of Mombasa at **Bamburi**, where a private initiative to preserve them is being supported by the Kenya Wildlife Service. The nests and eggs are protected, and when enough of the small turtles have hatched and are ready, residents, tourists and scientists join in a ceremony to release them into the sea. Results from this project show that the turtle population is stabilising for at least four species: the green, hawksbill, loggerhead and giant leatherback. The turtles favour the seagrass and coral reef areas.

## Clear waters at Kisite

About 120 km (75 miles) south of Mombasa is the town of Shimoni, "the place of the caves", where slaves were kept while awaiting shipment. The **Mpunguti Marine National Reserve** was established near this small township in 1978, as Kenya's second marine reserve. Its boundary encompasses the Inner and Outer Mpunguti Islands and the sand bar of **Kisite**. Kisite itself has been designated a national park – understandably since it's unrivalled on the Kenya coast for clarity of water. One first-time snorkeller is reported to have popped up exuberantly and exclaimed: "It's like being in a gin and tonic."

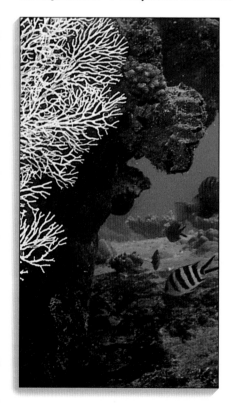

The Kisite-Mpunguti Park can be reached only by boat, and low spring tides provide the ideal conditions. The boat trip from Shimoni takes approximately 1˘ hours. Bottle-nosed dolphins can frequently be seen during the ride out, but they rarely stay close when people enter the water.

The journey is along the edge of one of the finest deep-sea fishing areas on the East African coast, the **Pemba Channel**, which drops away to a depth of more than 300 metres (1,000 ft). Not infrequently, schools of yellow-fin tuna can be seen in the area. Boats – but not equipment – can be hired from the park base near the jetty to the west of Shimoni village, or from the Shimoni Reef Lodge. This lodge arranges daily dhow trips to the reserve, calling on the way back for a leisurely and gargantuan seafood meal at their restaurant on **Wasini Island**.

Accommodation at Shimoni itself is limited. The Pemba Channel Fishing Club is small, homely and comfortable, catering for deep-sea fishing trips rather than snorkelling or diving forays into the reserve. The nearest commercial operators with diving equipment and compressors are at **Diani Beach**, some 50 km (30 miles) to the north. These may be persuaded to take large groups to Shimoni, but will not hire out their diving equipment to people who do not also utilise their boats.

## Safety first

In addition to taking basic precautions against sunburn, you should take great care when walking in rock pools and swimming. Wear stout shoes and avoid sea urchins in shallow water. The spines are mildly toxic and tend to break off in a hand or foot, resulting in discomfort for days.

You may encounter stone fish, particularly in areas of dead coral, so keep an eye open for these very poisonous masters of camouflage. Their dorsal fins inject a dose of venom into anything that touches them, and the excruciating pain that follows will cause severe symptoms of shock, even unconsciousness and sometimes death. After a sting, immerse the wound in *very* hot water and seek medical help immediately. Several other fish also have poisonous defence mechanisms and, although few are aggressive, it is best to avoid touching any of them.

Minor discomfort can be caused by stinging coral, which in Kenya is a fern-like hydroid, growing abundantly on hard corals. The pain is sharp but soon disappears. Jellyfish and other small organisms, known as standing plankton, cause blisters on the skin and if possible you should apply alcohol. This counteracts the action of the stinging cells, whereas water aggravates it. It is unwise to poke into holes or under coral rocks. Do not handle shells, particularly the cone shell, which has a poisonous barb at the sharp end.

All in all, it is safer – and more responsible – to leave the underwater world exactly as you find it, and touch nothing at all. ❑

Map on pages 280 & 288

*You can observe sea creatures without getting wet at Kenya Marine Land, by Mtwapa Creek, north of Mombasa. The huge aquariums contain sharks, turtles, barracudas, sting rays and a host of smaller fish.*

**BELOW:** a manta ray glides across the ocean floor.

# Travel Tips

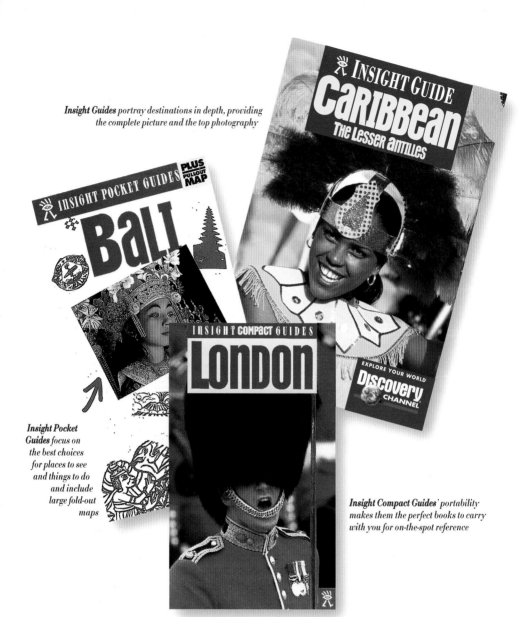

*Insight Guides portray destinations in depth, providing the complete picture and the top photography*

**Insight Pocket Guides** *focus on the best choices for places to see and things to do and include large fold-out maps*

*Insight Compact Guides' portability makes them the perfect books to carry with you for on-the-spot reference*

# Three types of guide for all types of travel

**INSIGHT GUIDES** Different people need different kinds of information. Some want *background information* to help them prepare for the trip. Others seek *personal recommendations* from someone who knows the destination well. And others look for *compactly presented data* for on-the-spot reference. With three carefully designed series, Insight Guides offer readers the perfect choice. Insight Guides will turn your visit into an experience.

**The world's largest collection of visual travel guides**

# CONTENTS

# Getting Acquainted

## The Place

**Area**: 582,644 sq km (224,959 sq miles) and 13,600 sq km (5,250 sq miles) of inland water.
**Population**: 26 million; Nairobi: 1.5 million.
**Languages**: Swahili, English, Kikuyu, Luo and many others.
**Religion**: traditional religions; 25 percent Christian; 6 percent Muslim.
**Capital**: Nairobi.
**Currency**: Kenya Shilling (Ksh), divided into 100 cents. At time of going to press, there were around 100 Kshs to £1 sterling, 60 to US$1. Money must be bought locally.
**Electricity**: 240 volts, three-pin plugs.
**Weights and measures**: metric.
**Dialling Codes**: 254 + 2 (Nairobi), + 11 (Mombasa).
**Time Zone**: 3 hours ahead of GMT. Daylight is almost a constant 12 hours with fast sunrises and sundowns at around 6.30am and 6.30pm.

## Geography

Kenya is bounded in the north by the deserts of Somalia, Ethiopia and the Sudan; to the east by Somalia and the Indian Ocean; and to the south and west by Tanzania and Uganda. Broadly, the country may be divided into four main physiographic regions:
• **Rift Valley and Central Highlands**: Fertile, mountainous, lake-studded, and the most developed region economically and in human settlement.
• **Northern and Eastern Kenya**: A vast T-shaped swath of country from west of Lake Turkana across the north to the Somalia border and to the Tanzania border in the south. This is mainly semi-arid rangeland for nomadic pastoralists and wildlife.
• **Western Kenya**: Low plateau farmland east of Lake Victoria.
• **The Coastal Belt**: 480 km (300 miles) of Indian Ocean littoral, including coral reefs and beaches and a narrow fertile strip for sub-tropical agriculture, giving way to bush and semi-desert.

• **Principal Mountains**:
Mt Kenya (Batian) – 5,199 metres (17,057 ft)
Mt Elgon (Wagagai) – 4,321 metres (14,177 ft)
Aberdares (Ol Doinyo Lesatima) – 3,999 metres (13,120 ft)
Cheranganis (Chemnirot) – 3,581 metres (11,749 ft)
Sekerr Range (Mtelo) – 3,334 metres (10,938 ft)
Mau Range (Melili) – 3,098 metres (10,164 ft)

• **Principal Waterfalls**:
Gura – 273 metres (896 ft)
Kindaruma (Seven Forks) – 135 metres (443 ft)
Nyahururu (Thomson's Falls) – 73 metres (240 ft)
Swift-Rutherford – 67 metres (220 ft)

## Kenya's Major Lakes

Victoria (Kenya section) – 3,785 sq km (1,461 sq miles)
Turkana – 6,405 sq km (2,473 sq miles)
Baringo – 130 sq km (50 sq miles)
Naivasha (minimum) – 115 sq km (44 sq miles)
Amboseli (seasonal) – 0–115 sq km (0–44 sq miles)
Magadi – 104 sq km (40 sq miles)
Jipe – 40 sq km (15 sq miles)
Bogoria (formerly Hannington) – 34 sq km (13 sq miles)
Nakuru (seasonal) – 5–30 sq km (2–11½ sq miles)
Elmenteita – 18 sq km (7 sq miles)

**Principal Rivers**:
Tana – 708 km (440 miles)
Athi-Galana-Sabaki – 547 km (340 miles)
Suam-Turkwel – 354 km (220 miles)
Arror-Kerio – 350 km (218 miles)
Ewaso Ngiro (north) – 330 km (205 miles)
Mara – 290 km (180 miles)
Nzoia – 258 km (160 miles)
Voi – 210 km (130 miles)
Ewaso Ngiro (south) – 140 km (87 miles)

## Climate

With an altitude ranging from sea level to 5,199 metres (17,057 ft), the temperature, rainfall and humidity variations in Kenya are extreme. In relation to the four main physiographic zones, the climate and land-types can be generalised as follows:

### Rift Valley and the Central Highlands

This highland region of Kenya is generally fresh and invigorating overall, rather like a Swiss summer. The climate ranges from temperate in the Central Rift Valley to arctic on the Mount Kenya peaks.

The land here is the most productive in Kenya. In the uplands, between 1,500–2,000 metres (4,900–6,600 ft), the greater part of Kenya's agricultural output is produced. In the Rift itself, production is mixed – arable, dairy and livestock.

The central massif of Mount Kenya and the high Aberdares form the country's main water catchment area, with rainfall of up to 3,000 mm (120 ins) a year on the mountains, producing run-offs to the main Rift lakes.

Statistics for Nairobi, at the centre of the region, are:
• Altitude: 1,661 metres (5,450 ft).
• Rainfall: Minimum 20 mm/0.8 ins (July); maximum 200 mm/8 ins (April); average annual 750–1,000 mm (30–40 ins), mainly in two seasons March–May and October–December.
• Sunshine: Averaging from maximum 9½ hours daily in

February to minimum 5 hours (April).
• Temperature: Minimum
10°C–14°C (50°F–58°F); maximum
22°C–26°C (72°F–79°F).

## Western Kenya

Hot, wettish, with the rain spread fairly evenly throughout the year. Most of the rain falls in early evening. The climate at Kisumu, the centre of the region, may be taken as indicative of the region:
• Altitude: 1,157 metres (3,795 ft)
• Rainfall: Minimum 60 mm/2½ ins (June); maximum 200 mm/8 ins (April); annually between 1,000 and 1,300 mm (40–50 ins).
• Sunshine: Between 7 and 9 hours daily throughout the year.
• Temperature: Minimum 14°C–18°C (57–64°F); maximum 30°C–34°C (86°F–93°F).

## Northern and Eastern Kenya

The land ranges from bleak lava desert around Lake Turkana, where west of the lake rainfall averages below 255 mm (10 ins) a year and temperatures rise to 104°F (39°C), to sand desert at the Chalbi in the north; from arid pastoralist bush, vast dryish grass and acacia rangeland, down to the baking soda lake of Magadi in the south, where again temperatures will be as high as 100°F (38°C). It is difficult to set an average climate for this vast T-section of the country, but one indicative example may be Garissa, at the eastern edge of the dry savannah belt.
• Altitude: 128 metres (420 ft).
• Rainfall: Minimum zero (July); maximum 80 mm/3 ins (November); average annual, 255–510 mm (10–20 ins).
• Sunshine: Averaging 9 hours a day over the year.
• Temperature: Mean annual minimum, 22°C (72°F); mean annual maximum 34°C (93°F).

## Coastal Belt

The coral beaches are hot with about 70 percent humidity but tempered by sea breezes. Then comes a thin plain, suitable for agriculture (fruits, nuts, dairy, cotton), but this soon gives way to thorn scrub and semi-desert. The climate of Mombasa is typical:
• Altitude: 17 metres (57 ft)
• Rainfall: Average minimum 20 mm/0.8 in (February) to 240 mm/9 ins (May); average annual 1,000–1,250 mm (40–50 ins).

• Sunshine: Average max of 9 hours a day in March, 7 hours in May.
• Temperature: Mean annual minimum 22°C (72°F); mean annual maximum 30°C (87°F).

## Economy

On its own account, Kenya is among the world's leading exporters of quality coffee, teas and pineapples. Other primary exports are horticultural produce, pyrethrum, sisal and other cash crops. Tourism is an important source of foreign exchange, with further substantial receipts from Kenya's position as the regional centre for communications, banking, insurance and general commerce.

## Kenyan Politics

President Daniel arap Moi, elected for his final term of office in 1997, holds executive power assisted by a Vice-President and Cabinet chosen from the legislature, the National Assembly. This body consists of 188 members elected by universal suffrage, 12 Presidential nominees, the Speaker and the Attorney-General. The Assembly's term is for five years unless dissolved by the President or its own majority "no confidence" vote.

The process of government in Kenya is democratic and the first multi-party elections for 25 years took place in December 1992. There are now 11 registered political parties in Kenya, although the Kenya African National Union (KANU) has held power since Independence.

The constitution guarantees certain rights, including the freedom of speech, assembly and worship, but it also allows the President to detain without trial persons who have been deemed a threat to public security.

The country's record of stability, as well as its development performance since independence in 1963, has made it among the most prosperous nations in Black Africa. It is a major recipient in Africa of international development aid.

Kenya is an independent republic, a member of the Organisation for African Unity (OAU), the United Nations and the Commonwealth.

# Planning the Trip

## Visas and Passports

All visitors must be in possession of a valid passport. Visas are required by everyone except citizens of most Commonwealth countries and certain other countries with which Kenya has reciprocal waiver arrangements. The Commonwealth exceptions are Australia, Nigeria and Sri Lanka.

Citizens of the UK of Indian, Bangladeshi or Pakistani origin also require visas, as do all arrivals from the Republic of South Africa.

At present, visas are not required from nationals of Denmark, Ethiopia, Finland, Germany, Holland, Ireland, Italy, Norway, Spain, Sweden, Turkey and Uruguay.

Since these arrangements may change, it is essential to double-check on visa requirements with airlines, tour operators or Kenya Government offices abroad well ahead of the trip. Normally it takes up to six weeks to process a visa application. Visas are usually issued for a period of three months.

Arrivals holding onward or return tickets may obtain a "Visitor's Pass" on arrival at any Kenya port of entry for a fee of US$20 or the equivalent in convertible currency. Its validity is normally for three months.

No visitor is permitted to take up work or residence in Kenya without the authority of the Principal Immigration Officer.

These are the normal entry requirements, but before you intend to travel, visitors are advised to consult Kenyan embassies or representatives abroad in case of changes in immigration regulations.

## Customs Regulations

Unused personal effects, unexposed film, cameras and accessories (except cine and slide projectors) may be temporarily imported duty-free.

Among items which must be declared, but will be admitted duty-free, are: 250 gm of tobacco, or the equivalent in cigarettes (200) or cigars (50); one litre of alcohol; and one litre of perfume.

Refundable deposits may be required for the import of radios, tape-recorders and similar equipment, musical instruments, etc. Firearms may only be imported if accompanied by a permit issued by the Central Firearms Bureau, PO Box 30263, Nairobi.

The import of agricultural or horticultural produce, or pets, is not permitted.

## Health

### *Malaria*

Malaria is endemic in Kenya below altitudes of 1,800 metres (6,000 ft), so prophylactics are essential. Take pills as prescribed two weeks before arrival, during the stay and for two weeks after departure.

Unless your intention is to stay for the duration in Nairobi, where malaria is rare, there is a risk of being bitten by a carrier mosquito outside the capital – especially at the coast or up at Lake Victoria.

### *Yellow Fever and Cholera*

Protection against yellow fever and cholera is recommended but not mandatory to enter Kenya. Consult your doctor at home for advice.

## What to Bring

Besides a **camera** and **binoculars** for viewing game, other equipment is not necessary, unless you intend to engage in some particular activity such as golf or fishing. Field guides to East African birds and mammals will enhance your enjoyment when on safari: there are some recommendations for such guides at the end of Travel Tips.

**Film** in Kenya is very expensive, so the best advice is to bring your own. Kodak, Agfa and Fuji have laboratory services, so there are no problems in having film developed on the spot should you wish to.

**Toiletries** and make-up are available locally but are mostly imported and comparatively expensive. It is best to bring your own. Also bring enough personal prescription medicines to last through your stay in Kenya.

US visitors should bring a small step-down **voltage converter**. Sockets in Kenya are 3-pin square, so adaptors for other types of sockets will be needed.

If you want to hire a vehicle, an **international driving licence** is required. Alternatively, a national licence is valid for 90 days, provided it is endorsed at the Road Transport Office, Nyayo House, Kenyatta Avenue, Nairobi.

## Kenyan Diplomatic Missions Overseas

**Australia,**
6th Floor, QBE Building, 33–35 Ainsli Avenue, Box 1990, Canberra, ACT 2601.
Also:
PO Box 1990, Canberra, ACT 2600.
Tel: (02) 647 4788,
**Canada,**
Gillin Building, Suite 600, 141 Laurier Avenue, West Ottawa, Ontario KIP 5J3.

Tel: (250) 563 1773–6.
**United Kingdom,**
45 Portland Place, London, WIN 4AS.
Tel: 0171-636 2371.
**United States,**
2249 R Street, NW, Washington DC 20008;
Tel: (202) 387 6101/4. Also:
866 United Nations Plaza, New York 10017.
Tel: (212) 421 4740.

## WHAT TO WEAR

For much of the year, Nairobi is like a European city in summer. If you are travelling on business, you'll be too hot in a jacket during the day, but can put it on for a smart dinner in the evening. Some months (June, July, August) can be overcast: cool in the daytime and chilly at night. So, if you are visiting at this time of year, you should make sure you have some warm sweaters.

If you are planning to spend most of the time **on safari**, you should bring a small, select wardrobe for all seasons – depending, of course, on where you intend to go. Light and casual for the coast and game park safaris, and not necessarily the full professional hunter rig-out; muted colours, shirts, jeans and the like will do, plus, of course, a hat for protection against the sun. For the forest lodges, dress (almost) as for evening in a European ski lodge, or at least well wrapped up.

Drip-dry clothing is recommended, and plenty of it. Soil in Kenya is red and dusty just about everywhere, so clothes get grubby quickly. Don't bother bringing rainwear, even if the safari is timed for the rainy season. If necessary, a light waterproof can be picked up locally.

Safari clothes and boots for both men and women are available throughout Nairobi, and are very reasonably priced. Tailor-made safari suits can be run up in a few days: while not to everyone's taste, they look smart, feel cool, and cost only a fraction of a regular suit, with the added bonus of being washable.

**Women** will probably find cotton dresses cooler and more comfortable than trousers, particularly for daytime. If you prefer to wear trousers, make sure they are baggy enough to allow plenty of ventilation. The local *kanga* dresses or loose blouses are available in an infinite variety of designs and are good value. The *kikoi* – local wrap-around sarong – is also useful.

For **footwear**, comfort should take precedence over style, as pavements are often uneven in the cities and towns – and non-existent, of course, in the bush. Take any specialised **sports clothes** you might want. While these are available in Nairobi and Mombasa, the range is limited and the cost high.

On the coast, shorts are just about all right for visitors in Mombasa during the day, but the rule is to keep in mind the Muslim ethic for "decency" in dress. This, incidentally, precludes nude or topless bathing on the beach – although this is sometimes practised in flagrant breach of both the law and local sensibilities.

## Public Holidays

**January 1** – New Year's Day
**March/April** – Good Friday
**March/April** – Easter Monday
**April** – Id al-Fitr (Muslim holiday to mark the end of Ramadan)
**May 1** – Labour Day
**June 1** – Madaraka Day (anniversary of self-government)
**October 10** – Moi Day (anniversary of President Moi's inauguration)
**October 20** – Kenyatta Day
**December 12** – Jamhuri (Independence Day)
**December 25** – Christmas Day
**December 26** – Boxing Day

## Getting There

### BY AIR

Kenya runs its own national airline, Kenya Airways, and there are also 35 international airlines currently providing regular air services to and from the country. In addition, there are many charter flights, particularly from Europe, full of passengers travelling on all-in package holidays.

International flights serve both Nairobi and Mombasa, from where you can fly all over the country.

**From London** Flights leave regularly from London (Heathrow) for Nairobi; some are direct, while others are with European stopovers. Passengers from Ireland must connect in London.

**Fares** APEX fares (cheaper than other fares) can be reserved one

## Kenya Airways

**In Kenya:**
Barclays Plaza, Loita Street, PO Box 41010, Nairobi.
Tel: (02) 229291/210771.
Airways Terminal, PO Box 99302, Mombasa.
Tel: (011) 221251;
PO Box 634, Malindi.
Tel: (0123) 20237.
**In the United Kingdom:**
Cirrus House, CSC Building, Bedfont Road, Staines, Middlesex TW19 7NL.
Tel: 01784 888222.
**In the United States:**
KLM Office, 437 Madison Avenue, New York, NY 10022.
Tel: 212-681 1200;
Fax: 212-681 1206.
9150 Wilshire Boulevard, Beverly Hills, Los Angeles, CA.
Tel: 310-278 0850.

month in advance, and allow stays of 19 to 90 days. The cost obviously varies according to the season, with June–September and December–January considered "high" seasons.

Note that reconfirmation of return flights is essential.

### *Airports*

Kenya has two main points of entry: Jomo Kenyatta Airport in Nairobi, and Moi International Airport in Mombasa. The capital's airport is one of the most modern in Africa. Mombasa's is not so prestigious, but big enough for the wide-bodied jets with full passenger facilities. Both airports are in the process of being upgraded: there is a new passenger terminal at Moi International.

See page 315 for more information about Nairobi airport, its facilities and so on.

### BY SEA

Long gone are the days when a leisurely cruise to Mombasa was an everyday event.

It is conceivable that a passenger berth can be found and negotiated on a cargo ship out of

London or one of the European ports, but you'll have to work hard to find a passage. Most people who arrive in Mombasa by sea are on a luxury cruise liner and stop over for just a few days. These trips usually include short safaris around the country if desired.

Short cruises are available on the *Royal Star* from Mombasa to Lamu or Zanzibar (book through African Safari Club in Mombasa, tel: 472021). It is also possible to take a dhow or catamaran from Mombasa to Zanzibar or Dar es Salaam in Tanzania.

## BY ROAD

Access by road from the north is difficult because of problems of uncertain transit through northeast Africa. But it is not impossible. A handful of companies in London seem to be the market leaders for group overland safaris to Kenya, though such trips are designed for the adventurous. Advertisements can be found in the national press.

If you are tempted to organise your own private overland expedition, thorough advance planning is necessary, and you would need to consult with the embassies of countries on the selected route. Bold travellers have done the journey solo by motorbike, but most people would be advised to travel with two or more four-wheel drive trucks, fully rigged for long desert crossings.

If you do want to attempt the road access, the required documents for entry into Kenya are:
• International Touring documents: Carnet de passage and Triptique
• International Certificate of Insurance
• International Driving Licence (visitors may use their domestic licence for up to 90 days providing that it has been endorsed at the Road Transport Office in Nairobi).

**From Tanzania and Uganda:** Overland entry into Kenya from Tanzania and Uganda is less problematic. Buses run from Dar es Salaam to Mombasa, or you can take a train to Tanga and a bus over the border. A well-used and popular route is from Arusha or Moshi to

## To Kenya By Rail

Railway access to Kenya is not really feasible – except by an unlikely roundabout route from Dar es Salaam in Tanzania, up to Mwanza on Lake Victoria, then by lake steamer operated by the Kenya Railways Authority to Kisumu, and from there down the old "Lunatic Line" to Nairobi and Mombasa. It is difficult to imagine anyone doing this trip as part of a run-of-the-mill holiday, though it might possibly appeal to anyone interested in the relics of the old imperial railways!

Nairobi, which takes about five hours by bus or minibus, with a straightforward border crossing. There are regular bus services between Nairobi and Kampala in Uganda.

Advice can be obtained by writing ahead to the Automobile Association ("AA") of Kenya, PO Box 40087, Nairobi, tel: 720382.

## Special Information

### WILDLIFE AND CONSERVATION

East Africa has a number of non-governmental organisations (NGOS) which complement official conservation efforts. They include:
**African Conservation Centre**
PO Box 62844, Nairobi.
Tel: 224569. Fax: 215969.
**African Fund for Endangered Wildlife (AFEW)**
PO Box 15124, Nairobi.
Tel: 891658.
Fax: 890973.
**African Wildlife Foundation (AWF)**,
PO Box 48177, Nairobi.
Tel: 710367–71.
**David Sheldrick Memorial Appeal**
PO Box 15555, Nairobi.
Tel: 890053.
**East African Wildlife Society**
PO Box 20110, Nairobi.
Tel: 574145.
Fax: 570335.
Email: eawls@elci.sasa.unon.org.
**Elsa Wild Animal Appeal**
PO Box 30092, Nairobi.
Tel: 742121.

**Friends of Conservation**
PO Box 59749, Nairobi.
Tel: 339537/334868.
**Kenya Wildlife Services**
PO Box 40241, Nairobi.
Tel: 501081/ 506671.
Fax: 505866.
**Gallmann Memorial Foundation**
PO Box 45593, Nairobi.
Tel: 520048.
**Wildlife Clubs of Kenya**,
PO Box 40658, Nairobi.
Tel: 891903/4.
**Worldwide Fund for Nature (WWF)**,
PO Box 62440, Nairobi.
Tel: 229945/230012.

## INTERNATIONAL ORGANISATIONS

Most of the **United Nations Organisations** represented in Kenya are located in the UN complex at Gigiri, about 11 km (7 miles) from the centre of the city close to the suburb of Muthaiga. Some addresses are given below:
**Food and Agriculture Organisation of the United Nations (FAO)**
Utumishi Co-operative House, Mamlaka Road, PO Box 30470, Nairobi. Tel: 725128/725069.
**Organisation for African Unity (OAU)**
5th and 6th floor, Mandeleo House, Monrovia Street. Tel: 338544.
**United Nations Children's Fund (UNICEF)**
Gigiri. Tel: 520671/3.
**United Nations Development Programme (UNDP)**
KICC Building, Harambee Avenue, PO Box 30218, Nairobi.
Tel: 228776–8.
**United Nations Educational, Scientific and Cultural Organisation (UNESCO)**
Tel: 621234. Fax: 215991.
**United Nations High Commission for Refugees (UNHCR)**
Chiromo Road, Westlands, PO Box 43801, Nairobi.
Tel: 443028–34.
**World Bank and Affiliates (IBRD)**
View Park Towers, Monrovia Street, PO Box 30577, Nairobi.
Tel: 714140.
**World Health Organisation (WHO)**
6th Floor, Afya House (Ministry of Health), Cathedral Rd (off Ngong Road), Nairobi. Tel: 720050.

## ROTARY CLUBS

### Mombasa

**Eldoret,**
PO Box 220, Eldoret.
Tel: (Sec) (0321) 2936.
**Kilindini,**
PO Box 99067, Mombasa.
Tel: (Sec) (01) 25157.
**Mombasa,**
PO Box 90570, Mombasa.
Tel: (Sec) (01) 25924.

### Nairobi

**Host:** tel: (Sec) 742269;
**North:** c/o PO Box 30751, Nairobi.
Tel: 21624.
**South:** c/o PO Box 46611, Nairobi.
Tel: (Sec) 337041.

## OTHER CLUBS

### Nairobi

**African Cultural Society**
PO Box 69484, Nairobi.
Tel: 335581. (Cultural Festivals
Lectures and Theatre.)
**American Women's Association**
PO Box 47806. Nairobi.
Tel: (membership chairman) 65342.
**The Caledonian Society of Kenya**
PO Box 40755, Nairobi.
Tel: (Sec) 520400 (evenings).
**Geological Club of Kenya**
PO Box 44749, Nairobi.
**Geographical Society of Kenya**
PO Box 41887, Nairobi.
**Nairobi Branch of the Royal
Society of St George**
PO Box 48360, Nairobi.
Tel: 891262.
**Nairobi Photographic Society**
PO Box 49879, Nairobi.
Tel: 337129.

## Tourist Information

For tourist information about
Kenya before you leave home,
contact the following addresses:
**United Kingdom,** 25 Brooks
Mews, London W1Y 1LF. Tel:
0171-355 3144.
**United States,** 424 Madison
Avenue, New York, NY 10017.
Tel: (212) 486 1300; 111
Doheny Plaza, 9100 Wilshire
Boulevard, Beverly Hills, CA
90121. Tel: (213) 274 6635.

# Practical Tips

## Business Hours

Working hours in Kenya are
something of a movable feast:
shops and so on open any time
from 8am to 5.30pm, with some
general stores or Indian shops
(*dukas*) staying open well into the
evening and also most of the
weekend. In Mombasa, shops and
businesses may open as early as
7am, shutting for a long siesta any
time from 12.30 to 4pm, and then
opening up again until after dark.
(Buying in the retail trade has a
touch of the Persian market about
it, with haggling possible in Nairobi
and mandatory in Mombasa.)

Normal banking hours are 9am
to 3pm, Monday to Friday. Some
banks open 9–11am on the first
and last Saturday of each month.
Banks at Nairobi's international
airport run a 24-hour service.

## Money Matters

Exchange rates are best at banks
and exchange bureaux. Avoid
changing currency at hotels unless
you're desperate. However, most
hotels, lodges and tented camps –
even out in the bush – can change
currency, though they may limit the
amount you can change. Of course
it is a bad idea to carry around a lot
of cash, so plan accordingly.

All major credit cards are widely
accepted, and most credit card
companies have offices or agents
in Nairobi and Mombasa.

Currency restrictions for visitors
have been abolished, so there are
no tedious currency declaration
forms to fill out. But do not take a
large amount of Kenya Shillings out
of the country, since you will have
trouble exchanging them abroad.

## Tipping

As far as tipping is concerned, the
rules that you probably use at home
should apply in Kenya. For instance,
add 10 percent to a restaurant bill
unless a service charge is included.

The biggest tip will probably go to
your tour driver if he or she has been
helpful and responsive on the trip.
As much as £3/US$5 per person
per day is expected on safari.

## Media

### Radio and Television

There is one English-speaking radio
station and one television station
operated by the government. There
are also two privately-owned
television stations, Kenya Television
Network and Stellavision, which
offer a good variety of programmes,
including CNN and BBC.

There are a number of private FM
radio stations, including Capital FM,
and the BBC.

### Newspapers

There are three English-language
daily newspapers: the *Standard*, the
*Nation* and the *Kenya Times*. There
is one weekly newspaper, the *East
African Chronicle*, which contains
news from all around East Africa.
Foreign newspapers and magazines
can be picked up easily in Nairobi.

## Telephone and Telex

Kenya has developed an excellent
communications system for both
domestic and international
services. Direct dialling is available
between most centres in the
country, and a full international STD
system has been introduced.

There are also internal and
external telex facilities, providing
direct dialling to most major
capitals and many nations on a 24-
hour basis. This service operates
through the Mount Longonot earth
satellite station.

## Postal Services

There is a post office in most major
shopping centres in Nairobi, and

the system is efficient. Mail can also be sent from major hotels. International and local speed post and parcel services are offered by several independent operators.

**Poste Restante** is free; the main pick-up point is the Central Post Office, Haile Selassie Avenue, Nairobi.

**Telegrams** can be sent by phone; call the operator (900) and ask for assistance.

## Tourist Information

There are two official bureaus for tourist information: one in front of the Hilton in Nairobi centre; the other close to the street-spanning tusks on Moi Avenue in Mombasa.

Most private tour companies scattered around the urban centres are fairly liberal with information and there are plenty of publications available – in the form of maps, guides of varying quality, brochures, pamphlets and a *What's On* magazine. The newspapers also provide information on any available "special offer" tour packages or cut-rate accommodation.

## Security and Crime

Kenya is usually considered among the safest countries in Africa, though recently there have been an unprecedented number of attacks on visitors, including hijackings and armed robbery.

Crime is not insignificant in the towns, and tourists should take care, especially in Nairobi and when arriving in the country. The common-sense rules are to keep out of dark back-streets at night, wherever you are, and to avoid Nairobi's sleazier bars and dance dives.

Some of the African dance halls are the liveliest places in town, and there is no reason why the visitor can't partake of the sweaty, exotic experience. But go in a group, if possible, and leave the "professional ladies" alone (*see page 314*).

Don't carry too much money or valuables around, and avoid wearing

## Looking for a Ride?

A message-board in the New Stanley's **Thorn Tree Cafe** in Nairobi offers lifts or shared-cost safaris for youngsters and others on tight budgets.

expensive jewellery, whether you are walking in town or on the beach.

Rape and sexual assault are uncommon in a society which has fairly liberal access to sex. Should you be accosted, it's more likely that the villain is after your property than your body.

Problem areas of violent crime are deserted beaches and drunken, mixed-company parties. Probably the commonest urban crime in Kenya is car theft, followed by house-breaking. For tourists, expert pickpockets and confidence tricksters are the most common problem. Elaborate and convincing stories involving money can catch out even the most experienced traveller.

In any threatening situation, the rule is don't panic or make any sudden moves in attack or retreat. Keep quiet and do what you're told

(within reason) – basically, apply common sense.

### *Tourist Police*

The rise in crime against visitors has led to the establishment of a Tourist Police Force. This force is doing a good job, especially at the coast, but bag-snatching and muggings do happen, and there's a rather savage deterrent for it. Someone shouts "thief" and suddenly it's a Roman holiday, with the mob giving chase and meting out summary justice when they catch up. Shout for help only if you really think the situation warrants the severe beating the accused will receive.

### *Problem Areas*

Up-country, theft from the Somali *shifta* gangs is a problem and thus tourists have been warned to stay out of the northeast area. Gangs have also attacked in Maasai country, but there has usually been some serious provocation.

Recently, there have been a spate of incidents on the Mombasa to Lamu road, with *shifta* gangs holding up the buses. Armed convoy buses now sometimes accompany

## Embassies and Consulates in Kenya

**Australia**
Riverside Drive,
PO Box 39341, Nairobi.
Tel: 445034–39.
**Austria**
City House, Wabera Street,
PO Box 30560, Nairobi.
Tel: 228281–2.
**Canada**
Comcraft House,
Haile Selassie Avenue,
PO Box 30481, Nairobi.
Tel: 214804.
**France**
Embassy House,
PO Box 41784, Nairobi.
Tel: 339783–4.
**Germany**
Wiliamson House,
4th Ngong Avenue,
PO Box 30180, Nairobi.
Tel: 712527–30.

**India**
Jeevan Bharati Building,
Harambee Avenue,
PO Box 30074, Nairobi.
Tel: 225104/225180
**Italy**
Prudential Building,
PO Box 30107, Nairobi
Tel: 337356–7
**Ireland**
Maendeleo House,
Monrovia Street,
PO Box 30659, Nairobi.
Tel: 226771–4.
**United Kingdom**
Upper Hill Road,
PO Box 30465, Nairobi.
Tel: 719082/719107.
**United States of America**
Haile Selassie Avenue,
PO Box 30137, Nairobi.
Tel: 334141–50.

the regular services as a pre-caution. Travelling by road to Lamu independently is not recommended.

In general, the vast bush areas in Kenya amount to one great camp site and are entirely safe providing people stick to the fundamental safety rules.

## DRUGS

Kenya's soft smoke is called *bhang* locally. Like most plants in Kenya, it grows wild and abundantly. Needless to say, smoking or dealing in pot is against the law, and don't even think about exporting it: Customs officers are wise to all the tricks.

Hard drugs are virtually ignored by the youngsters in Kenya, and the only stuff in common use is a mild narcotic called *miraa*. It is grown extensively in the wet hills above Meru and Embu and small sticks are chewed for mild stimulation, mostly by the northern nomads; it is supposed to keep them awake through the long night looking after the camels.

## Medical Treatment

### Medical Services
Overall, medical services are better in Kenya than in most other African countries. There are several first-rate hospitals in Nairobi and on the coast, with a surprising number of specialist physicians and surgeons, as well as some fine dentists and opticians.

For **emergency services**, including ambulance, dial 999. In Mombasa there is a Police Hotline, tel: 222121/222811.

### Medical Insurance
Medical insurance can be bought locally at reasonable cost from indigenous and locally based multinational insurance firms.

Another option (which would also be a supportive gesture) is to buy inexpensive insurance from the famous **Flying Doctor Service** in Kenya. In the event of serious illness or accident on safari, a doctor will fly out from the service's headquarters at Wilson Airport and either treat the casualties on the

spot or fly them to a hospital back in Nairobi.

**Africa Air Rescue** sells visitors insurance packages that include the use of their service's health facilities throughout the country, including medical evacuation in conjunction with International SOS Assistance, mobile casualty units and air evacuation within Kenya. For information contact Africa Air Rescue at PO Box 41766, Nairobi. Tel: 715319. Fax: 715328. Email: aar@ken.healthnet.org.

### Pharmacies
There is no shortage of chemists or pharmacies in Kenya, and all of them are staffed by qualified pharmacists.

Most drugs are available, although sometimes you may encounter unfamiliar brand names. If your specific prescription is not available, the pharmacist will often be able to prescribe a suitable alternative without the need of a visit to the doctor. Advice and treatment for minor ailments is always generously available.

Most chemists close on Saturday afternoons, Sundays and public holidays. When closed, the name and location of the duty chemist is usually posted on the shop door, or may be obtained at the nearest

## Hospitals in Kenya

**The Aga Khan Hospital**
3rd Parklands Avenue,
PO Box 30270, Nairobi.
Tel: 740000.
**Nairobi Hospital**
Argwings Kodhek Road, PO Box 30026, Nairobi. Tel: 722160.
**Gertrude's Garden Children's Hospital**
Muthaiga Road, PO Box 42325, Nairobi. Tel: 763474/763475.
**Mater Misericordiae Hospital**
Dunga Road, South B,
PO Box 30325, Nairobi.
Tel: 556666/556298.
**M. P. Shah Hospital**
Shivachi Road, Parklands,
PO Box 14497, Nairobi.
Tel: 742763; fax 746177.

**Coast General Hospital**
PO Box 90231, Mombasa.
Tel: (01) 314201.
**Mombasa Hospital Association**
PO Box 90294, Mombasa.
Tel: (01) 312191/312099.
**Galana Hospital**
Lamu Road, Malindi.
Tel: (0123) 20837/30575.
**Consolata Hospital**
PO Box 25, Nyeri.
Tel: (0171) 31011/21010.
**Nakuru War Memorial Hospital**
Tel: (037) 211990.
**Nanyuki Cottage Hospital**
Tel: (0176) 32666.
**Uasin Gishu Memorial Hospital,**
Eldoret. Tel: (0321) 22691/61511.

## Religious Services

Cathedrals, churches of many denominations, synagogues, chapels, mosques and temples are located all over the country – in rural villages as well as in larger towns and cities. Locations and times of services etc, are published in the national newspapers.

hospital. Weekend chemist opening times are advertised in the local newspapers.

## Health Hazards

### The Equatorial Sun
Tourists often feel that the sun in Kenya is no stronger than, say, on the west coast of America or on the European continent in the summer. But, being directly overhead in Kenya, the sun is unexpectedly powerful and pale skins must be exposed very gradually.

On the coast, the drill is to start your sun-bathing in the early morning and late afternoon, extending the exposure time each day as your skin begins to tan. Protection for your eyes, head, the nape of the neck and back (when snorkelling) are strongly recommended. Also, insist that children swim in T-shirts for peace of mind and peaceful nights.

## HIV and Aids

HIV infection is rife in Kenya, amongst both the homosexual and heterosexual population. Some figures estimate that as many as 1 in 4 people is infected, but this has not been confirmed by official figures, partly for fear of upsetting Kenya's vital tourist trade. If you have a pre-existing illness which may require hospital treatment, think twice before going to Kenya because blood supplies in smaller hospitals may be infected. Larger private hospitals are much more likely to have reliable blood supplies. You are advised to take a first aid kit which includes syringes and so on, available from any good chemist's or outdoor shop.

As HIV infection is common in the general population, you should avoid having sex not only with prostitutes, but also with anyone whose sexual history you do not know.

### Tap Water
In Nairobi, the water is drinkable, but the chances are that new arrivals are going to get diarrhoea anyway – from the change of diet as well as the water. Anywhere outside the city, the water should be boiled unless it has been drawn from ice-cold mountain streams. Bottled mineral water is widely available.

### Altitude Sickness
It generally takes a couple of days to acclimatise to high altitude locations such as Nairobi. The relatively thin oxygen can cause new arrivals to feel tired around the middle of the day, or at least experience a certain light-headedness. On the higher reaches of Mount Kenya, above 4,000 metres (13,000 ft), there is a risk of pulmonary oedema, a capricious

suffusion of the lungs which might bring down an athlete and yet leave an habitual smoker to go on blithely to the summit. The only antidote is a swift retreat back down the mountain; otherwise the consequences can be fatal.

## Etiquette

Visitors should show respect to the local people by exercising tact, tolerance, and common sense. A few "don'ts" might be helpful:

**Don't** show disrespect for authority, starting with the president. Don't try to take his picture – or that of any of Kenya's other leaders, and don't tear up his portrait on a banknote. Visitors have sometimes destroyed the last of their Kenyan cash at the airport before their departure – and have got into trouble for doing so.

**Don't** photograph anyone without their consent, not even the tribesmen way out in the bush. A smile, waving your camera around and the offer of a few shillings is normally enough to get consent. These days, the Maasai are wise to the habits of tourists, and they may ask for up to $10 for a photo of their handsome profile. In reality, the going rate for one photograph is 10 to 50 shillings.

**Don't** make a show of your wealth anywhere. The obvious temptation is to relieve you of some of it in one way or another.

**Don't** break the law, of course. For tourists, the main hazards are the Exchange Control Act (illegal deals with money), the traffic regulations, and the ordinances against prostitution, sexual offences and drug taking.

The law is in fact fairly benign in Kenya, especially in its application to tourists. Where there is a problem, it is dealt with through the due process of law modelled on the British system: there is no arrest without a warrant; no holding without a charge; no detention without trial.

When a visitor is in trouble, he or she is usually handed over to the care of his or her embassy; then, in an exceptional case, he or she may

be escorted to the airport and requested not to return. Very few are actually jailed, unless they are charged with murder or mayhem. For criminal and some civil offences, there would probably be an appearance in court, a fine and an order to depart the country.

## Photography

Don't forget always to ask permission before attempting to photograph people.

In addition to your usual preferred film, you may want to consider taking out faster films – up to 1000 ASA – for those tricky lighting conditions where you cannot use flash, e.g. artificially lit water-holes. Lenses for 35mm cameras should include telephoto and/or zoom up to 300mm. Keep films in a cool box when it's very hot.

The best light for photography is in the early morning and late afternoon. Midday vertical shadows tend to have disastrous effects.

Finally, a "foolproof" compact camera is a useful backup. After all, there are times when you will miss a good shot if you're not quick.

## Forms of Address

The masses in Kenya are known as the *wananchi* – the "people" – and the word carries a connotation of respect. Do not use "blacks" or "coloureds"; the terms are "Africans" or "Asians".

In addressing an old man – anyone over 35 – call him *mzee* pronounced "mu-zay". It is a term of respect, meaning "old man" or "elder" and you can use it in shops, restaurants, anywhere. Call a mature woman (over 21) *mama* and a child *toto*. A word you will hear constantly is *wazungu,* meaning "white people" (*mzungu* in the singular).

A waiter is addressed as "steward" or maybe *bwana,* which means "mister".

# Getting Around

## By Air

Kenya Airways, the only national airline, runs scheduled services from Nairobi to Mombasa, Malindi and Kisumu.

In addition, private air charter companies based at Wilson Airport, just outside the capital, operate regular, scheduled services in five- to ten-seater light aircraft to destinations like Lamu and the Maasai Mara. Half a dozen companies at Wilson charter aircraft, from small monoplanes to Learjets. Some of them have branch operations in Mombasa and Malindi, where there are also coast-based air charter companies.

Another possibility for qualified pilots is to rent a plane at the Wilson-based Aero Club of East Africa.

For information on charter flights, try contacting one of the following:
**Airkenya Aviation Ltd**, PO Box 30357, Nairobi. Tel: 602951/ 501601.
**Boskovic Air Charters Ltd**, PO Box 45646, Nairobi. Tel: 501210/9.
**Eagle Aviation Ltd**, PO Box 32553, Nairobi. Tel: 822924/505015.

### Nairobi Airport
Nairobi airport offers all the usual services, including 24-hour currency exchange, a post office, shops, restaurants, coffee stations, duty-free shop and bars. A porter service is available both inside and outside the customs area. Tip about Kshs 20 per bag.

For visitors without health certificates, a vaccination service is available in the arrivals building.

The Kenya Airways bus service no longer runs, so you now have to take a cab. Taxis cost at least Kshs 1,000 to the centre of town, and are of course cheaper if shared.

### On departure
Your air ticket now includes a departure tax of US$20 cash per person, so there is no need to pay this separately at the airport. On domestic flights, Kshs 50 must be paid before boarding.

## By Rail

Train travel is exceptionally good value, and comfortable in both first and second class.

The overnight trip between Mombasa and Nairobi takes about 12 hours, with two- or four-bunk sleeping compartments and a fully serviced bar and restaurant car. The service extends up-country from Nairobi to Kisumu and Lake Victoria, where Kenya Railways run a lake steamer service to Mwanza and other Tanzanian ports.

## By Bus

Buses are the cheapest form of travel in Kenya, with a nationwide network wherever there are reasonable roads. The long-haul buses out of Nairobi and Mombasa are by no means excluded to visitors, but they are definitely rough and ready.

It may be difficult for visitors to find their way about the urban routes on the local buses, and be warned that urban buses also tend to be jam-packed during the rush hours: 7–9am and 4.30–6.30pm.

## Taxis

The only properly organised taxi service is a fleet of Mercedes, operated by the state Kenatco Transport Company from the international airports and main urban hotels. You can take the driver's word (usually) for the set per-kilometre rate.

Other than this, taxis are something of a free-for-all in Kenya. All are marked with yellow stripes but otherwise they are a decidedly

## Caution!

If you travel by public transport, never accept any food or drink from fellow-passengers, however generous the offer may seem. It has been known for thieves to lace the "gift" with drugs, causing the unsuspecting recipient to fall asleep, and allowing the thief to make off with his or her possessions.

motley collection of vehicles, in various stages of dilapidation, and none with meters. The fares are always negotiable, which presumes foreknowledge of reasonable rates. At the airport, ask advice at one of the hotel or tour operator booths and, in town, from your hotel porter or the Tourist Information Bureau.

## Other Vehicles

*Matatus* are private vehicles that offer a cheap service around the urban centres and between towns. They are crowded, sometimes dangerous, and generally not recommended to visitors.

A long-distance Peugeot taxi service is a better prospect to take you out of Nairobi to towns in the Rift Valley and elsewhere. A number of luxury coaches, also privately operated, run between Nairobi and Mombasa. One enterprising local runs a 4- or 5-day safari aboard his "Turkana Bus" to the northern desert and the lake.

## Driving

It is perfectly possible for even first-time visitors, who do not want to be "packaged" by a tour firm, to simply hire a car and set off for a safari or to the coast. There is nothing particularly hazardous about driving around Kenya. Even so, try not to be too ambitious about the distances you want to travel in a day; pre-book your accommodation; and make sure you have sufficient maps, tools, food and water (for yourself and the car). Be sure also to fill your tank with petrol whenever you have the opportunity, since petrol stations are few and far between in some areas.

This isn't standard advice, however. Most locals will probably warn newcomers instead about the poor state of Kenya's bush roads, the kamikaze drivers, the chances of getting lost and so on. But you should not take such advice too seriously. Sensible drivers should be able to find their way around the country's main tourist circuits – Amboseli, Tsavo and so on – without too many problems. If you plan to do the 483-km (300-mile) drive from Nairobi to Mombasa, note that the road is in a bad state of repair, with disintegrating tarmac, huge holes and temporary bridges. Allow plenty of time and be prepared to drive slowly.

Driving in the more remote areas, such as north to Turkana, is a different story. On these out-of-the-way safaris, you need a four-wheel drive vehicle and many more supplies, equipment and local experience, plus someone else driving in convoy.

### Car Hire

Hertz, Avis and National operate in Nairobi and Mombasa, together with numerous other local entrepreneurs offering everything from Range Rovers to small saloons. In many cases, you will have the choice between the chauffeur-driven or self-drive option.

## Timing Your Safari

Tourists visit Kenya all year round, but during the "long rains" (end of Mar to mid-Jun) and the "short rains" (end of Oct to early Dec) safari travel is restricted due to the soggy state of the roads. On the other hand, these are low seasons for hotel and lodge operators, and many offer correspondingly low rates.

The high seasons, when coast and safari accommodation may be difficult without pre-booking, are Dec–Mar and the school holiday period from Jul–Sept.

At the coast, vehicles for hire include breezy Mini-mokes, which are ideal for running up and down the beach strip.

## Travel Packages

Tour operators who charter blocks of seats on scheduled flights (thus greatly reducing the per-head ticket price) usually offer an all-in holiday "package". The packages include a stay on the coast, or safaris, or a combination of both – with the price varying according to, for example, length of stay, distances covered, type and style of accommodation and transport, etc. The big expenses – flights, internal travel, food and accommodation – are included in the tour cost, leaving

the traveller to pay just for beer, tips, shopping and so on.

"Packaged" safaris are often organised for groups with special interests, such as zoologists, ornithologists, historians, anthropologists or geologists.

At the top end of the package tour market are tour operators offering deluxe, hand-tailored safaris for individuals or small groups. These can cost up to $1,000 a day, but you will be marvellously pampered, with private safari vehicles and light aircraft for transport, fully serviced camps or lodge accommodation, superb food, a retinue of staff, and the freedom to go when and wherever you decide.

These operators are generally not into mass-marketing their safaris; to find out about them, you should ask the larger Africa tour retailers or the overseas tourist offices of the Kenya Government.

At the other end of the price scale, the large mass-market tour operators sell reasonably-priced packages to Kenya, which take in beach hotels and safari trips into the more popular parks.

## Local Safaris

There are literally scores of tour operators in Nairobi, and more in Mombasa, offering minibus safaris on various permutations of itineraries round the country. The

## Mini-Safaris from Nairobi

Most of Kenya's tour operators run a system of regular minibus safaris in and around Nairobi. In this case, you simply buy seats on these set departures, joining up with whoever else goes along. Samples of "Safaritrail" tours are as follows:

**Nairobi City Tour:** Two hours' orientation – main shopping area; principal buildings; the Railways and National Museums, and Snake Park.

**Bomas of Kenya:** Traditional dancing, building styles and

artifacts at the cultural complex 14 km (9 miles) from the centre.

**Nairobi National Park:** Just 13 km (8 miles) out of the city, but authentic Africa on the doorstep of Nairobi. Resident wildlife includes lions, cheetahs, rhinos and hippos, with various antelope species migrating in and out from the open Kitengela-Athi plains to the south.

**Orphan Elephants:** A half-hour drive from the city to Daphne Sheldrick's home, at the edge of the Nairobi National Park, where the orphan animals are cared for.

**The Giraffe Centre:** About 20 minutes' drive from the centre of Nairobi in the suburb of Langata. An education centre for children and also a sanctuary for the endangered Rothschild's Giraffe. Feeding the giraffes is one of the main attractions here.

**Karen Blixen Museum:** the former home of Karen Blixen has some items from the film Out of Africa.

**White Water Adventures:** for the more adventurous: 90 minutes' drive from Nairobi to the Tana River for a day of fun and daring!

tour cost normally includes full board at lodges or tented camps in the parks and reserves. The duration of the tours can be anything from two to 14 days.

## SAMPLE SAFARI TOURS
### 2-Day Tours
• **The Forest Lodges:** Around 161 km (100 miles) north of Nairobi on the slopes of the Aberdares Range and Mount Kenya. These are Treetops, The Ark and Mountain Lodge, all offering a nightly parade of wildlife at floodlit water-holes and salt-licks. A typical tour is: Nairobi to the Outspan Hotel, Nyeri, for lunch, on to Treetops for the night, back to the Outspan for breakfast, then return to the capital – about 24 hours in all.
• **Amboseli:** A 500-km (310-mile) round trip with an overnight stay at one of the five lodges and camps in the park.
• **Maasai Mara Game Reserve:** Hemingway's "Green Hills of Africa" and the most spectacular of Kenya's game areas – especially in the season of the migration of the wildebeest and other plains animals out of the contiguous Serengeti. "The Mara" is 275 km (170 miles) from Nairobi, so you would be hard pushed to visit on a weekend road safari. A more comfortable alternative is to travel by light aircraft. A possible schedule would be: morning flight from Wilson Airport to a lodge or luxury tented camp in the Mara; game drives in four-wheel-drive safari vehicles; overnight in the camp or lodge; return to Nairobi after lunch on the second day.

### Longer Safaris
These can be pre-booked with travel or tour operators in the States or Europe, or alternatively booked after arrival in Kenya. Basically, you decide where you want to go, then shop around for preferred itinerary, duration of the tour and price. Decide also on what you can afford so as to determine how you will go on your safari – minibus, light aircraft or combined air and road.
The following are Kenya's

principal tourist destinations:
• **North of Nairobi:** The forest lodges on Mount Kenya and the Aberdares; Mount Kenya Safari Club; Samburu and Shaba National Reserves; Marsabit, Maralal and Meru National Parks. The Rift Valley Lakes – Naivasha, Nakuru, Bogoria, Baringo and Turkana – are also spectacular.
• **West of Nairobi:** The Maasai Mara Game Reserve, Lake Victoria.
• **Southwards** (south, southwest and southeast): Amboseli and Tsavo National Parks; the Taita Hills Game Sanctuary and on to the coast.
• **Principal Beach Attractions** (from south to north): The Pemba Channel/Shimoni for deep-sea fishing; Diani (superb 19-km/ 12-mile, palm-fringed beach); Mombasa Island (cosmopolitan town and fine beach at Nyali); Bamburi, Shanzu and Kikambala beaches immediately north of Mombasa; Kilifi Creek, Watamu and Malindi (good facilities for fishing); and the fascinating ancient Arab town of Lamu well to the north.

## SAFARI NOTES
Caution and common sense must be exercised in both national parks and reserves. The Ministry of Tourism and Wildlife has compiled some rules and regulations and these are for the protection of the animals as well as the people. Many tourists from time to time forget that a reserve or park is not an open zoo with invisible bars. The rule is to stay in the car and if animals approach, close roofs, doors and windows.
• Touring the parks and reserves is restricted to daylight hours – from 6am to 6pm. Before dusk, when the light turns a golden orange, is the time the carnivores begin their hunt for dinner and the nocturnal animals come out of hiding. The best time for game viewing is in the early morning or late afternoon.
• Driving speeds in the parks and reserves are limited to 48 kph (30 mph), but driving slower is better as you'll be able to see more.
• Rangers are available as guides on game runs, and it's often a good

idea to employ one since they know the area and the animals like the back of their hands.

## Tour Operators

Further information about safaris throughout Kenya can be found at the following specialist tour companies:
**Abercrombie & Kent Ltd,** PO Box 59749, Nairobi. Tel: 334955. Fax: 215752. Email: akkenya@attmail.com.
**Africa Expeditions Ltd,** PO Box 24598, Nairobi. Tel & Fax: 561457/561054.
**Archers Tours & Travel Ltd,** PO Box 40097, Nairobi. Tel: 223131/331825. Fax: 212656/227758.
**Bunson Travel Service Ltd,** PO Box 45456, Nairobi. Tel: 221992–4. Email: bunson@form-net.com.
**Express Travel Group,** PO Box 40433, Nairobi. Tel: 334722–7. Fax: 334825. Email: expressk@africaonline.co.ke. Web: http://www.etg-safaris.com.
**Ker & Downey Safaris Ltd,** PO Box 41822, Nairobi. Tel: 553222/556466. Fax: 552378.
**Let's Go Travel Ltd,** PO Box 60342, Nairobi. Tel: 340331. Fax: 336890. Email: info@letsgosafari.com Web: http://www.kenya-direct.com/letsgo.
**United Touring Company,** PO Box 42196, Nairobi. Tel: 331960. Fax: 216871. Email: utcn@attmail.com.

# Where to Stay

## Choosing a hotel

Hotels and lodges are officially graded in Kenya, each being given a classification from E to A and a star rating from 1 to 5. Anyone after a reasonable to high level of comfort should choose from Classes A, B and C. If cheapness is of top priority, as well as D and E establishments, there are unclassified places where you can get a bed (and bugs) for just a few shillings.

Generally, you can expect to pay upper-middle level European or American prices for the 5-star accommodation in Kenya, and a little less for the best of the beach hotels and lodges.

## Hotel Listings

The hotels below (in Classes A, B and C only), are listed in alphabetical order by region, with separate listings for game lodges and tented camps. Many of the places listed are described in more detail in the relevant section of the main guide.

### NAIROBI

**5-star (Class A)**

**The Grand Regency**
PO Box 40511, Nairobi.
Tel: 211199. Fax: 217120.
In the city centre, with lots of brass and a formal atmosphere.

**Hilton International Hotel**
PO Box 30364, Nairobi.
Tel: 334000. Fax: 339462.
In the centre. All you would expect from this multinational chain. Used mostly by businessmen.

**Hotel Inter-Continental**
PO Box 30353, Nairobi.
Tel: 335550. Fax: 210675.

Email: nairobi@interconti.com
Within the central city grid. A businessman's hotel along the lines of the Hilton.

**Nairobi Safari Club**
PO Box 43564, Nairobi.
Tel: 251333. Fax: 224625.
Up-market, suites-only hotel in the centre of town.

**Nairobi Serena Hotel**
PO Box 48690, Nairobi.
Tel: 710511/711077.
Fax: 718103.
Email: serenacr@africaonline.co.ke
Stylish enterprise of the Aga Khan; set in a park on the edge of the city grid. Excellent food and service.

**Norfolk Hotel**
PO Box 40064, Nairobi.
Tel: 335422/33. Fax: 336742.
Email: norffoh@nbnet.co.ke
Historic favourite of visitors; fully modernised and just a short walk to the city centre.

**Safari Park Hotel & Casino**
PO Box 45038, Nairobi.
Tel: 802493–6. Fax: 802477.
Email: safariht@arcc.or.ke
Out of town on the Thika Road. Large, very well-appointed hotel with all the facilities.

**Windsor Golf & Country Club**
PO Box 45887, Nairobi.
Tel: 862300. Fax: 802322. Email: windsor@users.africaonline.co.ke.
Fifteen minutes' drive from the centre of Nairobi. Very attractive hotel with the main feature being the 18-hole championship golf course.

**4-star (Class B)**

**Holiday Inn Mayfair Court Hotel,**
PO Box 74957, Nairobi
Tel: 748288/748290.
Fax: 748823.
Newly refurbished hotel in the suburb of Westlands.

**New Stanley Hotel**
PO Box 30680, Nairobi.
Tel: 333248–51. Fax: 229388
In the city centre; its pavement café is Nairobi's safari epicentre.

**Panafric Hotel**
PO Box 30486, Nairobi
Tel: 720822–8. Fax: 726356
On a hill overlooking the centre of the city. Provides full amenities and services.

**3-star (Class C)**

**Boulevard Hotel**
PO Box 42831, Nairobi
Tel: 227567–9. Fax: 334071.
A small garden hotel just beyond the 5-star Norfolk Hotel; excellent value for money.

**Fairview Hotel**
PO Box 40842, Nairobi
Tel: 723211. Fax: 721320.
A long-established hotel set among pleasant lawns; suitable for families.

**Hotel Ambassadeur**
PO Box 30399, Nairobi.
Tel: 336803–9. Fax: 211472.
Close to the Hilton. Has a good Indian restaurant, the Safeer.

**Jacaranda Hotel**
PO Box 14287, Nairobi.
Tel: 448713–7. Fax: 448977.
Family-style hotel in the suburb of Westlands. Now run by a major local hotel chain.

**Six-Eighty Hotel**
PO Box 43436, Nairobi.
Tel: 332680. Fax: 332908.
Modern town hotel that is reasonably priced.

### MOMBASA TOWN

**Polana Hotel**
PO Box 41983, Mombasa.
Tel: 222168/229171.
Fax: 314506.

**Royal Court Hotel**
PO Box 41247, Mombasa.
Tel: 312389/312317.
Fax: 312398.

**Hotel Sapphire**
PO Box 1254, Mombasa.
Tel: 494841/494131.
Fax: 495280.

### SOUTH COAST

**5-Star (Class A)**

**Diani Reef Grand Hotel**
PO Box 35, Ukunda.
Tel: (0127) 2723.
Fax: (0127) 2196.
Email: dianireef@form-net.com

**Golden Beach Hotel**
PO Box 31, Ukunda.
Tel: (0127) 2625/2054.
Fax: (0127) 2321.

**Indian Ocean Beach Club**
PO Box 73, Ukunda.
Tel: (0127) 2622/3201.
Fax: (0127) 3557.

**LTI Kaskazi Beach Hotel**
PO Box 135, Ukunda.
Tel: (0127) 3725/3170.
Fax: (0127) 2233.
**Leisure Lodge Club**
PO Box 84383, Mombasa.
Tel: (0127) 2011/2.
Fax: (0127) 2159.
Email: leisure@africaonline.co.ke

*4-star (Class B)*
**Africana Sea Lodge**
PO Box 84616, Mombasa.
Tel: (0127) 2622.
Fax: (0127) 2145.
**Jadini Beach Hotel**
PO Box 84616, Mombasa.
Tel: (0127) 2622.
Fax: (0127) 2269.
**Safari Beach Hotel**
PO Box 90690, Mombasa.
Tel: (0127) 2726.
Fax: (0127) 2357.

*3-star (Class C)*
**Beachcomber Club**
PO Box 54, Kwale.
Tel: (0127) 2426.
**Two Fishes Hotel**
PO Box 23, Ukunda.
Tel: (0127) 2720/2101.

## NORTH COAST
*5-Star (Class A)*
**Mombasa Inter-Continental Hotel**
PO Box 84383, Mombasa.
Tel: 485811/486721.
Fax: 485437/485918.
**Mombasa Beach Hotel**
PO Box 90414, Mombasa.
Tel: 471861.
**Nyali Beach Hotel**
PO Box 90581, Mombasa.
Tel: 471551.
**Reef Hotel**
PO Box 82234, Mombasa.
Tel: 471771–2.
Fax: 471349.
**Serena Beach Hotel**
PO Box 90352, Mombasa.
Tel: 485721.
Fax: 485453.
**Whitesands Hotel**
PO Box 90173, Mombasa.
Tel: 485926/485911.
Fax: 485652.
Email: sarovamwgm@
whitesands.sarova.com

*4-star (Class B)*
**Bamburi Beach Hotel**
PO Box 83966, Mombasa.
Tel: 485611. Fax: 485900.
**Plaza Hotel**
PO Box 88299, Mombasa.
Tel: 485321/2. Fax: 485325.
**Severin Sea Lodge**
PO Box 82169, Mombasa.
Tel: 485001. Fax: 485212.
**Traveller's Beach Hotel**
PO Box 87649, Mombasa.
Tel: 485121.
**Silver Beach Hotel**
PO Box 74888, Nairobi.
Tel: 716628.
Fax: 716457.
Email: prestigehotels@form-net.com
**Silver Star Hotel**
PO Box 74888, Nairobi.
Tel: 716628.
Fax: 716457.
Email: prestigehotels@form-net.com

*3-star (Class C)*
**Kenya Beach Hotel**
PO Box 95748, Mombasa.
Tel: 485821. Fax: 485574.
**Neptune Beach Hotel**
PO Box 83125, Mombasa.
Tel: 485704.
**Sun 'N' Sand Beach Hotel**
PO Box 2, Kikambala.
Tel: (0125) 32621/32008.
Fax: (0125) 32133.
Email: sunsnd@africaonline.co.ke.
**Whispering Palms Hotel**
PO Box 5, Kikambala.
Tel: (0125) 320045.

## KILIFI, WATAMU, MALINDI AND LAMU
*5-star (Class A)*
**Hemingways** (Watamu)
PO Box 40433, Nairobi.
Tel: 334722–7.
Fax: 334825.
Email: expressk@africaonline.co.ke

*4-Star (Class B)*
**Peponi Hotel**
PO Box 24, Lamu.
Tel: (0121) 33421/33154.
Fax: (0121) 33029.
**Turtle Bay Beach Hotel**
Box 10, Watamu.
Tel: (0122) 32622/32226.
Fax: (0122) 32268.
Email: turtles@africaonline.co.ke

*3-Star (Class C)*
**Mnarani** (Kilifi)
Tel: Kilifi 22061
**Ocean Sports**
PO Box 100, Watamu
Tel: (0122) 32008. Fax: 32266.
**Driftwood Beach Club**
PO Box 63, Malindi.
Tel: (0123) 20155.
**Kipungani Bay** (Lamu)
PO Box 74888, Nairobi.
Tel: 716628. Fax: 716457.
Email: prestige@form-net.com
**Lawfords Hotel**
PO Box 20, Malindi.
Tel: (0123) 20441.
**New Lamu Palace Hotel**
PO Box 83, Lamu.
Tel: (0121) 33272.
Fax: (0121) 33104.
**Watamu Beach Hotel**
PO Box 300, Malindi.
Tel: (0123) 32001/32010.

## Up-Country Hotels
*5-Star (Class A)*
**Mount Kenya Safari Club**
PO Box 35, Nanyuki.
Tel: (0176) 22960/1.
Nairobi.
Tel: 216920/40.
Fax: 216796.
Email: lonhotke@form-net.com.

*4-Star (Class B)*
**Aberdare Country Club**
PO Box 58181, Nairobi.
Tel: 216920/40.
Fax: 216796.
Email: lonhotke@form-net.com
**The Outspan Hotel**
PO Box 40075, Nairobi.
Tel: 335807. Fax: 545948. Email:
block3@users.africaonline.co.ke
**Lake Baringo Club**
PO Box 47557, Nairobi.
Tel: 335807.
Fax: 340541/545948. Email:
block3@users.africaonline.co.ke
**Lake Naivasha Country Club**
PO Box 40075, Nairobi.
Tel: 335807. Fax: 545948. Email:
block3@users.africaonline.co.ke
**Naro Moru River Lodge**
PO Box 49839, Nairobi.
Tel: 227103/337508.
Fax: 219212/244199.
Email: alliance@africaonline.co.ke

### 3-Star (Class C)
**Golf Hotel Kakamega**
PO Box 42013, Nairobi.
Tel: 229751.
Kakamega, tel: (0331) 20125.
**Imperial Hotel**
PO Box 1866, Kisumu.
Tel: (035) 41455–6.
Fax: (035) 40345.
**Isaac Walton Inn**
PO Box 1, Embu.
Tel: (0161) 20128–29.
**Lake Bogoria Hotel**
PO Box 541, Nakuru.
Tel: (037) 42696
**Sportsman's Arms Hotel**
PO Box 3, Nanyuki.
Tel: (0176) 32347–8.
Fax: (0176) 22895.
**Hotel Sirikwa**
PO Box 3361, Eldoret.
Tel: (0321) 31655.
Fax: (0321) 61018.
**Sunset Hotel**
PO Box 215, Kisumu.
Tel: (035) 41100–4.
**Tea Hotel**
PO Box 75, Kericho.
Tel: (3618) 30004–5.
**Tsavo Inn** (Mtito Andei)
PO Box 30139, Nairobi.
Tel: Loitokitok (0302) 22451.

## Game Lodges

### 5-Star (Class A)
**Amboseli Serena Lodge** (Amboseli)
PO Box 48690, Nairobi.
Tel: 710511/711077.
Fax: 718103.
Email: serenacr@africaonline.co.ke
**Borana Ranch** (Timau)
PO Box 24397, Nairobi.
Tel: 574689/567251.
Email: ras@swiftkenya.com
**Keekorok Lodge** (Maasai Mara)
PO Box 40075, Nairobi.
Tel: 540780. Fax: 545948. Email:
block3@users.africaonline.co.ke
**Mara Serena Lodge** (Maasai Mara)
PO Box 48690, Nairobi.
Tel: 710511/711077. Fax: 718103.
Email: serenacr@africaonline.co.ke
**Ol Pejeta Ranch House** (Nanyuki)
PO Box 58582, Nairobi.
Tel: 216920/40. Fax: 216796.
Email: lonrhotke@form-net.com
**Ol Tukai Lodge** (Amboseli)
PO Box 40075, Nairobi.

Tel: 540780. Fax: 545948. Email:
block3@users.africaonline.co.ke
**Rusinga Island Fishing Lodge**
(Lake Victoria)
PO Box 24397, Nairobi.
Tel: 574689/567251.
Email: ras@swiftkenya.com
**Taita Hills Lodge** (Tsavo)
PO Box 30624, Nairobi.
Tel: 334000/(0147) 30270/43.
Fax: (0147) 30007.
**Salt Lick Lodge** (Tsavo)
PO Box 30624, Nairobi.
Tel: 334000/(0147) 30270/43.
Fax: 339462/(0147) 30007.
**Sarova Shaba Lodge** (Shaba)
PO Box 30680, Nairobi.
Tel: 333233. Fax: 211472.
Email: reservations@sarova.co.ke
**Samburu Lodge** (Samburu)
PO Box 40075, Nairobi.
Tel: 540780. Fax: 545948. Email:
block3@users.africaonline.co.ke
**Samburu Serena Lodge** (Samburu)
PO Box 48690, Nairobi.
Tel: 710511/711077.
Fax: 718103.
Email: serenacr@africaonline.co.ke

### 4-Star (Class B)
**Amboseli Lodge** (Amboseli)
PO Box 30139, Nairobi.
Tel: 227136/337510.
Fax: 219982.
**The Ark** (Aberdare NP)
PO Box 58581, Nairobi.
Tel: 216920/40. Fax: 216796.
Email: lonhotke@form-net.com
**Loi Saba Lodge** (Rumuruti)
PO Box 24397, Nairobi.
Tel: 574689/567251.
Email: ras@swiftkenya.com
**Il Ngwesi Lodge**
(north of Mount Kenya)
PO Box 60342, Nairobi.
Tel: 340331/213033.
Fax: 214713/336890.
Email: info@letsgosafari.com
**Kilimanjaro Buffalo Lodge**
(Amboseli)
PO Box 30139, Nairobi.
Tel: 227136/337510.
Fax: 219982.
**Kilimanjaro Safari Lodge** (Amboseli)
PO Box 30139, Nairobi. Tel:
227136/337510.
Fax: 219982.
**Kilaguni Lodge** (Tsavo West)
PO Box 40433, Nairobi.

## Hostels

**Kenya Youth Hostels
Association**
PO Box 48661, Nairobi.
Tel: 723012/721765.
**Youth Hostel**
Ralph Bunche Road, Nairobi.
Tel: 723012.
**YMCA Hostel**
PO Box 30330, Nairobi.
Tel: 713599/724066.
Fax: 728825.
**YWCA Hostel**
PO Box 40710, Nairobi.
Tel: 724789/724699.
Fax: 710519.
**Yare Safaris Hostel**
Maralel.
Tel: Maralel 2295.

Tel: 334722–7. Fax: 334825.
Email: expressk@africaonline.co.ke
**Lion Hill Lodge** (Lake Nakuru)
PO Box 30680, Nairobi.
Tel: 333233. Fax: 211472. Email:
reservations@sarova.co.ke
**Mara Sopa Lodge** (Maasai Mara)
PO Box 72630, Nairobi.
Tel: 336724/336088.
Fax: 223843.
**Ngulia Lodge** (Tsavo West)
Kenya Safari Lodges,
PO Box 42013, Nairobi.
Tel: 340894. Fax: 227815.
**Shimba Lodge** (Shimba Hills)
PO Box 40075, Nairobi.
Tel: 540780. Fax: 545948. Email:
block3@users.africaonline.co.ke
**Treetops Lodge** (Aberdare NP)
PO Box 40075, Nairobi.
Tel: 540780. Fax: 545948. Email:
block3@users.africaonline.co.ke
**Voi Safari Lodge** (Tsavo East)
Kenya Safari Lodges,
PO Box 42013, Nairobi.
Tel: 340894. Fax: 227815.

### 3-Star (Class C)
**Buffalo Springs Lodge**
Motto Tours,
PO Box 70739, Nairobi.
Tel: 335154. Fax: 335154.
**Elsa's Kopje** (Meru)
PO Box 39806, Nairobi.
Tel: 748307/748327.
Fax: (0154) 22553.
Email: chelipeacock@attmail.com

Mountain Lodge (Mount Kenya)
PO Box 123, Kiganjo.
Tel: (0171) 30785.
Fax: (0171) 30785.
Lake Nakuru Lodge
PO Box 70559, Nairobi.
Tel: 224998.
Maralal Safari Lodge
PO Box 45155, Nairobi.
Tel: 211124. Fax: 214261.
Olkurruk Mara Lodge
(Maasai Mara)
PO Box 40433, Nairobi.
Tel: 334722–7. Fax: 334825.
Email: expressk@africaonline.co.ke

## Tented Camps

### 5-Star (Class A)
Africa Expeditions Private Tented
Camps (Loita Hills/Maasai Mara)
PO Box 24598, Nairobi.
Tel: 561959. Fax: 561457.
Finch-Hatton's Camp (Tsavo West)
PO Box 24423, Nairobi.
Tel: 604321–2. Fax: 604323.
Email: finchhattons@iconnect.co.ke
Governor's and Little Governor's
Camps (Maasai Mara)
PO Box 48217, Nairobi.
Tel: 331871–2. Fax: 726427.
Email: govscamp@africaonline.co.ke
Kichwa Tembo Camp
(Maasai Mara)
PO Box 74957, Nairobi.
Tel: 441001–5. Fax: 750780.
Email: conscorp@africaonline.co.ke
Larsens Tented Camp (Samburu)
PO Box 40075, Nairobi.
Tel: 540780. Fax: 545948. Email:
block3@users.africaonline.co.ke

## Private Ranches

Some of the best accommodation
is on private farms and ranches.
Usually these are near, but out-
side, national parks and reserves,
so it's possible to go walking and
take night drives (both forbidden
in national parks). The farms and
ranches below offer "homestays":
Ol Malo – Laikipia
Lewa Downs, Wilderness
   Trails – Isiolo
Kitich Camp – Mathews Range
Patrick's Camp – Solio
Rekero – Maasai Mara

Mara Intrepids Club (Maasai Mara)
PO Box 74888, Nairobi.
Tel: 716628. Fax: 716457.
Email: prestige@form-net.com
Mara Safari Club (Maasai Mara)
PO Box 58581, Nairobi.
Tel: 216920/40. Fax: 216796.
Email: lonhotke@form-net.com
Mara Sarova Camp (Maasai Mara)
PO Box 30680, Nairobi.
Tel: 333233. Fax: 211472.
Email: reservations@sarova.co.ke
Samburu Intrepids Club (Samburu)
PO Box 74888, Nairobi.
Tel: 716628. Fax: 716457.
Email: prestige@form-net.com
Siana Springs Camp
(Maasai Mara)
PO Box 74957, Nairobi.
Tel: 441001–5. Fax: 750780.
Email: conscorp@africaonline.co.ke
Sweetwaters (Nanyuki)
PO Box 58581, Nairobi.
Tel: 216920/40. Fax: 216796.
Email: lonhotke@form-net.com
Tortilis Camp (Amboseli)
PO Box 39806, Nairobi.
Tel: 748307/748327.
Fax: (0154) 22553.
Email: chelipeacock@attmail.com

### 4-Star (Class B)
Campi ya Kanzi (Chyulu Hills)
PO Box 60342, Nairobi.
Tel: 340331. Fax: 214713.
Email: info@letsgosafari.com
Cheli & Peacock's Camp
(Maasai Mara)
PO Box 39806, Nairobi.
Tel: 748307/748327.
Fax: (0154) 22553.

Lokitela Farm – Mt. Elgon
Deloraine – Western Rift Valley
Mundui Estate – Lake Naivasha
Sirata Siruwa – South Kajiado
Tana Delta Camp – North Malindi
Takaungu – Kilifi
Al Qasr – Kilifi
   Accommodation at the above
can be booked through: Bush
Homes of East Africa Ltd,
PO Box 56923, Nairobi.
Tel: 571647/49/61.
Fax: 571665. Email:
bushhome@users.africaonline.co.ke

Email: chelipeacock@attmail.com
Delamere Camp (Lake Elmenteita)
PO Box 48019, Nairobi.
Tel: 229009. Fax: 330698.
Email: eaos@user.africaonline.co.ke
Desert Rose Camp
(Mount Niro, South Lake Turkana)
PO Box 24397, Nairobi.
Tel: 574689/567251.
Email: ras@swiftkenya.com
Fig Tree Camp (Maasai Mara)
PO Box 40683, Nairobi.
Tel: 220592/220593.
Gala Tented Camp (Tsavo East)
PO Box 48019, Nairobi.
Tel: 229009. Fax: 330698.
Email: eaos@user.africaonline.co.ke
Galdessa Camp (Tsavo East)
PO Box 24397, Nairobi.
Tel: 574689/567251.
Email: ras@swiftkenya.com
Island Camp (Lake Baringo)
PO Box 60342, Nairobi.
Tel: 340331/213033.
Fax: 214713/336890.
Email: info@letsgosafari.com
Kitich Camp (Mathews Range)
PO Box 60342, Nairobi.
Tel: 340331/213033.
Fax: 214713/336890.
Email: info@letsgosafari.com
Lerai Tented Camp (Isiolo)
PO Box 48019, Nairobi.
Tel: 229009. Fax: 330698.
Email: eaos@user.africaonline.co.ke
Mara River Camp (Maasai Mara)
PO Box 48019, Nairobi.
Tel: 229009. Fax: 330698.
Email: eaos@user.africaonline.co.ke
Mugie Camp (Laikipia)
PO Box 39806, Nairobi.
Tel: 748307/748327.
Fax: (0154) 22553.
Email: chelipeacock@attmail.com
Patrick's Camp (Solio)
PO Box 56923, Nairobi.
Tel: 571647/49/61.
Fax: 571665.
Email:
bushhome@users.africaonline.co.ke
Satao Camp (Tsavo East)
PO Box 90653, Mombasa.
Tel: 220737/227581.
Fax: 314082.
Tana Delta Camp (north Malindi)
PO Box 56923, Nairobi.
Tel: 571647/49.
Fax: 571665. Email:
bushhome@users.africaonline.co.ke

**Tsavo Safari Camp** (Tsavo East)
PO Box 30139, Nairobi.
Tel: 332334/227136.
Fax: 219982.
**Umani Springs Camp** (Kibwezi)
PO Box 60342, Nairobi.
Tel: 340331/213033.
Fax: 214713/336890.
Email: info@letsgosafari.com
**Ziwani Tented Camp** (Tsavo West)
PO Box 74888, Nairobi.
Tel: 716628.
Fax: 716457.
Email: prestige@form-net.com

## Central Booking

Many up-country hotels, lodges and
camps have a central booking
system based in Nairobi. Below is a
list of the principal management
groups and the accommodations
that they handle:

**Alliance Hotels**
PO Box 49839, Nairobi.
Tel: 227103/337508.
Fax: 219212/244199.
Email: alliance@africaonline.co.ke
Africana Sea Lodge – Diani Beach
Jadini Beach Hotel – Diani Beach
Naro Moru River Lodge – Naro Moru
Safari Beach Hotel – Diani Beach

**Block Hotels**
PO Box 40075, Nairobi.
Tel: 540780.
Fax: 545948. Email:
block3@users.africaonline.co.ke
Indian Ocean Beach Club – Diani
Beach
Keekorok Lodge – Maasai Mara
National Reserve
Lake Baringo Club – Lake Baringo
Lake Naivasha Country Club – Lake
Naivasha
Landmark Hotel – Nairobi
Larsens Camp – Samburu National
Reserve
Nyali Beach Hotel – North Coast,
Mombasa
Ol-Tukai Lodge – Amboseli National
Park
Outspan Hotel – Nyeri
Samburu Lodge – Samburu National
Reserve
Shimba Lodge – Shimba Hills
National Park
Treetops – Aberdare National Park

**The Conservation Corporation**
PO Box 74957, Nairobi.
Tel: 746707/750298/750780.
Fax: 746826.
Email: conscorp@africaonline.co.ke
Kichwa Tembo Camp – Maasai Mara
National Reserve
The Mayfair Court Hotel – Nairobi
Siana Springs Tented Camp –
Maasai Mara National Reserve
The Windsor Golf & Country Club –
Nairobi

**Hilton Lodges & Hotels**
PO Box 30624, Nairobi.
Tel: 334000.
Fax: 339462/226477.
Nairobi Hilton Hotel – Nairobi
Salt Lick Lodge – Taita Hills
Taita Hills Safari Lodge –
Taita Hills

**Let's Go Travel**
PO Box 60342, Nairobi.
Tel: 340331/213033.
Fax: 214713/336890.
Email: info@letsgosafari. com
Island Camp – Lake Baringo
Lentolia House – Lake Naivasha
Patrick's Camp – Meru National
Park
Umani Springs – Kibwezi

**Lonrho Hotels**
PO Box 58581, Nairobi.
Tel: 216920/40. Fax: 216796.
Email: lonhotke@form-net.com
Aberdare Country Club – Mweiga
The Ark – Aberdare National Park
Mara Safari Club – Maasai Mara
National Reserve
Mount Kenya Safari Club –
Nanyuki
Norfolk Hotel – Nairobi
Sweetwaters Tented Camp –
Nanyuki

**Mellifera Bookings**
PO Box 24397, Nairobi.
Tel: 574689/567251.
Email: ras@swiftkenya.com
Borana Lodge – Timau
Desert Rose – Mt Niro, South Lake
Turkana
Galdessa Camp – Tsavo East
National Park
Loi Saba (formerly Colcheccio
Lodge) – Rumuruti

**Prestige Hotels**
PO Box 74888, Nairobi.
Tel: 716628. Fax: 716457.
Email: prestige@form-net.com
Kipungani Bay – Lamu Island
Mara Intrepids Club – Maasai Mara
National Reserve
Samburu Intrepids Club – Samburu
National Reserve
Silver Beach Hotel – North Coast,
Mombasa
Silver Star Beach Hotel – North
Coast, Mombasa
Ziwani Tented Camp – Tsavo West
National Park

**Savannah Camps & Lodges**
PO Box 48019, Nairobi.
Tel: 229009.
Fax: 330698.
Email: eaos@user.africaonline.co.ke
Delamere Camp – Lake Elementeita
Gala Tented Camp – Tsavo East
National Park
Indian Ocean Lodge – Malindi
Lerai Tented Camp – Lewa Downs
Conservancy, Isiolo
Mara River Camp – Maasai Mara
National Reserve
Sangare Ranch – Mweiga

**Sarova Hotels**
PO Box 30680, Nairobi.
Tel: 333233. Fax: 211475.
Email: reservations@sarova.co.ke
Ambassadeur Hotel – Nairobi
Lion Hill Lodge – Lake Nakuru
National Park
Mara Sarova Lodge – Maasai Mara
National Reserve
New Stanley Hotel – Nairobi
Panafric Hotel – Nairobi
Sarova Shaba Lodge – Shaba
National Reserve
Whitesands Hotel – North Coast,
Bamburi

**Serena Hotels & Lodges**
PO Box 48690, Nairobi.
Tel: 710511.
Fax: 718103.
Email: serenaacr@africaonline.co.ke
Mara Serena Lodge – Maasi Mara
National Reserve
Nairobi Serena Hotel – Nairobi
Samburu Serena – Samburu
National Reserve
Serena Beach Hotel – North Coast,
Shanzu

# Where to Eat

Restaurants serving mainly African, European and Asian cuisine can be found throughout Kenya. In general, the food is of excellent quality and is reasonably priced.

## NAIROBI

**African Heritage Café**
Banda Street. Tel: 337507.
Local specialities.
**Akasaka Restaurant**
Muindi Mbingu Street. Tel: 220299.
Japanese.
**Alan Bobbe's Bistro**
Koinange Street. Tel: 224945.
French and expensive.
**Carnivore Restaurant**
Langata Rd. Tel: 501775.
Barbecued meats and great atmosphere.
**Daas Ethiopian Restaurant**
Ralph Bunche Rd. Tel: 727353.
**Dawat Restaurant**
Shimmers Plaza, Westlands.
Tel: 749337.
Indian.
**Gringo's Restaurant**
Limuru Road. Tel: 521231/2.
Tex-Mex.
**Haandi Restaurant**
The Mall, Westlands. Tel: 448294.
Excellent Indian but not cheap.
**Hardrock Café**
Barclays Plaza, Loita Street.
Tel: 220802.
Fast Food.
**The Hong Kong Restaurant,**
Koinange Street. Tel: 722394.
Chinese.
**Horseman Restaurant**
Ngong Road. Tel: 882033/882133.
International cuisine and karaoke bar.
**Ibis Grill**
Norfolk Hotel, Tel: 335422/33.
International cuisine, expensive.

**La Galleria**
International Casino. Tel: 744477.
Italian, expensive.
**Lord Errol's**
Runda Estate. Tel: 521308.
Continental cuisine, expensive.
**Minar Restaurant**
Banda Street. Tel: 330168.
Indian.
**Nawab Tandoori**
Muthaiga Shopping Centre.
Tel: 740209.
Indian.
**Pagoda**
Shankardass House, Moi Avenue.
Tel: 227036/230230.
Chinese.
**The RaceCourse Restaurant,**
Ngong Race Course. Tel: 561002.
International Cuisine.
**Siam Thai Restaurant**
Unga House, Westlands.
Tel: 751727/28.
**Steers Restaurants**
Muindi Mbingu Street, City Centre
and Mpaka Plaza, Westlands.
Tel: 214300/222239.
Steak and hamburgers.
**Tamarind Restaurant**
Harambee Avenue. Tel: 338959.
Seafood specialities, expensive.
**Toona Tree**
International Casino. Tel: 744477.
Italian/International.
**Trattoria**
Kaunda/Wabera Street. Tel: 340855.
Italian.

## MOMBASA

**Blue Room**
Haile Selassie Road. Tel: 223029.
Indian.
**Galaxy**
Archbisop Makarios Road.
Tel: 226132.
Chinese.
**Hong Kong Restaurant**
Moi Avenue and Malindi Road.
Tel: 226707/486137.
Chinese.
**Hard Rock Café**
Nkurumah Road. Tel: 222221/28.
International Cuisine.
**Minar**
Nyali Golf Club. Tel: 471220.
Indian.
**Singh Restaurant**
Membe Tayari Road. Tel: 493283.
Indian.

Wine is imported, and so is expensive by Kenyan standards, but not so much for European or American visitors. South African wines are particularly good value.

Local beers are cheap and refreshing. "White Cap" and "Tusker" are lager-type beers and come in large and small bottles. "Premium" is the strongest of the Kenyan beers. In Nairobi at least, you can be guaranteed they will be served icy cold.

**Tamarind**
Cement Cilo Road, Nyali.
Tel: 471747. Seafood.
**Tamarind Dhows**
Ratna Square, Nyali. Tel: 471948.
Seafood.
**La Terrazza**
Mbuyuni Road. Tel: 312828.
Italian.

## DIANI BEACH

**Ali Barbour's Cave**
Diani Beach Road.
Tel: (0127) 2033/3003. Seafood.
**Forty Thieves Beach Bar and Restaurant**
Diani Beach Road.
Tel: (0127) 2033/3003.
**Tropicana Resaurant/Pizzeria**
Diani Beach Road.
Tel: (0127) 2303.
**Wasini Island Restaurant**
Diani Beach Road.
Tel: (0127) 2321. Seafood.

## MALINDI

**La Malindina**
Ngowe Street off Lamu Road.
Tel: (0123) 20045/30126.
Italian seafood.
**I Love Pizza**
Vasco Da Gama Road.
Tel: (0123) 20672. Italian.
**Old Man of the Sea**
Vasco Da Gama Road. Seafood.

# Culture

## Art Galleries

There are some good artists at work in Kenya, particularly younger artists, but you may have to hunt down their work. East Africa has nothing like the tradition of West Africa for any of the arts. This would obviously be disputed locally, but many of the paintings, batiks, carvings and sculptures offered to tourists look as though they came off an assembly line.

The best of the indigenous art is usually found in small galleries, mostly in Nairobi – notably a store called **African Heritage Ltd** on Kenyatta Avenue, which also brings in artifacts from all over Africa, including *makonde* carvings from Tanzania.

Local artists, including Europeans, occasionally exhibit paintings in places like the **New Stanley Hotel**, the cosmopolitan **French Cultural Centre**, the **Exhibition Hall** at the Village Market and the **One Off Gallery**, on Rosslyn Lone Tree Road (tel: 520752).

Recommended places for up-

## Theatre and Cinema

In Nairobi, the **National Theatre**, **Phoenix Players**, **Braeburn Theatre** and **French Cultural Centre** all offer good quality classical, traditional and contemporary stage productions. There are 13 cinemas in Nairobi (including two drive-ins), and four cinemas in Mombasa. In the capital, the **Nairobi**, **Kenya** and **20th Century** cinemas offer the best facilities and latest films.

Check the daily newspapers or the *What's On* guide for listings.

market art and artifacts in Nairobi are **Gallery Watatu** on Standard Street, and **Paa-ya-Paa Gallery and Workshop** on Ridgeways Road (just out of town).

## Concerts

The **Nairobi Music Society** promotes performances by local amateurs and, occasionally, by foreign professionals. The **Nairobi Orchestra** is renowned in Africa and holds symphonic concerts three times a year and combines with the Music Society several times a year for choral events.

## Other Entertainment

Check the entertainment page of daily newspapers for listings of live bands. Most hotels provide traditional dancing and, occasionally, live music.

The **Carnivore** (Langata Road) has nightly live entertainment, with rock music on Wednesday nights, African night on Friday, an all-night disco on Saturday and soul music on Sunday. There's a nightly floor-show of modern and traditional African dance at the **Safari Park Hotel** on the Thika Road.

The **International Casino** complex has a disco as well as three restaurants and a casino. If you feel like Karaoke, then try the **Zanze-Bar** in the Kenya Cinema building or the **Horseman Restaurant** in the Nairobi suburb of Karen.

## Cultural Centres

Several foreign countries maintain Cultural Centres in Nairobi featuring book, record and video libraries. Many offer local theatrical productions and musical entertainment open to the public. Check with the individual centres or the entertainment section of daily newspapers for activities.

**American Cultural Centre**
National Bank Building,
Harambee Avenue,
PO Box 30143, Nairobi.
Tel: 337877/334141.

## The National Museum

Before you go on safari it is worth visiting Nairobi's **National Museum of Kenya**, where the displays of stuffed animals will help you to familiarise yourself with the animals that you may see in the bush. The displays are live in the museum's **snake park** and **aquarium**. Books and leaflets on just about everything to do with Kenya's flora and fauna are also available.

There are much smaller versions of the National Museum in several up country towns:
- Kisumu – tel: (035) 40803
- Eldoret – tel: (0321) 20670
- Maralal – tel: (0368) 2092
- Meru – tel: (01643) 20482.

On the coast there are museums at:
- Lamu – tel: (0121) 33073
- Gede, on the Old Malindi–Mombasa Road – tel: (0123) 32065
- Fort Jesus, Nkrumah Road, Mombasa – tel: 312839/225934. Has a particularly impressive collection.

**Bomas of Kenya** (near Nairobi National Park entrance)
PO Box 40689, Nairobi.
Tel: 891801.
**British Council Library**
ICEA Building, Kenyatta Avenue,
PO Box 40751, Nairobi.
Tel: 334855–7
Biashara Bank Building, Nyerere Avenue, Mombasa.
Tel: 223076.
**Italian Institute of Culture**
Chiromo Road, Nairobi.
Tel: 746739.
**Japan African Culture Interchange Institute**
Kamburu Drive, Nairobi.
Tel: 566262.
**Nairobi Cultural Institute**
Ngong Road.
Tel: 569205.

# Shopping

## What to Buy

A popular item with tourists is the *kiondo* **basket**, which is handwoven in sisal. These baskets are often made by old Kikuyu women, who can sometimes be seen weaving as they walk along the street, without even breaking their stride. Some of them produce small masterpieces which find their way into stores in London and New York – at heavily marked up prices. Bought locally, the baskets are excellent value.

**Soapstone carvings** from Kisii District are also popular with visitors. Some are polished black, but they are arguably better left in their natural greys and pinks.

There are a few good local buys at the coast – such as the intricately carved, brass-bound and studded **Zanzibar chests**, varying in size from a small jewellery box to a steamer trunk. Coastal **jewellery**, in sterling silver, can also be very attractive.

**Ethiopian rugs** in brown-sandy tones are worth buying – except that they have been known to carry unhatched insect eggs.

## Where to Shop

You will have collections of curios thrust upon you at every street corner by casual street traders. You should establish prices in the shops before haggling with the hawkers in order to get genuine bargains.

Almost all hotels and lodges in Kenya have small shops selling curios and artifacts – as well as films, sun screen and other essential personal items. In general, however, you will find by far

## Illegal Trading

Don't ever be tempted or conned into buying any item that is made from wild animal. You will almost certainly be offered "elephant-hair" or "giraffe-hair" bracelets, but often these will in fact be made of plastic. It is actually illegal to export elephant or giraffe hair.

Trade in ivory, rhino horn, skins and all other anatomical relics of wildlife is prohibited. Similarly, at the coast, the selling of sea shells, corals and so on is also prohibited by law, although hawkers will openly try to sell these items.

It happens occasionally that some local "entrepreneur" will offer this type of curio for covert sale to tourists, but both parties risk prosecution if caught.

The export of live animals, birds and reptiles is similarly banned, except where the dealer is a professional and licensed.

The same rule applies for diamonds, gold and gemstones.

the biggest range of goods in the capital.

The **City Market** in Nairobi has a good broad selection of curios and basketwork for sale, but be prepared to be hassled and harassed and to engage in bazaar-style buying (starting with an offer of about half the asking price).

Also good is the open-air **Maasai Market,** held every Friday at "The Village Market" at Gigiri, where you can buy tribal artifacts such as spears, shields, gourds, masks, cow bells and jewellery.

For a wide selection of ceramic beads, a trip out to **Kazuri Beads** in Karen is well worth the effort. For safari wear, try **Colpro** on Kimathi Street, and **Legend Lives Ltd** at Wilson Airport.

In addition, Nairobi has a wide range of souvenir and curio shops. Below is just a small selection:
**African Heritage Ltd**, Kenyatta Avenue; or at Libra House on the Mombasa Road (towards the airport)

**The Collector's Den**, Hilton Hotel.

**The Craft Market**, ABC Centre, Waiyaki Way.

**Kashmir Crafts**, Biashara Street.

**Rowland Ward's**, Standard Street.

**The East African Wildlife Society Shop**, Museum Hill Centre.

**Hitesh D Shah**, Mokdar Daddah Street.

**Undugu Society Shop**, Westlands

**Kumbu Kumbu**, Hilton Arcade.

**Utamanduni**, off Langata South Road.

# Sport

## SPORTS CLUBS

Temporary memberships are offered to visitors in most sports clubs around Kenya. Below is a list of some of these clubs and the sporting activities that they offer:

**Impala Club**
Ngong Road, PO Box 41516, Nairobi. Tel: 568573.
(Tennis, squash, rugby, football, hockey, cricket)

**Nairobi Club**
Ngong Road, PO Box 30171, Nairobi. Tel: 336996.
(Squash, tennis, cricket, hockey, bowls, basketball)

**Parklands Sports Club**
Ojijo Road, PO Box 40116, Nairobi. Tel: 742829.
(Tennis, squash, rugby, hockey, cricket, snooker)

**Mombasa Sports Club**
PO Box 90241, Mombasa.
Tel: 224705.
(Squash, snooker, bowling, rugby, football, hockey, cricket, tennis)

**Nanyuki Club**
PO Box 139, Nanyuki.
Tel: (0176) 31896.
(Tennis, squash, rugby, golf, snooker)

**Rift Valley Sports Club**
PO Box 1, Nakuru.
Tel: (037) 42264/43821.
(Tennis, squash, cricket, snooker, swimming).

## WATER SPORTS

Deep-sea fishing and other water sports can all be arranged on the spot through hotels along the coast. River and lake fishing can be booked through specialist travel agents. Or you may like to contact:
**Kenya Association of Sea Angling Clubs**
PO Box 267, Watamu

**Malindi Sea Fishing Club**
PO Box 364, Malindi.
Tel: (0123) 20410

**Mfangano Island Camp**
Lake Victoria,
PO Box 48217, Nairobi.

**Mombasa Deep Sea Fishing Club**
PO Box 84958, Mombasa
Tel: (011) 311532

**Mombasa Sea Angling Club**
PO Box 82345, Mombasa.
Tel: (011) 220823.

**Fisherman's Camp, Naivasha**
PO Box 60342, Nairobi,
Tel: 340331

**Oasis Club**
Lake Turkana
PO Box 56707, Nairobi (book through travel agent).

**Pemba Channel Fishing Club**
PO Box 86952, Mombasa (book through travel agent).

**Rusinga Island Camp**
Lake Victoria (book through travel agent).

**Watamu Sea Fishing Club**
PO Box 197, Watamu.

**Kenya Divers Association**
PO Box 95705, Mombasa.
Tel: (011) 471347.

**Nairobi Sailing & Sub Aqua Club**
Nairobi Dam, Langata Road,
PO Box 49973.
Tel: 501250.

**Mombasa Yacht Club**
PO Box 90391, Mombasa.
Tel: (011) 313350.

### *Swimming*

Swimming is not recommended in slow-moving rivers or at the edge of lakes with reeds, no matter how inviting the water appears. The risk is bilharzia, which is carried by a parasite that moves from host water snails to man, attacking vital organs such as the liver.

Swimming in the Indian Ocean is almost entirely safe, mainly because sharks and other predators rarely get past the reef that fringes the coast. On the reef itself, however, you need to take more care and wear protective footwear. The worst of the pests on the reef is the stone fish, which is well camouflaged to look like a lump of coral. If you step on one, you can receive a painful and highly

Members of the **Mountain Club of Kenya** (PO Box 45741, Nairobi; tel: 501747) and the **Cave Exploration Group of East Africa** (PO Box 47583, Nairobi) meet every Tuesday from 7.30pm at the Mountain Club of Kenya Club House, Wilson Airport.

venomous injection which requires immediate medical attention. Another reef creature to watch out for is a feathery fish with a variety of names but most commonly known as the dragon fish.

## GOLF CLUBS

**Karen Country Club**
Karen Road. PO Box 24816, Nairobi.
Tel: 882801/2. Fax: 884088

**Muthaiga Golf Club**
Kiambu Road. PO Box 41651, Nairobi. Tel: 762414/761262.

**Royal Nairobi Golf Club**
Mucai Drive, off Ngong Road,
PO Box 40221, Nairobi.
Tel: 725768/725769.

**Railway Golf Club**
Haile Selassie Avenue,
PO Box 40476, Nairobi.
Tel: 724084.

**Windsor Golf & Country Club**
Garden Estate, Kigwa Road,
PO Box 45587, Nairobi.
Tel: 862300. Fax: 802322.

**Sigona Club**
Naivasha Road, PO Box 10, Kikuyu.
Tel: (0154) 32431/32462.

**Aberdare Country Club**
PO Box 449, Nyeri.
Tel: (02) 216940

**Mombasa Golf Club**
Mombasa Island, sea front.
PO Box 90164, Mombasa.
Tel: (011) 313352

**Nyali Golf & Country Club**
PO Box 95678, Mombasa.
Tel: (011) 471038/471589.

**Limuru Country Club** (Tigoni)
PO Box 10, Limuru.
Tel: (0154) 40033.

**Malindi Golf & Country Club**
PO Box 320, Malindi.
Tel: (0123) 20404.

**Nakuru Golf Club**
PO Box 652, Nakuru.
Tel: (037) 40803.
**Nanyuki Sports Club**
PO Box 139, Nanyuki
Tel: (0176) 31896.
**Nyeri Club**
PO Box 74, Nyeri.
Tel: (0171) 7425.
**Eldoret Club**
PO Box 78, Eldoret.
Tel: (0321) 31395.

## Spectator Sports

### Horse racing
Horse racing takes place most
Sundays at the **Ngong Road Racecourse** – check in the newspapers
for dates. The first race normally

begins at 2.15pm. Admission Is
Kshs 100 (adults) and Kshs 20
(children). For advance information
you could try contacting the
**Jockey Club of Kenya** PO Box
40373, Nairobi (tel: 566109).

### Motor Sports
The **Safari Rally** is held at the end
of February or at the beginning of
March, and is internationally
acknowledged as the most
gruelling race of its kind. For
information contact **Safari Rally
Limited**, PO Box 59483, Nairobi
(tel: 723127).

The local **Rally Championship**
races are organised by recognised
motor clubs around Kenya all year.
A specialised off-road

endurance event called the **"Rhino
Charge"** is held every year at the
end of May in different parts of
the country. It is the toughest and
perhaps the most glamorous event
of its kind in Kenya. It does not
count towards Rally Championship
points, but all revenue accrued is
donated to the organisation
building the fence around the
Aberdare Rainforest, to protect the
rhino, elephant and other animals
that thrive there.

Championship Motocross
events, **Rally-X** and **Quatro-X** (4x4
assault course driving)
competitions are also held
throughout the year at several
sites around Nairobi.

## Kenya's Sporting Calendar

**January**
*mid-Jan* – Mnarani Formula, Kilifi;
Ladies Kennel Association Dog
Show, Nairobi.
*late Jan* – Mtwapa Cup, Mtwapa.
*end Jan* – Lady Delamere Fishing
Competition, Kilifi.

**February**
*early Feb* – CMC Festival,
Mtwapa.
*mid Feb* – Malindi International
Billfish Tournament, Malindi.
*end Feb* – Kilifi Classic Fishing
Competition, Kilifi.
*end Feb/early Mar* – Safari Rally

**March**
East Africa Kennel Club Dog Show,
Nairobi.
Kenya Open Golf Championship,
Nairobi.
*early March* – Watamu Sea Fishing
Club Festival.
*mid March* – Broadbill Competition,
Watamu.

**April**
*Easter* – Mnarani Easter
Competition, Kilifi; Horse Racing,
Derby; Easter Horse Show,
Nairobi.

**May**
Mombasa International Marathon.

Anti Stock Theft Unit Horse Show,
Gilgil.

**June**
International Safari Sevens Rugby
Tournament, Nairobi.
North Kenya Polo Tournament,
Timau.
*early June* – Rhino Charge
*mid-June* – Agricultural Society of
Kenya, Nakuru Show.

**July**
*2nd weekend* – Concours
d'Elegance (Cars & Motorcycles),
Nairobi.
Maralal International Camel
Derby.
Nairobi Polo Tournament, Nairobi.
Kabete Happening, Nairobi.
Timau Horse Show, Timau.
Silverdale Show, Nairobi.

**August**
Laikipia International Camel Derby,
Rumuruti.
Mugs Mug Polo Tournament,
Nairobi.
Horse of the Year Show, Nairobi.
Agricultural Society of Kenya,
Mombasa Show.

**September**
International Polo Tournament,
Nairobi.

*late Sept* – Peter Darnborough
North Kenya Bank Tournament,
Watamu; Agricultural Society of
Kenya, Nairobi Show.

**October**
Football, Moi Golden Cup Final.
*beginning Oct* – Equator Rally.
*mid-Oct* – Malindi International
Fishing Festival.
*end Oct* – East Africa Kennel Club
Dog Show, Nairobi.

**November**
Manyatta Polo Tournament, Gilgil.
Sanctuary Farm Horse Show,
Naivasha.
*early Nov* – Billfish On Fly, Kiwayu.
*mid-Nov* – Moorings Competition,
Mtwapa.
*mid-Nov* – Matthews/Devilliers
Memorial, Malindi.

**December**
Uhuru Trophy, Malindi.
*1st weekend* – Pemba Channel
Fishing Club Billfish Tournament,
Shimoni.
*mid-Dec* – Open Boat, Mtwapa.
*Boxing Day* – Kids Competition,
Watamu.
*27 Dec* – Mnarani Christmas
Competition, Kilifi.
*28/29 Dec* – Christmas
Competition, Watamu.

# Language

## General

English is understood by many people in up-country Kenya, but not so much at the coast, which is predominantly Muslim, speaking the Afro-Arab-Indian mix Swahili (more formally called Kiswahili). It's not a difficult language and it's worth learning a few words.

English is taught in schools all over the country, so there is always someone who will understand you, even in the remote bush. At the coast, more locals are responding to the European continental tourist invasion and many speak some German, French and Italian. Up-country, "kitchen Swahili" (unrefined) is spoken and understood.

## Useful Phrases

Hello/*jambo*
How are you?/*habari?*
I am well (good, fine, etc)/*mzuri*
Thank you (very much)/*asante (sana)*
Goodbye/*kwaheri*
Where is the hotel?/*hoteli iko wapi?*
Where does this road lead to?/*njia hii ina-enda wapi?*
Please help me push this car/*tafadhali nisaidie kusukuma gari*
Please change this wheel/*tafadhali badilisha gurudumu hili.*
Good morning/*habari ya asubuhi*
Good afternoon/*habari ya mehana*
Good evening/*habari ya jioni*
Please come in/*karibu ndani tafadhali*
Please sit down/*keti tafadhali*
You're welcome/*una karibishwa*
Where do you come from?/*ume kuja kutoka wapi?*
I come from.../*nime toka...*

What is your name?/*jina lako nani?*
My name is.../*jina langu ni...*
Can you speak Swahili?/*waweza kuongea kiswahili?*
Yes/*ndiyo*
No/*hapana*
Only a little/*kidogo tu*
How do you find Kenya?/*waonaje Kenya?*
I like it here/*hapa napenda*
The weather is hot, isn't it?/*hewa hapa in joto, sivyo?*
Yes, a little/*ndiyo, kidogo*
Where are you going?/*una kwenda wapi?*
I am going to.../*nakwenda...*
Turn right/*geuka kulia*
Turn left/*geuka kushoto*
Go straight/*enda moja kwa moja*
Please stop here/*simama hapa tafadhali*
How much?/*ngapi?*
Wait a minute/*ngoja kidogo*
I have to get change/*ni badilishe pesa kwanza*
Excuse me/*samahani*
Where is the toilet?/*wapi choo?*
Where may I get something to drink?/*naweza kupata wapi kinywaji?*
One cup of coffee/*kikombe kimoja cha kahawa*
How much does this cost?/*inagharimu pesa ngapi?*
That's quite expensive/*waweza kupunguza*
Fine/*sawa*
I will buy it/*nita nunva*

## Useful Words

Mr/*bwana*
Mrs/*bibi*
Miss/*bi*
I/*mimi*
you/*wewe*
he, she/*yeye*
we/*sisi*
they/*wao*
What?/*nini?*
Who?/*nani?*
Where? (Place)/*mahali gani?*
Where? (Direction)/*wapi? (upande gani?)*
When?/*hini?*
How?/*vipi?*
Why?/*kwanini?*
Which?/*ipi?*

to buy/*kununua*
to come/*kukuja*
to drink/*kukunywa*
to eat/*kukula*
to go/*kuenda*
to sell/*kuuza*
to sleep/*kulala*
to stop/*kusimama*
quickly/*haraka*
slowly/*pole-pole*
street/road/*barabara*
shop/*duka*
money/*fedha/pesa*
hotel/*hoteli*
room/*chumba*
bed/*kitanda*
hospital/*hospitali*
police/*polici*
bad/*mbaya*
good/*mzuri*
today/*leo*
tomorrow/*kesho*
now/*sasa*

### Food and Drink

beer/*tembo* (or *pombe*)
bread/*mkate*
butter/*siagi*
coffee/*kahawa*
cold/*baridi*
fish/*samaki*
food/*chakula*
hot/*moto*
meat/*nyama*
salt/*chumvi*
tea/*chai*
sugar/*sukari*

## Numbers

1/*moja*
2/*mbili*
3/*tatu*
4/*ine*
5/*tano*
6/*sita*
7/*saba*
8/*nane*
9/*tisa*
10/*kumi*
11/*kumi na moja*
12/*kumi na mbili*
20/*ishirini*
21/*ishirini na moja*
30/*thelathini*
40/*arobaini*
50/*hamsini*
100/*mia moja*
1,000/*elfu moja*

# Further Reading

## Landscape & History

**Kenya: The Magic Land** by Amin, Willetts and Tetley; London, 1988. Fantastic photographs fill this coffee-table book that takes the reader on a tour of the country.
**The Beauty of Kenya** by Amin, Duncan and Willetts; Nairobi, 1984. Fabulous photos in this pocket-size guide to Kenya. In the same format by the same team: *The Beautiful People of Kenya* (Nairobi, 1989) and *The Beauty of the Kenya Coast* (Nairobi, 1986).
**The Great Rift: Africa's Changing Valley** by Anthony Smith.
**Cradle of Mankind** by Amin and Tetley; London, 1981. A colourful guide to life in and around Lake Turkana.
**Railway Across the Equator** by Amin, Willetts and Matheson; London, 1986. Great photography gives added depth to the story of the "Lunatic Line".
**The Prehistory of Africa** by Desmond J. Clark; London, 1970.
**The Prehistory of East Africa** by Sonia Cole; London, 1964.
**The Tree Where Man Was Born** by Peter Mattiessen; New York, 1972.
**Fort Jesus and the Portuguese in Mombasa** by C.R. Boxer, and Carlos de Azevedo; London, 1960.
**Malindi, the Historic Town on the Kenya Coast** by E.B. Martin; Nairobi, 1975.
**The Green Hills of Africa, The Snows of Kilimanjaro** by Ernest Hemingway.
**The Scramble for Africa** by Thomas Pakenham. A great tome that sets out to disentangle the complicated story of the emergence of the nations of Africa.
**The Beauty of the Maasai Mara** by David Round-Turner; Nairobi 1994. Pocket guide with colour photos provides a close-up look at Kenya's most popular wildlife theatre.

**Safari: A Chronicle of Adventure** by Bartle Bull. Fascinating history of African safaris, full of adventure and tales of daring, with many historical photographs.
**Memories of Kenya: Stories from the Pioneers** by Arnold Curtis; London, 1986.
**The Kenya Pioneers** by Errol Trzebinski; New York, 1985.

## Kenyan People

**Portraits of Kenya** by Moll Amin; Nairobi, 1995. A lavishly illustrated look at the peoples of Kenya.
**The Last of the Maasai** by Amin, Duncan, Willetts and Eames; London, 1987. An in-depth look at the Maasai people and customs, with many full-colour photographs.
**Maasai** by Beckwith, Carol and Ole Saitoti, Tepilit; London, 1980. This lavishly illustrated coffee table book tells the Maasai story in great detail through the eyes of a Maasai tribesman.
**The Maasai** by S. S. Sankan; Nairobi, 1995.
**Maasai Days** by Cheryl Bentsen; USA, 1991.
**The Maasai: Herders of East Africa** by Sonia Bleeker, London, 1964.

## Personal Accounts

**Out of Africa** by Isak Dinesen; New York, 1981. The famous auto-biographic account of Isak Dinesen/Karen Blixen's life in Kenya, which inspired the Oscar-winning film of the same name.
**Journey to the Jade Sea** by John Hillaby; London. The well-known account of one man's adventurous 1,100-mile walk to Lake Turkana, the "Jade Sea".
**Flame Trees of Thika** by Elspeth Huxley; New York, 1987. Also *Out in the Midday Sun* and *Mottled Lizard*. Elspeth Huxley's collection of wonderfully told tales about her childhood in East Africa.
**In the Shadow of Man** by Jane Goodall; Boston, 1971. The famous account of Goodall's life among the wild chimpanzees.
**I Dreamed of Africa** by Kuki Gallman; New York, 1991. A

biographical account of one woman's love affair with Kenya.
**Facing Mount Kenya** by Jomo Kenyatta; London, 1965.
**West With The Night** by Beryl Markham; UK, 1942. Fascinating memoirs of a remarkable and adventurous woman who made Kenya her home.
**An Unfinished Journey** by Shiva Naipul; New York, 1987.
**My Kenya Days** by Wilfred Thesiger. This well-known British explorer is also the author of *Visions of the Nomad*.
**A Far Off Place** by Laurens Van der Post; New York, 1978.

### Biographies
**Ancestral Passions: The Leakey Family** by Virginia Morell; Mountain Club of Kenya.
**Diana, Lady Delamere and the Lord Errol Murder** by Leda Farrant; Nairobi, 1997. A look at the colourful life of Lady Delamere, particularly with regard to the "unsolved" murder of her lover, Lord Erroll.
**White Mischief** by James Fox; New York, 1984. Fascinating account of the murder of Lord Erroll, which inspired the much inferior film of the same name.
**The Man Whom Women Loved: The Life of Bror Blixen** by Ulf Aschan; New York, 1987. Biography of Isak Dinesen's (Karen Blixen) ex-husband, written by his godson and illustrated with photographs from family archives.

## Wildlife

**The Hunters and the Hunted** by Karl and Katherine Ammann. Incredible photographs tell the story of Kenya's predators and their prey.
**The End of the Game** by Peter Beard; USA, 1988. Beard's dramatic photographs and story tell of the history – and questionable future – of African wildlife.
**Run, Rhino, Run** by E. & C.B. Bradley-Martin; London. 1983. A detailed look at the rhinoceros and its plight. Many colour photographs.
**A Leopard's Tale. Kingdom of Lions** by Jonathan Scott. Detailed accounts of the lives of big cats in

the wild, complemented with photographs and illustrations.

**The Orphans of Tsavo** by Daphne Sheldrick; London, 1966. Famed conservationist Daphne Sheldrick tells of the ups and down of raising orphan elephants – and the equally fascinating trials and tribulations of Kenya's largest game park, Tsavo.

**East African Coast and Reefs;** Nairobi, 1975.

**Among the Elephants** by Ian and Oria Douglas-Hamilton; London, 1975.

**The Last Elephant** by Jeremy Gavron; London, 1994.

**Solo: The Story of an African Wild Dog** by Hugo Van Lawick; London 1973. A real-life animal saga follows a wild dog pack across the Serengeti.

**With My Soul Amongst Lions** by Gareth Patterson; London, 1996.

## Guides

### FIELD GUIDES

#### General

**National Audubon Society Field Guide To African Wildlife** by Knopf.

**Jonathan Scott's Safari Guide To Eastern African Animals** by Jonathan Scott.

**Collins Safari Guides: Larger Animals of East Africa** by Martin B. Withers and David Hosking; London, 1996.

**The Butterflies of Kenya and Their Natural History** by Torben B. Larsen.

#### Trees and Flowers

**African Trees** by Bob and Dorothy Hargreaves.

**African Blossoms** by Bob and Dorothy Hargreaves.

**The Beautiful Plants of Kenya** by John Karmali; Nairobi, 1986.

**The Wildflowers of East Africa** by Michael Blundell; London, 1992.

**Collins Photo Guide: Tropical Plants** by W. Lotschert and B. Beese; Hong Kong, 1994.

**Trees of Kenya** by Tim Noad and Ann Birnie.

#### Mammals

**A Field Guide to the Large Mammals of Africa** by Jean Dorst and Pierre Dandelot; London, 1970.

**Collins Field Guide: Mammals of Africa** by T. Haltennorth and H. Diller; UK, 1996.

**Know Your Monkeys: A Guide to the Primates of Kenya**, Institute of Primate Research; Museums of Kenya, Nairobi, 1989.

**The Kingdon Field Guide to African Mammals** by Jonathan Kingdon.

**The Behaviour Guide to African Mammals**, University of California Press.

#### Birds

**The Beautiful Birds of Kenya** by John Karmali; Nairobi, 1985.

**Birds of Kenya: a Photographic Guide to Birds in East Africa** by Dave Richards; London, 1995.

**Jonathan Scott's Safari Guide To Eastern African Birds** by Jonathan Scott; 1997.

**Collins Field Guide: Birds of Eastern Africa** by Van Perlo; London 1996.

**A Field Guide to the Birds of East Africa** by J.A. Williams; London, 1967.

**Collins Safari Guides: Common Birds of East Africa** by Martin B. Withers and David Hosking; London, 1996.

**Birds of Kenya and Northern Tanzania** by D.A. Zimmerman, D.A. Turner and D.J. Pearson; South Africa, 1996.

### OTHER GUIDES

**Kenya's Best Hotels, Lodges and Homestays** by B. Glenday, S. Southwick and J. Westley; Nairobi, 1994. A thorough guide that includes many wonderful off-the-beaten-track places.

**Gemstones of East Africa** by Peter C. Keller. A comprehensive illustrated guide to the gemological wealth of the region; a must for the potential gemstone buyer.

**Beauty of Samburu, Shaba and Buffalo Springs** by Jan Hemsing; Nairobi, 1997. Colourful pocket-size guide to these northern Kenyan game parks.

**Guide to Mt. Kenya and Mt. Kilimanjaro.** Nairobi, 1991.

## Other Insight Guides

The main series of nearly 200 *Insight Guides* has been joined by more than 100 *Insight Pocket Guides,* and an exciting range of miniature travel encyclopedias – *Insight Compact Guides,* which present key information in a user-friendly highly portable guide.

Three *Insight Guides* make essential reading for a successful African safari:

*Insight Guide: East African Wildlife* focuses on all facts necessary for a rewarding and unforgettable journey and contains superb photography.

*Insight Guide: South Africa* paints a complete portrait of what is currently one of the most exciting destinations in the world, with insightful reporting and superb and vibrant photography.

*Insight Guide: Namibia* is a comprehensive guide to this dramatic and beautiful country, which is being increasingly discovered by discerning travellers.

# ART & PHOTO CREDITS

**AKG** 178T
**Iain Allan** 136, 232
**Mohamed Amin & Duncan Willets**
1, 2B, 6/7, 14, 16, 19, 23, 24, 30,
31, 32, 34, 36, 37, 38, 40, 41,
42, 43, 44, 45, 46, 47, 48, 49,
50, 51, 52, 53, 54/55, 57, 58, 59,
60, 62/63, 64, 66, 67, 68, 71,
72/73, 74/75, 76, 77, 78/79, 80,
81, 82, 103, 105, 106, 144/145,
146, 147, 148, 149, 150,
152/153, 154, 155, 156, 159,
160/161, 162/163, 164/165,
166/167, 180/181, 182, 183,
186, 187, 189, 194/195, 196,
197, 199, 200, 204/205, 210,
212, 213, 214T, 218/219, 221,
227, 228/229, 230, 231, 234,
238/239, 240, 241, 243T, 243L,
243R, 244, 245, 246, 247,
250/251, 254T, 256, 257, 258,
262/263, 264, 268, 281L, 281R,
282, 284/285, 286, 287, 292T,
293, 294, 295, 296/297, 298,
299, 300L, 300R, 301, 304
**Karl Ammann** 4/5, 10/11, 12/13,
69, 88, 90, 91, 92, 93, 94, 95,
96, 97, 98, 99, 100, 101, 104,
107, 108, 109, 110, 111, 112,
113, 114, 115, 117, 125, 135,
157, 172, 184, 188, 190T, 192,
193, 201, 206, 207, 210T, 216,
220, 223, 224, 225, 226T, 233T,
235, 237, 253, 302, 303
**Courtesy of Ulf Aschan** 134
**James Ashe** 121
**Alan Binks/ABPL** 18, 29, 177
**David Breed** 256T

**Bill Campbell** 138
**Camerapix** 4B, 33, 35, 61, 120,
123, 142, 158, 175, 178, 179,
248T, 258T, 269, 270, 275, 282T,
290
**David Coulson** 226
**Gerald Cubitt** 5BL, 184T
**Peter Davey** 116, 126, 127, 141,
233, 249
**Roger De La Harpe/ABPL** 8/9
**Christopher Dracke** 279
**Mary Evans Picture Library** 132
**Dave Hamman/ABPL** 15
**Dirk Heinrich/ABPL** 56
**Chris Hillman** 122
**David Keith Jones** 20/21, 22, 27,
28, 83, 86/87, 89, 102, 124,
128/129, 130/131, 137, 139,
140, 143, 168, 185, 190, 191,
208T, 209, 215, 217, 236, 248,
255, 257T, 275T, 302T
**Nicky Martin** 276/277, 283T, 289
**Jeffery Pike** 198T, 216, 278
**Royal Geographical Society** 39
**Anup Shah/ABPL** 236T
**Daniel Stiles** 26
**Wendy Stone** 2/3, 17, 70, 173,
176, 259, 271, 273, 291, 292
**P Thompson/Allsport** 151
**Topham Picturepoint** 25, 84/85,
133, 176T, 192T
**Duncan Willetts/Camerapix** 5BR,
65, 211, 265, 267, 267T, 268T,
272, 283

**Map Production** Berndston &
Berndston Productions.
© 1999 Apa Publications GmbH & Co.
Verlag KG, Singapore.

## Picture Spreads

**Pages 118–19**
*Top Row, left to right*: Gerald Cubitt,
Duncan Willetts/Camerapix, Gerald
Cubitt
*Centre Row, clockwise from left*:
Martin Harvey/ABPL, Gerald Cubitt,
Gerald Cubitt, Duncan
Willetts/Camerapix
*Bottom Row, left to right*: Gerald
Cubitt, Duncan Willett/Camerapix,
Camerapix, Clem Haagner/ABPL
**Pages 202–203**
*Top Row, left to right*: Roger De La
Harpe/ABPL, Roger De La
Harpe/ABPL, Duncan Willetts (*top*),
Roger De La Harpe/ABPL (*top*),
Trip/D Saunders
*Centre Row, left to right*: Roger De
La Harpe/ABPL, Roger De La
Harpe/ABPL, Duncan
Willetts/Camerapix (*top*), Roger De
La Harpe/ABPL (*bottom*)
*Bottom Row, left to right*: Duncan
Willetts/Camerapix, Camerapix,
Roger De La Harpe/ABPL, Gerald
Cubitt
**Pages 260–61**
*Top Row, left to right*: Thomas
Dressler/ABPL, Gerald Cubitt,
Malcolm Funston/ABPL, Trip/R
Daniell
*Centre Row, left to right*: Malcolm
Funston/ABPL, Camerapix, Peter
Chadwick/ABPL, Gerald Cubitt
*Bottom Row, left to right*: Gerald
Cubitt, Gerald Cubitt

*Cartographic Editor* **Zoë Goodwin**
*Production* **Stuart A. Everitt**
*Design Consultants* **Carlotta
Junger, Graham Mitchener**
*Picture Research*
**Hilary Genin, Monica Allende**

# Index